Game Design
Secrets of the Sages

MACMILLAN
DIGITAL PUBLISHING USA

Copyright © 1999
by Macmillan Digital Publishing USA

First Edition
First Printing—1999

ISBN: 1-57595-257-2

01 00 99   4

Interpretation of the printing code: the rightmost double-digit number is the year of the book's printing; the rightmost single-digit number, the number of the book's printing. For example, a printing code of 99-1 shows that the first printing of the book occurred in 1999.

Printed in the United States of America

Screen reproductions in this book were created using Collage Plus from Inner Media, Inc., Hollis, NH.

PRESIDENT
Douglas S. Bennett

PUBLISHER
Stacy L. Hiquet

PRODUCER
Steven M. Schafer

PRODUCTION EDITOR
Robin Drake

DESIGN MANAGER
Robin Lasek

DESIGNERS
Gary Adair and Jason Grisham

PRODUCTION MANAGER
Brad Chinn

Overview

Dedication

This book is dedicated to Kellie Sherman for her endless love and support.

Acknowledgments

A very special thank you goes out to all of the members of the electronic gaming industry who have taken the time and effort to contribute to this book.

Thanks to Steve Schafer for his affability and professionalism, and for believing that people who play games might also want to know how to create them. And thanks to Robin Drake for her proficient editing and encouraging words. Finally, thanks to Brad Chinn for his hard work on this book. We literally could not have done it without him!

About the Authors

Marc Saltzman, Compilation Editor

Marc Saltzman is a freelance journalist for over 40 game-related and consumer publications, including *USA Today*, *Playboy* magazine, *PC Gamer*, *PC Accelerator*, *PC Games*, *Gamecenter*, *Yahoo! Internet Life*, *Next Generation*, *Happy Puppy*, *Family PC*, and many more. He has also written two books on Internet gaming for Macmillan Publishing and two in-game manuals: *Quake II* and *Sin*.

Contributors

The following game and level designers, programmers, musicians, producers, sound engineers—and many other titles and job functions could be added here—provided the core of this book: their insights into and experiences with the fascinating world of game design. (For biographical information on many of the contributors, see the Appendix at the end of this book.)

Peter Akemann	Liz Bell	Louis Castle
Kurt Arnlund	Mark Bernal	Jim Charne
Marc Aubanel	Eric Biessman	Jason Chu
Ted Backman	Cliff Bleszinski	Kevin W. Cloud
Kelly Bailey	Dan Bray	Steven Coallier
Sinjin Bain	George Broussard	Bryce Cochrane
Andrew Barnabas	Chip Bumgardner	Vance Cook
Bob Bates	Melanie Cambron	Nick Corea
Tom Bazzano	Carol Caracciolo	Brad Crow

Matthew D'Andria
Stuart Denman
Vince Desiderio
Barry Dorf
Scott Easley
Sacha Fernandes
Chad Freeman
Jamie Fristrom
Toby Gard
Alex Garden
Richard "Lord British" Garriott
Ron Gilbert
Rick Goodman
Charles Gough
Mark A.C. Green
Mario Grimani
Tom Hall
Torsten Hess
Evan Hirsch
Rodney Hodge
Bryan C. Horling
Sean House
Matt Householder
Marc Hudgins
Allen Jackson
Paul Jaquays
Jane Jensen
Todd Johnson
Matthew Lee Johnston
Adam Kahn
Michael Kelly
Geoff Kirk
Joe Koberstein
Marc Laidlaw
Michael Land
Franz Lanzinger
Tim Larkin
The Levelord (Richard Bailey Gray)
Adam Levesque
Susan Lewis
Bill Linn
Mark Linn
Carin Lockrem
Doug Lombardi
Al Lowe
Tony Lupidi
Jean-François Malouin

Michael McCart
Mitzi McGilvray
Michael McGrath
Seumas McNally
Sid Meier
Ellen Meijers-Gabriel
Michael Meyers
Harry A. Miller
Shigeru Miyamoto
Richard Moe
Peter Molyneux
Steve Moraff
Peter Moreland
Ray Musyka
Gabe Newell
Mike Nichols
Mike Nicholson
Paul O'Connor
Scott Orr
Genevieve Ostergard
Alexey Pajitnov
Rob Pardo
Alan Patmore
David Perry
Kurt Pfeifer
Bobby Prince
Matt Pritchard
Josh Resnick
Brian Reynolds
Hugh Riley
Chris Rippy
Seth Robinson
John Romero
Stuart Roseman
Michael Rubinelli
Haiko Ruttmann
Michael Saladino
George (The Fat Man) Sanger
Ragnar Scheuermann
Kevin Schilder
Carl Schnurr
Joe Selinske
Lee Sheldon
Bruce C. Shelley
Toby Simpson
Chris Sivertsen
Brandon Smith

Joshua Staub
Phil Steinmeyer
Timothy J. Stellmach
Jay Stelly
Jonas Stewart
Greg Street
Gonzo Suarez
Tommy Tallarico
Chris Taylor (Gas Powered Games)
Chris Taylor (Interplay)
Chance Thomas
Joel Thomas
Matthew Toschlog
Rick Vandervoorn
Jeff Vogel
Wolfgang Walk
David Walls
Robin Ward
Roberta Williams
Tim Willits
Jay Wilson
Mike Wilson
Jon Zuk

So You Want to Make a Game, Huh?

Quite simply, there has never been a better time to create your very own computer game. The tools have never been easier and better, the industry has never been more ripe, and the Internet, as a medium, is one of the most incredible technologies for gamers and game developers everywhere. Strike the iron while it's hot, as they say.

Creating games for a living may sound like a dream job, but thousands of people are doing it as you read this, and many quite successfully. And you don't need millions of dollars to design a hit game, either. Take for instance Wizard Works' *Deer Hunter*. One of the cheapest retail games to develop was also one of the best-selling titles of 1998, with over one million units sold in the United States. Think about that for a moment—that's as if 1 out of every 272 people have this game! Why did it do so well? Because it was a great idea coupled with clever marketing and a relatively low price tag. And once you have a success like that, you can imagine the sequel and franchising opportunities. *Deer Hunter II*, for example, has already sold close to a million units.

According to the NPD group, a marketing information provider, the reported retail sales for computer and console game software and hardware in 1998 exceeded $6.3 billion in the U.S. alone. As if that wasn't impressive enough, this is a growth rate of 27% compared to the year before. Needless to say, this young and bustling industry is absolutely booming, so the big question remains—what do *you* want to be doing in the 21st century?

As far as the publisher and I know, this book is unlike any other book ever published. First, let's cover what this book *isn't*. This book will *not* require budding game programmers to be familiar with advanced concepts such as data structures, algorithm analysis, or anything like that. For the most part, the entire book is in easy-to-comprehend language; if acronyms, technical jargon, or industry slang are used, the word(s) are followed with a brief definition or clarification.

In addition, while the book is called *Game Design: Secrets of the Sages*, it covers much more than just *game design*. Sure, it explains how to write a perfect design doc and how to decide what kind of game to create, but it also caters to all the members of a development team—programmers, artists and animators, sound engineers and musicians, *plus* the entire business side of gaming. This includes how to properly market your game, working with the press, the best ways to test your product, why a killer Web site for your game is essential, the do's and don'ts of technical support and customer service, and much, much more. Furthermore, a good chunk of the second half of the book is devoted to breaking into the exciting gaming industry, whether you want to be a sole shareware game designer, you want to start your own full-blown development company and need to pitch your idea to a publisher, or perhaps you prefer to squeeze in at an existing development studio or publishing company.

Because this book covers so much ground, you may or may not want to read it all the way through. Feel free to jump back and forth from chapter to chapter as dictated by your personal tastes.

Also, be sure to keep in mind that each chapter could really be expanded into a book itself—or even a series of books, for that matter. Therefore, in case further reading is desired, most chapters contain a handful of great Web links and Usenet newsgroups to surf to or books to pick up, plus there's a chapter toward the end of the book reserved for the best game design resources out there.

Whether you're into action games or strategy, sims or sports, adventure or role-playing games, or puzzles/classics, we've got over 100 of the gaming industry's savvy developers ready to pour out advice in a myriad of topics, pooled from their many years of experience in the limelight.

So go ahead, dive right in and get in the game. With help from our sages over the next few hundred pages, the only thing between you and your hit game is your imagination...

SECTION I

Pre-Production

CHAPTER **1**

Game Genres and Playing Perspectives

Before diving into this book, we should cover a few of the basics. The first section of this chapter clarifies the differences between gaming *genres*. This is very important so that we're all on the same wavelength. Plus, before you sit down to design your game, you will ultimately need to choose a genre or a combination of genres to help solidify your vision.

There will be a number of terms thrown around over the next few hundred pages to explain how the game is played and/or the view the player has of the action. Words like *top-down*, *first-person perspective*, *third-person perspective*, and *isometric* will be explained and illustrated with an example.

So, as Duke Nukem says, "Come get some…"

Game Genres

Action

Action games (or "twitch" games) typically rely more on hand/eye coordination than on story or strategy. They're generally fast-paced and reflex-oriented. The most popular type of action game for the PC is the first-person perspective 3D shooter (more on this in a moment). id Software's *Quake* series and Epic Games' *Unreal* are recent examples. Fighting games, such as the *Tekken* series from Namco or Midway's *Mortal Kombat* series, fall into this category, as do "platform" side-scroller games (GT's *Oddworld: Abe's Exoddus* or Interplay's *Heart of Darkness*) and "over-the-shoulder" games such as the *Tomb Raider* series from Eidos Interactive.

Action games are arguably the most popular genre for both PC and console systems these days. But there are many different flavors of action games. Half-Life, for example, is a 3D shooter but adds a deep, involving story element. (Used with permission by Sierra Studios)

Strategy

Strategy games emphasize logical thinking and planning. They often stress resource and time management, which usually take precedence over fast action and character involvement. Tactical organization and execution are necessary, and the game creators usually place the decision-making skills and delivery of commands in the player's hands.

As opposed to *turn-based games* such as Microprose's *Civilization* or 3DO's *Heroes of Might and Magic*, *real-time strategy* (*RTS*) games add an active element and force the player to consider multiple events occurring at the same time. Examples of such games are Blizzard's *StarCraft* and Ensemble Studios' *Age of Empires*.

Blizzard's Warcraft and Warcraft II (pictured here) were a couple of the first breakthrough real-time strategy games, alongside Westwood Studios' Command & Conquer and the game that started it all—Westwood Studios' Dune II. (Used with permission by Blizzard Entertainment, Inc.)

Adventure

Adventure games involve the player in a journey of exploration and puzzle-solving. These games usually have a linear storyline in which you, the protagonist, set out to accomplish a main goal through character interaction and inventory manipulation. Some traces of the action genre may be found in these games. Good examples of adventure games are LucasArts' *Grim Fandango* and Brøderbund's *Myst* or *Riven*.

Role-Playing Games (RPGs)

Role-playing games (*RPGs*) are similar to adventure games, but rely more on character growth and development (usually involving player statistics), conversation, and strategic combat than on puzzle-solving. Huge, epic quests and fantasy worlds with *NPCs* (*non-player characters*) are common, and storylines are not always linear as in traditional adventure games. Side quests are also not uncommon to the genre.

Note >> Often computer role-playing games are referred to as CRPGs.

Action may play a significant role in an RPG, as in Blizzard's *Diablo* and Squaresoft's *Final Fantasy VII*, or more strategic elements may be necessary, as in Bullfrog's *Dungeon Keeper*. Older RPGs, referred to as *MUDs* (short for *multi-user domains* or *multi-user dungeons*), are exclusive to the Internet and are text-only. The majority of them are played via Telnet instead of over the World Wide Web. Most gamers, however, have shifted interest over to the more graphical proprietary online RPGs such as Origin's *Ultima Online* or Sony's *Everquest*.

Squaresoft's Final Fantasy VII, above, and Interplay's Baldur's Gate, below, are two popular RPGs of late, though their look and gameplay are quite different. (© 1997/1998 Square Co., Ltd. FINAL FANTASY and SQUARESOFT are registered trademarks of Square Co., Ltd. All rights reserved. Baldur's Gate image used with permission by Interplay Productions)

Sports

Sports titles simulate a single-player or team game from an instructional or player perspective. Realism is important, as are fast action and tactical strategy. Examples of popular sports games include the *NHL* series from Electronic Arts, Acclaim's *WWF: Warzone*, Sierra Sports' *PGA Championship Golf*, and Midway's *NFL Blitz* (though the "realism" gets blown right out of the water on this one).

Simulations or Sims

Sims realistically simulate a given animate or inanimate object or process. Most often, sims place the gamer in a 3D first-person perspective and re-create machinery such as planes, tanks, helicopters, and submarines. Examples include Jane's Combat Simulations' *WWII Fighters* and NovaLogic's *Armored Fist*.

There are also sims that mimic the animal kingdom, such as Sanctuary Woods' *Wolf* or Maxis' *SimEarth*. "God-game" sims are those that require the (often megalomaniac!) gamer to build and manage cities, communities, and other resources on a grander scale; Maxis' *SimCity 3000* and Bullfrog's *Populous: The Beginning* are good examples.

Microprose's popular Falcon 4 is an example of the most popular kind of sim—aerial combat simulations. Realism is the number one objective when designing these kinds of games. (Used with permission by Hasbro Interactive)

Puzzle or "Classic" Games

The *puzzle* or *"classic" games* include older, more historic games of leisure such as cards, tile games, trivia, word, or board games. Chess, checkers, backgammon, Mahjongg, and Solitaire are perfect examples. Recently, "classic" games have also included simpler and smaller-scale computer games, such as older arcade favorites and games that may lack a deep story or player commitment (*Tetris*, *Bust-A-Move*, and *Minesweeper* are great examples). Keep in mind that some of these games borrow elements from multiple genres (as illustrated in the RPG examples) or toy with different playing perspectives.

A "new" genre of games has evolved lately, known as the *music* genre. Games such as 989 Studios' *Bust a Groove* or Sony's *Parappa the Rapper* focus on music, singing, and dancing. This is an exciting new trend that's sure to continue well into the future.

Playing Perspectives

Here's a quick rundown of all of the varied playing perspectives.

First-Person Perspective

As touched on earlier, this is an approved choice among the action game designers. In 3D shooters, the view of the gaming environment is as though the player is seeing it through the character's eyes, such as 3D Realms' *Duke Nukem 3D* or Acclaim's *Turok: Dinosaur Hunter*.

Genres other than action games take advantage of this popular perspective, too, including most simulations (e.g. Microsoft's *Combat Flight Simulator*), adventure games (Mindscape's *John Saul's The Blackstone Chronicles*), strategy games (Activision's *Battlezone* or 3DO's *Uprising*), and role-playing games (Westwood Studios' *Lands of Lore III*).

A first-person perspective view is often preferred since it adds to the believability of the world and overall immersion factor. Pictured here is a screen shot from Deer Hunter II. (Used with permission by GT Interactive Software Corp. and Wizard Works, Inc.)

Third-Person Perspective

Also known as the "over-the-shoulder" view, the third-person perspective is another popular choice among game designers these days, especially since most games are in 3D. A third-person perspective is when the player can see onscreen the character he or she is playing. This has its advantages, too, since more of the environment can be seen while playing, plus you can see the moves your character can make—impossible in a first-person perspective view.

Many console and PC games use this view, including the *Tomb Raider* series, *Mario 64*, *Legend of Zelda: Ocarina of Time*, *Crash Bandicoot: Warped*, *Metal Gear Solid*, and *Resident Evil*.

Eidos Interactive's Tomb Raider was one of the first big hits to use a third-person perspective with an "intelligent" camera that followed heroine Lara Croft around. This is a screen shot taken from the latest game in the series, Tomb Raider III. (Used with permission by Eidos Interactive, Inc.)

This perspective is not limited to just action/arcade games: Sports games (almost all of them) honor this view, as well as RPGs (*Heretic II*, *Final Fantasy VII*) and adventure games (*King's Quest: Mask of Eternity* and *Gabriel Knight III: Blood of the Sacred, Blood of the Damned*, to name two).

Top-Down Perspective

This perspective is exactly as it sounds. The game is viewed from a *top-down perspective*, as if the "camera" was hovering over the game itself. The genre that uses this perspective the most is the strategy game genre—both turn-based and real-time versions. This is because of all the minute micro-management details and tactical placement of troops on a landscape for battle. The player must be able to access the units and survey the situation with one glance. Good examples of top-down games are Blizzard's *StarCraft*, Microprose's *Civilization*, and SSI's *Steel Panthers* and *Panzer General*.

Non-strategy games that use this perspective include Monolith's retro RPG *Get Medieval*, older *Ultima* and *Zelda* games, and many classic 2D games of yesteryear, including arcade hits *Centipede* and *Frogger*.

Don't forget about pin-ball simulations. Most of these games utilize a top-down view as well. Pictured here is a table from the Balls of Steel expansion pack. (Used with permission by 3D Realms/Apogee, Inc.)

Isometric

Often confused with top-down is the *isometric* point of view. This is a slightly tilted "three quarter" view that hovers up and off to the side of the gameplay and gives the impression of 3D. Good examples of this kind of perspective are Blizzard's *Diablo*, Interplay's *Baldur's Gate*, and Activision's *Twinsen's Odyssey*.

ASC Games' Sanitarium is an iso-metric adventure game. Many game developers prefer this view because both the player and the environ-ment can be seen by the player at the same time. (Used with per-mission by ASC Games, Inc.)

Flat, Side-View

This is the traditional two-dimensional "side view" of the action, a perspective that has become less and less popular over the years for its gameplay and aesthetic limitations. This view was popularized with the once-common *"side-scroller"* or *"platform"* games in the late '80s and early '90s, such as a few *Mario Brothers* and *Sonic the Hedgehog* games.

Some current games still use this perspective, and it may prove to be a refreshing change from all the first-person and third-person perspective games these days. Examples include Epic Games' *Jazz Jackrabbit 2*, Microprose's *Worms 2*, Monolith's *Claw*, and GT's *Oddworld: Abe's Exoddus* or *Oddworld: Abe's Oddysee*.

Monolith's Claw, above, and Mindscape's Creatures 2, below, use traditional 2D flat screens for the gameplay. (Used with permission by Monolith Productions, Inc. and Mindscape Entertainment, Inc., respectively)

Text-Based Games

There are very few of these games which don't use graphics at all, or very sparingly. Aside from the classic text adventure from the early '80s, such as the famous *Zork* series from Infocom or Douglas Adams' *Hitchhiker's Guide to the Galaxy*, today's *You Don't Know Jack* is a good example of this type of game.

Berkeley Systems' You Don't Know Jack is an extremely popular trivia CD-ROM series and online game series. Most of what's seen on the screen is in text, coupled with audio narration. (You Don't Know Jack is a registered trademark of Jellyvision, Inc., image used with permission of Jellyvision and Berkeley Systems, Inc.)

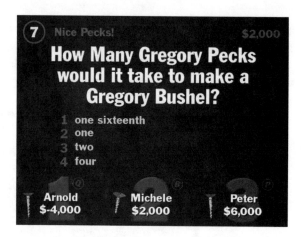

It should be noted that many games allow players to change the playing perspective, depending on what's going on in the game. Examples from different genres include Microprose's *European Air War*, Electronic Arts' *Need for Speed III: Hot Pursuit*, LucasArts' *Jedi Knight*, and Red Storm Entertainment's *Rainbow Six*.

There is also a lot of experimentation these days with both genre mixing and playing perspectives.

CHAPTER 2

General Game Design:
Action and Strategy Games

Considering that good game design is more of an art form than a science, it can often be difficult to ask someone to "teach" it to you. As an analogy, it's like asking Lennon or McCartney how they write a song like "Yesterday," or how Salvador Dali conceives a painting such as *Persistence of Memory*. In fact, it's often more difficult to analyze and tutor on game design, since it incorporates more senses than any other art form, not to mention that it's often a group effort *and* an interactive medium to boot.

Having said that, we are very fortunate to have some talented game designers who *are* able to put their avenues of inspiration into words and game design processes onto paper. Naturally, there are as many ideas on approaching game design as there are developers, but over the next two chapters, we've got some inspiring and enlightening advice from some of our young and bustling industry's finest.

>> Before diving into these words of wisdom, remember one thing—all the glitz and glitter poured into games these days, such as expensive art, animation, real actors, or the best musicians, cannot cover up for poor gameplay.

This chapter features designers from the action/arcade and the strategy game genres.

Action/Arcade Games

Shigeru Miyamoto, Nintendo

The honorable Shigeru Miyamoto is the general manager of entertainment analysis and development at Nintendo Co. Ltd. in Kyoto, Japan. He has created and designed some of our industry's most beloved series, including *Donkey Kong*, *Mario Bros.*, and *Zelda*. At the 1998 Electronic Entertainment Exposition (E3), Miyamoto was honored as the first inductee into the Academy of Interactive Arts and Sciences Hall of Fame.

Asked what are the most important pieces of advice to give new game designers, Miyamoto responds as follows:

> What is important to understand is that those who are making games are completely devoting themselves to the games. Because of such devotion, they can make unique, independent games. On the other hand, because of too much involvement, they are unable to objectively comprehend how the actual players would feel when they play the game for the first time. It is important to note that devotion to game creation has these effects.

> Another important element is a belief that creators are artists. At the same time, however, it's necessary for us creators to be engineers, because of the skills required for the creations.

Miyamoto says making games "fun" is Nintendo's only objective, and they're always making an effort to accomplish this goal. (Used with permission by Nintendo of America, Inc.)

➤ In Chapter 4, Miyamoto discusses how he creates such time-withstanding characters as Mario and Link.

Kurt Arnlund, Accolade

As a programmer on *Mechwarrior 2: NetMech*, the *Interstate '76* series, *Heavy Gear*, and now Accolade's *Slave Zero*, Arnlund has learned a thing or two about game design. He has two key pieces of advice to share:

Immersion

> Create a game environment that is so detailed that the player can get lost in it and forget he's even playing a game. This doesn't mean having the finest, most detailed texture maps of any game. This means creating the illusion that the game universe is bigger than it really is. Cracks in walls that hint at whole other areas of the world where life continues as usual. Cars and people on the streets going about their every day business. If you can create the illusion that the game is a living puzzle and the player is but a small piece of the puzzle, then the player is likely to get drawn into this puzzle even more. I'm constantly sucked in by games that make me feel like I'm really there. Good examples would be *Half-Life*, *Duke Nukem*, *Jedi Knight*, *Monkey Island*.

Have Fun Doing It

Second, Arnlund reminds designers that if the game isn't fun, it's not going to get attention.

> If it doesn't get people's attention, then they're not going to tell their friends about it. If they don't tell their friends about it, it probably is not going to sell well. You want to create a game that people are going to tell their friends about. The slightest bit of tedium and the player is most likely going to put it on the shelf and forget about it. There are few things I love more than calling up friends when I've discovered XYZ in a game, or I was completely amazed by how they executed feature B in a game. I love getting people riled up with the same excitement I have about a game.

Arnlund says he'd like to continue to work on creative projects that don't just push the technological limits of the available hardware, but also give the game players new experiences that are different than anything they have seen before.

Toby Gard, Confounding Factor

You may not be familiar with the name Toby Gard, but chances are you're aware of his most beloved creation—Lara Croft. Toby Gard left Core Design as lead graphic artist and game designer on the revolutionary title, *Tomb Raider*, to launch his own development studio alongside fellow Core Design lead programmer Paul Douglas.

Concerning general game design, Gard says your objectives should be contingent upon your resources. He explains:

> If you are forced into using a type of technology, e.g., a certain engine, or are limited in any other way by your platform or programming, then you have to come at your design from that direction first. For instance, at its most severe, if you're making a Game Boy game, then you already know you're limited to it being 2D and having pretty serious speed and memory restrictions. No *Quake 12* for you then.

"Assuming that you'll be making a game for the PC or one of the newer 3D consoles, however, as is more often the case these days, your restrictions are pretty loose." That said, he offers the following:

> I prefer working from this direction, because you can take a pure idea and you know that in some form you will be able to make it happen, however hard that route is. So then you need an idea, right? Well, I think we all have about a million of them each—it's whatever gets you excited, like wanting to be in *Star Wars* or showing people how much fun snowboarding is. Then all you need to do is go down to the pub and talk endlessly about what would be cool about it with your mates, or preferably with whoever you're going to make the game with.
>
> During that time, you need to be constantly solving the "How the hell can we do that?" technical questions. Even if you're just saying stuff like, "Well, we need shadows. *Quake* does shadows, so how are they doing that, and can we use a similar technique?" During this period you should be thinking an awful lot about how your control system will work. I'm a believer in compressing your control system down to the minimum number of buttons to achieve your aims; that way you tend to get an elegant rather than a cumbersome control system. You're basically aiming to be in the position where you have such a clear idea of what the game will be like, that you can actually play it in your head. When you can do that, if you're visualizing it hard enough, you'll be able to see and address loads of the flaws in the idea before you've implemented a damn thing!
>
> Therefore, the three most important things for me are a) visualize the control system, including game mechanics; b) have technology ideas for how to implement all of the above; and c) write it all down!

➤ Gard divulges how to create a successful lead character in Chapter 4.

Carl Schnurr, Red Storm Entertainment

As producer on the award-winning PC hit *Rainbow Six* and the *Eagle Watch* expansion pack, Carl Schnurr has plenty of enlightening words to share with budding designers, in a number of areas.

Features

It's not hard coming up with scads of cool features to add to your game, but it's hard to narrow them down to the ones that truly make a difference. Every feature included in your game should be considered extremely carefully. What other features does it affect? Does it add enough to the experience to justify the cost in development time? Does it truly add to the fun factor without obscuring the overriding vision?

Levels

I've always enjoyed games that allowed me to approach them how I wanted to, rather than forcing me down a narrow path. The trick is to make a level that's rich with possibilities—give players a handful of balanced ways to beat the level rather than telling them, "This is how you must beat the level." We used this design philosophy with the levels in *Rainbow Six* with great success.

Rainbow Six's Carl Schnurr says he has received email from people who've spent days playing the same level over and over again, just to try out all the different ways to beat the level. (© Red Storm Entertainment, Inc.)

Voice Talent

Pay good money for good talent. It's worth every penny. Sure, you could get a friend to do the voices, but it will probably show—if not in the final quality, then in the time it takes for them to get it right. Get yourself a good casting person (preferably in L.A.) to get samples for you, and be willing to pay Screen Actor's Guild (SAG) rates for professional talent. You'll be glad you did.

Contractors/Freelancers

Treat all of your contractors just like you would an employee. Interview them thoroughly before signing anything and always check references. Make sure that each of you clearly understands the deliverables verbally before committing signatures to the contract. Ensure that the contract contains specific references to reworks and redos. Monitor their progress closely and don't be afraid to fire them if they breach the contract.

Game Vision

If you can't get someone excited about the game with a five-minute talk and a one-page sell sheet, either rework the concept or trash it entirely. This is the time in the project when it's cheap to do that—before you've committed resources.

Focus

Game before glitz. If the core game is flawed, who cares if you have beautiful cut-scenes or killer music? People may buy the game based on glitz, but they'll love it or hate it (and tell others their opinion) based on the game itself. Make sure you have a killer game first, then add the polish. Too many game companies do it the other way round.

Gabe Newell, Valve Software

Half-Life was Valve Software's debut product, racking up a number of "best of" awards from around the world. Gabe Newell, managing director at Valve, shares some tips on creating successful games:

The first thing you need to understand is, "Why is this an interesting game? What about the experience we're providing for a customer is unique or worth their time and money?" This is a very serious question, and most game designs fail at this point.

Part of the reason that game designs are led astray is that some choices—such as rehashing an existing game design with a slightly modified gameplay or art direction—will work under certain circumstances and not others. People doing a sequel to a hit game can get away with a much less innovative game design. (As an aside, this kind of "looting the franchise" approach is likely a pretty bad idea in the long run, even though version 2 of something [popular] will still sell pretty well.) Other companies seem to think that they can do game designs that are sequels to other people's games, and that has a much lower likelihood of being successful, for a variety of reasons.

With *Half-Life*, Newell says they started from an experiential definition of what they wanted to build. "We knew how the player was supposed to feel playing *Half-Life*, and used that to make a whole bunch of decisions." *What* exactly did you want the player to feel, and *how* did you accomplish it?

Prior to starting work on *Half-Life*, I had been reading a bunch of Stephen King. In particular, there was a novella he had written called "The Mist." The primary aspect of the story that really appealed to me was this sense of an ordinary world spinning out of control. Setting a tentacle monster in a grocery store, for instance. There were elements of science fiction crossed with horror, which I really liked. And in general the main character was struggling with realizing he had to be the main actor in the situation, that people who should be on his side were turned against him, and that even though bad things were happening, the shape of the catastrophe wasn't very clear for a long way into the story.

Given how I had felt playing *Doom*, it seemed possible to put a player into that kind of intense, scary action experience. I wanted to get away from the notion of "shooter," where the player is the deadliest thing in the universe, who just jogs around killing everything.

The character of Gordon Freeman [was left] as transparent as possible to the player. There's no voiceover, no third-person camera or mirrors. We tried never to pull the player out of the experience through cut-scenes, voiceovers, or even Easter eggs or other obviously authorial devices. We made the other characters in the game sympathetic and helpful, and then we did horrible things to them to try to get the player to feel both loss and the sense that the world was actually dangerous. We left a lot of ambiguity in the story to allow the player to write the story however he wanted to, from what he was experiencing.

Is Valve's latest *Half-Life: Team Fortress 2* one of these games that "loot the franchise," as Newell puts it? No, indeed it isn't—this is a multiplayer-only, stand-alone, nail-biting team-based game.

In Valve's Half-Life: Team Fortress 2, there are nine classes of players to chose from, each with their own particular skills: Commander, Light Infantry (Scout), Medic, Heavy Infantry, Rocket Infantry, Sniper, Commando, Spy, and Engineer. (Used with permission by Sierra Studios)

Cliff Bleszinski, Epic Games

Beginning at the age of 17, Cliff Bleszinski developed games for Epic Games. In 1993, Cliff designed the popular platform title *Jazz Jackrabbit*; then he began work on *Unreal* and a sequel to *Jazz Jackrabbit*, both of which were released in 1998. At last check, Bleszinski was tweaking the semi-final touches to *Unreal Tournament*.

Bleszinski says there are three things that he believes are key for designing and building a game:

No One Is Bigger than the Band

Making a game involves an entire team of talented and dedicated individuals. No one person makes any product; much like a Super Bowl-winning football team is not all about the quarterback, a game is not about a programmer or designer. A good team works well together, hangs out together occasionally, and acts like a well-oiled machine.

As an example, Bleszinski reveals that building *Unreal* took 20 people from start to finish. "Games are far more complex and involving than ever before."

Design Documents and Concept Art Are Invaluable

They outline your game plan and provide a "to do" list for the entire team. If anyone ever finds themselves twiddling their thumbs during the development cycle, you can just refer them to the documents or concept art for direction. A game needs a central starting point—although the team builds the game and makes it great, it needs focus and direction, and design documents and concept art do this.

A conceptual rendering of a level in an upcoming and undisclosed Epic Games title. Bleszinski says a team will often work around artist's sketches to create a unique style for that product. (Used with permission by Epic Games, Inc.)

The Ability to Separate Good Ideas from Bad Ideas Is Highly Underrated

You can sit down and dream up "the most incredible game ever," but can it be done realistically in a development cycle? Do you think you can *really* make 40 guns that all interlock and make infinite combinations of weaponry? Be realistic, and don't be afraid to shoot down an idea you don't like or an idea that's not feasible in the timeframe. Remember, every month your project is delayed is a month that you're paying a team and not earning money back.

David Perry, Shiny Entertainment

As game designer and president of Shiny Entertainment, David Perry has been responsible for many adored games, such as Disney's *Aladdin*, the *Earthworm Jim* series, *MDK*, and *Messiah*. Although most of Perry's input for this book is found in Chapter 4, he shares some words on general game design here:

A good *hook* is essential. A good hook means that you can describe your game in one sentence. For *MDK* it was, "He has a weapon so accurate, you can shoot your enemy in the eye from a mile away"—sniper mode was born.

A good ambiance. Take the gamer off into a world that he can explore and have fun in. It can be the real world, but if so, he must be able to do things that he doesn't personally have the skill to perform. If it's a fantasy world, make sure that everything makes sense and has consistency.

Keep the gameplay challenging, but don't let players get lost or blame the game for their problems. A good game designer always knows what the player is thinking and is looking over their shoulder every step of the way.

➤ David Perry's personal Web site is at www.dperry.com, plus Shiny's official site is at www.shiny.com.

Matthew Toschlog, Outrage Entertainment

Matthew Toschlog is president of the newly formed Outrage Entertainment. Prior to the name change and development team split, they were known as Parallax Software, the savvy group who developed the vertigo-inducing *Descent*, *Descent II*, and now, *Descent III*. (The other half of Parallax formed Volition to work on *Descent: FreeSpace*.)

Concerning general game design, Toschlog believes the most important thing when developing any game is *finishing*. He explains:

> I know this has nothing to do with games *per se*, but many small developers (and some big ones) let their games get out of control. If a game takes too long, your technology can get out of date, competing games can steal your market, and your team can get discouraged and quit.

With this in mind, Toschlog says his three bits of advice are a) know what you're going to do when you start, b) cut extraneous junk, and c) don't insist that everything be perfect. "It doesn't matter how cool your game is if you don't ship it."

I'm sure many game designers are curious as to how the idea for *Descent* was conceived. Were *Doom* and other first-person shooters a major influence? Toschlog sheds some light:

> I started in the game industry working on flight games, and *Descent* came out of the desire to combine a flying game with an interior engine. We had seen *Doom* and thought it was cool, but didn't really think of Descent as improving on it. *Descent* and *Doom* both used interior engines, but I think of them as different types of games: *Doom* is a walking game and *Descent* is a flying game.

We obviously get a lot of inspiration from other games. Anyone who plays a game notices problems or thinks of things that would make the game more fun, so pay attention when playing games. Any art form can provide inspiration: movies, books, painting, sculpture, comic books.

"The trick is to combine your original idea with the appropriate elements from art and culture to produce a unique product," says Toschlog, with a shot from Descent III as evidence. (Used with permission by Interplay Productions)

Toschlog provides examples from his past experiences on the need for focus and cutting "extraneous junk":

> We made a lot of mistakes on *Car & Driver*, the game I worked on before *Descent*, and the things we learned on that project helped make *Descent* successful. Perhaps the biggest mistake we made on *Car & Driver* was developing the game from multiple sites—we had programmers and artists all over the country. When we started *Descent*, we realized it was crucial to have everyone in one spot, and it made a huge difference.

> You should have a clear idea of what you're going to do in your game. If you have an unfocused design, you can waste an enormous amount of time. You'll add features you don't need, and you'll spend time on code that gets ripped out later. The more you think about things ahead of time, the more focused you'll be later, and the sooner you'll finish. This was another big mistake on *Car & Driver*—we were making things up as we went along, instead of working toward a clear goal.

> Don't overemphasize technology. Technology is your tool, but it's not a game. Fun is the key, and you don't have to have the best technology to make a fun game.

And finally, Toschlog advises, "Don't be afraid to cut stuff. For most games, simpler is better. Pare down your design as much as you can before you start, and resist the temptation to add every cool idea you think of."

Alan Patmore, Surreal Software

Alan Patmore is the president and design director at Surreal Software, the company behind Psygnosis' action/adventure title, *Drakan*, where he served as lead designer.

In a lengthy interview, Patmore touches on game design recommendations, where to look for inspiration, and the issue of 2D versus 3D games:

> Game design has been evolving over the past four years. Traditionally, designers would create a design document and sketch the levels. Artists and programmers would then build the game based on the design. *Doom* changed the way games are designed by providing easy-to-use tools that combined the art and programming, creating a level. This took gameplay to the next level; gameplay iterations took minutes instead of days. Surreal has followed this model by building tools specifically designed to allow for maximum gameplay iteration. With all that said, game designers at Surreal are both environment architects and gameplay gurus.

> The first thing you need to do when designing a game is to get all of your ideas down on paper. Even with the most incredible tools, it's important to have a well-thought-out game. This means writing everything down before diving in and building the game. By sketching out levels before you build them, you eliminate a lot of potential design problems.

According to Patmore, the next step is to build a demo, the first real implementation of your design. He explains:

> While building the demo, it's important to tackle the major game mechanics. If you're building a third-person action/adventure, you need to figure out how the camera is going to work. Implement the control system and combat system, figure out the world scale. When this is done, you will have a really good feel for how the game will play and feel.

> Once in full development, the most important thing is to figure out what your game does well and build on it. The best games are usually based on five or six play mechanics that, when combined, create the basis for the majority of the game. Essentially, stay focused! It's very easy to "feature creep."

"If you want to be a designer, there are several things you need to ask yourself," advises Patmore.

First, do you LOVE games? You really have to eat, sleep, live games to survive in this industry. You will have no life other than games. Do you like to work long hours? The game industry is not a 9-to-5 job. It's not uncommon to work 100-hour weeks when under the gun. Do you take criticism well? If you answered "yes" to all of these questions, you may be able to survive a job in the game industry.

The next step is to figure out what you want to/can do in game development. All too often I receive résumés from people who don't have the slightest idea what they want to do: "I program a little, but I want to design and do animation." Focus! Focus! Focus! The best game designers I know focus on game design. That's all they want to do. The best programmers program. Everybody has input into the game. It's important to figure out what you want to work on for the game and focus on it. The best way to get into design is to get the latest *Quake II/Unreal/Half-Life/Drakan* editor and build levels. With complete levels, you can demonstrate your ability to create 3D geometry, your mastery of level flow, creature placement, and game balance.

What about inspiration? Where does it come from?

Ideas for games come from everywhere. When I play games I think, "Wouldn't it be cool if they did this?" or "Why didn't they do this?" That sort of thing. Movies, books, and simply imagination are the greatest sources of inspiration. I am always daydreaming about alternate worlds. That's how *Drakan* was created.

After *Drakan* was conceived, what was the next step in the game design process? Has the vision of the game remained the same over the past two years?

Drakan has had two distinct designs. Originally it started as a fast action dragon shooter. That's right, Rynn wasn't even in the game. We chose this direction more from publisher pressure than our own creativity. Early in development, while we were creating a playable demo, we realized that the current design of the game wasn't going to have the depth that we desired. Our publisher, Virgin, was going through financial problems, and wasn't treating us very well. They eventually told us to start shopping the game around. We took this opportunity to start fresh. We redesigned the game, and the world of *Drakan* was created. We immediately created a demo demonstrating the new play mechanics, the look of the world, combat system. From there we took the play mechanics that we had established and built on them. *Drakan* was always an action game, so we focused on air combat first.

After getting the flight mechanics tight and solid, we focused on the ground section of the game, i.e., Rynn's combat system. This was the most difficult part of the game to design. We chose to develop a system that had not been implemented by any other game, so we had no model to use as a baseline.

"It was a snap pitching Drakan to publishers with a playable demo," says Patmore, because "there were no questions; the gameplay had been implemented." (Used with permission by Psygnosis, Inc.)

Do games need to be in 3D these days? Does a 2D game have a chance in succeeding? Patmore says games don't need to be 3D, and titles such as *StarCraft* and *Diablo* are perfect examples of 2D games that have been incredibly successful. That said, Patmore suggests the following:

> However, with 3D cards standard on all new machines, and the power and flexibility that 3D allows the development team, there's really no reason to build a game in 2D. 3D allows you to create environments that are much more immersive than 2D. After all, we live in a 3D world. There are tried-and-true 2D game mechanics that transition well into 3D. Mario 64 is a perfect example of how 2D platform elements can work incredibly well in 3D.

Patmore says he's been an avid game player and designer since he was eight years old. (Hence the fantasy game where you can ride the back of a dragon?)

David Walls, Hasbro Interactive

As creative director at Hasbro Interactive over the past two years, David Walls had the opportunity to design and direct many games, such as *Frogger*, *Centipede*, *Game of Life*, *Jeopardy*, *Wheel of Fortune*, *Clue*, the *Tonka Series*, and more.

Concerning general game design, Walls says to adhere to the following rules:

Study Games

Don't just play games, study them. Many people play lots of games, but the key to game design is understanding them. Why do some hold you for hours while others have you running back to the store to return them? Why do some games have a look and feel that makes you want to play them, while others disgust you at first sight? The problem is that there are really no tried-and-true rules to game design; in fact, many great games are designed by feel alone. But by studying games and trying to pick out those things that work and don't work, you can begin to develop a feel for game design. But, remember, this feel doesn't come from just playing alone; you must actively think about the design of the games, the reasons they do what they do.

In addition, don't just play one type of game, play all types. Many people are just like, "Dude, I'm an action guy" or "I only play the hardcore strategy games." I feel that you definitely limit your thinking by playing only one style of game. You can gain so much by playing lots of different games. Here at Hasbro Interactive, we work with everything from *Candyland* to *Frogger* to *Axis and Allies* to *Civilization*. It's awesome to be surrounded by so many great games because you can learn so much from different styles of game. You discover that even a game like *Sorry!* can teach you something about great multiplayer game design.

So play everything from console to PC to board, from action to strategy to family. Go from an action game like *GoldenEye* to a strategy game like *Civilization*. Think about what works with these games, find similarities. Find things that work for one type of game but not for another, and discover the reasons why. Study as many games as you can and you will begin to get the *feel*.

Develop Written Skills

More often than not, game design ends with a design document. This is a doc that outlines the whole game: rules, style, interface, characters, story, etc. As much as possible should go into the design doc before the project begins.

This requires that game designers have good written skills, especially the ability to organize information in a document form.

Develop Visual Skills

Most designers use game design docs to communicate the vision, but visual skills are very important. Now, you don't necessarily have to go out and become an artist, but the ability to draw and/or use a drawing program such as Visio is important to outline interfaces, levels, maps, character design, game structure, etc. Words are great, but a picture of how something works is always better. The ability to think visually is key.

Is it easier or more difficult to work with a well-known franchise, such as a board game, arcade game, or TV show? What are the pros and cons? Walls responds simply with the following: "It's fun to work with well-known franchises that are great games, but it's really hard work to get it right." He expands:

> You would think that working with well-known franchises is easy, but they often prove to be just as challenging as developing a new game from scratch. At Hasbro Interactive, we work with many well-known games in different forms. We develop games from many sources, such as *Frogger* and *Centipede* from the arcade world, games such as *Monopoly*, *Scrabble*, and *Clue* from board games, *Jeopardy* and *Wheel of Fortune* from TV, and even *Tonka* from the world of toys. Each of these formats has its own challenges, but the trick is to remain true to the brand, the play pattern, the look and feel, while updating where necessary for the computer games market. Here are some examples and lessons learned.

On *Frogger*

> Sometimes, the biggest mistake, and the one that is always easy to make, is to really "blow out" the game and try to update it too much. *Frogger*, as many remember, is really just a simple but addictive game where you hop little Frogger across the road. We were given the task of taking this game and "updating it for the '90s." Fun? Yes. Simple? No. *Frogger* started with the concept "*Frogger* as *Mario*"—a hop-everywhere sort of frog that you could steer in any direction. After all, who would want to play that old game as it was? We need to update the game play! Sounded like good strategy, but we quickly discovered that this just didn't feel right. It just didn't have the frantic *Frogger* feel. So we said okay, let's give him an eight-way hop! That sounded good—Marketing could probably put it on the box: "*Frogger*! Now with Eight-Way Hop!"—and it would make the game feel updated. But even that just didn't work gameplay-wise to allow *Frogger* to hop diagonally. So we made the grand leap—do nothing. Stick to the basics: forward, backward, left, and right, and keep the levels in a grid format. And that did the trick—it was *Frogger*! (of course).

> But the big question was, "Would people still want to play a game with these simple controls?" After selling a million-plus copies, the answer was definitely "YES!" and there was a reason for that. A game like *Frogger*, that has simple, addictive game play, is still a blast to play!

There were many lessons learned from creating *Frogger*. First, when dealing with classic properties, sometimes it's best to stick with the core gameplay and resist the urge to fit it into today's gameplay design. Second, as more people get computers, the audience for computer games is becoming wider, and games that have a combination of ease of use, ease of control, and simple, yet addictive gameplay patterns have the potential to become huge.

2

Walls and company at Hasbro Interactive decided not to toy too much with the winning formula that made the original Frogger such a hit in the arcades 15 years ago. (Used with permission by Hasbro Interactive)

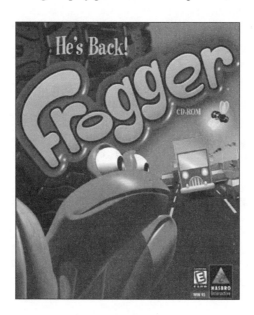

On *Jeopardy* and *Wheel of Fortune*

TV shows and movies have their own set of challenges. The primary urge is to re-create the show on the computer. For example, with game shows, you would get video contestants, do lots of different cuts, shoot lots of video, make a full-blown interactive television show. When we started *Jeopardy* and *Wheel of Fortune*, I'm sure we would have gone down this route had it not been for two games: the previous computer rendition of *Jeopardy*, and *You Don't Know Jack*.

When we started, we sat and played each game. In the old *Jeopardy*, the game tries to mimic the show and features video contestants. But since you're playing the game through characters, you never really feel "in the game." It just didn't flow. *You Don't Know Jack*, on the other hand, talks to you. It's first person. You are the contestant. You are playing. Everything is directed at you as "the player." We quickly arrived at the conclusion that the *Jack* format was the way to go with the new *Jeopardy* and *Wheel of Fortune*.

But wouldn't people want that "watching the TV show" experience? Don't we need video contestants? Don't we need Vanna spinning the letters? The answer was no, people want to play the game, and they don't want to watch TV when they're playing a game. Beyond being great TV, *Jeopardy* and *Wheel* are awesome games, tons of fun to play, and anything that gets in the way of that game-playing experience just gets in the way. So our direction was: These are not the television shows, these games are computer games. Approach it from the point of view that the game knows it's a game and it knows that the players playing are sitting around a computer. Avoid anything that bogs down the game.

This approach freed us from many binds. By relying on the power of the games themselves, we didn't need lots of video footage, we didn't need video contestants, we didn't need tons of bells and whistles, we didn't even need Vanna spinning the letters (fun to watch on TV, but murderous to game pacing). This approach allowed us to make very playable games.

Lesson learned: When designing games, always look at it from the player's point of view. Avoid anything that doesn't support the game play. Make things "player focused."

In conclusion for this thought, Walls says while it's challenging getting the right mix of brand essence, gameplay, and look and feel, working with these *old* games is great fun and a real gamer education. Says Walls: "There is a reason why these properties are still around; they're all simply amazing games!"

Walls was asked how he and the creative folks at Hasbro Interactive come up with new games. That is, are they brainstormed in a meeting or individually conceived? Walls says both, "but it's good to go to many sources for inspiration." What sources?

Other games: Depending on the genre for which you're making the game, it's good to immerse yourself just playing games in that genre to get you in the right frame of mind. But instead of just jumping into making the game, question everything about the current games. Try to go beyond the current thinking. This is always hard to do. Sometimes it helps to do crazy mental exercises to free your mind. For example, "I'm making a first-person shooter; what if I had to do that without any weapons?"

Other people: Get a bunch of people together and brainstorm. Believe it or not, at this point, include everyone: producers, programmers, sales, marketing, executives, anyone with ideas. But always start the meeting by saying that this is a brainstorming meeting. No bad ideas, but also no decisions. It's just an "idea collection factory." These type of meetings are great, but you want to avoid designing by committee.

Hard thinking: Most great ideas come from just plain hard mental work. It is good to lock yourself up in a quiet room with a pad and pencil and just think. Image what the game will be like from the title screen on. Think about characters. Think about gameplay mechanics. Try to think of the game as a whole entity. And then, challenge your assumptions. Got something good? Try to make it incredible. Got something incredible? Shoot for amazingly amazing.

What is Walls' take on 2D versus 3D? He retorts: "3D only matters if you need 3D to make a great game. Can a 2D game make it in 1999? If it's a great game, yes."

So why do people tend to run to 3D? According to Walls, it depends on the genre and demographic: "Action currently is about 3D. Strategy can take or leave it. Families don't want 3D because they typically don't have the hardware to run it."

And finally, what about multiplayer gaming? A must-have these days? "Again, depends on the game," answers Walls. He continues:

> There will always be an audience for the single-player game. If *Half-Life* had shipped without multiplayer, it probably would still have been successful, because the game was about an action/adventure story. The multiplayer in that game was just a bonus. But other games are beginning to be defined as multiplayer games, such as *Quake III: Arena*. It's all about the online competition.

David Walls says his future aspirations are to continue to make top-quality games for Hasbro Interactive—and along the way, add some original games to the mix.

Jay Wilson, Monolith

Monolith's Jay Wilson had plenty of axioms to share with newbie designers when asked "What makes a great PC game?" These assorted pointers are as follows:

1. Play a lot of games, *understand* them, and love them. "This seems obvious," begins Wilson, but says it's a necessity. "You all have to have the passion to take it one step further. The gaming industry is very competitive and everyone *must* want to do it."

2. You *can* improve on a good thing. Wilson draws the analogy to movies, where there are large categories, such as action, drama, or comedy, but the implementation of each is very different (slapstick comedies, dark comedies, dry comedies, etc.).

   It's a young industry, so everyone has their own idea on reinventing the wheel. It's evolutionary, not revolutionary. With *Blood 2*, we added RPG elements to the action game genre; with *Shogo: Mobile Armor Division*, it was an animé element to the action game genre.

3. More importantly, ask yourself what's realistic. Mirroring other designers' opinions in this chapter, Wilson says it's key to understand whether you can realistically pull off what you plan to do.

   You may want to make an online role-playing game—do you have the resources to do it and compete against others? You either have to scrap your idea if it's not realistic, or change the idea.

4. And finally, "Organization is key. I can't stress this enough," asserts Wilson. "I believe in that saying, 'work better, not harder.' Know exactly what you're going to do when you're making a game, and everything will run much smoother."

Jon Zuk, Raven Software

Gathered from his experience as lead designer on *Heretic II*, and on past games as a designer, Zuk says he certainly has some advice to pass on to junior designers. He offers these three quick pointers:

> I believe that the number one thing to keep in mind when creating a game is whether or not it's fun. No matter how good your idea or how many little extras you manage to stuff into your game, if it's not fun, it won't last. We spent time every step of the way to ensure that *Heretic II* would be fun. We had focus groups on the character, we tested key configurations, we tweaked the camera over and over, and so on. We as a development team knew that it wasn't the hook that was ultimately going to make the game successful, but the fun factor. The hook only gets people looking at it and trying it out. People most likely aren't going to play *Broccoli 2000: The Garden Simulation*, because it doesn't sound fun.
>
> You'll notice that I brought up the word "hook." While fun is most important of all, the hook is probably second. What's going to make people look at your game over the other 4,000 on the market? If you really think about it, there aren't a lot of original game ideas out there. So how do you make it stand out from the other 20 *Quake*-killers, or 50 racing games, or 100 real-time strategy games? The hook. Games always need a hook and a style of play that people can relate to. Take for example *Heretic II*. The hook is that it's a third-person action game. It's not *Tomb Raider*, and it's not *Quake*. The style, though, is closer to *Quake*, and people can relate to it.
>
> Finally, after you know (or think you know) your game will be fun, and you've got that perfect product hook, you need a team. Team chemistry is

very important. At Raven, almost everyone gets along well with each other. If there is someone that doesn't, at least everyone is professional. I've heard and read stories about other companies that have terrible chemistry. There's constant infighting, the managers yell at everyone, and no one wants to work. This causes schedules to slip, and the game to suffer as a whole. If you're going to put a team together to make your dream game, make sure you can put up with them for a year or more.

Strategy Games

Sid Meier, Firaxis Games

There is a very good reason why Sid Meier is one of the most accomplished and respected game designers in the business. He has pioneered the industry with a number of unprecedented instant classics, such as the very first combat flight simulator, *F-15 Strike Eagle*, then *Pirates*, *Railroad Tycoon*, and of course, a game often voted number one game of all time, *Civilization*. Meier has contributed to a number of chapters in this book, but here he offers a few words on game inspiration.

"Find something you as a designer are excited about," begins Meier. "If not, it will likely show through your work." Meier also reminds designers that this is a project that they'll be working on for about two years, and designers have to ask themselves if this is something they want to work on every day for that length of time. From a practical point of view, Meier says, you "probably don't want to get into a genre that is overly exhausted."

To Meier, it all boils back down to passion:

> What do you get excited about and what are you good at? Do an RPG, not an action shooter just because it's in style. Perhaps find something new and fresh—publishers want to be leading edge, too, so they're usually receptive to new ideas. But remember, for every 20 guys that walk into the door, maybe only two ideas are worth considering.

Meier's last two releases were *Gettysburg!* and most recently, *Alpha Centauri*.

➤ Be sure to flip to the chapters on user interface (12), testing (15), and breaking into the industry (20) for more from Meier.

Peter Molyneux, Lionhead Studios

Peter Molyneux is a household name for hardcore gamers because of his string of continuous successes at Bullfrog Productions. At this U.K. development studio, Molyneux served as a game designer, programmer, and often producer, for the following international hits: 1989's *Populous*, 1990's *Powermonger*, 1991's *Populous 2*, 1993's *Syndicate*,

1994's *Theme Park* and *Magic Carpet*, and last, 1997's *Dungeon Keeper*. His number one current aspiration is to make Lionhead Studios' first release, *Black & White*, "the best computer game ever."

When asked to offer advice for budding game designers, Molyneux responds with the following:

> The art of game design is not so difficult as people might imagine. The first piece of advice I would give anyone designing a game is use every source of inspiration available to you—from films, books, and music to everyday life. For example, I got the initial inspiration for *Dungeon Keeper* after seeing the films *Pulp Fiction* and *Interview with a Vampire*, where the bad guy was the hero. Once I've been inspired and have the idea, then I always spend at least six months turning it around in my head. Personally, I never write anything down; once I do that, it seems to solidify, and I'd rather keep it developing until I'm completely happy with it. Once this happens, I write down the idea, keeping to two pages and just listing the exciting parts of the game. (If you need more than two pages to do this, your idea is too bulky.) Only at this stage do I feel ready to reveal my idea to friends and colleagues, and if they're excited by that idea then I know I'm onto a good thing. In conclusion, I would point out that my game ideas are evolutionary, as they grow as the game is developed.

➤ For more from Molyneux on breaking into the industry, see Chapter 20.

Rick Goodman, Stainless Steel Studios

While at Ensemble Studios, a company formed in 1995 with his brother Tony, Rick Goodman was the lead designer on the tremendously popular *Age of Empires* for Microsoft. He has since left to form another development house, Stainless Steel Studios, and is currently working on an epic real-time strategy (RTS) game known as *Empire Earth*.

Goodman offers us his "Ten Commandments of RTS Game Design," here in its entirety. Thou shalt pay attention:

The Healthiest Plants Have the Strongest Roots

Goodman says to know your roots, whether they're comic books, sci-fi, board games, puzzles, toy soldiers, Chess, *Dungeons & Dragons*, or anything else, for that matter.

Paper Never Refuses Ink

The key here is how to separate your good ideas from bad, otherwise known as, "Hey—I have this great idea for a strategy game."

Goodman says anyone can write a good design document, but there are four keys to success: Play the game through in your head, model everything in a spreadsheet, prototype user interfaces, and compose your "strike team" of play testers. In fact, Goodman used the Internet to recruit 12 savvy *Age of Empires* players and uses them all the time for guidance on *Empire Earth*, and to flush out bad ideas. Goodman reminds designers to welcome advice from others, with the adage "It's hard to see the picture when you are inside the frame."

A Person Who Walks in Another's Tracks Leaves No Footprints

To innovate or to clone? Goodman reminds budding designers that we tend to criticize clones, then religiously follow up with new ones. He cites a phrase coined by Sid Meier, "innovative continuity," who came up with this term to not preclude him from doing anything he wanted. "Balance is key—add some innovative new things but make players comfortable in the game's surroundings so that they understand the rules and won't have to read the manual."

Finally, Goodman says to "enhance the positive, eliminate the negative, and don't fiddle with the middle."

If I Really Wanted Reality, Would I Have Booted Up the Computer?

The point of this commandment is to reinforce the fun factor over reality. Goodman refers to *Computer Gaming World* magazine polls that suggest fantasy strategy games are often more popular than historical or reality-based ones. He reminds game designers that although *Age of Empires* is a historical strategy game, not everything is realistic: priest conversions, moving catapults, naval units attacking land units, and so forth.

If a game is too realistic, does it take away from the fun factor? Goodman pokes fun at his own Age of Empires by asking "Where are the women? Doesn't anyone eat food?" and "Soldiers always fight to the death?" (Used with permission by Ensemble Studios, Inc.)

2

If I had Been Present at Creation, I Would Have Given Some Useful Hints

Goodman advises knowing your limits—look at yourself, try to recognize your strengths and passions, and take advantage of them. For example, Goodman knew his knowledge of board games was very strong when he approached *Age of Empires*.

By the Mile It's a Trial, by the Inch It's a Cinch

Creating a game usually follows a top-down methodology, with game vision on top of the pyramid, game ideas and features in the middle, and low-level game mechanics on the bottom. Goodman explains:

> There *is* a method to this process. The top is where the vision is generated (e.g. "How about a game where you're on a desert island?"), the middle is the game's features ("And this is what we'll do on this island"), and the bottom, the most crucial out of the three, is how to implement these ideas in the game.

According to Goodman, many game designers concentrate too much on the top two levels and not enough on how the play mechanics will work in the game. "The bottom level is the hardest; the implementation of the details is key," says Goodman. He also says most design docs seem to rely on the first two levels, when the emphasis should be on the implementation of the ideas into the computer and not just the ideas themselves.

Take Note of the Future; You'll Spend the Rest of Your Life There

Basically, Goodman says for the RTS genre to move forward, there has to be more to the game, and not just more of the same. He cites 3D action shooters as a genre that has evolved graphically, but not in gameplay, barring a few recent exceptions. With RTS games, try to foresee what will come down the pike and work toward bettering the genre.

Trees That Are Slow to Grow Bear the Best Fruit

"Time is your friend," says Goodman. "Use your project schedule well. *Age of Empires* was a 1,000-day project, with roughly a quarter of that time devoted to play testing 500 games."

"Beware—the only thing that can kill a good game is a great game." Be realistic at the beginning of your project and keep in mind many of the great RTS games, such as *StarCraft* and *Age of Empires*, took longer than average to complete, but look at the outcome!

Communicate Your Vision

One of the most important considerations while developing a game is communication. This is not only between a designer and his team, but between a designer and publisher, the public, marketing, game critics, and testers.

Never Put a Glazed Donut on a Mouse Pad

"…and other lessons learned the hard way," says Goodman. Some of his other lessons are "Schedules are not more important than quality," and "'Let's not tell them and maybe they won't find out' always backfires; it's no different than when you were a kid."

➤ For more information on *Empire Earth* and the design team at Stainless Steel Studios, visit www.stainlesssteelstudios.com.

Bruce C. Shelley, Ensemble Studios

Bruce Shelley is a senior game designer at Ensemble Studios who helped shape the mega-successful *Age of Empires* series. Prior to moving to Ensemble Studios, he co-designed many games at Microprose, including *Railroad Tycoon*, *Covert Action*, and the one and only *Civilization*, alongside Sid Meier.

Before diving into game design advice, Shelley was asked to discuss how he goes about researching a game, such as *Age of Empires I* and *II*. (Ever see the bibliographical references in the game?) Must it cost a lot of money? Shelley responds with the following retort:

> For most games, don't go into great detail. Don't try to amaze gamers with your deep knowledge. The player should have the fun, not the designer or researcher. The information in your game should be at a level of detail accessible by the average person. I begin researching games in the children's section of the local library. This works because children's books include a lot of graphics and computer games are intensely graphical. You can pick up graphic hints as well as research information. The level of detail regarding history presented in children's books is very well suited for mass market games. If you want to do a detailed simulation for only the hardcore, then you have to dig into more detailed sources. Eventually I do read a lot of adult books as well, to help with the overall understanding of events and the period.
>
> Research should not cost a lot of money. Microprose had a very limited budget for books and other sources. I learned this business making do with what I could find at the library. Ensemble Studios has been much more willing to buy books and videotapes to help our designers and animators. We have two bookshelves full of resources for *Age of Empires II*.

Shelley believes too much research is definitely a risk because people have preconceptions of historic topics based on movies and TV, in large part. If you stray too far from that paradigm, you risk frustrating them. The following is an expansion of this suggestion, and an example:

> When the game plays differently from what they expect, they're confused and begin to question the game. Always give precedence to creating fun over re-creating history. That's the clear lesson of entertainment media, especially movies and TV.
>
> An example from *Age of Empires* would be the catapult unit, which is able to move and fire with an area effect. There was nothing like this in ancient times, to my knowledge, but it worked for our game and stayed in. Also in *Age of Empires*, we adjusted the range, number of attacks, and movement of the different units so that there were interesting relationships between the units. We approached this balancing from the play test side, not by calculating real ranges and movement speeds. Flight sims designed for fun usually compress the time flying from base to dogfight and back because that's no fun. They usually also allow the player to carry way more fuel and ammunition than they do historically. This is to emphasize the fun part of play, which is combat, versus just flying in formation for hours to the engagement.

I reminded Shelley that it can be quite intimidating as a new designer to create a game with so many great titles on the market. Is there any advice he can give to ensure success? Shelley offers this assorted collection of general game design tips:

> Design games that you want to play and hope that a million people or more have the same taste.
>
> Try to make the game attractive to both hardcore and casual gamers; hardcore people create the buzz, but the big sales come from the casual market. Blood, gore, and foul language kill much of the casual gamer interest, and severely limit the potential sales of your game.
>
> Provide the player with interesting decisions, not trivial or random ones. This is the essence of gameplay.
>
> Analyze what the competition is doing very well and plan how you will meet or exceed them; determine where the competition is weak and plan how you can be very strong in those areas. For *Age of Empires*, we determined that none of the other RTS games had a non-cheating AI, random maps, or multiple victory conditions. Including those features in our game helped differentiate our product and went a long way toward creating the perception of value that made *Age of Empires* successful.

Avoid random events that adversely impact a player. These just increase frustration and add very little of interest.

Work toward two goals: maximum player fun (gameplay) and minimum player frustration (random events, poor interface, bugs).

And finally, Shelley's last truism is possibly the most pointed:

A new design (perhaps not a franchise sequel) has to have a great first 15 minutes. *Age of Empires* did, but many of our competitors didn't.

When it comes to balancing units in a real-time strategy game, are there any do's and don'ts a new game designer should bear in mind? Answers Shelley:

There are no real do's and don'ts. You simply rely on your instincts and thousands of hours of testing by different types of game players. Fix things people complain about, and leave things alone where they don't. If people don't find a unit useful, you improve it. If everyone wants to use only one unit, you scale back its effectiveness. We use this evolutionary process because it gives us the best chance of developing a game that's a lot of fun to play and is deep. The downside of this process is that it's very hard to predict. We don't know when we'll be done until we get very close to being finished. For most publishers, this is unacceptable because they must plan ahead for marketing, advertising, budgets, etc.

For *Age of Empires II*, we wrote a small routine that lets us quickly set up battles between different types of units. They fight it out in high speed and we quickly get empirical evidence of how they fight against each other. It can be a difficult problem to solve when you see A always defeat B one-on-one but 10 B's always defeat 10 A's.

➤ Strategy game designers interested in learning more about unit balancing should read Chapter 7 for additional advice on this important matter.

Brian Reynolds, Firaxis Games

"Okay, here are a few general thoughts," begins Brian Reynolds, vice president of software development of Firaxis Games.

Being a professional game designer (probably much like being a professional anything) is not nearly so *difficult* as you might think; it's more a question of scale and the amount of time you put into it. If you're good with a computer, you can probably already write a simple and fun game in a weekend or a week. Now imagine hiring 10 more people and spending an extra year or two polishing it—that's really the main difference between doing it strictly for fun and doing it for both fun and profit. So all of the tricks that professional game designers use work just as well for games written at home. In fact, you have a lot of advantages—the most successful professional game designers are usually the ones who both design the games and write the code personally. If you've got a cool idea for a game, no one can bring it to life the way you can.

Secondly, Reynolds says to get in there and make something you can play right away. He expands:

> Don't try to write everything out on paper or make fake interface screens, thinking you'll come back and write some code for it later. Try to put something simple together that you can actually *play* right from the very beginning. Play your game and see which parts are fun, what the strong and weak areas are. Then get back into the code, improve the strong points, and eliminate the weak points (or sometimes start all over with a different idea entirely). At Firaxis, we create a working prototype in the first few weeks of a project, and then play-and-revise-and-play-and-revise-and-play-and-revise for the rest of the project. We call this "prototyping" and the "iterative design process" and it really works. If you want to end up with a game that's really *fun*, there's no substitute for playing it yourself.

His third and final piece of advice covers the fun factor, interaction, and challenges:

> One way to describe a computer game is "a series of interesting decisions." Computer games are so much fun because they allow us to *interact* with a story rather than simply sit passively and receive it; so when you're creating a game, try to present the player with lots of opportunities to react. I've seen lots of games, even some famous ones, make the mistake of creating an elaborate "game system" that nonetheless leaves the player with nothing important to do. If a game spends most of its time performing elaborate calculations to simulate complex events, but doesn't spend much time allowing the player to participate and control the process, we say that "the computer is having all the fun," and that's bad—the player isn't getting to make enough interesting choices. Likewise, if a game leads you along one particular linear path, essentially forcing you to make particular decisions in order to succeed, we say that "the game designer is having all the fun," and that's bad, too, since a decision where A is always the right answer is really a non-decision, and isn't much fun. That's why we say a game needs to be a series of *interesting* decisions. When you present the player with three different options, each option should be a plausible path, and you should be able to succeed and win (at least sometimes) using each option. If you present your players with the choice "Fight, Bribe, or Flee," then each choice should lead to victory in at least some circumstances. The best games allow the *player* to

call the shots: The *player* picks a strategy, and then makes choices to bring his or her goals to fruition. If your game can be won using not just one, but a whole variety of strategies, people will want to play it more than once.

Chris Taylor, Gas Powered Games

By the time Chris Taylor launched his own company, Gas Powered Games, he had been in the gaming industry over 11 years, working at Electronic Arts for most of this time. Four years ago, he hooked up with Ron Gilbert to begin work on *Total Annihilation* at Cavedog Entertainment.

2

Though he was on vacation in his native province of British Columbia, Taylor was eager to share his knowledge on game design, inspiration, and how to become market sensitive. He begins as follows:

> Well, the first [principle] has to be an overall vision of the game that they're about to design. It's really hard to design something if you just have the mandate to make a great game. The second is that implementation is very important and that you have to find the right team of people to build the game. Third is understanding a long list of principles when designing. Principles like not designing it all up front, working with the team, experimentation, paying attention to the market, breaking some rules, not being afraid of copying what the competition has proven to be fun, and not being afraid of throwing stuff away if it sucks!

On inspiration, Taylor says that it often comes from the gamer inside of yourself:

> What do you like? What makes you nuts? How could you change something to make it better? I play games and always ask myself those basic questions. I also try to learn from movies, books, and music. These are areas where artists struggle to create new ideas, tell new stories, or evoke emotions that have never been felt before.

Taylor offers the genesis of *Total Annihilation* as an example:

> After playing *Command & Conquer*, I wanted to do an RTS game, but in 3D. I didn't know how much of the game would run in 3D at the time but I knew that if I could get the units to render at any angle, then things like being able to shoot while retreating would be possible. I also knew that if the units were 3D, I could have many more of them in memory than if they were all pre-rendered bitmaps.
>
> When I told Ron [Gilbert] about the idea, he immediately liked it and supported the project by having me join Humongous [Entertainment, Cavedog's sister company] and start working on it.

Note >> The terrain in *Total Annihilation* is 3D but it's pre-rendered so the camera has to maintain the same relative position and angle.

Being market sensitive is often an important determinant of a game's success, believes Taylor, and he explains how to achieve this without having to compromise the designer's original vision.

> Well, first of all, let's define "market sensitive." I see this as meaning "paying attention to what people are buying, what people are ignoring, and an extra sensory perception of what people might want if it were there to buy."

> I think if you have a strong vision of the product you want to build, nothing will get in the way. Even a market with a constantly shifting focus.

Says Chris Taylor, "Know what the market is currently excited about and add some of that to the design, subtract some of what they are tired of, and add a little of something wild and new that they have never seen before." (Used with permission by Cavedog Entertainment, Inc.)

> I don't think it will ever pay to jump off the deep end and deliver a new experience that's so alien that [players] can't relate. Creating a means of allowing the gamer to relate to the game is one of the most important things that a designer should keep in mind. People need to feel comfortable with what they're seeing and interacting with.

Taylor was reminded that this book was meant to also cater to budding game designers with little or no money. How can someone begin building his/her development team on a shoestring budget? Answers Taylor:

> Well, if you have no money, then everyone involved should have another job to pay the rent, and a lot of spare time afterwards to devote to the project. If you have that, then you have a chance.

> Someone on the team should have the vision, someone else should be an ace at code, and someone else should kick some huge butt in the art department.

Sound is important but that can come later, and be damn sure they know what they're doing, because nothing can make a game come alive like sound and music.

When you're working on something on the sly, you'll need to have something special, something that's brilliant and that makes the difference in a way that high production values won't. Think of an art film that captures the imagination of the audience for $100 grand, not $100 million. Even when you're in the business, you need to come up with tricks to cut corners and make a thousand dollars look like something that cost ten times that. Heck, I think that's where the magic can come from. A limited budget can help to focus you on the game experience and not all the expensive fluff that so many games have.

Peter Moreland, Hothouse Creations

Peter Moreland is the director of this U.K. game development company, plus he assumes the roles of game producer, team leader, and game designer. Their latest release is the controversial strategy game, *Gangsters: Organized Crime*. Moreland starts off by confessing, "I don't consider myself to be a game designer. In fact, I'm not even sure I know what a 'game designer' is." He expands on the admission:

> I've been in the games software industry for over 15 years, and don't think I've met the mythical beast that delivers all the concepts, implementation ideas, detailed equations, game flow plans, scripts, level designs, audio briefs, art briefs, and all the other things that make a game design. I know a couple who come close. But for mere mortals, game design is usually a team effort. The reason for this is that the range of skills needed to design a good game is unlikely to be found in a single functioning carbon unit! The most successful designers listen to and use the skills of people around them.

Moreland says one of the most fun tasks is creating the game concept:

> The first step is deciding the genre, subject matter, and basic content. This is the design stage people tend to zoom through, and it's one of the most important parts of a design. It's the foundation of the game. Bad foundation, bad game—simple as that. You will spend all your time retrofitting things and trying to patch a game up. Most of the time this is a recipe for disaster, so spend the time to get the foundations right.

> At Hothouse, we try to keep the game concepts reasonably simple. Be a prohibition gangster, a cutthroat pirate, or a special-ops marine. These subject matters are not plucked out of the air; they are chosen carefully. The game

player will have read books and watched films about these subjects, and probably have played these characters in make-believe games as children.

The benefit here, says Moreland, is that the player knows something about these characters, what they do, how they do things, how they behave. Before you load *Gangsters* you know what you will get to do in the game. Says Moreland:

> The player doesn't have to learn a complex world with all new values and rules that are alien to the player. This isn't rocket science, just common sense. Ease the player's path into the game world as much as you can.

> Think big for the original concept; if needed you can trim it back before full design or production starts. When I was at Microprose, we were lucky enough to work with Nick and Julian Gollop of Mythos Games to produce the best selling *X-Com* series. When they suggested the first game to us it was proposed to be purely the combat section, taking place on alien planets. We loved the idea but thought that the game should be bigger and that the player should be able to relate more closely to the plot. So Rob Davies, the Gollops, and I locked ourselves away for an afternoon's brainstorming. Rob and I suggested to them that setting the game on Earth, protecting the Earth, commissioning research, having the ufopedia would turn it from being a great tactical battle game into a top strategy title that players would really have a feel for. Mythos agreed to it all, went away, expanded on the theme, and produced one of the best strategy games ever.

Is there any advice you can give on the best way to nurture these concepts? Does the Hothouse team brainstorm often? They do, and Moreland offers these simple pointers:

> When you're having a brainstorming session, make sure that you get the lot on audiotape or whiteboard. If a session is really cooking, you don't want to lose the impetus by going into too much detail. Get the big picture down and come back for the detail.

> You should review these sessions after a few days' break, to see if things still look as good as they did when you held the meeting! Put them in front of a peer group for comment. Keep the cool stuff, dump or rework the ideas that don't get a positive reception. It will probably take several sessions to get something you're happy to move forward with.

"Once you've done this, you should be able to distill the concept into an overview document that presents your vision of the game," but he warns, "no more than a couple of pages." If the focus group is still excited by this document, it's worth carrying on; otherwise, there's probably something missing. Fix it or dump it and start again.

The design document—or, as Moreland calls it, the "pitch document" comes next, and should do the following:

> It explains the whole game concisely, and should have as its intended audience potential publishers. The finished pitch for *Gangsters* only consisted of about a dozen pages, but those dozen pages contained the framework for the entire game. What the player's goals are, what the player gets to do, the game flow, what the player gets to see, how the player can manipulate the game world.

> Not only should this document convey your vision to others; it must also state clearly what's unique about it. Identify a small handful of "golden nuggets"—the gameplay features that make your game really cool; then others will know why the game will be great. If you're doing a dreaded "me too" game, these must demonstrate why your game will stand head and shoulders above its predecessors.

Moreland reminds apprentice game designers to make sure that the design team is well balanced. "In the case of *Gangsters*, the framework was handed over to Martin Capel, who was able to extrapolate the ideas from the brief in detail (that dreaded word again)." But Moreland says more people are needed to shape the game in this stage:

> Don't forget the artists and programmers. Give them plenty of scope for R&D [research and development] while you're moving from the concept to pitch stage of the design. In *Gangsters*, all the artists and programmers experimented with different effects and styles of presentation. Maybe brief one artist and programmer as to how you imagine the game will look, but let others interpret the concept and pitch documents in their own way. Chances are they'll come up with a look and feel far better than yours, unless of course you're a top artist and programmer as well as game designer.

Concludes Moreland, "Use your skills, don't abuse them." And use your head:

> When you know there's someone on the team who can do something better than you, ask for their help, collaborate, share. Add to this thorough concept foundations, uncomplicated subject matters for your games, thinking big at the concept stage, regular reviews of your work, and not losing sight of your "golden nuggets," and you'll have learned some of the secrets of good game design.

Chip Bumgardner, Interplay

This producer at Interplay Productions contributed to this book's chapter on proper game testing (Chapter 15), but in this section he talks about general game design and what it's like to work on a well-known franchise. After all, he's currently working on *Star Trek: New Worlds* for the PC and PlayStation.

When it comes to designing a game, Bumgardner says, "Start off with a pretty good idea on where you want the game to go, but be open to change." He explains why:

> Very rarely does a product come out that was exactly like the designer intended. The team will always have ideas that pop up and should be weighed for the benefit of the project, but don't go nuts with it or you'll never finish (believe me, I have seen it happen).

Secondly, he reminds designers that what you're doing is a game, so "go nuts with it— the most memorable games to me are the ones that did something different than you would expect."

When asked how he approaches licenses, and if he finds it difficult to stick to the rules of the licensed universe, he responds as follows:

> I love working on *Star Trek*! There's such a huge and interesting history there. The question you asked is twofold; it *is* more difficult in one sense because everything you do has to be approved by Paramount, so we can't just go and do what we want with the story. Fortunately they're *really* fun to work with, and understand what we are trying to do. They really get into working on the titles, and I think they're a great place to start to see if the game is really *Star Trek*. In another sense, it's easier [to work with a license] because a lot of the history is already there. If we need to know how something works, we just look it up in their archives.

In closing, Bumgradner concedes he is "really excited" about *Star Trek: New Worlds*, because it's the first ground-based strategy game to use the *Star Trek* license. And they also were able to create some stuff that has never been seen before. Curious?

Chris Taylor, Interplay

Senior game designer Chris Taylor is currently working on the *Star Trek*-licensed computer game *Starfleet Command*, and offers these three pieces of advice for game designers starting out in the biz:

Play Games

> Always, always, always be playing games. You can't design for the market if you don't know what the market is doing. Play computer games in the genre you want to design for. Play other genres. Play the bestsellers. Play the games that fail. Analyze the games and see why they succeeded or why they failed. Make notes. Keep a journal of the games you play and notes about them. Also, play board games, card games, RPGs, whatever. Just play a *lot* of games.

2

Set Small Goals and Achieve Them

It's much easier to set smaller goals than to set one large goal. Try and divide the work up into smaller sections. Instead of setting a goal of designing 20 missions in one month, set a weekly goal of 5 missions or a daily goal of one mission.

Don't Try to Include the Kitchen Sink

Pick one thing about your game and make it the best thing in that genre. Always do something better than everybody else but don't try to do everything better than everybody else. In *Fallout*, we set out to do the best characters and character creation of any CRPG. We made it so that the character's statistics and skills actually mattered in the gameplay. A character's Intelligence stat actually made a difference in the dialogue options the player had. Because of this, people would play *Fallout* multiple times with different characters, and the game would actually change for them. *Fallout* didn't have the best environment because you couldn't pick up every single object in the game or blow down the walls, but it really succeeded in capturing the role-playing aspect that many previous computer games had failed to do.

Taylor discusses what it's like to work with a successful franchise such as *Star Trek*. Is it more difficult or easier to create a game with an established license?

Easier, since you have a background of material already created. More difficult, because you have to match that background material. You don't have to paint as much of the world to your players, since they already should understand that world (or universe, in the case of *Star Trek*). People know what a Vulcan is, for example. You don't have to describe a Vulcan in detail; you can get down to the important part of actually telling the story of what the Vulcan does. Makes life a little easier. But you can't go against those preconceptions randomly. You have to justify your design more when dealing with known parts of the franchise.

Mark Green, Psygnosis

Currently, Mark Green is the production and design liaison for Psygnosis' U.K. studio. Until late 1998, he was a lead designer and has now moved onto a wider role, with more dealings with marketing and input on all games that come out of the Leeds studio.

On game design, Green says the first and most important piece of advice he can give is that *design* is not an avenue for those who can't be programmers or artists. He explains:

In order to be a good designer, you need knowledge of both programming and art. If you can't talk to people on their level, they'll not believe you are any good, and you'll never understand why they're telling you that something is impossible. I'm not saying that you have to be the world's greatest programmer and artist rolled into one, but you do need to understand how programmers go about structuring and writing their code, and how artists create and texture their models, and what limitations are involved. Obviously the same is true from the other side of the fence—just because you're a great programmer/artist, don't assume that you'll be a good designer; each one involves its own set of skills.

Green says understanding and breaking down an idea is key:

It's not enough to know that this game is good and that game is bad. You must be able to analyze games in order to be specific about what it is that makes a game particularly good or bad. People in your team will come to you with ideas for the game that you're working on. They'll not accept "That won't work" as an answer. They want to know *why* it won't work. Programmers, artists, even producers all have their own vocabulary that they use when talking on their subject. Designers also need one; their vocabulary needs to include that used by all the other vocations but also extend into psychology, marketing, and game specifics.

"Designing a game is an evolutionary process," says Green. "You come up with an idea for the latest, greatest blockbuster that's going to knock everyone's socks off, you write your thoughts down on a couple of sheets of paper and other people get interested, and the project gathers speed." Then what?

Next, you sit down with your newly formed team and flesh out the initial design to a stage where everyone is on board with the idea. Since individuals all have their own opinions, likes, and dislikes, this phase will probably see your idea of a game changing from how you first envisioned it. As development progresses, you will probably find the fine detail of the game changing even further from the original. As long as the essence of the game remains, then this is good.

In closing, Green says if people don't challenge your ideas, "then something is very wrong! Either that or you're a design genius—and there are precious few of those around."

Wolfgang Walk, Blue Byte

Serving as project manager for the critically acclaimed *Incubation* and many other positions at Germany's Blue Byte studios, Wolfgang Walk says he has some simple advice to share for budding game designers:

Think for a long time about what it is exactly you want to create. Think for a long time about what you *don't* want to create. Take your results and think for a VERY long time how you can make your game mechanics as easy to handle as possible. Never bore or frustrate the customer.

"And then," continues Walk, "there's the usual stuff a beginner has to go through."

Look what the others are doing. Never be so arrogant as to think that you can't become better anymore. There's so much to learn that you literally will never reach the point where you're not a pupil anymore. You'll always be learning, even if you become a teacher for others some day.

Find talented people.

Become familiar with all the other related arts: movies, novels, comics, etc.

Walk saves his most important pointer for last: Be a gamer!

Torsten Hess, Blue Byte

Project manager and graphic artist Torsten Hess has worked on *Settlers III* and *Incubation,* and contributes his thoughts on game design. Hess says first and foremost the designer has to write a concept:

It should be as detailed as possible. There are certainly a lot of things to change later. But it makes it a lot easier to handle the project if you have a concept to begin with.

Read articles and books about game design, interface design, signs and symbols. You can avoid a lot of mistakes by reading this stuff. There are enough mistakes you can make yourself as the project grows. Maybe you'll find out that these articles are not boring at all. One of my first books was Brenda Laurels' *Computers as Theatre* [1993, Addison Wesley].

Next, think about the budget:

We get a lot of concepts from people who want to sell us a game. Even if they take the first hurdle (an understandable concept), a lot of them don't have project milestones and budget plans. Take a look at the market and understand the gaming industry. It doesn't mean that you have to make a first-person shooter when it's hip to make them.

Hess is currently working on a *Settlers III* expansion pack.

CHAPTER **3**

General Game Design:
Adventure, RPG, Sports, Puzzles, and Sims

This chapter continues the discussion of general game design and inspiration from Chapter 2, heading into the rest of the game genres: adventure, role-playing games, sports, puzzles, and simulations.

Adventure Games

Bob Bates, Legend Entertainment

Legend Entertainment studio head Bob Bates started his career in 1986 writing games for Infocom, the popular computer game company that specialized in text adventures. Since then, he has written many award-winning graphical adventures, including *Eric The Unready* and, most recently, *John Saul's Blackstone Chronicles*.

In the following composition, Bates divulges his strategies and secrets for creating successful adventure games:

Entertain the Player from Moment to Moment

The worst crime you can commit as a game designer is to bore the player. More specifically:

a) Don't make the player perform a complex action twice. Once he has completed the steps to a puzzle, if he needs to do it again give him a single input that will perform the entire sequence. I'll give you two examples:

If you have a combination lock on a safe, once the player has opened it the first time, don't make him reenter the combination thereafter. Just give him an "Open safe" command.

If you've created a maze that takes a 20-move sequence to get to the center and recover the sacred *foo*, when the player starts to go out, take him all the way out automatically. Don't make him go through that 20-move sequence in reverse. And if he decides he wants to go back into the maze later, take him right to the center.

Tip >> Bates says *foo* is a generic word game designers use to stand for any object, such as "thingamabob."

b) Don't create long action sequences where the player has to do a bunch of tricky stuff without being able to save, and then if he fails, make him go back and do it all again.

c) Make it easy for the player to move around. If you have large environments, build in shortcuts to get from one end to the other, and don't design your puzzles so the player has to continuously crisscross your world.

d) Similarly, if you have rendered transitions in the game, let the player hit the Escape key or right-click to bypass them. There's nothing worse than being forced to sit through the same cut-scene over and over. God gave us the Escape key for a reason. Use it. And restarting the game is another spot where we often cause the player tedium. I know you've created the most beautiful intro movie known to man, but hey—he's seen it already. Let him bypass it.

If you eliminate these and other boring activities that most game designers put players through, what you'll be left with is a tight, fast-paced game that will hold the player from start to finish.

Don't Try to Write if You Don't Know How

It turns out that writing well is hard. People spend a lifetime learning to do it. If you've never really given writing much thought, *don't do it*. This doesn't mean you can't be a good game designer, or that you can't do good puzzles. It just means that when it comes to writing your text and dialogue, you need to get someone else to do it.

Good writing is an art and a craft. It's a lot like game design, in that you're trying to create the maximum effect with the minimum output.

My own personal litmus test is this. If you've never read Strunk and White's *Elements of Style* [Allyn & Bacon], you shouldn't be writing your own text. If you've never studied writing, if you've never struggled to learn the difference between good writing and bad, then bring in someone else.

Player Empathy

When people ask me what it takes to be a game designer, I tell them the single most important skill is what I call "player empathy." You need to be able to put yourself in the player's shoes. To anticipate what he's thinking, what he's feeling. To know what he'll want to try and to let him. To know what he or she will think is exciting. To know what will feel boring and to cut it out.

Without this ability, I don't think you can make it as a game designer—in any genre.

3

"I tell designers they need to be able to close their eyes and play the movie in their head—all before a single line of code has been written," says Bates. This screen shot was taken from John Saul's Blackstone Chronicles. (Used with permission from Mindscape, Inc. All rights reserved.)

Ron Gilbert, Humongous Entertainment

This gentleman is personally responsible for many of our best-loved computer games, such as *Maniac Mansion*, the *Monkey Island* series, and a handful of children's adventure games for Humongous Entertainment. Here he talks about the root of it all—inspiration. Says Gilbert:

> Sometimes it comes from playing someone else's game, it may come from watching a movie or reading a book—just something will give you a spark. Adventure games are built on stories, and you must approach the game design from that angle, as if you were writing a script or a book.

> Also, be aware who the audience is; if you're making a game just to please yourself, you may not be too successful unless you're *really* in sync with the market. But, at the same time, it has to come from your heart and not your head. If you do market research, it may come out too much from the head.

Are there any examples Gilbert can give, based on his past works? How did the *Monkey Island* idea come about? According to Gilbert, it was a bit of market watching (there were no pirate games of this kind) but was more of a personal preference:

> I wanted to make a fantasy game, since *Maniac Mansion* was set in a contemporary world, and I liked pirates. It took me a couple of years for *Monkey Island*, actually. I wrote five stories before I settled on one. But on the other hand, *Monkey Island II* was done in less than a year.

➤ We hear from Gilbert in the next chapter on creating a hit character, as well as Chapters 12 and 15 on user interfaces and testing.

Chad Freeman, Dreamforge Intertainment

Chad Freeman has served as a programmer on a few well-known and celebrated games, such as *Anvil of Dawn* and *Warwind*, and most recently he was the lead programmer for ASC Games' *Sanitarium*. We hear from Freeman in the chapter on programming (Chapter 8), but he also has the following tips to share regarding general game design:

The Importance of Story

> Let me start out by saying that I believe the most important aspect of a great game is its story. While there have been successful games and even whole genres that have been lacking more than the most basic of plots, inevitably the best games will be the ones that have a great storyline. *Quake* is certainly a classic in the first-person shooter genre, but *Half-Life*, while having essentially similar gameplay, has a great story that puts it a level above.

Don't Work in a Vacuum

You need the input of other gamers on your design. During the development of *Sanitarium*, we held walkthroughs of the entire game from beginning to end for the rest of our company. Their lukewarm reaction to one of the game's chapters [in *Sanitarium*] led us to scrap it and start again. On the flip side of the coin, don't change something just because anyone (or everyone) says you should. If you believe in your heart that something will work, leave it in. It may and it may not, but you'll never find out if you haven't tried.

Know Your Limitations

You deserve to be optimistic, but you need to be hard on yourself as well. For *Sanitarium*, we tried to identify our strongest and weakest points as a company and designed the game with those in mind. One thing that happens in every project is that features get cut in order to finish the game. In *Sanitarium*, we designed whole portions of levels that could be cut if necessary, without affecting the overall game. When the time came, we were prepared, and the game didn't suffer because of it.

Freeman's future aspiration is to create a game that surpasses *Sanitarium* in both gameplay and storyline.

Lee Sheldon, SouthPeak Interactive

Lee Sheldon is a writer and game designer who has worked on a number of well-known adventure games, including *Dark Side of the Moon*, *Temujin*, and the award-winning *The Riddle of Master Lu*. Sheldon was asked what are the most crucial things to bear in mind as a game designer, and to give a personal example to illustrate each of these words of guidance:

Why Make a Game?

Ask yourself why you want to make this game. That's the most important question you can ask. Do you want to make money? Do you want to entertain? Do you want to say something about the human condition in a unique and creative way? To answer this question, you need to look into your own heart, and know yourself. That's the first step. It's essential, if you want to create anything worthwhile. It can be extremely difficult. It's often overlooked.

To support this often-overlooked question, Sheldon provides the following example:

I was given my current game, *Dark Side of the Moon* (*DSOM*), as an assignment. This makes it even harder to invest yourself in a game, because you didn't develop it from scratch. It was science fiction set in outer space. We've seen a lot of games that can say the same. For *DSOM*, I asked myself the first question, "Why do I want to make this particular game?" What could I explore that would make it interesting to me? I came up with a theme. It was a simple one, not even very original, but it appealed to me. It was this: We humans need families. They nurture us, give us strength to face life. But our traditional concepts of "family" don't always succeed. I created a player/character who, through the course of the game, loses his blood family either through death or betrayal, but discovers a new family in a very unexpected place. So far, no reviewer has even noticed. I don't blame them. Themes in games are not as common as they are in literature. But it was that theme that made me want to do the game.

Who Is This Game For?

Make the game you want to make, but remember the player. If you hate first-person shooters, you won't have a good time designing one. At the same time, realize that you're not designing in a vacuum. Be aware of the genre's requirements and your audience's tastes. Don't try to make a strategy game idea into an RPG. Elevate your audience's tastes, if you can, but don't ignore them. The people who will ultimately buy your game don't care how you poured your heart and soul into it. They only want to know if it's fun. For them.

I started out in the game industry doing titles for children. *Once Upon a Forest* was an adventure game for young kids. I thought the puzzles and activities were pretty easy, and didn't need a hint system. But I also knew how frustrating a puzzle that stopped me dead could be. So I added a simple on-demand help system. If the child didn't know how to proceed, or didn't even want to think about it, she or he could click on a candle (the pre-electric-technology equivalent of a light bulb) on the interface, and the puzzle would solve itself. I had to put myself into the player's shoes, no matter how small those shoes turned out to be!

Challenge yourself

Don't set out to make a game that's "just like xyz, only better." Some common genre elements may be expected, and don't neglect those, but find a new way of approaching them. Raise the bar in as many different ways as you can: technical, story, characters, whatever. You'll need as many things as you can find to stand out from the crowd.

How did I challenge myself in *Dark Side of the Moon*? I created a system of modular storytelling in an experiment to see if I could tell a complex and involving story that can be experienced in any numbers of ways, but the ultimate experience the player takes away is still firmly in my control. Of the many virtues of adventure games, one is certainly *not* their non-linearity. If a game has it, there is usually little story. If there's a lot of story, things pretty much follow one after another in a single, predetermined path. I tried to create a full, rich, non-linear story. Nobody asked me to. It was incredibly hard to track all the possible variables to make sure the player didn't experience a "wrong" or apparently out-of-sequence moment. And since I couldn't predict exactly how anyone would play it, it requires far too much disk-swapping! It's an evolutionary step in adventure game design, by no means revolutionary, but I wanted to see if it could be done. Now that I know it can, and it *is* something reviewers and players have noticed and praised, next time I'll stretch the envelope just a little bit further.

And a final word on striving for excellence:

I started out in television. When I would go speak to groups about how to break into TV, I would invariably find many who felt that because TV was "so bad," it must be easy to create. They were convinced they could write down to the medium. They were wrong. Nobody should start out dumbing down their own work because of other dumb work they've seen wind up on the tube. You have to give it your best shot. Pour every ounce of craft and talent into the effort. There are a lot of other people waiting out there to "help" you. Consensus and democracy and reactive notes from non-creative sources will take care of all the dumbing down you need. Start with a peak, or you'll never end up with a reasonably decent hill.

What's next for Sheldon? An action/adventure game based on a major license ("but still shrouded in secrecy," says Sheldon) and *20,000 Leagues: The Adventure Continues*, due out before Christmas, 1999.

Roberta Williams, Sierra

We're privileged to hear from this veteran game designer throughout this entire book, but here she comments on game inspiration and ties her advice to a couple of fairly recent projects. Williams says a successful game designer is part marketer. She expands, "It's important to make a game you want to make, a game that will please you, but you must also know your audience and at the same time, know what niches can be filled."

With Williams' latest, *Kings Quest: Mask of Eternity*, she explains why she made a few changes with the game's design:

> I was getting the sense that people were growing tired of slow-paced games, or "plodding" through an adventure game, and it seemed there was a need for more "instant gratification." I didn't think *King's Quest: Mask of Eternity*, if created in the same vein as past *King's Quest* titles, would fly in today's world. Therefore, I did something to spice it up—adding an action element and making it in 3D, with no limitations. Again it goes back to understanding the marketplace. Although I think *MOE* straddles the fence well to appeal to longtime fans of the series, while attracting a new audience... it's very tough, but I wanted to inject some new blood into the adventure game genre.

With Mask of Eternity, Roberta Williams felt that it was time for a change, so she added an action element and made the game 3D, while at the same time aiming to please long-time fans by keep the story and dialogue fairly similar. (Used with permission by Sierra On-Line, Inc.)

As an additional example on niches that can be filled, Williams sheds some light on her design behind *Phantasmagoria*:

> I realized there was a popular genre going on in books and movies—horror— but this niche wasn't being met in the computer game industry. So *Phantasmagoria* became an interactive horror movie using full-motion video, with real actors.

Role-Playing Games (RPGs)

Matt Householder, Blizzard Entertainment

Blizzard North recruited Matt Householder to produce *Diablo II* and bring onboard a hand-picked group of programmers, artists, and sound/music artists for the project. Householder has worked in the gaming industry for many years and on varied platforms.

As a special treat to this chapter, Householder has written a large set of assorted truisms for game designers to follow. The list applies not just to RPGs, but to all genres.

Householder's Axioms of Interactive Game Design

Design for the target market—the players. Well, it may be obvious, but sometimes this basic principle gets lost during the dynamic process of game implementation. Of course, this axiom is true of all products, games or not.

Game design is an incremental process—you make changes to the game's code, artwork, or sound. Then you evaluate whether the changes improved the game or not. You try to predict which changes will be most valuable, of course, to avoid wasting time on things that add little/no/negative improvement to the game while requiring significant time or effort. In this way your game design "climbs the ladder of fun."

All design elements in a game must be judged by the standards of the target market. After all, players are going to spend most of their game budget and game-playing time on things that they enjoy. The best way to ensure that all your design decisions *increase* the amount of fun in your game is to test each one on the target market. But this is impractical for two reasons. One, the target market is huge. And two, it takes too long to get feedback. To make testing of design changes practical, you must choose a subset of the target market and poll it instead. Then the problem becomes one of choosing the best, most representative subset that can be *quickly* polled. The only subset that you can poll quickly enough is your game design/implementation team. So it is essential that your team represent as faithfully as possible the target market. That is, they must know games and know what is fun.

Householder recommends, "During development, make a playable build and criticize it thoroughly. Then, stop everything, analyze the criticism, and make the changes needed. Repeat as necessary." (Used with permission by Blizzard Entertainment, Inc.)

When you get into the beta process of bug-fixing and game-tuning, widen your market subset to include a well-selected group of beta testers. The Internet is probably the best way to find and communicate with these beta-testers.

Study the classics of game design. For coin-ops: *PacMan*, *Centipede*, *Asteroids*, *Defender*, *Robotron 2084*, *Joust*, *Street Fighter*, *NBA Jam*. Computer games: *Pinball Construction Set*, *Jumpman*, *John Madden Football*, *Doom*, *Quake*. Handheld/console: *Mario*, *Zelda*, *Bomberman*, *Tetris*.

Take something familiar to the audience and combine it with something novel. Beware, though, of an idea so original that you've never seen it in a game. Maybe it's such a bad idea that any game containing it is a guaranteed failure—kind of like a fatal genetic mutation.

Don't frustrate the player's desire for perfect control within the game world. Any sense by the player of lack of control (however brief) can be fatal.

The user interface must be intuitive and consistent. This makes it easy for new players to learn and encourages experienced players to become experts.

Reality is vastly overrated. Don't try to re-create reality. After all, if reality were that much fun, people wouldn't play games.

Don't interfere with the player's suspension of disbelief. And try to keep the game world (and interaction with it) self-contained and self-consistent. Although in this post-modern world, maybe the audience is only pretending to suspend their disbelief.

Make sure your player character is likable. If your audience looks at the character they control onscreen and thinks "Is that me? I don't like me!" your game won't sell well. Game players tolerate neither bad art nor the nagging feeling that they don't get the joke.

Make sure the frame rate is high enough and consistent. This is more important (and harder to do) for action games than strategy or simulations.

If you can't compute it, pre-compute it. Don't make the programming job even harder by calculating unnecessarily during runtime. Whenever possible, pre-calculate algorithms into tables and just look up the results at runtime.

Make everything (that must be) in the game adjustable.

An important part of game design and implementation is deciding how to model the game world—that is, the game variables and how they interact.

Anyway, put these variables into tables. This includes all the attributes of the players, enemies, and environment.

Balance the game by adjusting everything until it's maximally fun. Obviously, this is easier said than done. And economic realities will force you to stop sooner or later.

Have fun.

If all goes well, you will get to try it again.

Ray Muzyka, BioWare

Baldur's Gate, released at the tail-end of 1998, proved to be one of the true instant classics in the computer gaming industry. And successful, too—over 200,000 copies of the game sold through its first two weeks. Dr. Raymond Muzyka, one of the three founders of BioWare, is here to discuss what it's like to work with a licensed property (that is, *Forgotten Realms* and *Advanced Dungeons & Dragons*), and whether it helps or hinders game development and consumer recognition. The following is Dr. Muzyka's response in its entirety:

> Interesting question. A little bit of both at the same time, generally. I suspect that the answer will vary greatly depending on who you are licensing the property from, as well as the type of property. Wizards of the Coast (and TSR, which WOTC purchased in the past year) have been great to work with, actually (our publisher, Interplay/Black Isle, holds the license of *Forgotten Realms* with them, and BioWare developed *Baldur's Gate* in this universe). WOTC/TSR were very receptive to most of our ideas. If they had been difficult to work with, this would have made things a lot more complex—thankfully we didn't have to worry much about that, since we had a lot of fun working with them.

> One of the things we did early on was to involve WOTC/TSR in the design process—several representatives from TSR flew out to BioWare to see some of our art, design, and writing, so that they became more comfortable with the direction that we wanted to take with *Baldur's Gate*. They actively participated, suggesting things that would help out with the storyline. This ensured that they knew what we wanted to do, and also ensured that we knew how they felt about different design directions—we had to take care to develop the property in a manner consistent with their internal developments. It seemed most useful to talk to them frequently—not only at the outset, but a few months into the project and again a few months later, so that they could stay involved and comfortable with how we were treating their property.

3

Now, certainly, developing a licensed property is not a simple task. One of the first hurdles we encountered with developing in the AD&D world was complying with TSR's strict code of ethics—and this did limit some of the design a little. However, it didn't prevent us from coming up with a novel concept for the storyline, and in the end it didn't really impair any of the development. It was more something we had to stay aware of at all times.

We definitely benefited from the large variety of areas and characters that were already well developed in the *Forgotten Realms* universe—it simplified the task of picking locales, and we used the source books very heavily in this regard. We placed towns and cities, buildings, characters, and even scenery in *Baldur's Gate* according to how they were laid out in the sourcebooks for the game. Yet, this didn't constrain us too much because there was still a lot of scope for new characters or areas to be added in.

One of the largest hurdles was figuring out how to actually implement the *AD&D* rule system on a computer. We made the task more challenging for ourselves because we elected to make the game real time, rather than turn-based. We also decided early on to aim to not change any rules that we didn't need to change. Since AD&D is largely a series of exceptions to rules rather than merely a set of rules, this caused a lot of headaches. In the end, though, the benefit of staying true to the complete rule set became evident in the QA process: The game was largely balanced using all of the statistics of creatures and items "as is" out of the sourcebooks. If we had changed a lot of rules, the game would have been a lot more difficult to balance.

Finally, there are cost considerations. I'm not at liberty to say how much it cost for Interplay/BioWare to use the *Forgotten Realms/AD&D* license, but suffice to say, it wasn't cheap. A big-name license will cost a fair amount.

Overall, the process of developing a licensed property has both good and bad aspects. Certainly we plan to work (via our publisher, Interplay) with WOTC/TSR in the future, so in our case, at least, it was a very good collaboration.

 From a consumer standpoint, developing a game based on a well-known and loved franchise can work for you *and* against you. On one hand, the customer is already familiar with the characters (e.g., Fox Interactive's *X-Files* game), the environments (e.g., the *Star Wars* or *Star Trek* universes) and the rules (such as *D&D*). Therefore, the game may fly off the shelves faster because of the instant recognition, and the game may be easier to understand. On the other hand, there is a level of expectation by the consumer that, if not met, will surely disappoint the player more than an unknown set of characters, environments, and rules would.

Tom Hall, ION Storm

Before leaving to work on his RPG *Anachronox*, Tom Hall, the always-informative game designer extraordinaire at ION Storm, cofounded id Software, the birthplace of 3D shooters.

Concerning general game design, Hall admits there are many things that are important, but following are three good ones:

The Game Is for the Player

It's cool if you want to tell a story with the game, or have things go a certain way, but it needs to be fun and under control of the player as much as possible. It's okay to have arbitrary rules (like you can carry only four widgets), but never let them feel led by the nose. Never let the player see the man behind the curtain. They should always feel they're participating. If they ever feel they're watching and can't do anything about it, you've lost them. And what you actually get to do must be fun. Some designers seem preoccupied with the new or bizarre or detailed aspects of the game, and forget that the player is supposed to be having fun somewhere in the process.

Grab the Player in Thirty Seconds

Within the first half-minute of gameplay, you should really have an idea of the coolness of the game. If you're stuck in boring exposition, or you have to do boring things to get to any cool stuff, again, you'll lose the audience. What you want to hear when they start, and every few minutes after: "Oh—no way! Cool!" *Half-Life* did this well.

Your First Ten Games Will Suck

Get them over with. Make a bunch of small different games and learn your craft. I must've made 50 little games before working at Softdisk. Just finishing a game is a great accomplishment. It teaches you the whole process, and gives you incremental confidence.

To learn more about *Anachronox*, visit www.ionstorm.com.

Sports Games

Sean House, Electronic Arts

Sean House is an associate producer at Electronic Arts, in charge of the award-winning *Madden NFL Football* series for the PC. He says his advice applies to sports games as much as other genres. The three top things to keep in mind as a new game designer?

House says it's "detail, conciseness, and innovation," with the emphasis on the first point. He continues:

> The main factor to successful design is detail. Programmers and artists will take something that's unclear and always put their own spin on it, often in a different direction than that of the designer. A design that runs on with little focus will be hard to read and unsuccessful. Many of the main points will be clouded by the ramble. A design that's innovative will grab the attention of those that need to interpret it, and will have the greatest chance of being put into a product.

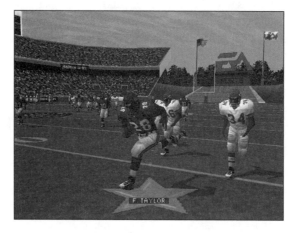

EA's Sean House believes detail and the implementation of the detail by talented members of a development team will ultimately lead to a better game. This shot is from Madden NFL Football '99. (Used with permission by EA Sports)

As an illustrative example, House recalls his experiences while working on *Madden NFL Football '97*:

> We had given to the developer a rough idea of a main screen's functionality. We wanted it to function similar to the Windows 95 dialog box with tabs (Display Properties uses this). The rough idea we had given them was quite rough, although we did go over what we were looking for at length in a meeting. We also told them we wanted it to have a "metallic look" and to make "metallic sounds" when you clicked on it. A month or so later, we got a screen that had a standard 3D Studio metal texture (dull with no reflectivity, no texture, very drab looking) and sounds that were similar to a musical triangle instrument (very high pitched and tinny). The main thing we were looking for in the screen was a hard, strong feel of steel with sound effects that were low toned, sounds you would hear in a steel mill or something, all of this depicting the hard, brute force of the NFL players and the game. What we got was a nice clean-looking screen that had some interesting sound effects, but something that would have been suitable for a techie

application or something. Moral of the story—if you have a particular idea about something, chances are that without a detailed, concise, and innovative design about it, you will get something out of it that is exactly the opposite of what you are looking for.

House was asked how important are cheat codes, secrets, and Easter Eggs in games. He says, "Coming from a PC background, I would say they're not very important," but admits that's merely his opinion. At the same time, he acknowledges its benefits:

> Cheat codes provide replay value. After people get bored playing a game with the default players or something, they can use the code to get a little more enjoyment out of it, and it makes them feel a bit more in control of their own game. This is what I have heard from our customers, and not a personal opinion of mine regarding my views on the games I play.

In closing, House says his aspirations include "moving up the proverbial ladder, taking on more responsibility, and developing new and innovative entertainment software."

Steve Coallier, Electronic Arts

This software development manager works for an in-house development group (Scoreboard Productions) at Electronic Arts. He has worked on a number of games at EA, from action titles to space sims to sports games. Coallier was asked to give his opinion on the current status of sports games and what a game designer should bear in mind while creating one. He responds as follows:

> Well, I don't think I've seen any sports game at all for the PC that I thought were well-tailored to the platform. There's a vicious circle with sports products: They don't sell well on the PC, so companies don't devote much effort into developing them, which affects their quality, so they don't sell well, etc. I believe the key to developing a successful PC title is to take advantage of the capabilities of the PC: There should be a well-developed network multiplayer version, there should be downloadable sets of stats, users should be able to import their own bitmaps to texture the players with, the graphics should push the PC envelope. Currently, just about all PC sports titles are not much more than you would see on a console system, and that's sad. This includes some of EA's own titles, such as *FIFA* and *Madden*, and it's an important thing that we're thinking about as we try to capture more sales going forward.
>
> As for console games, it seems like the focus of effort in most of the games is on providing a million features, which is a mistake on a console system because of the hardware limitations involved. We were somewhat guilty of this on the last game I completed (*NCAA March Madness '99*)—everyone

felt that the '98 product, which launched the franchise for EA, was fairly thin in hindsight, and so we sought to add anything you could possibly want in a college basketball game. As a result, we didn't have time in the end to do some of the polishing and tweaking that should be a part of any game's development.

So what's the answer?

A game should have a limited but extremely well-done scope of features, with most of the effort spent on the time the user spends actually playing the sport involved—keeping it fast and intuitive to control, with the user feeling like a part of what's being played. Our *NBA Live* franchise is an excellent example of this. They know that it's going to be an every-year product, and so they settle on a reasonable number of improvements each year. One year it might be adding plays to the AI and refining the Create Player feature; another year it might be adding facial animations and more dunks. You add enough each time to add value, and make it worth buying over last year's game *without* the updated stats, and then you add those as well. If you tailor what you're trying to accomplish to the schedule you're trying to accomplish it in, you're going to come out a lot better in the end.

Coallier's last point ties the two platforms—PC and console—together:

All of the time spent (on any platform) making a game look good, or sound good, or including every conceivable feature—all of that is simply wasted if the game is not fun and engaging to play. Take *Doom*—the number of features was extremely limited. Instead, they focused entirely on making an immersive, entertaining product, and because they kept that focus, they succeeded.

Puzzle Games

Alexey Pajitnov, Microsoft

This famous game designer, who is now creating puzzle games for Microsoft, is best known as being the author of *Tetris*, one of the most popular (and most imitated) video games of our time. During a telephone interview with Pajitnov, he divulged his top three game design secrets and admits he adheres to them when creating puzzle games.

Nothing Is Too Simple

Pajitnov says nothing is too simple for players and mentions this first because "when you get too close to your work and you're involved with it for so long, things tend to look simple to you." With the puzzle games Pajitnov has worked on in the past, everything looked to be trivial after a while, but he later realized someone who hasn't seen the game yet would likely find it challenging.

Don't Neglect the Hard Puzzles, Either

"No matter how difficult the task, there will be the player who figures it out," says Pajitnov. He admits this is contradictory to the first point, but they're both correct. "Don't neglect the hard puzzles because you don't think someone will figure them out; there will always be a smarter gamer than you."

Is the Game Fun?

Finally, Pajitnov believes if *you* don't get fun from your game, nobody will. "I tell all three of these things to my team all the time."

What about inspiration? Is there a way to find it? Pajitnov says, "Inspiration cannot be rationalized; it usually comes during the work, I am never waiting for it."

Do puzzle games need to be in 3D these days? How about multiplayer games? Does a single-player game stand a chance in the 21st century? Pajitnov's reply:

> 2D games still have great chances: The technology has been changing dramatically for the last 10 years, but not the human brain. And there are lot of people enjoying the Solitaire games, but multiplayer mode is such a great advantage that it's a crime to skip it.

Franz Lanzinger, Actual Entertainment

An independent game developer for nearly 10 years, Franz Lanzinger is responsible for games such as *Gubble 1* and *2*. Now with Actual Entertainment, he offers some comments that may be more sobering than you would want to hear, but it's the truth, according to Lanzinger:

From a creative standpoint, what are the three most important things a budding game designer must keep in mind when creating a puzzle game such as yours?

> First, make your puzzles easy early on. This helps beginners and gives players a chance to learn the game mechanics. Many designers fail here and think that their early puzzles are easy, when in fact they're not.

> Second, if you must make ridiculously hard puzzles, make them optional. You'll still get support calls about them, but not quite as many. Or better yet, include cheats or hints in the product itself. After all, nobody sells crossword puzzle books without the solutions!

Franz Lanzinger advises, "Even if you're absolutely sure that the game is really easy early on, don't forget to test this with young kids and adults who don't play many games." This screen is from the original Gubble game. (Used with permission by Actual Entertainment, Inc.)

Third, whenever possible use the game itself to teach your players how to play it! In *Gubble* we were concerned that players wouldn't know how to fly and would get stuck on levels where it was necessary to fly. Game designers often solve this kind of problem by putting a note in the manual or by putting text or even speech into the game to teach the players. This is okay, but there's a better way. For *Gubble*, we created a level whose whole purpose was to teach players that there was a fly button, and that they had better use it or they would have no chance at completing the level.

Stuart Roseman, nineCo

nineCo, Inc. are the producers of the popular multiplayer network Gamesville. Products include *The Bingo Zone*, *Picturama*, *AceyDeucey*, *Crystal Ball*, and many more. Stuart Roseman is the CTO (Chief Technical Officer) for the company and joins us to discuss multiplayer gaming and general game design.

Roseman was asked if he thinks a game must have a multiplayer component these days. What about multiplayer-only games? Are they harder to program than solo games? He responds:

> Our games are actually a step beyond multiplayer. Multiplayer has come to mean 2–4 players in a bridge game. To differentiate our products, we call them "large-arena, massively multiplayer games." Essentially we aren't satisfied unless we have thousands of people playing against each other in the same game.
>
> The race conditions, context switch issues, CPU cycle optimizations are different and more difficult when you're trying to organize that many players,

but we think it's a unique experience that's well worth the effort. Large-arena, massively multiplayer is something that you can only experience on Gamesville through the Internet. It's a wonderfully *human* feeling. You are genuinely part of the whole human race at that moment—competing with people from the Russian steppes to the Philippines—in a venue that allows everyone to feel connected.

In light of general game design, Roseman says there are two areas that can contribute to a successful game: figuring out who the audience of the game is, and being conscious of the code you're writing:

We decided early on to be as inclusive as possible—shooting for games that everyone can enjoy and play. If that audience is your target, then remember to keep it simple. Our guiding policy has been "less is more." We usually spend a lot of time taking stuff out of the interface.

Second, I know that various really successful software companies have made it fashionable to write games that use up all of your facilities and send your computer screaming for more RAM and CPU cycles, but it's possible to write software that is small and fast and efficient. It is a little harder, but imagine trying to explain your last egregious memory leak to the geek at the pearly gates.

Roseman discusses the simplicity of Gamesville's *E-mercial*:

This is a TV-like commercial broadcast to our players between games. It has a control panel. This control panel used to have two buttons—stop and go. You'd think this was a really simple interface, but not simple enough for us. We redesigned the software to get rid of the stop button. If you think about it, there was really no good reason to have that stop button. The final design was that each action should be initiated by the players clicking a go button. They never had to stop because they didn't go until they wanted to.

And on Gamesville games in general:

There are no downloads, no expensive system requirements, all you need is a computer attached to the Internet and the ability to click. We get emails from people all the time thanking us for being their refuge from clutter and plug-ins on the Web.

For *AceyDeucey*:

This is a large-arena, massively multiplayer card game. You get dealt two cards and you bet points on what the third card will be. There comes a point in this game where we have to figure out who has the most points. At first, we felt that this calculation had to be instantaneous, which would have forced us to run extra gatekeepers and careful action queuing. Instead we created an extra "Please wait while we calculate the winner" page—it's a fun page with music and graphics that everyone loves. And, as we all know, those things that are horribly difficult to do instantaneously become wonderfully easy when you have, say, five extra seconds.

Simulations

Adam Levesque, Blue Fang Games

Before leaving Papyrus to become president of the newly formed Blue Fang Games, Adam Levesque served as a 3D artist on *IndyCar Racing*, a producer/designer on *NASCAR Racing 1* and *2*, and an executive producer on all Papyrus products. Levesque was asked what three pieces of advice he can offer a budding game designer who wants to create a racing simulation. His reply is as follows:

Decide Who Your Market Is

If you're going after the hardcore sim market, make sure you understand what they want. The game will have to be realistic. The physics model, the rules of the racing (especially if modeling a real racing series) will all have to be spot-on. On the other hand, if you're going after the casual gamer, make sure that the game is easy to get into and not too complicated. Give the player early success and build from that. Also, the physics model will probably be more arcade-like; it's important to keep the frustration factor very low.

Do Lots of Research

Learn the type of racing you are trying to model. This follows more for modeling an existing race series like *NASCAR* or *Formula 1*. If you're inventing a new series, this is less important. Make sure you know all the rules of the series inside and out. Make sure you understand all the little nuances of the series—who are the best drivers? what are the most difficult tracks? etc.

Stick to Your Design Goals

This really applies to all games. At the beginning of the project, come up with a set of goals (usually no more than five) that the game *must* follow through on. Make sure every team member knows the goals and buys into them. Then, when a major decision about the game must be made, refer to the goals to help make the best decision.

Levesque provides an example of this five-goal rule as it pertains to *NASCAR 2*:

> Our goals were to: a) make the interface easier to use, b) add the spotter fea-
> ture, c) add the crew chief feature, d) make the race weekend more realistic,
> and e) improve the graphics to current standards. I think we stayed pretty
> true to those goals. The degree of success we had on each varied (in particu-
> lar with the race weekend) but for the most part we achieved what we set out
> to do.

When Levesque created *NASCAR Racing*, did he look at older racing sims and think,
"Hmmm… I think I can make one better"? In other words, should game designers try
to reinvent the wheel, or is it possible to simply improve on a good thing? Answers
Levesque:

> No matter what type of game you're making, to some extent, you're always
> getting inspiration from other games, past and present. The challenge is tak-
> ing those designs and adding your own interpretation on them. I believe it's
> critical for games to have their own *twist* to them. I mean, who cares if some-
> one does a game that's essentially a copy of EA's *Need for Speed*? Wouldn't
> it be better to take that concept and add a different *twist* to it? Maybe make it
> a game about racing those sports cars across country, dodging other vehicles
> and the police. Maybe about racing those cars around major cities in the
> world. With regards to *NASCAR*, we knew we had a good thing with *IndyCar
> Racing*. We also knew that *NASCAR* was an up-and-coming series. Heck,
> there was an old game called *Bill Elliott's NASCAR Challenge* (not regarding
> it as a stellar game) and it sold very well, because it was NASCAR. The
> main thing with *NASCAR* was to build on the success of the *IndyCar* engine,
> and make sure we were as true to life with the representation of the sport as
> we could be.

> *NASCAR 2* was a similar process. We knew we had a good franchise, and we
> wanted to make sure we could add some new and different things to it. That's
> why I'm pleased we were able to get the spotter/crew chief feature in the
> product. Not only was it something that could really help the player, but it
> was something they really do. In fact, it's a very big part of the sport.

In closing, Levesque says the most important thing is to identify the goals of the project
and stick to them. "In addition, add something new to the genre. Don't just rehash the
same old stuff."

Levesque left Papyrus to start his own company and work on other genres. He and his
team are currently working on *Dragon Hoard*, a strategy/RPG in which the player takes
on the role of a dragon.

Allen Jackson, Origin Systems

This dedicated Origin Systems employee has served as a software engineer on a number of high-profile and best-selling titles, including the *Crusader* series and the *Wing Commander* series. He has contributed to the chapter on programming (Chapter 8), but joins us here with an extensive essay on game design and all of the components that go into the exhaustive process. So kick back and enjoy the read:

Tools and Editors

There are three development-type jobs in constructing a computer game: designing, programming, and art. Many times each team member will do a little of all three of these duty types, especially in small or core development teams.

In all three areas, one of the most important considerations is the tools that will be used to make a game application. Programmers need to consider which compiler and system tools they are going to use—system tools like memory managers, exporting tools, and the SDKs needed to develop the game. For example, if the game is going to be developed for a Windows 95 environment, the programmer should become as familiar as possible with the DirectX tools from Microsoft.

The most ideal way of creating games is to have 70% of the game developed by designers who generate the data that the game engine presents to the players. All games with a large scope should be data-driven in such a way that the entire game could be created with just the editors, tools, and exporters created for the game engine. The game code should know very little about the actual game data, so that it's forced to parse the data in a general manner, which allows the game to become expandable and robust.

A good thing to remember is that the designers will need a scripting language of some kind to generate some basic artificial intelligence, scripted scenes, and menus. There are many kinds of scripting languages out there, including Python and JavaScript. The designers could script out a scene using the game objects in a sequence of dialogs that explain a plot point in one of these scripting languages, then the programmer would be responsible for interpreting the script and adding functionality in the game. The code could become isolated from the design of the game this way.

There are a number of responsibilities for the programmers on a project. There will need to be some sort of low-level interface to the operating system for things like files, video, audio, and networking. These low-level interfaces will need to be assembled into a game system that presents the game data to the user.

Jackson says a game designer can't design unless he or she is aware of the tools allotted by the programmer. This screen shot is from Wing Commander: Prophecy. (Used with permission by Origin Systems, Inc.)

There are few reasonable game-developing tools out right now because there are so many types of games that could be made, and nobody wants to have a clone-type game. Since the idea of game creation is to be original—as new as possible—most of the time the developers will need to create the technology for the first time. For example, if you wanted to make a *Quake* clone, there are a number of 3D engines that will have tools specifically for you to make *Quake*–type action, fast-paced games. On the other hand, if you wanted to make a football game using the same engine, the programmers would need to rewrite tools to allow for this kind of design. Further, the main engine would most likely need to be rewritten in a way that allows for the kind of gameplay that the game is designed for.

Never underestimate the art that will be needed for a game. Even a simple game that will only require 2D sprites will need a good 2D-sprite generator. So here, too, the artist tool consideration is paramount. It would be extremely convenient if the art tools supplied a user-defined way of tagging certain things like frames of animation, hot spots, script commands. For example, if the artist was working on a walking animation and wanted to place a "play footfall sound here" on a certain frame, then being able to place a save off that information inside of the art file somewhere would really speed up game software development.

The programmers and designers should also be able to use the art tools in order to make temporary art. While this is a relatively small problem in the long run, it really is convenient for the programmer to tweak his code by trying to import different art objects into the game that he created.

While designing tools for the game, it's important to develop intermediate file formats that will allow for future upgrades and features. Later, the game tools could use these files to generate specific, optimized game files. For example, maybe the current 3D engine that a development team is using only uses one texture map per polygon, but later it may be possible to use multiple textures per polygon. In this case, it would benefit both the artists and programmers if the art could be exported out to an intermediate file that would include all the textures for that mesh. Then, as the 3D engine becomes more sophisticated, the 3D art would not need to be remade to utilize the additional features of the engine.

The Core Game and Audience

At the center of every entertainment product—including movies, television sitcoms, books, games, and amusement park rides—is the core clever idea that will make the product entertaining. This core game design is important, since the player will likely be playing the games for hours on end. The audience must be able to recognize, embrace, and become engaged with the central themes, routine gameplay, and overall plot of the game.

Probably one of the first things developers think of when creating a game is the audience it will reach. The structure of the game develops in order to attract as wide of a range of consumers as possible, while staying true to the core design all along.

The best way to examine how the targeted audience influences design is to compare two games with similar premises but different gameplay. *Diablo* and *Fallout* both feature a main character that the player uses to interact with a fictitious world. *Diablo*'s audience is attracted to the quick fix. They like games that are simple to learn with a constant stream of action, preferably over the Internet. *Diablo* is an action-based game, which features nonstop animation and action, while relying on an intuitive, simple interface to learn in randomly created dungeons. While trolls, goblins, and gargoyles pour into the dungeon that the player is exploring, the player only needs to click on the monster to attack it. The inventory system is as simple as it can be, by ignoring things like weight allowances and backpacks inside backpacks. A simple grid allows players to place items; if the player can't fit the item in the grid, he can't store it.

On the other hand, *Fallout*'s audience is more concerned with character and story development where the gameplay is slower, more deliberate, and completely non-Internet capable. To this end, the development of the game is based around the character statistics and attributes, as well as the overall plot and setting of the world that the player is going to explore. Though the interface is still simple, the number of ways a player can interact in the game is much more wide and varied.

Both of these games are designed well, and it's conceivable that both games would be appealing to the same person, but for different reasons. Though the games look similar and the click-and-go mouse interfaces for moving are almost identical, the core designs are targeting different game experiences. The best thing to remember is that the features for the game should never make the original core design suffer.

The core game should be fun from the start. There should never be a time when the players will have to "suffer" until they can "acquire" the privilege to have fun. For example, if you're designing a military game that features gameplay in a tank, the player shouldn't have to go through boot camp or any kind of boring exercise for the sake of "realism." There should be tutorials and in-game instruction that ramp up the players, but they should not go through a dull, tedious time at any time they're playing the game.

Some features in a game are important to hammer out early so they won't rear their ugly heads later in development. If the game is going to have a multiplayer aspect to it, the basic core game will need to allow for it. If the game is primarily to be played with a joystick, there will be a need to design an interface that doesn't include a joystick, such as a keyboard or mouse solution. When the design of a game is complete, there will be a lot less hassle during true coding and data-creation development.

Presentation

A very important part of developing a game is how you plan to present the game menus, sound, and graphics. The presentation of the game should be crisp and simple without too many special effects that bog down the application's response time. For example, if clicking on a button in a menu system brings up another menu's beautiful animation but it takes two minutes, the beautiful menu animation will need to be shortened.

An important choice is the type of graphics engine. I would like to state that 2D art is not dead. If the gameplay calls for simple 2D sprites running around the screen, that's fine. In fact, there are many games that are using a 2D sprite-based engine, such as *Crusader*, *Ultima Online*, *Fallout*, *Diablo*, *Civilization 2*, and *StarCraft*. Though the 2D sprites look 3D, they're only 2D sprite representations of a 3D object.

The emergence of hardware 3D cards for personal computers really took off about a year ago. And some game genres have really flourished using this new technology—*Thief: Dark Project*, *Tomb Raider*, *Wing Commander: Prophecy*, and *Quake*. In addition, there are quite a few good 3D engines that have been written that take full advantage of OpenGL, Glide, and DirectX drivers.

The presentation of a game is not complete without sound. Great sound effects, moving cinematic music, and the right sound bites are extremely important. The choice of the type of graphics engine should be important, but assuming that you're developing for a Windows 95 platform DirectSound is your only choice. This doesn't mean that the technology for audio is any less important. The next generation of 3D sound cards are coming out, and after a while there will be no more ISA audio cards.

The one thing to remember about presentation is to focus on the development team's strength. If the only art that can come out of the group is 2D sprites, then you might want to design with that in mind. Further, if you have a musician in the group who can generate excellent music, it might be worth the time and effort in creating a dynamic music system that changes the mood of a game. This also includes the strengths of the programming staff, who may have extensive networking experience, which means that the design should incorporate a great multiplayer feature.

One last note about presentation. Don't make an interactive live-action video (LAV). Unless your game specifically needs to have LAV, it's too easy to annoy an audience rather than entertain them by using amateur video sequences.

Two last questions were proposed to Jackson: Should newbie game designers license a game engine or create their own? And is it feasible to make a game with no money behind you? Jackson responds to both queries in order:

On Licensing a Game Engine

My advice for persons who simply want to make a game is to use an existing 3D engine. If a programmer is interested in building his own 3D engine, that's a very daunting task in itself. In fact, without any prior experience with 3D math and/or complex coding architecture, building a 3D engine would become its own project, since it's a very large beast to tackle by itself.

I would suggest searching www.cg.cs.tu-berlin.de/~ki/engines.html for a 3D engine to start. Many of the engines offered there are free to use, and some even come with source code. For right now, most 3D engines are structured around how to pipeline a series of polygon and textures to 3D acceleration cards. Sometimes you'll also be able to find audio and collision code that will further simplify your game-coding timeline. This site also has plenty of suggestions about how 3D engines work.

What If You Have No Money?

Assuming that you already own a computer, have a compiler, and have access to the Internet, there really is no reason that you should have to spend another dime. Though it's likely that you may want to buy an existing "game builder." Many professional game houses are buying their 3D engines from out-of-house development companies. Usually the reason for this is that the out-of-house company has already spent a lot of time and money on the technology, which the game house then doesn't have to spend.

"Further," Jackson concludes, "if the out-of-house company has created a number of good editors and support tools, getting down to making the core game becomes much easier."

3

CHAPTER 4

Creating Characters, Storyboarding, and Design Docs

Lara Croft. Mario. Sonic. Pac Man. Earthworm Jim. Crash Bandicoot. Leisure Suit Larry. Duke Nukem.

What do these words have in common? The answer is simple—all of them are household names, but they're not famous actors from a Hollywood movie or some hit TV show. They're not Saturday morning cartoon characters (okay, some of them went *on* to that) and they're not the latest doll craze for kids. These are the video game heroes, the stars of the interactive screen whose marketing potential has keep them in the limelight for many years, and lined the pockets of their creators with green.

Many developers and publishers have tried desperately to create the next billion-dollar game icon, but a catchy name or cute look often isn't enough. So what's the secret? This chapter contains words of wisdom from many of those aforementioned characters. But that's not all we're going to explore here.

If there was a common theme running through this chapter, it would be "how to get your ideas down on paper." Some game designers prefer to sketch out rough characters or backgrounds on paper (or work with artists to do so); others draw sequential storyboards to help shape the vision and flow of the game; and in other cases, designers write fiction or game screenplays (usually for adventure games or RPGs when there's a lot of dialogue). *Design documents* are often lengthy paper reports used to communicate the entire blueprint of the game, covering all its features, story elements, characters, locations, dialogue, puzzles, artwork, sound effects, music, and much more. These documents are usually designed in a modular fashion so they can be updated and modified if the design of the game takes a new form.

This chapter highlights how some of the more famous characters in the gaming industry were born, plus we talk with game designers and artists about storyboarding, script writing, design documents, and other ways to flesh out your hit game before you type your first line of code.

Al Lowe, Al Lowe Associates

Al Lowe has been a game developer for Sierra On-Line since 1982, and it was five years later when he introduced a lovable loser of a character, Leisure Suit Larry. Eight games have been created based on this successful franchise; the latest is 1998's *Leisure Suit Larry's Casino*.

Lowe was asked if he can offer any tips for those who want to create a successful lead character such as Leisure Suit Larry. He replies:

> Clarify the character in your own mind before you begin. Describe him in writing, in great detail, fleshing out his background, his hopes and dreams, his desires, his strengths and weaknesses, his personality, etc., etc., etc. (Of course, I did *none* of this for Larry. Instead, I just made things up as I went along. But look at how *he* turned out!)

But where exactly did Lowe find the inspiration for him?

> Inspiration, hell! I had to ship a game in six months from start to finish, with nothing but a set of locations and weak puzzles to start with. It wasn't so much inspiration as pure unadulterated fear!

> That said, I'll give you a little more detail. In late 1986, I felt the time was ripe for a game that I didn't see anywhere else. Something that dealt with mature subject matter, and was funny. At the time, every computer game was

terribly serious: save the princess, save the galaxy! And all were set in fantastic settings: medieval times or other planets. I thought the world was ready for a funny game set in modern times, with modern people. Larry's loser image grew as I developed the game. Was he based on someone I know? No, he's based on the jerk everyone knows. (Well, okay, there *was* this guy who worked for Sierra as a traveling software salesman…

When Al Lowe created Leisure Suit Larry, he wanted to create a character that people could laugh at, but the difficult part was to make him someone they could also relate to. It's that balance that made Larry a success. (Used with permission by Sierra On-Line)

4

Lowe says sketching out a lead character prior to writing the game is essential:

If you can't write it down, you don't really know it yet. And if it's not written down, how can anyone else know what you're talking about? Every game I've done (at least since the old days of "Al does everything including the art") has had a game "bible," containing everything about everything in the game. The only exception to this is the actual dialogue, which I write later, while the art and programming are progressing.

Was the first Leisure Suit Larry game storyboarded?

In a way. *Larry 1* was based on a text-only game called *Softporn* that Sierra published in the Paleolithic period of home computers (1980). Sierra wanted an updated, fully graphical version of that design. When I examined it carefully, I realized I just couldn't do it. There was no protagonist at all! The writing was terrible. It took its mission seriously: your goal was really to "score three chicks." It was so out of touch, I said there was only one thing I could do: parody it. Mock it. Laugh at it. So I created a hero so out of it, he thought leisure suits were still hip.

So was there a storyboard? No. Mark Crowe and I determined all the elements that were needed in a scene, he drew it, I programmed it, then I wrote dialogue to fit what was there.

The rest, as they say, is history.

➤ Be sure to watch for the next Leisure Suit Larry adventure, Lust in Space, sometime in 1999 or 2000. Until then, fans of the series can visit a number of Larry tribute pages, beginning at www.sierrastudios.com/games/larry/links.html.

Toby Gard, Confounding Factor

Toby Gard is the creative director at the newly-formed Confounding Factor, but most gamers know him as the creator and designer of *Tomb Raider* and the Lara Croft character, when he was employed at Core Design.

When creating a lead character for a video game, Gard says to be sure you really like what you've designed; then other people have a good chance of liking it too. He expands:

If you aren't sure about your character, dump it. If you experiment all the time, drawing without any particular purpose, and explore avenues that look good in a fairly freeform sort of way, at some point you'll get something that you just instinctively know works. Then, you see, you'll start to love the character, and that will shine through in your work because the character starts to take on its own personality through your drawings. I think that's probably it—you need to design and redesign again and again, until you can't anymore. Then just draw that character about a hundred times (having fun with it) and you'll be there. Well, that's the method I use.

Toby Gard says a winning character will start to take on its own shape and personality after ample experimentation. (Used with permission by Eidos Interactive)

Are there any specific do's or don'ts Gard can offer when creating a hit character like Lara Croft?

> Make a character simple and clear; look at comics to see why. Your art should be an iconic piece of graphic art, as well as a nicely rendered piece of art. Example: gray, black, and yellow = Batman. Bold sections of color and a simple overall design. Whatever style you draw him in, Batman is always Batman because he's so iconic he's almost a logo in his own right.

> Do something radical. Almost everything can work equally well turned on its head. Most people are sick of seeing the same sorts of characters, so break the rules.

> If you want people to take to your character, then *you* should have respect for it; i.e., it should have admirable qualities, it should be something you kind of wouldn't mind spending a few hours stepping into the shoes of.

> After all, that's the whole point, right?

Shigeru Miyamoto, Nintendo

The honorable Mr. Miyamoto is a living legend in the interactive entertainment industry. He has conceived some of our most beloved electronic characters, such as Mario and Link. When asked how to create such internationally recognizable and deeply loved characters, Miyamoto says it all boils down to the fun factor:

> Making games "fun" is our only objective, and we are always making an effort to accomplish this goal. I believe that the creation of game characters is simply one of the processes to achieve this goal. If Mario games hadn't been fun to play, the character wouldn't be popular at all.

Miyamoto also warns that designers may not be able to objectively comprehend how the actual players will feel when they play the game for the first time, because they're so close to the project themselves.

4

Characters such as Link must be fun to play above all else, says Shigeru Miyamoto. This seems obvious, so why are there so many lackluster characters in computer and console games? (© 1998 Nintendo. Images courtesy of Nintendo of America, Inc.)

David Perry, Shiny Entertainment

President of Shiny Entertainment and game designer extraordinaire David Perry has brought to life a number of hit characters over the years. This includes protagonists from the *Earthworm Jim* games, *MDK*, *Wild 9*, *Messiah*, and others.

Perry was asked to provide three (in)valuable pieces of advice on creating a successful game character, and all three of his answers are thought-provoking:

1. Humor is a very important part of entertainment. So if you can make it amusing, that's the easiest way to go. Unique abilities are also good. Earthworm Jim's suit would use him to achieve its goals. Funny stuff like that adds spice to the characters you're creating.

2. Somebody once said that a great character has a unique silhouette—if you can identify a character just by its outline, you know you've made something that will stand out in a crowd.

3. New and interesting weapons are also important. Nothing is worse than playing a game with a leaky peashooter. So great firepower is a good way to pat a gamer on the head.

Finally, how important is storyboarding a game? Perry says it depends. "Storyboards dictate the direction of the game and the pacing, but it ultimately comes down to how well the game plays. Storyboards make a great starting point, but you can't rely on them 100% of the time. What works for films doesn't always work for games."

The many faces of David Perry. Earthworm Jim, MDK, and Messiah all have memorable characters because Perry adhered to his three rules. (Used with permission by Shiny Entertainment, Inc.)

4

George Broussard, 3D Realms

George Broussard is the president and partner of 3D Realms, one of the most sought-after development studios in the world. After all, they created the franchise known as Duke Nukem, and they're currently working on their fourth official title, *Duke Nukem Forever* (six if you count the PlayStation and Nintendo games they licensed).

What are the most important pieces of advice Broussard can give to someone trying to create a successful lead character in a game?

> It really depends on the type of characters you want to make. We typically create over-the-top characters that lean more toward what you might find in comic books or high-action movies. Characters that are larger than life, and for those types of characters there's a pretty basic starting point.

Broussard says you can break down any character into the following characteristics:

- **Personality traits.** This defines the character's personality and how he or she reacts to situations.
- **Appearance.** There should be a distinctive look to your character, so people will learn to recognize the character from appearance alone. Examples: Lara Croft, Superman (almost any super hero), Darth Vader.
- **Motivation.** Why do your characters do what they do? What drives them? Once this is established, your characters will get stronger from doing things the way people expect them to.
- **Catch phrase.** The best characters become famous and well known for a simple catch phrase that sticks in people's minds, and usually becomes part of pop culture. Remember the "Where's the Beef?" commercials for Wendy's? Examples: "What's up, doc?" (Bugs Bunny), "Up, up, and away!" (Superman), "Holy hand grenades, Batman!" (Robin), "I'll be back" (The Terminator), "Go ahead, make my day" (Dirty Harry).
- **Name.** A character's name should be "catchy" and unique in some way, so people hear the name and get an instant image in their mind. Rhyming and alliteration are good tools to come up with a catchy character name. Examples: Duke Nukem, Sonic the Hedgehog, Earthworm Jim.

To illustrate his point on the personality, appearance, motivation, catch phrase, and name of a distinguishable character, Broussard provides three excellent examples:

> See if you can guess the character before the name is given, simply from the basic elements.

Personality trait: Egotistical

Appearance: Sunglasses, red muscle shirt, bandoliers, blond flattop

Motivation: Kick alien ass/Score with babes

Catch phrase: "Come Get Some"

Name: Duke Nukem

Duke Nukem is one of the few characters to make the leap from a game to action figures and movies. (Used with permission by 3D Realms, Inc.)

4

Personality traits: Determined, inquisitive, loner

Appearance: Black suit, white shirt, tie, cell phone

Motivation: FBI agent/uncover conspiracies

Catch phrase: "The Truth Is Out There"

Name: Fox Mulder, from *The X-Files*

Personality traits: Lazy, devious, self-centered, meek

Appearance: Middle aged, gray hair

Motivation: Space explorer, shirk duties, cause mischief

Catch phrase: "Oh, the pain"

Name: Dr. Smith from *Lost in Space*

Says Broussard, "The above is merely a starting point for developing your own characters, and you can make them more or less complex depending on your needs. But in the end, these characteristics are needed for a really memorable character.

When it comes to artwork, how do you translate your sketches to real characters in the game? Is it necessary for a series such as *Duke Nukem*? Broussard responds:

> As video games have gotten more and more complex, we've started to adopt the ways that movies do things. A lot of games today have scripts much like a movie, where all the action, cut-scenes, and dialogue are carefully laid out in every detail. Another thing that has been adopted is the idea of concept sketches. These sketches serve to solidify the look and feel of elements in the game, such as characters, locations, and action sequences.

> The old adage "A picture is worth a thousand words" is certainly true.

This is a concept sketch for a character known as "Gus" in Duke Nukem Forever. Next to it, you can see how it translated into the game. The sketches provide the 3D modelers with a solid base to build on. (Used with permission by 3D Realms, Inc.)

Remember this controversial pre-rendered cut-scene from Duke Nukem 3D? Broussard gives us its origins with this very rare storyboard sequence. (Used with permission by 3D Realms, Inc.)

4

Here's an early representation of some locations in the highly-anticipated Duke Nukem Forever. (Used with permission by 3D Realms, Inc.)

But what about design documents? Does Broussard think they're necessary for all types of games?

Let me tell you about design docs. *Duke 3D* didn't even have one. We did stuff as we went, adding bits that were cool and discarding ideas that didn't work. Look how the game turned out. All we had was a vague notion that the game would be based in a future, seedy L.A. The rest came from a dynamic development process.

Duke Forever has substantially more on paper from the start because it's a much more cohesive and large game. But people who write 300-page design docs beforehand are wasting their time. The game design process (for most) is an evolutionary process. You refine and redesign as you go, learning and making things better. It's insane to write a 300-page doc, then just make the game. There is no way you can think of every cool idea before you make the game, and you have to be flexible enough to roll with the punches and add and refine ideas as you go, all according to the timeline.

Speaking from our experience, design docs are merely a general guideline that gets more and more polished as you go. You just try to stay 3–4 months ahead of things as you go. The design doc isn't done until the game is.

Also bear in mind that 3D action games are not that complex. They have bad guys, guns, items, and level locations. Not exactly rocket science, or something needing 300 pages.

➤ Be sure to read all about the exciting Duke Nukem happenings at 3D Realms' official Web site (www.3drealms.com).

Jane Jensen, Sierra On-Line

As a game designer at Sierra On-Line, Jane Jensen has created one of their most memorable identities—*Gabriel Knight*—and has had plenty of experience in writing scripts for her award-winning adventure games. She joins us here to talk about designing characters and writing stories.

I think this is a very similar process to writing in any medium. Yes, I do try to work through the characters' backgrounds and motivations, as well as, hopefully, having some change in the character that results from the story.

I do maintain a fairly tight control on characters during production. I review the character models, write the dialogue myself, and participate in the casting. It's critical to get the characters right. There's also some greater challenges and rewards, specifically in interactive characters. On the downside, you must do voiceover messages and responses to a lot of unimportant details (like the door or magnifying glass) and remain in character. There's also usually dialogue paths that lead nowhere. On the plus side, using these kinds of messages, which are not really story-related, you can really flesh out a character for the player in a way that might be difficult in a book or movie, where you have to stick directly to story-related events.

There must be considerable storyboarding in the *Gabriel Knight* mysteries, no? "We do some storyboarding of the large scenes for artistic reasons," answers Jensen, "to get the animation and cameras right. But most things are not storyboarded." So how then does it all come together?

4

The design process goes something like this: My first job is the design "bible" or story outline. Usually this ends up being about 100 pages and takes me five months. It lays out every scene and what happens in that scene. The big puzzles, such as the treasure map in *Gabriel Knight III*, are laid out in this document, though smaller ones often will be added later.

The team reviews this document and any necessary changes are made. At this point, I do "room descriptions," which lay out each location in the game and describe everything in the location and what animations take place there. This is for the background artists. I then begin the scripting process. We have a tool in-house that's like a Microsoft Access database. Each scene, whether a large story scene or a one-line voiceover message, gets its own entry. These are keyed by noun, verb, case, sequence number, in that order. For example, in the location KITCHEN you might see an entry for STOVE LOOK ALL 1 "It's a stove." Or:

CHIMNEY CLIMB NOT_HAVE_ROPE 1 "How would I do that?"

CHIMNEY CLIMB HAVE_ROPE 1 "I guess I could try it."

CHIMNEY ROPE FIRST_TIME 1 "I guess I could try it."

CHIMNEY ROPE FIRST_TIME 2 <Gabriel takes out the rope and throws it up the chimney.>

CHIMNEY ROPE FIRST_TIME 3 <Gabriel climbs up the rope. CUT TO: Rooftop>

CHIMNEY ROPE OTHER_TIME 1 "I don't need to go back up there."

In this fashion, each interactivity in the game is laid out with the logic (what triggers the response and under what conditions), the dialogue, and the description of the action for the animators and programmers.

After I see the art that's done for the backgrounds, I also add "incidental messages," that is, simple LOOK messages or whatever, for items that the artists put in the room that I hadn't called for (or sometimes I'll have them take it out if it's too leading or confusing).

Jane Jensen's database program also spits out a script for voiceover recordings or for actors, such as Dean Erickson, pictured here, when filming games. (Used with permission by Sierra On-Line, Inc.)

Jensen says many people wonder how to tell a real story interactively. In fact, she has been to conferences where Hollywood types claim it can't be done. She explains why they believe this is:

The reason is this: A real, defined plot and story is by nature linear and inflexible. People ask why *Gabriel Knight* (*GK*) does not really have the ignorantly lauded "multiple endings." The answer is simple. It's because a *real* story has a natural flow and a natural termination. If in *GK I*, for example, I decided that the hero died at the end or the "bad guy" lived or some such variation, the players would have been frustrated—they would know that was not the "right" ending. Indeed, *GK I* had a "false" ending in which the hero died; players instinctively knew this was not the "right" ending and that they'd done something wrong. They would even write to me in those words: "I saw the wrong ending once but then I replayed and got the real ending." Take, for example, the movie "CLUE." It had multiple endings, but most of them seemed pretty fishy. You knew the last one was the "real" one. And even to provide those multiples, the story was not so much a story as a series of red herrings.

Another problem is the natural linearity of storytelling. Gabriel can't confront his mistress with her sins until he has learned about them. And she can't threaten his life until he has confronted her. And he can't respond to that threat until she has threatened him. And so on. A story, by its nature, is a sequence of action/reaction, with the stakes and the pressure building more and more at each arc. How, then, to make it interactive?

The answer is the old "string of pearls" approach, which was first described to me by Roberta Williams when we were working on *King's Quest VI*. The idea is to picture each major plot point as the beginning of a pearl on a string. It is one central point, which is fixed. This could, for example, be the beginning of the game, or the beginning of a chapter or time block. You know where the player is at this point, you're in control of what he knows, and you convey the next large chunk of story. After this comes the "wide part" of the pearl. There may be 3 or 8 or 15 different little scenes or actions the player can trigger, and he can trigger them in any order. Thus these smaller actions are "non-linear." But once the player has done all of these things (or, at least, all that are required for the story—some might be optional), the game registers this fact and comes back to a central point— ending the chapter or section of the game by giving another big story chunk and thus "closing" the pearl.

4

As an example, Jensen offers the following:

The first chapter of *GK II* opens with a scene in which the villagers of Rittersberg come to ask Gabriel to take on a new *Schattenjäger* case: the hunting of an alleged werewolf that has killed a young girl. I know where the players are mentally—they have just started the game and as of yet know nothing. So the scene is simple; it's just like the opening scene of a book or movie. After the scene ends, Gabriel is left in the farm house of the murdered girl's parents. At this point we are "interactive." The player can move Gabriel around and explore the surroundings. During this chapter, [you as] Gabriel will do the following plot points:

- Read a newspaper that tells about the case, mentioning that wolves that escaped from the local zoo are the suspected culprits and giving the name of the detective on the case.

- Write to your assistant and mail the letter.

- Examine the crime scene at the farm; take a cast of a wolf-like print and pick up some animal hair.

- Go to the zoo and look around at the wolves in the habitat—eventually interviewing a boy who feeds the animals and the man in charge of the animals, and getting in to examine a wolf up close in order to get some hair for comparison.
- Go to the police station and ask to see the detective in charge.
- Take the samples of the wolf hair along with the hair and print from the crime scene to a local lab for analysis.
- Look up your family lawyer and ask for help translating some German you find.
- Follow the man from the zoo to a men's club and figure out a way to get in.

"This is all greatly simplified," admits Jensen, "but it illustrates how things are linear or not within the body of the chapter or the 'wide part' of the pearl." Keeping with the examples from *Gabriel Knight II*, Jensen expands on the "string of pearls" analogy:

> Gabriel can't get to the zoo until he's read about it in the newspaper, so those two actions are linear. However, he can do the zoo sequence independently of the police station sequence and writing to his assistant. He can't accomplish much at the lab until he's completed the zoo and gotten the hair sample, but he can go there and have the crime scene finds analyzed even if he doesn't have the hair from the zoo. The lawyer can be visited at any time, though you need the German note to get him to translate it. You can go through the entire zoo sequence without ever having found the hair and print at the crime scene. And so on. What all these actions lead to is getting into the men's club. That needs to be disallowed until all other actions are done, because that's where we "close the pearl" and end the chapter. This is taken care of as follows: You can go visit the club, but in order to be admitted you need family papers from your lawyer. You can visit the club earlier (after visiting the man at the zoo and asking your lawyer for the German translation, which gives you the name of the club), but the concierge asks for these papers. If you go to your lawyer to request them, he accepts the request but claims that his secretary needs to "find them in the file and Xerox them." No matter how often you go back to the lawyer, these papers will not be ready until the game finds that all other actions have been done (write to assistant and mail it, visit police station, etc.). Once all these things are done, the lawyer will give you the papers, and with these you can get accepted into the club. At this point (Gabriel gives papers to concierge), I once again know where the player is in the story—he has completed all actions for the chapter, so now we "close the pearl" and have the chapter close with a large story scene in which Gabriel meets the members of the club. This completes the chapter as well as setting up the intrigue for the next chapter (by introducing many new characters that the player will want to check out). It's not, perhaps, infinitely

non-linear, but it does provide enough variety and freedom for the player to explore in his own manner and learn things in a number of different ways. More importantly, it allows us to have lesser and greater plot points, which, in turn, allows us to tell a story.

Jensen has published novels based on the *Gabriel Knight* series, and she also gives us a special treat—excerpts from the design doc of the latest *Gabriel Knight* adventure, dubbed *Gabriel Knight III: Blood of the Sacred, Blood of the Damned.*

Excerpts from the *Gabriel Knight III* Design Document

Examples of fleshing out characters:

Detective Mosely

Mosely is from the New Orleans Police Department and is an old friend of Gabriel. Mosely just happens to be in Rennes-le-Château, having come on a "treasure hunt" vacation package. "It sounded like a lark," he says, but his behavior is decidedly strange. He keeps disappearing, for one thing. For another, he seems a little too interested in Gabriel's case. Mosely further bewilders by insisting that Gabriel not let anyone on the tour know that he's a cop, which, to Gabriel's thinking, is the only remotely interesting thing about him. Why does Gabriel get the feeling he's not *really* as "off-duty" as he claims?

Madeline Buthane

Beautiful, strong-willed, and erotically French, Buthane has down cold the mix of outdoorsy-yet-quintessentially-feminine womanhood that few men can resist. She certainly has her nearly all-male tour group wrapped around her little finger. Still, she is *awfully* enthusiastic about—one might even say *obsessed with*—the Rennes-le-Château treasure. Could the tour group be a ruse? A way to get free labor for a personal mission or get frequent access to the region for her own purposes? And is her interest in the ideas of every male she runs into really coquettishness? Or is she hunting for something specific?

John Wilkes

Wilkes is an Australian of the exceedingly macho variety (as if there were any other kind). In his late 40s, Wilkes has been all around the world—at least the desolate parts of it. He's a real treasure hunter, that's quite obvious. Although he won't talk about it unless exceedingly drunk or well seduced, Wilkes believes he has the secret of the treasure of Rennes-le-Château. He

4

believes the secret will make him incredibly wealthy. He's dead wrong about that.

An example of a scene and puzzle:

Catch Emilio spying in hallway (3D puzzle).

When talking to Mosely about the case, if you zoom in on the keyhole in Mosely's door during the conversation, you can see an ear.

When you go outside after the conversation, you can see Emilio just stepping away from the door. He has a glass in his hand. He pretends to finish drinking what was in it (the glass was actually empty), then he puts it down on a service tray in the hall and walks away.

If Gabriel misses this scene, he can still get the glass, as it will be on the tray when he exits.

Take glass from hall tray.

The glass goes into inventory.

This glass can be used on any of the hotel room doors at any time to see if someone is in the room or not. (We'll play various sound effects to indicate their presence in the room.)

And finally, an example of a conversation tree:

Jean, the hotel desk clerk

Talk to Jean

Topic: Rennes-le-Château

Jean recommends that Gabriel check out the museum.

Topic: Two men with a trunk

He wasn't on duty last night so he doesn't know how people came in or what luggage they had, but there are only seven rooms and a tour group takes up the other six rooms (besides Gabriel's).

Topic: Tour group check-in

Jean only knows that the rooms were reserved and filled, not what time people arrived.

➤ The official *Gabriel Knight III: Blood of the Sacred, Blood of the Damned* Web page is at www.sierrastudios.com/games/gk3.

➤ A very well-written and informative guide to writing design documents is available on the Gamasutra Web site. It's written by DigiPen's Tzvi Freeman and was originally published in *Game Developer* magazine in mid-1997. You can access the entire step-by-step tutorial at www.gamasutra.com/features/game_design/091297/design_doc.htm. Special thanks to editor Alex Dunne for the link!

Roberta Williams, Sierra On-Line

During a telephone interview, Williams gives her take on storyboarding and creating characters.

> Storyboarding works when you're creating a cut-scene or intro movie, when there's less (or no) inventory. Storyboarding seems to interfere with game-play since it's hard to show all the options visually.

Williams says she has done very little storyboarding and writes more in script form for her games, such as the *King's Quest* series or the *Phantasmagoria* titles. The design document is written rather than drawn and will describe with words what a character or room should look like. Concept artists may take it over from there to sketch the visuals. Williams also writes in a language so that the programmers will understand what she wants at that spot in the game.

Williams fleshes out the history of the other characters in the game much more than the main protagonist—the one that the player assumes the role of. Why is this?

> This is so you can put yourself in their shoes. Main characters are the least fleshed out in the game, so you don't know where they're from or who they are, really. I make them more open to interpretation."

➤ For more on how to create a great design document, flip over to Chapter 20, "Breaking Into the Industry."

Marc Hudgins, Yosemite Entertainment

Also at Sierra is Marc Hudgins, who is employed at the Yosemite Entertainment studios in Oakhurst, California. As an art director and game designer, he has worked on many celebrated PC titles such as *Quest for Glory I*, *III*, and *IV*, *The Realm*, *King's Quest VII*, and *Babylon 5*, to name a few.

4

In the following passage, Hudgins maintains that it's important to clarify what *kind* of storyboarding is required, and for whom it's meant:

> As applied in game development, storyboarding generally falls into two categories : interactive sequences and non-interactive sequences. Additionally, storyboards could be made for different audiences—team members, management staff, or outside contractors. Each of these factors affects the degree and kind of detail you might include. The idea is to spend just enough time on the boards to make sure they're 100% effective at communicating what they need. Storyboards are a tool, not an end product. Their job is to convey visual ideas to others.
>
> Non-interactive sequences tend to be boarded from one POV [point of view]. They require a step-by-step diagramming of the action. In these cases, the boards are more mechanical and specific. Non-interactive sequences are more like traditional storyboards. They can require camera moves, cuts, and other transitions. Timing is often a key ingredient. Most often, non-interactive sequences carry emotional and dramatic content, so the artist needs to be keenly aware of the visual language of film and be able to use it to advantage.
>
> The audience dictates the degree of polish and detail in a storyboard. If I'm trying to spec out a step-by-step sequence of events for another artist, I can usually churn out very quick, shorthand sketches to get the idea across. If the work is for a programmer, I need to make sure that the images are clear and that the proportions and visual relationships are correct. Programmers tend to take your board pretty literally, so I try to be as clear as possible. Still, within the team, I don't tend to put the degree of polish on the images that I do for other audiences.
>
> If I'm preparing art for a presentation to management or for implementation by an outside contractor, I put a lot of effort into them. The same amount of information is in them; they're just very clear and "finished." The idea is that someone can read them without needing me to explain the basic sequence. The images should be clear and indicate the proper perspective, attitudes, behaviors, timing, and relationships of their elements. For this kind of audience, you're usually trying to either sell them on the idea or, in the case of a contractor, trying to make sure they give you back exactly what you want. Either way, all the details need to be there, both visually and conceptually.

These storyboards are taken from King's Quest VII: The Princeless Bride. The first sketch is a non-interactive sequence; the second highlights dialogue and locations. (Used with permission by Sierra On-Line, Inc.)

4

When sketching out these ideas, Hudgins says, "Ideas pop in [my] head, and I make lots of doodles until what's in my head is in some kind of visual form. From there it varies. I might make very detailed drawings on paper and scan them to act as templates, or I might just work from scratch on the computer."

➤ To see some of Hudgins' creations, drop by his Web site at www.marchdesign.com.

Ron Gilbert, Humongous Entertainment

The gaming genius behind many of our most lovable characters, such as *Monkey Island*'s Guybrush Threepwood, *Maniac Mansion*'s Bernard, and *Pajama Sam*, believes that "there has to be something about the character that is visually recognizable, and simply understood." Gilbert continues:

> We don't have the bandwidth yet for complex characters like in film, so we simplify and often rely on stereotypes, and then we build them up through storytelling. In action or RTS [real-time strategy] games, we rely on these stereotypes for you to instantly understand who the character is. The story is secondary, more of an afterthought, but not for adventure games, of course.

➤ Many of Gilbert's latest and greatest characters can be found and downloaded at www.humongous.com.

Tom Hall, ION Storm

ION Storm's Tom Hall take some time out from working on *Anachronox* to give his opinion on creating a successful computer or console game character. He comments:

> Good lead characters must have recognizable motivations, have personalities that are engaging, represent a player's fantasy, and have an interesting quirk/Achilles' heel/pet object that makes them interesting. Their humor should be from within. Cracking jokes is cool, but if you hear them again and again, they wear thin. If something is funny because "that guy is just being that guy," then it's funny every time. Ben from *Full Throttle* is consistently cool. Any jokes or comments make sense within his tough biker world. And the free life on the road is a common fantasy—the player wants to be Ben. His pet object is his cool bike.
>
> Manny Calavera and other Tim Schafer lead characters always have wonderful references and non-sequiturs that keep every interaction interesting. They also have wonderfully expressive faces, which most games lack. This helps the player, because you don't have to tell them how the character is feeling, or use excessive voice work or exaggerated body movement—they can just look dejected. Tim is very good at presenting characters that are very unique and instantly familiar at the same time.

Manny Calavera and the other memorable personalities from Grim Fandango are great examples of rich, expressive characters, says ION Storm's Tom Hall. (Courtesy of LucasArts Entertainment Company LLC. © 1998 LucasArts. All rights reserved. Used by permission)

On the action game front, Duke Nukem is always crass and full of machismo—a refreshing break for many people when times are so politically correct. He's basically Arnold [Schwartzenegger] mixed with Ash from *Evil Dead 2*.

Lara Croft has that wonderful accent, the tough adventuring female angle (like a British Ripley [from the "Alien" films]), and the ridiculously proportioned measurements, which are the stuff of teenage fantasy. For men, you want to adventure with her, and be with her. For women, she's a strong female role model—a rare thing in gaming.

"Another great thing is a sense of mystery," continues Hall. "If there's more to their story than just what happens in the game, that's great." What exactly does he mean by this? Answers Hall:

If you give the character a history, even if you don't mention it, the character and your writing will feel deeper. And if you do have foreshadowing, like Cloud freaking out once in a while in *Final Fantasy VII*, questions are raised in the player's mind. This is wonderful, and makes the player yearn to know what happened, and what's next.

Are there things a game designer should *not* do when creating a lead character?

I would say don't rely on punchlines, and don't just trot out the usual stereotypes. Make something new. If you steal a recognizable stereotype, give it a twist that makes it fresh. If you're going to have an old Gabby Hayes prospector, have him knowledgeable in quantum mechanics. Have your action hero brake for pets. Have the old lady confess her torrid love affair with the character's father. Set up expectations and go against them, and you'll always get people's interest.

4

Joe Selinske, Ritual Entertainment

To complete this chapter on "getting ideas down on paper," Ritual Entertainment's Joe Selinske offers an example on fleshing out a character's dossier prior to creating the game. The femme fatale from Ritual/Activision's *Sin* is the beautiful but deadly Elexis Sinclair.

The following is an excerpt from her file:

Name: Elexis Sinclair

Sex: Female

Age: 31

Eye color: Green

Hair color: Black

Marital status: Single

Occupation: Bio-geneticist, chemist, and head of SinTEK Industries

Distinguishing marks: Tattoo on right buttock, tattoo around ankle, and navel ring

Family relations: Thrall, father (whereabouts currently unknown). Diane, mother (living in Europe).

Ritual Entertainment's Joe Selinske submits Elexis Sinclair's dossier as an example of how budding game designers can breathe life into game characters. (Used with permission by Activision, Inc.)

Background history:

Born in the sumptuous suburb of Freeport to Dr. Thrall Sinclair and Diane Kettle Sinclair on April 12, 1996. Elexis' mother abandoned them when Elexis was two to go out and "find herself." Her father, Thrall, a university professor and research scientist for a large pharmaceutical company, raised Elexis. She attended various boarding schools until the age of six, at which time her mother returned to partake in Thrall's good fortune. Thrall gathered up all of his and Elexis' worldly possessions, liquidated all of his assets, hid his money, and disappeared into the wilds of various jungles to escape from his estranged wife.

Not much is known of this time in Elexis' life, except that they both traveled around the world while Thrall studied all of the mystical and wondrous native sciences. For four years they traveled, learned, explored, and studied. One experience changed all that when Elexis contracted a rare sickness that was running rampant through one of the towns that they were currently in. Thrall feared for his daughter's life and rushed his little girl back to Freeport and the best medical help that money could buy. Elexis underwent extensive medical treatment and almost died due to complications.

Thrall wept by her bedside as she lay at death's door. This should never happen to anybody. Death is the cruelest of masters and on this day he vowed to find some way to prolong or even conquer this specter. He returned to his work with a newfound passion: to conquer death.

Many new challenges and situations help mold the woman that Elexis would become. Her mother's return (yet again), the problems and pain that Diane caused Elexis and her father. The fights over money, the struggle over control of Elexis' upbringing, and the tearing of her poor fragmented soul into a million pieces. She turned her attention away from family and began to study. She was soon swept up in a new passion—a passion for knowledge. She grew up fast and never looked back.

She had an affinity for the sciences and worked long and hard to learn everything there was to learn at the university. She graduated in three years with degrees in both chemistry and biology and entered into the masters program that summer. In only a year and a half, unheard-of at this or any other university, she completed the masters programs for both chemistry and biology. She manipulated her way into a lucrative research project that she was then able to use to obtain her Ph.D. in biochemistry and genetic engineering. She had become an equal to her father in cunning and talent.

She joined her father again and together they brought the smaller but growing SinTEK Industries to the forefront of the medical and scientific community. They diversified the business even more and expanded their market into the global economy. They stunned the world with a new product, Vanity, which seemed to stop and almost reverse the aging process. Their lives were set; Thrall quietly retired from the scene, and Elexis leaped to the forefront of the media to continue to push SinTEK Industries.

Little is known about her current genetic research. Rumor has it that she is experimenting in areas where many scientists fear to tread. SinTEK Industries is a virtual fortress, so even the local law enforcement has had no luck in getting even remotely close to speaking with Elexis about this. You can be sure that, whatever Elexis is involved in, it's something that's not even close to moral.

She's a gorgeous and mysterious woman. A genius who uses every faculty at her command to control and manipulate the situations to her benefit. She has her finger in so many different places that even an octopus would be envious.

Is sex often used to sell a game character? It's hard not to argue that sex appeal had something to do with the success of Sin's Elexis Sinclair, Tomb Raider's Lara Croft, and pictured here, Drakan's Rynn. Why should games be any different than movies, TV, music, or comic books?

CHAPTER 5

Puzzle Design

You look through the keyhole into the next room and there it is—the book of spells you've been yearning to find throughout this treacherous journey. With this precious collection of magic potions and chants, you will surely be able to get past the grunts guarding the castle up ahead. Alas, the door is locked, but a second glimpse into the keyhole reveals something sticking out of the other side. It's the key! You hastily look around the room, to find a scrap piece of paper lying on the table. And then it hits like a bolt of lightning. You slide the paper halfway under the locked door and bang your fists on it until the key falls out of the keyhole and onto the paper. Slowly sliding it back toward you exposes the key, and into the room you go to snag the book.

This hypothetical example is meant to illustrate *puzzle design*. That is, a game designers' sneaky way of inserting a challenging obstacle the player must solve with brains and not brawn (usually) to continue playing the game. These kinds of puzzles are found in adventure, role-playing, and some action games. There are usually different kinds of these puzzles littered throughout games:

- *Environmental puzzles* can be solved by analyzing and often altering your surroundings in the game. In Nintendo's *Legend of Zelda: Ocarina of Time*, the player must light torches on each side of a door to enter a new area of the cave.

- In *inventory puzzles*, objects in your possession may solve the puzzle. It's fair to say that environmental and inventory puzzles work together quite a bit, such as in the example above (or in a game like LucasArts' *Day of the Tentacle*, where you must place your bottle of wine in a time machine and pick it up in the future if you need vinegar).

- *Conversation-based puzzles* are usually solved by saying the right piece of dialogue when conversing with a character, or perhaps recalling an exchange between characters in the game that may be used in the present situation. An example of this is Mindscape/Legend Entertainment's *The Blackstone Chronicles*, where the ghosts of tortured psychiatric patients must be talked to in order for the player to find his/her kidnapped son.

- Finally, many adventure games, especially those that came out in the mid-1990s, used puzzles that had no relevance whatsoever to the task at hand. For instance, in DreamWorks Interactive's *The Neverhood Chronicles*, the player must solve a sliding tile puzzle in one instance and play a game of Concentration in another, though it had nothing to do with the game.

Bob Bates, Legend Entertainment

Bob Bates is the studio head at Legend Entertainment, and he shares the duties of running the organization with Mike Verdu, who has been his partner at Legend since they founded the company in 1989. Altogether, he has written, co-designed, or produced over 20 games that have won more than 30 industry awards.

Bates begins by explaining how puzzles relate to gaming, and the best ways to insert them smoothly into the game world:

> When you set out to write a game, you first design the major structural elements—the story, the setting, the characters, the major threat to the player's world, and the final goal that the player is striving for. Once you've done that, you've got to put obstacles between the player and his goal. These are the puzzles, and they must flow up naturally out of the setting you've created and the story that you're telling.

> Some think this requirement is unique to the adventure game genre, but it's not. Putting obstacles in the way of the hero has always been a fundamental part of storytelling. Ulysses didn't get back from the Trojan wars in a weekend.

The important thing is that each puzzle be appropriate to its setting, that it be reasonable for the obstacle to be there, and that, when we solve it, we know why what we did worked.

Bates believes that the villain should be at the center of the puzzle. He explains:

> Probably the single most useful piece of advice I can give about designing puzzles is to think about the villain. Something doesn't want your hero to succeed. Whether it's a person, the gods, the government, or the ultimate bad guy—whatever that thing is, is the villain. The villain is in active opposition to your hero/heroine. He's the one creating the obstacles. He says to himself, I do not want the hero to succeed, and I will stop him by doing *this*. The material he uses is material from the environment. His purpose is clear, and it's up to the hero/heroine to overcome the obstacle. So when you're designing a puzzle, ask yourself why it should be there. Who would have put it there? Why? Who is this bad guy and why is he threatening your hero/heroine?

The villain in John Saul's The Blackstone Chronicles is the spirit of the player's deceased father, Malcolm Metcalf. By understanding Malcolm's ways, it may be easier to get out of the many puzzles in the sanitarium. (Used with permission by Mindscape, Inc., All Rights Reserved)

5

"And remember to have your puzzles make sense." reminds Bates. "Give the player enough clues to solve them, don't make them too hard, and make sure that every puzzle advances the story."

Bates gives an example of a character-based problem to solve in order to advance the story:

> For example, think of a locked door. Sure, you could put a "move the blocks around" combination lock on the door. But what if you had a woman sitting on the floor in front of the door, crying? Clearly you need to talk to her to

learn why she's crying. And then you're going to have to solve her problem to get past her.

So suddenly we have introduced character development. Probably the very same bad guy who is making your life miserable did something nasty to her. The player learns more about her, the environment, and the villain—all because you designed a really good puzzle.

Bates concludes by suggesting that story and/or character-related puzzles may be the best way to go when creating an adventure game. "If you think of each puzzle as a story-telling opportunity, then it will fall naturally into the game, and your players will accept it as an integral part of the story, instead of an arbitrary roadblock put there to slow them down."

Jane Jensen, Sierra

Jane Jensen has talked with us quite a bit throughout the pages in this book, offering her expertise in many areas, including game design and character development (Chapter 4), and now she wears the hat of puzzle designer extraordinaire. Her flagship series for Sierra Studios is the *Gabriel Knight (GK)* franchise.

Jensen says it helps to choose a story concept in the first place that's inherently loaded with "puzzles." She explains:

Detective mysteries work well. What does a detective do? He examines evidence at the scene, tracks down and interviews suspects, perhaps follows people, gets news back from the lab, looks up the files on his suspects, etc. All of this natural work is easily converted into puzzles. "Quests" of the kind that *The Odyssey* or *Sinbad* made popular work for similar reasons. It's in the nature of a quest to explore foreign lands, have fights with bad guys or monsters, find treasure, and so on. A love story is a good example of a genre that's harder to make puzzles from. This is not to say that every game should be a detective story or a quest, but do be aware of how the puzzles will flow from your story before you spend a great deal of time writing it.

Jensen believes that puzzles are best when they flow naturally from the plot. Why is this, exactly? And why have so many game designers added puzzles that don't make any sense in relation to what's going on? Is there room for both?

A story with a bunch of logic puzzles (like *7th Guest*) has its place, but it probably won't be much of a story. It's not realistic to have your detective keep running into Chinese boxes and complicated puzzle locks. Of course, one or two aren't bad. In fact, you must put in more interesting puzzles than simply interviewing people and finding keys or reading letters. Just try to integrate them with the story.

In *GK I*, there was a clock in Gabriel's grandmother's attic that used to belong to his grandfather (now deceased). The clock was a German mechanical clock and it looked like it might do something, but what? On the outer dial was a series of images: a dragon, a lion, a moon, etc. To open the hidden drawer in the clock, you had to set the dragon to the top (12:00) position and set the hands of the clock to 3:00. A puzzle? Yes. But it was worked into the plot. "Three snakes" was a recurring theme in Gabriel's dreams—dreams he shared with his father and grandfather. This imagery was a key one to their enemies, being a sort of sacred symbol to them. This little puzzle not only emphasized the importance of this image in Gabriel's family dreams; it acted as a hint to a later, more important puzzle where "three snakes" had to be set in the enemy temple to get back the family talisman. Thus the "three snakes" ideas provided two very "logic puzzle" type puzzles, but it was also an important plot point and felt like part of the story—not a tack-on.

Also in *GK I*, Gabriel could visit the tomb of Marie Laveau in New Orleans. He finds odd symbolic marks on the tomb that he can copy. By copying these marks, he can find a voodoo expert to tell him that it's a code and translate the message for him. It's a direct letter-for-symbol translation, and the message is a hint pointing toward a suspect—but nothing definitive. That's because that first message is not the main point of this puzzle. Later on in the game, Gabriel finds a second message left on the tomb that he can copy (but not have translated at that point—the "expert" is now unavailable). Still later, he needs to have the voodoo cult take something specific with them to a meeting. How to accomplish this? He can leave his *own* message on the tomb, which will be assumed to be from the code writer. The problem? To leave the message, he needs some letters that weren't used in the first, translated version. But by transferring the letters he knows from the first message to the second message, he gets something like this: "I would l_ke to h_ve." Thus giving him by deduction the symbols for *i* and *a*. Now he can leave his complete message. This is a hard puzzle sequence, quite complex. And yet it does work with the story.

In *GK III*, I found a story idea that was naturally chockfull of puzzles. The story was about an obscure little place in France called Rennes-le-Château. The real-life mystery involves a number of riddles that supposedly point the way to buried treasure in the region. Not only was this a great mystery plot idea, but it provided the game with a main body of puzzles (deciphering riddles, laying out a treasure map) that were inherent to the story.

5

Note >> Jane Jensen's eagerly-anticipated *Gabriel Knight III: Blood of the Sacred, Blood of the Damned* should be out by the fall of 1999.

Louis Castle, Westwood Studios

We now turn our attention to Louis Castle, vice president of creative development at Westwood Studios. This experienced producer, programmer, artist, and art director explains how some of the creative puzzles were conceived for *Lands of Lore 3*:

> The storyline and the gameplay evolve hand in hand. We try to map out the emotional experiences the player will have while playing the game. Puzzles figure heavily into this, since they will slow down a game and take the player into a different range of emotions than the action sequences. The story and the puzzles are usually thought of in the abstract first—"At this point we need a task that will help the player improve xyz skill." Then each designer reaches into his or her bag of tricks to offer some ideas on how to accomplish the goal.
>
> Many times a designer will have a great idea for a puzzle but can't find a place for it. I encourage designers to flesh out their ideas and set them aside. It's amazing how the need for that idea will come up within a few weeks.

Castle says that puzzle designing is really a collaborative effort:

> We have in-house writers and have used contract writers. As long as the designers know the emotional beats of the story and the basic actions that take place, the writers can go to town on characters and situations. Many times a puzzle or task comes out of reading and interpreting the story.
>
> In *Lands of Lore 3*, you have the opportunity to travel to the underworld, where spirits are trapped in limbo due to the circumstances of their deaths. You meet a maiden who bemoans her fiery fate and that of her sisters. She implores you to end her suffering. As you explore the house, the rooms catch fire, and you're caught in an inferno that spreads down the halls and into the sleeping chambers. The puzzle? To find the lamps and empty the oil before the event begins. As with all quests in *Lands of Lore 3*, care was taken to reset the events should you fail and "perish" in the flames. In this case, the flames are but phantoms—in all cases there is a way out of your position so that no situation is a dead end, where the player is stuck with no way to progress. This prevents players from feeling they have to restart the game to succeed. It's always possible, although sometimes far more difficult, to finish the game.

Instead of punishing the player for not solving this real-time puzzle in Lands of Lore 3, the designers at Westwood Studios have written an alternate way for players to beat the situation. (Used with permission by Westwood Studios, Inc.)

Roberta Williams, Sierra On-Line

"Designing good puzzles is an art. To jog the player's mind without giving it all away or making it so tough that they give up—that perfect balance is a very fine line." Williams should know; after all, she's often referred to as the godmother of graphical adventure games. *Mystery House* was one of the first graphical adventure games, released on the Apple IIe in 1980.

Williams maintains that being obtuse isn't bad, but "it's how you give messages and arrange your clues, dialogue, inventory, and environment." Williams believes it's important to "remember to repeat hints, in case the player missed the first one; do this until the puzzle is solved, then the clue can go away."

 >> Ever play an adventure game and because you couldn't figure out a puzzle, you "cheated" by finding a walkthrough on the Internet or calling a hint line? The most frustrating part of all this is when you find out the answer to the puzzle was related to something you didn't notice onscreen. Because of this, Roberta Williams says when she's writing environmental puzzles, she always makes sure that the object that must be noticed is twice the size it should be, and center screen, if possible. She also believes in "message clues" through dialogue or through items that say something when you click on them.

Following suit with the other members of this chapter's puzzle-writing round table, Williams says she prefers real-world puzzles to abstract ones, and she cites Trilobyte's *7th Guest*, where the puzzles have no relevance to the story.

An example of a good environmental puzzle (and one that relates to the story) can be found in Williams' latest adventure, *King's Quest: Mask of Eternity*. Explains Williams:

5

At one point in the game, you have to look for a Stone of Order. It was stolen and it must be retrieved, as it [represents] law and order for these people.

Later on, the stone is found, but it's high up on an altar with lava below, and the player is on a plank suspended above the lava. Between the gamer and the stone hang seven gong-like objects. There are also message clues when you click on objects such as the stone in the distance, your inventory, and the gongs, which allude to the solution. The player then realizes that his bow and arrows can be used to shoot at these gongs. When a gong is hit, a musical tone plays and color flashes. If the player hits the right one, the platform extends out toward the stone. If the second one is wrong, it brings the game back again.

Roberta Williams says some of her puzzles in King's Quest: Mask of Eternity may be solved in different ways, with plenty of messages given to the player as feedback. (Used with permission by Sierra Studios)

The solution can be figured out by trial and error (for example, writing down which one is first, second, third, etc.), but the tones also represent a musical scale beginning with C, and they go in order up the scale, and the colors represent the seven colors in the rainbow. Hence, the "Stone of Order."

➤ For a playable retrospective of Roberta Williams' fruitful career, be sure to pick up Sierra's *The Roberta Williams Anthology*.

CHAPTER 6

Level Design

The worldwide PC gaming community hasn't been the same since id Software's *Wolfenstein 3D* was unleashed in the spring of 1992. More than a quarter million people scrambled to download this racy, 700KB shareware game from their local bulletin board system (BBS), and thus, the first-person perspective 3D "shooter" was born.

The next seven years yielded many memorable shooters—*Doom*, *Dark Forces*, *Duke Nukem 3D*, *Quake*, *Jedi Knight*, *GoldenEye 007*, *Unreal*, *Sin*, and *Half-Life*—and in so doing, it launched a specialized and necessary art form, known as *level design*. Loosely speaking, level design pertains to creating the architecture of maps in the game, plus dealing with object placement, mission or goal of the map, and often mini-missions within the level as well.

So what makes for a well-laid-out and challenging level to complete? What are some of the more common mistakes found in amateur level design? Is there a science to it? You bet. This chapter features the world's top level designers and their invaluable opinions on what makes or breaks level architecture in 3D shooters. Keep in mind that many of these pointers can also apply to other 3D games, such as third-person perspective action/adventure hybrids (e.g. *Tomb Raider*).

The classic Wolfenstein 3D almost single-handedly diffused side-scrolling "platform" games on the PC. But with this new perspective came new obstacles... (Used with permission by id Software)

Tim Willits, id Software

As level designer on *Ultimate Doom* and *Quake* and lead level designer on the legendary *Quake II* and the upcoming *Quake III: Arena*, Tim Willits has gathered quite a bit of knowledge (and respect in the industry) on how to create a successful map for 3D shooters. He shares with us his words of wisdom on this exciting facet of 3D game development. Before Willits sits down to create a map he asks himself, is this going to be a single-player map or Deathmatch map? He expands:

> Before you can do anything, you need to figure out what kind of level you want. It's a lot easier if you stick to either Deathmatch (DM) or single player (SP). Though it can be done, making a map great for both DM and SP is a very difficult task. Usually if it's great for DM it'll be too circular for SP, and if it's a fun SP map it's usually too straight for DM.

Note >> Deathmatch, or DM, refers to non-team-based multiplayer maps typically played over the Internet or on a LAN with other human players. It's a "kill or be killed" scenario where the goal is to stay alive and rack up as many "frags" (points) as possible. Kill a player, get a frag; die yourself, lose one. Hence the name "Deathmatch."

While many of the same principles can be applied to creating both SP and DM maps, Willits breaks up his advice into separate groups for SP and DM:

Single-Player Levels

According to Willits, there are a number of rules to adhere to when devising successful single-player levels. The following are the most significant rules to keep in mind.

Focus and Continuity

Of the utmost importance in Willits' opinion is focus and continuity of the task. And as he explains, it can be easy to lose both during a game's cycle:

> Every game has one overall mission or goal. The game then is made up of many single levels. Every level in turn must also have one overall mission. And every map must have a reason why it exists. It's important that the designer doesn't forget this—it happens a lot. A designer will be working on a level with a goal in mind. And then something happens—sometimes a technology is introduced into the game or a technical problem arises and the focus of the map shifts. Sometimes the designer doesn't even realize that they've lost focus on their original goals of the level, but they have. When this happens, the designer must step back, look at where things are going, and focus more attention on the overall design and goals of the level, sometimes reworking areas or changing the goals to accommodate the map's mission. Basically it's crucial that designers stay focused on their ultimate goals in designing a level.

As a side note, Willits reminds level designers that there must be one person who focuses on the entire design process, to ensure that levels don't stray too far from their original goal. A fresh set of eyes from someone not too close to the level designing is ideal for all games.

Architecture Design and Gameplay Elements

According to Willits, SP maps require a pretty linear flow, and they need to guide the player through the level with both architecture design and gameplay elements. To clarify, *architecture design* is basically how the areas are constructed. There should be natural breaks in levels that separate the major components of that level, as well as the level's mini-missions (Willits gets to this in a moment). *Gameplay elements*, on the other hand, follow the events orchestrated by the story of the level within the game. Willits cites an example:

> If the player's mission on the power station level is to destroy the nuclear reactor, then the level may be broken down into areas such as the control center, waste pumping station, core reactor, and coolant subsystems. Each one of these areas must look like they're supposed to look, as well as perform some function in the overall level. The player may need to enter the security codes in the control center to grant access to the coolant subsystems. Once in the coolant subsystems, the player could drain the core reactor's

6

coolant, causing an unstable heat exchange within the core. Finally, the player could reverse the waste in the waste pumping station, creating a chain reaction that would destroy the entire nuclear reactor.

Risks and Rewards

Risks and rewards must be peppered throughout SP maps to challenge the gamer while plowing toward the end of a game. Willits believes it's essential that each new area contain these kinds of obstacles. Here's an example:

> The player enters a new area of a map and there's a slime pool that's too far to jump across. On the other side of the slime pool is a button that extends the bridge, but it's guarded by a monster. The player's mini-mission is to extend the bridge. The obstacles to accomplishing that mission are the monster and the fact that the button is on the other side of the slime pool—too far away to push. To accomplish this mini-mission, all the player needs to do is shoot the button from his side and then avoid the monster while crossing the bridge; that's it. Simple. It may not seem like a mission, but it is. It's a challenge that the player must face and overcome in order to continue with the game. A single-player level is a collection of these mini-missions tied closely around unique areas in some cohesive manner.

Levels should contain mini-missions within them—that is, obstacles and objectives aside from just enemies. In this example from Quake 2, the player must get across this broken bridge somehow without landing in the molten lava. (Used with permission by id Software, Inc.)

As an example of *not* rewarding the player enough, Willits recalls:

> I once played a game where there was a tower in the middle of a courtyard with some monsters in it. It looked important and it was a centerpiece of that

courtyard. I killed the two guys in the upper portion and navigated to the top. I was pretty disappointed when I finally reached the top and there was nothing there. Every time you have an area in the map that looks important and there's a fight to reach it, you need to reward the player with some "goodie."

Environmental Feel, Teasers, and Flow

An important consideration of an SP map, according to Willits, is the overall environmental feel. Aside from looking good and playing well, what does he mean by this?

> A designer must make the level look the way the player expects it to. If the designer calls a map a *warehouse*, then there better be some crates lying around, because players will be looking for them. Also, a designer must try to make the level seem like it fits into the rest of the world. Don't mix time periods if you're not traveling in time, don't mix construction materials along similar time periods. For example, don't build your first map out of sheets of metal and have the follow-up map made mostly of brick and stucco. Players want consistency; they're comfortable with it because it surrounds their everyday lives.

Another nice touch in creating a good environmental feel is to build the map with the hint that there's more out there. "Create fake facades that can be viewed through windows but unreachable on foot. Have boxes come out of walls and vanish through other walls on the other side of the room. Create architecture that sweeps out past the playing area," says Willits. If these items are placed in the levels by the designers, players will feel like they're involved in something "bigger."

Along with these "teasers," a few outstanding visual scenes or landmarks will also help capture the environment that the designer wants to create, says Willits.

> Spend some time developing a spectacular view. Maybe a grand entrance, a detailed outer building, or even a super advanced control center. Make players turn a corner for the first time and say to themselves, "Wow." It stays with the players, and they remember the level long after they completed it if they were impressed by something cool-looking. This isn't so important in DM maps, mainly because once you run past it no one cares what it looks like time after time. Don't spend too much time on something visually stunning in DM; spend more time on flow.

6

Detailed outer buildings and other eye candy are important for the "wow" factor in games. Level designers and artists work together to create memorable locations, such as the top of this control center in Quake 2. (Used with permission by id Software, Inc.)

In terms of flow, the levels need to start out pretty easy and then advance in difficulty, maintains Willits. As a rule, he builds the first level as a training level.

> If you want to build some cool objects that move or some sort of complex geometry to showcase the engine, put it out of the path of the player. For example, air vents with spinning blades look just as good horizontal behind grates. Or moving pumps along side walls is another good use of moving things that are non-threatening. I know you want to add a lot of interesting things in the first couple of levels, but just keep them as non-intrusive as possible.

Perhaps you're only interested in creating top-notch multiplayer maps? If that's the case, pull up a chair to Willits' DM 101 and a few pointers on *Capture the Flag*–style games as well.

Deathmatch Levels

There are basically five popular styles of Deathmatch levels: arena, circular, linear, location-based, and theme-centered. Many of these styles can be included in one map, and some have crossover traits, according to Willits.

Arena

In a nutshell, arena levels usually have one central area where most of the combat takes place. Most of the hallways and passages either lead from this central area or to it. Says Willits:

> The map has very few other large rooms or areas of significance. The arena style of DM is very focused, very refined; the maps are quickly learned and

easy to master. Players will always know where they are and should never get lost navigating the hallways around the arena area. Players will find these maps fast paced with high frag limits, which will be reached quickly. An example level is *map07* from *Doom II*.

And a word of caution to designers:

> Try not to make the arena areas too architecturally complex. This is the area where all the fighting occurs, so it has to run fast. Complex architecture may look good, but it only slows down the game. Try to build this area as simple as possible.

Circular

As the name suggests, these maps are circular in design, or as Willits says, "built in such a fashion that the player would never need to stop and turn around along its main path." He expands:

> Build with as few dead ends as possible—they're best built with none. Use numerous entrances and exits around its central core, which would allow free-flowing movement without hitches. The map would also need good weapon distribution, where either side would not have an advantage. There would be as little holding ground as possible. (*Holding ground* is a place where a player can stock up on health and ammo in a room and camp.) An example level here is *dm6* from *Quake*.

Linear

Linear maps are built with only a few alternate paths. Willits amplifies:

> The architecture becomes a roadmap, where people instantly know which side of the map they're on. Nice open areas or wide hallways where players can enjoy jousting-type combat. Even weapon distribution to force players to move back and forth. Have the ammo for the weapons on the opposite side of the map, forcing players who want to stock to travel. An example level is *e1m1* from *Doom*.

Location-Based

Location-based DM allows players to always know where they are. You may not be able to figure out how to get somewhere else fast, but you immediately know your location. These maps are not free-flowing as in circular or linear maps, but instead are made up of many unique identifiable areas. Each area should have some distinct combat areas or mini themes included in it.

6

For example, in *dm3* from *Quake* is a water area for swimming, a thin stair-
case for vertical fighting, and a computer room made for close fighting. Each
area has a special weapon or power-up that fits the environment. These maps
are great for team games.

Theme-Centered

And last on the list for DM maps are theme-based maps. As Willits put it, a theme-based
map uses something unique to combat and over-exaggerates it all over the map. Perhaps
this is better explained by an example:

> An example of this is *e1m4* from *Quake*, a.k.a. The Sewage System. This
> map is covered with water; most of the fighting is in or around water.
> Everywhere the player looks, he sees water or something related to water. In
> almost every area, the player can enter or exit the water. The water is the
> "theme" or the special combat characterization throughout the map. Theme
> maps are great for players who enjoy something totally unique. Theme-based
> maps are also more difficult to navigate through, and should only be used for
> medium or advanced play. Themes need to enhance gameplay, not detract
> from it.

 Note >> Good id Software examples of theme-based maps include wind tunnels
(*Quake*, *e3m5*); low gravity (*Quake*, *e1m8*); low light, such as the mine levels
in *Quake 2*; hazardous materials such as lava, slime, or pits of death (*Quake*,
dm4); torturous devices such as spike shooters or security lasers (*Quake 2*);
wide and open areas (*Quake 2*); teleport craziness (*Quake*, *dm1*).

Capture the Flag

"Capture the Flag" is a popular team-based multiplayer game where the object is to steal
the other team's flag and bring it safely back to your own base. There are now many new
custom variations of Capture the Flag (CTF) games. In the following section, Willits
offers advice on creating maps for CTF fanatics.

Symmetric Levels

With CTF games, it's important that levels be nearly mirrors of each other to make
things even between the two teams. Willits maintains, "In theory it's possible to have two
bases look different, but even in practice this has rarely worked." He cites a *bad* example
of a CTF map from *Quake 2*, and why:

Strike is a fairly big failure in that regard due to BFG and teleporter placement (putting red team at a large disadvantage). Also, there are more methods of entering the red base than the blue base, making blue base easily defensible. This map also has uneven ammo and weapon placement; the blue base has far better resources within. All this is solved very easily by making both sides identical.

Asymmetrical Levels

Willits says if the level is not symmetrical there should be a balanced strategy that needs to be employed by each individual team. For example, if one side is largely covered by water, the team should be given rebreathers. Similarly, protective environment suits should be accessible on the slime side.

Random Tips for CTF Maps

Willits grants us an assorted medley of tips on creating CTF maps:

There should be a good supply of weapons and ammo near a base, but don't overdo it. This makes the base too easy to defend and difficult to attack. If a designer is using power-ups, they should never start off within the base.

While still making it defensible, there should be multiple entry points and exits to a base.

Centralized placement of major power-ups is a good idea. The power-ups still need to be located far enough from each other to prevent players from using a single power-up and crushing everyone on the map.

Create some good sniper locations but, if players are going to snipe, they should be vulnerable in some way, too.

There should be obvious color coding of areas, but don't rely on colored lighting, since colored lighting tends to neutralize player colors and you can't see what team they're on. Use colored textures instead.

Focus on good weapon placement and think it through. Weapon placement may be more important in CTF than normal DM because it can greatly shift the balance of power from one side to the other.

We'll return later to the masters at id Software. But first, we've got some divine intervention. Bow your heads because next up is The Levelord.

6

The Levelord, Ritual Entertainment

Much of the excitement and anxiety experienced during bouts of *Duke Nukem 3D*, *Quake: Scourge of Armagon*, and *Sin* can be directly linked to The Levelord's miraculous touch. So what's his secret for keeping you awake until 4 a.m.?

The Levelord's three commandments may seem obvious, but according to him they're quite often neglected or overlooked: the "fun factor," game action/player interaction, and authenticity of setting.

Note >> The Levelord has requested that we keep his written material the way it was submitted, so this is the Lord speaking throughout. Hear ye! Hear ye!

The Fun Factor

The first and foremost question to be answered about any game, whether it's a shooter or whatever, is "Is it fun?" This applies to the game itself, of course, but it also has great bearing on each and every component of the game, including level designing. As a game is developed, this question should be answered many, many times.

The Fun Factor is often forsaken for cutting-edge flash, and much effort is taken away from the game itself due to the ever-increasing computer performance on which games are played. Nonetheless, it seems paradoxical that many games simply are not fun; they look great, but they aren't worth playing. Cutting edge is indeed fun when it adds cool weapon effects and faster game performance, but it's not cool when a developer spends too much time with research and development, only to forget the main purpose of a game: fun!

The Fun Factor is also frequently back-seated to realism. This is not to be confused with a game being realistic or authentic, but is rather a seeming side effect of the "reality" portion of our games' virtual reality. Too often fun ideas and features are shelved because developers say things like "Hey, you can't change momentum in mid-air in real life!" or "A real bullet doesn't do that!" when the more important statement at hand was "That was so much fun!"

There are no defined rules for fun and the only way to ensure the Fun Factor is to play test. The easy part about adding the Fun Factor is that most all of us have the same concept of fun; that is, if you the game developer think it's fun, then the game audience is likely to think so, too. The Fun Factor is not transient or ephemeral, either. It should survive countless trials and tests and still be entertaining in the end. This is the only way to ensure that a game is fun—to play test it over and over.

Game Action and Player Interaction

First-person shooters are no longer the simple "shoot, find the key, and shoot some more" games that they were a few years ago. These games are now fully interactive environments, and what used to be considered randomly placed and sparse Easter Eggs are now the standard norm. If a level has a phone or computer, they had better be functional, and the player had better be able to blow them up.

The player must be able to destroy just about everything! As a level designer, I spend a lot of my time making things destructible, but it's always worth the while. Take the time to become a good demolitions expert, because destroying things is not only good action, it is also never-ending fun.

Another important aspect of the action in a first-person shooter is puzzle solving. A good level should be a series of challenges and rewards. The challenge can come before the reward, or after, but don't just haphazardly strew goodies and bad guys through your level. The players should feel as though they are being run through a gauntlet of contests and prizes.

Puzzle-solving is an integral part of 3D level design, says The Levelord. This "heated" scene is from Scourge of Armagon, the first official add-on pack for Quake. (Used with permission by Ritual Entertainment)

6

All of these forms should be as animated as possible to improve feel of action. Make the player work for the rewards. Do whatever you can to make the player say "Ah ha!" Make as many secret areas as possible, too, as discovering secrets is one of the most fun puzzles in a game.

Authenticity

Related directly to level designing, the third question to be answered is "Are you there?" First-person shooters in particular rely on the sense of immersion. The most important duty you have as a level designer is to bring the player "into" your level. It's not until after this submersion that issues like action, game play, and even the Fun Factor enter the game.

The more of your level to which the player can attach himself via familiarity, the stronger the player's sense of "being there" will be. Real-world situations usually make good levels because it's easier to capture the reality.

A strong sense of authenticity is the groundwork of any killer level. Remember the movie theater or football stadium in Duke Nukem 3D or the opening bank sequence from Sin? Here's a look at Sin's jungle level. (Used with permission by Ritual Entertainment)

The closer that the player can relate to your level, the deeper the player will be submerged into the level.

Continuity is also an important factor of a level's immersion. Continuity is related to the level's main theme, and this theme must be maintained throughout the entire level. Too often I see levels that are patchworks of various themes. Your level must seem like a continuous place.

The almighty Levelord has spoken, and deems these as the true foundations of any killer level. "These seem apparent, but they can be the biggest burdens a game designer, especially a level designer, can face... without them, most every other aspect of a level will be missed or forgotten, and the game as a whole will suffer."

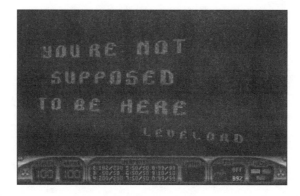

Littering your maps with secrets is also an important considera-tion in level designing, deems The Levelord. Anyone find this in Duke Nukem 3D? (Used with permission by 3D Realms, Inc.)

Paul Jaquays, id Software

Paul Jaquays is a "jack of all trades" (check out his bio in the appendix), but at id Software he provides level design for *Quake II* and game and level design for *Quake III: Arena*. Now who *wouldn't* want to be in his shoes, eh? When Jaquays heard about this *Secrets of the Sages* project, he wanted to offer a large collection of do's and don'ts on level design, as well as more general advice on the art of map creation. Without further ado, let's first jump into his collection of handy design tidbits.

Jaquays' 26 Level Design Tips

1. Know what you want to do with a level before you start. Don't expect a map that you start as a single-player map to be easily changed into a multiplayer map. The reverse holds true for trying to make a Deathmatch map into a single-player challenge.

2. Sketch out a diagram of the map to use as an initial guide.

3. Don't start with grandiose projects. Try making something fun with a few rooms.

4. If possible, build your level with a "gimmick" in mind—some tricky gamism bit that players will remember. Popular gimmicks that have been used in the past include wind tunnels, numerous portals, lava maps, trap maps, water-filled maps, maps with large, slow-moving hazards, and low-gravity maps.

5. Try to be fresh and original with every new design. Do something that you haven't seen done before.

6. Test gimmicks of gameplay, tricks, and traps in test levels before building them into your game level.

7. Do architecture and texture studies ahead of time to establish an architectural style. Stick to that style.

6

Above, Jaquays roughly sketched out a complicated puzzle and trap for Quake 2, involving modularized, moving prison cells as a part of the Laboratory sequence. The concept was not implemented in the final game. Below, Jaquays began one of his first Quake 3 arena maps by roughly sketching out the major game features and their relationship to each other. The final version of this arena map carried several of the original concepts through to fruition, even though much of the layout and geo-metry was changed. (Both images used with permission by id Software, Inc., copy-right 1998)

8. Block out your level with large pieces of geometry. Think of the architecture you'll use, but concentrate more on how gameplay will flow through the level. At this stage, I try to keep my map grid at the largest possible setting (in *Quake II* or *Quake III*, that's the "64" grid). Avoid fussy details at this point and go for mas-siveness. At this stage of development, try to keep your frame-rate speeds well below the amount allowed by the game (for *Quake II*, we aimed to be below a maximum count of 500 triangles of architecture in any view). A good rule might be to try for no more than a third of your total possible polygon count in the worst views in and near your larger rooms.

This 64-player map is taken from the Quake II DM Pack 1: Extremities expansion CD. Jaquays reminds level designers to make sure that large maps have distinctive, memorable play areas. (Used with permission by Activision)

9. Once the flow is established, you can start adding architectural detail and refining hall and room shapes.

10. Build in a modular manner. Make prefabricated pieces that be can fit together easily to make your level. Build tricky pieces of detailed architecture (such as door frames, complicated cornices, or furniture) once and set them outside the boundaries of your map. Clone them as needed for placement in the map.

11. When designing architectural elements, study the real world. Try to duplicate the look and feel of impressive works, but with less complicated geometry. Set yourself challenges in this regard.

12. Strike a balance between the use of real geometry and textures that imply three-dimensional depth when building architectural details. Textures that appear to be 3D should be used with caution. When viewed from a distance, they can fool the

6

eye into believing that the architectural geometry is significantly more complex than it actually is. But the same texture viewed up close and at eye level completely destroys the illusion of depth.

13. Compile the map often. Don't wait until everything is placed to see what things look like (or if you have leaks in the map hull).

14. Complete your map geometry before adding monsters and items.

15. When building single-player game maps, don't put every game feature in the level. Having every monster possible in the game in a single game level is a glaring sign of amateur work. Generally speaking, the only place you're going to see all the monsters at once is in the AI programmer's test level.

16. The same goes for tricks, traps, items, weapons, and power-ups. Unless your map is as massive as the 64-player DM maps created for *Quake II*, restrict the number of different items you put in the map. Use a few things cleverly, rather than many poorly.

17. Small maps can be relatively similar throughout. Large maps should have distinctive, memorable locations that the player can use to orient himself in the map. "City64," a large DM map for *Quake II*, featured a huge canyon area, a massive alien temple, underwater caverns, a vast deep tank with water in the bottom, and numerous stretches of twisty corridors. The corridors were often similar, but they ended in distinctive large play areas.

18. For DM maps, give the players frequent opportunities to avoid pursuit and dodge for cover. Long hallways with no exits are bad. Avoid forcing players to make long trips to dead-end rooms—even to get good power-ups.

19. Place lights to achieve drama. If you have a choice between under-lighting an area and over-lighting it, err on the side of darkness. Just don't go overboard. Dark levels may look nifty, but stumbling around in the dark while playing gets old fast.

20. Light as you go—even if you're only placing temporary lights.

21. Don't forget the audio elements of a map. Sounds can provide important game clues.

22. If possible, allow multiple solutions for puzzles. You can still reserve the greatest rewards for players who solve them in what the designer has decided is the "best way."

23. Give the player a variety of game experiences and challenges in each map. All combat or all puzzles can get old quickly.

24. Be kind to your players; don't over-challenge them unnecessarily. Well-placed environmental hazards add to the tension of game play, but falling into lava or

slime every third step or being crushed to death by falling weights every time you turn around quickly becomes frustrating.

25. Study maps you like and make an effort to duplicate or even improve situations and settings.

26. Finish what you begin.

As many other programmers, artists, animators, musicians, and level designers have stated in the past, this last point on finishing a project instead of starting 10 new ones is essential, and not easy for beginners.

Paul's Advice on Game Design

Throughout his career in the gaming industry, Jaquays has accumulated quite a bit of knowledge on the art of game design. While he covered many individual pointers in the preceding section on map creation, the following details serve as more broad advice on game design, drawing from his own personal experiences as well.

Stop Imitating Yourself

I started in the game business as a designer of game adventures for the new (at the time) game called *Dungeons & Dragons* and later for the game called *Runequest*. There was a time when I was considered one of the best adventure writers in the field. One of the reasons that I quit designing pencil-and-paper-type role-playing games was I found that I had started to imitate myself, rehashing the same storyline over and over. I was no longer fresh. Thankfully, I had other career options within the game business that I could pursue. But the problem still remains: how to keep your ideas alive and new.

Choose the Unconventional Solution

There's a tendency in game design to use familiar or tried-and-true solutions to design. In the latter part of the Golden Age of Video Games (the *classic* 8-bit years), the solution for nearly every game based on a character or movie license was to create a side-scrolling game. During my tenure at Coleco, we were given very few opportunities to create new games. Most of our work was to analyze and translate arcade titles.

The "War Games" movie license gave us the opportunity to create a game that broke the mold. The conventional solution would have been to make a side-scrolling "solve the puzzles, find the hidden goodies, and avoid the bad guys" game until at last you confronted the computer in the last scene. At that point, the game would start you back at the beginning and ratchet up the level of difficulty a notch. After seeing a special preview screening of the

6

movie "War Games," I was inspired by the sequence near the end of the movie in which the computer runs simulated scenario after scenario in which the outcome was always the same: nuclear war and complete world devastation. I was taken by the graphics that plotted the arcs of missiles as they approached their targets. If I could convince the powers-that-be, that short sequence of the movie would be our game. The actual gameplay derived from several unrelated concepts. The goal of the player would be to stop bombers, subs, and missiles (which were drawn on the fly as lines—no simple trick in the 8-bit pattern tile game systems of the day), from reaching their targets on a map of the United States. In a way, it had similarities to the popular arcade game *Missile Command*, where the player fires anti-ballistic missiles at incoming missiles dropping down from the top of the screen. Unlike the arcade, the play took place on six separate maps simultaneously. Like the juggler who keeps numerous plates spinning at once atop thin sticks, the player had to rapidly switch his attentions between a radar map showing the whole USA and six sub-maps that contained closer views of target cities and military installations. The player had to rapidly commit resources (missiles, interceptor planes, and attack subs) to deal with enemy attacks, then shift to the next map and do the same. If the player had the right stuff, he or she could defeat the game.

Blending Flavors

Some of the most popular foods are those that blend unlike or even opposite flavors together in one tasty package. Sweet-and-sour Chinese dishes and Chicago-style hotdogs are just two examples. What does this have to do with game design? One of the products of which I am most proud is a book series called *Central Casting*. The purpose of the products was to create vivid backstories or histories for characters in role-playing games. I created separate books that covered three distinct genre groups of games: fantasy, science fiction (or futuristic), and 20th century games. Players rolled dice and compared the results against a series of tables and lists. Roll by roll, they selected events and personality traits that they could use to define their game characters. Quite often, the results of dice rolls would seem unlikely to be combined together, but with a little creative thought the widely disparate events would blend together, like the myriad of flavors in a Chicago-style hotdog, into a uniquely original result.

Make It Real

Even if you plan on making your game setting wildly fantastic—that is, nothing you would ever see in the real world—take care to make it seem real. This is something I learned as a fantasy illustrator, painting covers for games and books. The way to make the fantastic elements of a painting believable is to realistically paint the mundane things in the picture. This establishes a setting that appears as if it could actually exist somewhere. You then paint the fantastic elements in the painting with an equal amount of care so that they partake of the *reality* of the rest of the painting. The same holds true when making 3D game levels. Give the player one or more familiar elements that he can relate to. By comparison with the *real* elements, the *unreal* things in the game should seem more real, or perhaps a better explanation is that they seem more plausible. And by contrast with the mundane, they will seem that much more fantastic.

John Romero, ION Storm

"A level designer has a very responsible position, because maps are where the game takes place," says John Romero, game designer, chairman, and cofounder of ION Storm. Having worked on such 3D shooter classics such as *Wolfenstein 3D*, *Doom*, *Doom II*, *Heretic*, *Hexen*, and *Quake*, Romero has plenty of opinions to share regarding level design.

Romero maintains that the inevitable breaking up of responsibilities at a development house can take away from the overall vibe and consistency of the level. "Some companies do their maps in stages, with many different people handling different tasks— architecture, texture placement, object placement… and this [specialization] can take away from the 'cool' factor."

Although most of his suggestions on what makes a good level are fairly universal (such as providing the gamer with landmarks throughout the map to give it personality, making the player totally immersed in this fictitious world, and so on), Romero also proposes an interesting rule that's broken more than it's obeyed, in his opinion. "The gamer must be in constant fear," believes Romero. "It's extremely important to keep gamers on their toes when playing shooters, with plenty of traps lying around so they're constantly in fear of dying…"

6

Tip >> Landmarks can serve a dual purpose in well-designed maps: They can add to the immersion factor while offering navigation cues to players, helping them know their direction and location in the level.

Romero cites specific examples such as *Quake*'s *E2M5* ("Wizard's Manse"), where players get locked into a cage and it slowly descends into water with no way out. Another *Quake* map, *E2M6* ("Dismal Oubliette"), also has a slow vertical sink, inspired by Disney World's Haunted House "elevator" ride. "The player panics because he's stuck in this room and after it stops completely, a Shambler is teleported into the room, spikes shoot out, then there's a Fiend to fight, and then Zombies. It's just one thing after another," says Romero with a smile. "*This* is key in good level design."

Romero will be able to show off these helpful tips with *Daikatana* when it ships in mid-1999.

Cliff Bleszinski, Epic MegaGames

At a mere 24 years old, Cliff has made quite a name for himself as a game designer and level creator on the award-winning PC titles *Jazz Jackrabbit* and *Unreal*. Although he agrees with John Romero that fear is an important element of level design, he believes that it's only a fraction of what makes a solid level. "Pacing is far more important. If the player is constantly in fear, then he'll become numb; if he's constantly surprised, then it will wear off and not be effective," explains Bleszinski. He continues:

> The key to scaring the player in a level is knowing when, where, and how often to spring a surprise. If there are, say, five minutes of idle time exploring and chatting with peaceful aliens, then, when the door bursts in and a lava monster stomps in screaming bloody hell, you can bet the player will be shaking in his boots. This is why good horror movies don't spring surprise after surprise on the audience, because it loses its impact.

> Good pacing is a skill that applies to every element of level design. Pace your flow of monsters, and have areas where the player feels like he is being engulfed by less intelligent "cannon fodder" foes, as well as areas that have just a few devious baddies that are hard as nails to take out. Know how often to reward the player with goodies or health. Don't cover the level with items; rather, give him the prizes after monsters are killed, doors are opened, or a ledge is reached.

Being chased by a deadly Skaarj adds to the fun and excitement of the level, but Bleszinski warns that fear should be used sparingly to break up the pace of a level. (Used with permission by Epic MegaGames)

Bleszinski recognizes that there's a lot more to level design than the "fear factor" and "good pacing," so he also provides his very own five-step crash course in good level design. Pencils in hand? Here we go…

Geometry Building and World Texturing

Naturally, you need to construct your environment first. Ideally, the texture artists should have a head start on the level designers so that the level designers have content with which to texture their areas while building. Then the level designers can tell the artists, "I need a 32×128 girder with three bolts on it and no directional rust, and please put it into the FACTORY texture set!"

Lighting the Environment

The right kind of lighting can make or break a beautiful scene. Low lights tend to illuminate monsters more dramatically, while bright rooms reduce fumbling around in the dark. A level designer needs to be creative with his lighting; if the player is going deeper into a volcano, then the lighting should get "hotter" the further you go by getting brighter and more orange and red, or if you're sending him through a swampy area, use drab, depressing colors, such as green and gray.

6

Pancho Eekels, one of the level designers Cliff Bleszinki works with, has managed to make this room well lit, yet moody and colorful. This shot is from Unreal Tournament. (Used with permission by Cliff Bleszinski)

Using the *Unreal* or *Quake* engine gives a level designer amazing control over realistic shadows. Building architecture that allows for shadows is essential; try putting support beams beneath a skylight to encourage sharp, moody shadows on the floor, or put a flame behind a polygonal grate to cast harsh shadows on the opposite wall.

Tricks, Traps, and Puzzles

Never force the player to learn by dying. Always give him a chance to figure out a puzzle without slapping his wrists. Remember, the person playing your game is playing it for *fun*, not for *work*. If you want to have slicing blades pop up from the floor of your Incan temple, make sure that you put some blood splotches and body parts around the exact spot that the blades spring forth, so that the attentive player will not be killed. Even if the player is killed, he will think "Oh, I should have seen those warnings, how stupid of me!" instead of "This game cheats! How was I supposed to know there was a trap there?"

If the primary objective of your game is to kill and kill fast, then don't slow the player down with boring, cumbersome puzzles. It's one thing to have three switches that need to be turned on in order to pass; it's another to have twelve switches that have a combination code three levels away that the player must physically write on a piece of paper to remember.

Monster, Ammo, and Health Placement ("Gameflow")

During the course of *Unreal*'s development, I've been harassing the level designers to always make their monsters patrol a local area, or to have them spring out of the dark, or even crash through glass at the player. If the player walks into a room and the monsters are just standing there waiting for him, he's not going to feel that this is a very believable world. However, if he walks into a room and his foe is just walking past him to go work on a computer terminal, he'll appreciate the extra effort that has been taken to further the believability.

Ammunition is always tricky to get right in a level. Too much ammo and the gamer breezes through the level without a sweat; not enough ammo and your gamer is running around the level hacking at your foes with his default weapon while pondering looking for cheats online. Right when the player is thinking, "Boy, I'm going to be needing some ammunition soon," there should be a box of bullets waiting for him. The same rules apply for health.

Drama!

In *Unreal*, we're trying to create a sense of being in a hostile alien world. This believability is greatly helped by what I refer to as *drama*. Hearing a scene occur behind a locked door. Watching an evil alien punish a friendly alien who assists the player. Witnessing the murder of a comrade before your eyes. Real events that occur real time in the game, many of which the player can interfere with. Well-done drama will stick in the player's head for years to come.

So how important is level design, anyway? Why is this such an integral part of the game design? "Level design is where the rubber hits the road," are the first words Jay Wilbur, former "biz guy" and CEO of id Software, told Cliff Bleszinski, during their initial telephone conversation a couple of years ago. This has stuck with Cliff as an "absolute truth." He expands on the analogy:

Game development can be compared to building a car. You have all these different parts that are created by talented people—programming, modeling, sound, and artwork—and at some point, everyone's hard work on a car comes together, and the tires hit the road. With a game, everyone's work is held together by the levels that use all of that, and they'd better be exceptional or the game falters.

6

Marc Laidlaw, Valve Software

Valve's first release, *Half-Life*, was a major evolutionary step in the history of the first-person perspective action genre. The game excelled in all key areas: storyline, art, animation, sound, music, pacing, and level design; combined, it made players feel like they were part of a living, breathing, populated world. The level design was instrumental in pulling off this effect, and even during the last third of the game, while on another planet with alien architecture, maps maintained their focus with lush outdoor and indoor environments and challenging obstacles to overcome.

Marc Laidlaw, the level team coordinator at Valve, was responsible for overseeing the six level designers who worked day and night to create *Half-Life*. Did you know there were a whopping 96 BSPs in the game? Laidlaw takes some time out of his busy schedule to discuss his own personal approach to level design:

Note >> BSP is an editing tool that converts map files into *Quake*-compatible level files. *Half-Life* is based on the *Quake/Quake II* engine, so they call the mini-levels in the game BSPs.

The Goal

The first on the list is the goal of the level. That is, the point of it all in the grand scheme of things. Says Laidlaw, "Everything in the level should somehow contribute to that goal—even detours, diversions, and distractions should figure into the overall scheme, thematically."

The Gameplay

Consideration of the gameplay is also important. What will players be *doing* as they go through the level? "Is this something that will engage, immerse, and interest them to the point that they absolutely cannot stop playing until they've accomplished their goal?" asks Laidlaw.

The Atmosphere

Laidlaw asks, "What kind of mood are you trying to create in the player? One of horror? One of pure action? Are you trying to create a mood that contrasts with preceding or subsequent levels?" The goal is to select and invent details that suit the mood you want to get across.

The following is a look at how Laidlaw's emphasis on the goal, gameplay, and atmosphere can be applied to some of the key levels in *Half-Life*.

"Office Complex"

The "Office Complex" level of *Half-Life* is a deliberately drab environment composed of offices, laboratories, corridors, and stairways. In other words, fairly mundane locales about as far removed as imaginable from the usual fantastic trappings of a science fiction action game. With that in mind, Laidlaw applies the level to each of his three approaches to map design:

> Goal: The goals in "Office Complex" are fairly obvious ones, such as exit doors, in plain sight. The layout of the maps are simple and, in essence, linear. However, by imposing obstacles, we force the player to take a devious route to the destination. For instance, you can peer through a pane of glass in a fire door and see your exit at the far end of a corridor; but since the fire door is locked, you'll need to explore other avenues. Clever use of obstacles can turn a completely obvious route into a complex non-obvious route. This technique was used numerous times in *Half-Life*. What's important is to make the goal obvious from the first, in order to give players a start on solving the problem of how to get there. And if they forget their goal somewhere along the way, they will experience a jolt of recognition when they finally gain the far-off door.

Marc Laidlaw stresses you must understand the goal, relevance to gameplay, and atmosphere for each level when making maps in a 3D shooter. These two images are from the "Office Complex" and "Questionable Ethics" levels. (Used with permission from Sierra Studios)

6

Gameplay: "Office Complex" occurs fairly early in *Half-Life*, and therefore gameplay was slanted toward the player who is still mastering basic skills, while preparing him for more dangerous encounters ahead. We force the player to crawl, dodge, and fight in tight quarters against ambushing *head-crabs*. Slow monsters, such as *mawmen*, give a steady sense of horror and menace, and allow the player plenty of opportunities to learn to team up with allies. He can talk to non-player characters (NPCs) and solve various small-scale room-based puzzles (such as shutting off switches to deactivate deadly turrets and electrical threats). In addition, we knew that the subsequent level would drop him into combat with extremely tough human soldiers, and in order to give him some experience fighting against squads of creatures with long-range attacks, we set up encounters with squads of *vortigaunts*, which are fun to fight and fairly easy to kill, thus allowing the player to develop some of the skills he'll need to survive encounters with human soldiers.

Atmosphere: The banal office atmosphere provides a perfect background for scenes of carnage and horror—the contrast with gruesome images is all the more striking because of the familiar setting. Most of the details were selected to evoke feelings of dread in the player. Scientists are dragged to their doom in airshafts; *mawmen* feed on corpses in the cafeteria. The one crucial atmospheric element that can't be conveyed in screenshots is that of sound. The first time the player steps into the walk-in freezer, he triggers music that evokes cold, echoing emptiness. And the claustrophobic echoing sounds not only reinforce the realism of the environment, but add to the sense of menace: Echoes are creepy.

Laidlaw then used another level in the game for contrast. This section of *Half-Life* takes place in a research and development lab, where the player catches a glimpse of some of the experiments that were in progress when disaster struck the Black Mesa Research Facility.

"Questionable Ethics"

The labs served numerous purposes in the game: To deepen the sense of conspiracy and cause the player to question what was actually going on at Black Mesa; to give the player access to a high-powered weapon that's crucial for battling powerful enemies in subsequent levels; and to force a style of puzzle-solving focused on protecting and working with human characters (scientists) rather than simply throwing switches.

Goal: This section of the labs is quite non-linear in layout, although judicious use of locked doors again gives it a linear flow the first time through. Non-linear areas tend to work against the usual dramatic virtues of pacing and rhythm and timing, and give rise to plentiful opportunities for boredom and confusion. They also make it easy for the player to miss or forget his goal. When designing the labs on paper, we decided that the player should see his goal (the exit) immediately upon entering the lobby. There's a scanner next to the locked exit, and by this time the player has been taught that only scientists or other NPCs can operate a scanner. Presumably the player will carry this knowledge with him as he moves away from the exit and fights his way through the other areas of the map, and by the time he encounters a group of hiding scientists, he'll understand that he's supposed to escort one of them through the labyrinthine labs back to the scanner. (To further aid the player in understanding the goal, we added a security guard to give a short briefing on the way into the area.)

Gameplay: Puzzles were built around a variety of enemy encounters, traps, and scientific devices, and assembled from elements that have some logical place in the environment: sterilizers, laser equipment, caged monsters. Getting certain weapons is tricky in that it requires exposing oneself to monsters, and then quickly working with the environment to neutralize the threat. The player must open a cage full of sharks, then retreat into a sterilizer control room in order to vaporize them before he is overwhelmed. In addition, the presence of enemy soldiers adds a constant threat and gives contrast to the alien menace. In some circumstances, the canny player may choose to wait out battles between aliens and other humans, and then deal with the weakened victor of those battles. In such cases, the player's best strategy is patience. This puts a twist on the usual action game tactic, where players usually can expect to solve all problems by direct, aggressive attacks.

Atmosphere: We selected details that seemed appropriate to the research environment, and that added to the underlying story. Certain areas were tailored specifically for the study of alien creatures, which tends to raise questions about how long the researchers at Black Mesa have known about the aliens, and what exactly they were doing with them. As much as possible, the details also provided opportunities for gameplay; for instance, sterilizers that were used by researchers to cleanse rooms of biohazards turn out to be just as effective at vaporizing pursuing soldiers. Since we wanted a mood of high-tech horror to pervade *Half-Life*, we avoided a lot of opportunities for wacky comedy, and instead tried to set up situations for suitably dark and ironic humor. The "Tau Cannon," for instance, is given to the player at the end of a macabre sequence. And as a bonus, in addition to the weapon itself, the player is "rewarded" with a unique piece of music that punctuates the action and puts a weird spin on the otherwise relentless mood of horror.

6

On Limitations of Tools

All of these aforementioned objectives must be accomplished with the tools at your disposal, and within the limits of your game engine. Laidlaw explains:

> Working within your limitations can seem restricting at first, but it also allows you to plan in advance and really get creative. It would seem as if having a team of programmers available to constantly implement new features would be utterly liberating, but sometimes this makes it hard to just get down to work and use what you have. It's very hard to anticipate what you might have one day. Level designers who have built a lot of *Quake* maps are used to working with known quantities; they know the limits of the *Quake* engine, they know the entities they have to work with, they know how to create spectacular effects that take both these factors into consideration. When the rules suddenly change, and a lot of new entities and features are in the works, and the engine itself is altered, a kind of paralysis can creep in. This is a predictable stumbling block for people who are moving from mapping as a hobby to level design as a profession; but being aware of it in advance, you should try to stay aware of your strengths and the known quantities, and master the new quantities a bit at a time.

Have a Plan

Laidlaw says if you can keep it all in your head, fine. But putting your ideas on paper is good.

> Sketches are helpful. You can evaluate your overall scheme more easily when it's clearly stated. If you can't sum it up in a few words, or sketch it out so that someone else will understand it, you might be painting yourself into a corner when you've put a lot of work into actual level construction.

Don't Work in a Vacuum

Laidlaw urges budding level designers to bounce ideas off a few like-minded people:

> A few brains working on the same problem will often come up with more interesting and varied ideas for gameplay than one person working alone. Each person tends to favor a particular style of gameplay, a particular design approach; in the course of a long game, you'll want to represent a variety of styles, to keep things fresh.

Get Creative

Finally, Laidlaw recognizes that it's important to study and learn from your favorites, but says to use them only as a springboard to invent something new.

Everyone starts out trying to re-create the great game experiences they loved, and this is a good way to learn the basics. But you won't get anywhere rehashing old ideas. Try to think in terms of the game you would love to play, if only someone out there would finally make it. Then make it yourself.

Eric Biessman, Raven Software

As project coordinator, lead designer, and level designer at Raven Software, Eric Biessman has received many e-mail messages from those who want to know how to create breathtaking levels, as seen in *Heretic II*. Here he sets the record straight:

- The level must be fun. This is a game, after all.

- Make sure that you have the level planned out before you start designing. To design in a vacuum usually means that you'll have a large amount of wasted time.

- Pay attention to the world around you. Find ideas in everything you do. Make sure that you aren't just making a level that plagiarizes another game. Detail is the key, but it has to be from your own imagination, not someone else's.

- I definitely sketch out ideas on paper first, but not the entire level. Usually, I will design smaller areas that are very important to the game and then go from there. I also like to flowchart the entire level before I even think about sitting down to the editor.

Key areas such as the Silverspring Docks in Heretic II should be sketched out on paper first, says Biessman. (Used with permission by Activision, Inc.)

6

- Be persistent. The more you practice, create, and build, the better your levels are going to be. Make contacts in the industry and touch base with them regularly. Play as many games, in as many different styles, as you can, and learn from them. Turn your hobby into a passion. If you can't do this, then you probably should think of another way to release your creativity. Dedication pays off 90% of the time but you still need to have creativity. Otherwise, there's really nothing that can be done.

Paul O'Connor, Oddworld Inhabitants

As lead game designer on *Oddworld: Abe's Oddysee* and *Oddworld: Abe's Exoddus*, Paul O'Connor has learned quite a bit about game design (not to mention that he's been designing games in some form since 1981). O'Connor provides a different take on this chapter, since the first two *Abe's* games are "side-scroller" platform games, in 2D.

O'Connor asks, "Will the player understand the level, puzzle, or situation? Is it clear to the player what he must do to solve the puzzle? Is it fun?"

> As each *Oddworld* designer works on his own levels, and as the order of those levels sometimes isn't determined until late in production, how does this particular level fit into the overall game flow in terms of difficulty and what you're demanding of the player? If this level requires mastery of a specific [mechanism], has that [mechanism] already been introduced earlier in the game? In other words, is the level design and difficulty level appropriate for the anticipated placement in the final game?

> How does this level advance the story of the game? What vital information does the player gain by completing this level? How does it connect with the preceding and following levels?

O'Connor comments on sketching out levels:

> I do, occasionally [sketch out levels] if the situation is novel. The level editor we used on the two *Abe* games was flexible enough for use as a composition tool. Usually, I'd just sit down in front of the editor with a rough idea of how many screens the budget would afford for this portion of the game, and a notion about the type of play I wanted to accomplish in this area, and then go from there.

CHAPTER 7

Mission Design

Mission design is an integral part of strategy games, simulations, RPGs, and, most recently, many action/adventure titles as well.

Whereas Chapter 6 deals with *level design*—that is, how a map is laid out architecturally (and the objects placed within it)—*mission* or *scenario design* refers to the specific objective(s) the player must carry out during the game. They can be historical in nature, such as in WWII combat flight sims or turn-based strategy war games, or purely fictional, as found in fantasy role-playing games. In many cases, each mission may have a number of smaller goals to complete. And it follows that the missions are part of a grander story.

Campaigns in a game refers to a string of single-level scenarios or missions, often in a sequential order to complete an overall goal. For example, Blizzard's mega-successful sci-fi strategy game *StarCraft* contains three campaigns for the different races—the Zerg, Protoss, and Terrans—each containing 10 scenarios, for a total of 30.

Dynamic campaigns means that the success or failure of missions is factored into the campaign, and should impact the future of the campaign as a result. For example, if Saddam Hussein's radar bases are destroyed in northern Iraq, it may be harder for them to detect U.S. and British forces approaching from eastern Turkey in future missions. Naturally, this breathes some life and additional satisfaction into the game experience, instead of the player feeling like he or she is part of a canned script. Hundreds of games a year fall short in this area, and the player often stops playing because of repetitive missions/campaigns, confusing situations, or missions that can be too easily completed or are painstakingly difficult.

Games such as Microprose's European Air War offer a dynamic campaign so the missions (and situations within missions) will change as the player progresses through the game. (Used with permission by Hasbro Interactive, Inc.)

This chapter contains advice from hand-picked professionals on what can turn your average game into a veritable masterpiece.

Rob Pardo, Blizzard Entertainment

Rob Pardo is a producer and designer at Blizzard Entertainment who was in charge of unit balancing in *StarCraft*. On the famed *StarCraft: Brood War* expansion pack, he became the lead designer. Pardo has a number of guidelines for his mission designers, and asks that they adhere to these rules closely:

Keep It Simple

Whatever the gimmick of the level is (countdown timer, must rescue a troop, etc.), make sure that it's very clear and that you don't use more than one. When designers try to put too many different gimmicks and/or goals into a level, the focus and objectives become confusing to a player.

Design on Paper First

You should always sketch out your level first and write down how the level should flow. This process will save you many hours in the long run, since it's much easier to change something on paper than it is to change in a mission editor.

Artistically Pleasing Levels

While the gameplay of the level is of primary importance, don't neglect the aesthetics of a game level. In *StarCraft,* there are a few guidelines that we follow:

- Lay down the terrain in isometric patterns. *StarCraft* tile sets are built along diagonal/isometric lines, so you don't want to have vertical or horizontal cliff faces for long stretches.

- Use a variety of tile types throughout the map. My general rule is that, on any given screen of map, if you can only see one tile type (water, dirt, etc.), then it's too much.

- Good doodad use. Doodads are important to make your map unique and interesting. It's very important, though, that they not be placed in a player's way. Keep them along terrain edges that the player will not be directly traversing frequently (cliff edges, water edges, etc.).

Clear Briefings and Objectives

After players have seen the briefing and read the objectives, they should be able to start the level and make progress very easily. If you have more than three objectives, I would classify this as "not clear." Players should never be frustrated with a level because they don't know what to do next. This is a major failing in many levels—and full-blown games, for that matter.

Here is a screen from Blizzard Entertainment's StarCraft: Brood War. Pardo says more than three objectives per mission may become too convoluted for the player. (Used with permission by Blizzard Entertainment, Inc.)

7

Avoid Pausing the Game for Story Elements

Any time the designer pauses the game on the player, it takes away the immersion factor of the game experience. If you have a "major" story point that you want to get across or you're changing the level objective, it's acceptable, but make this the exception, not the rule. On another note, though, it's perfectly fine to have a scripted cut-scene at the end of the level. This is a reward, and the player is usually pleased to sit and watch the story unfold at this point.

Ramp Up the Difficulty Appropriately

No matter what the relative difficulty for a given level, it should ramp from the beginning of the level at one point and become gradually harder as the level progresses. Try to avoid "killer" attacks that wipe out a player 30 minutes into a level.

Space Out the Mineral Placement (*StarCraft* Specific)

Due to the pathing algorithm that *StarCraft* uses, worker units can easily get stuck while harvesting unless the map designer places the mineral chunks in a pattern to prevent this. It's a good idea to play test every resource node before pronouncing the map "done."

Play Test, Play Test, Play Test

You should be constantly play testing your own levels to be sure that they work correctly and that they have the proper difficulty throughout the level. Levels at Blizzard are play tested by everyone in the company at the end of the project to make sure that we never release a level that's not up to our own quality [standards].

Also, be aware that you as the designer will be very close to the level and can't always be objective—get a friend who has never played your level to play test it. You may discover your friend never picks up on an objective that you thought was easy to understand, and he has becomes frustrated with the level.

Stages of *StarCraft: Brood War* Campaign Design

Pardo offers us a chronological overview of how they created the campaign for *StarCraft: Brood War*.

1. **Write the back-story.** Our first stage was to write the story for the campaign. It was important, though, to write a general story that could be modified as time goes

on. This process was to give us a starting point from which to think about the campaign as a whole.

2. **Define the campaign structure.** The *Brood War* campaign is a linear campaign that progresses through each of the three races, telling one unified story. We had to decide in what order the player would play the campaign. In our case, we chose to start the player as the Protoss, then go to the Terran, and end with the Zerg.

3. **Plot major story nodes.** Now we wanted to define the major events that were going to happen in the story: what characters were going to die, where betrayals were going to happen, etc.

4. **Start first-pass mission design on paper.** All the level designers would sit in a room and brainstorm on a level-by-level basis. When doing brainstorming, no idea is a bad idea. It's important for everyone to participate and to just get a ton of ideas down on paper. We would spend about 15 minutes per level just talking about the story for the level, how big the level should be, ideas for gimmicks, what units the player should have, and so on.

5. **Second-pass story design.** After the first round of discussions on a level-by-level basis, we found it necessary to tweak different parts of the story to accommodate certain goals we wanted to accomplish with the levels. In one case, it was necessary to add two more levels to the last campaign to better tell the story to the player.

6. **Second-pass level design on paper.** It was time to start locking things down. We went back through each level and talked about what the level should look like, where the player would start, how large was the enemy force, how we would program the AI and triggers. It's important to note that we have yet to lay out one level in the editor at this point. All work has been done in a conference room on paper.

7. **Start laying out levels!** Now it was time to divvy up the workload among the different designers and start work. Each designer would be responsible for laying out, placing enemy forces, and programming their own trigger actions.

8. **AI programming.** The AI programmers would take over the level and make the AI perform in interesting and different ways, according to the paper design and appropriate difficulty for the level.

9. **Play test.** For a level to be pronounced "done," it would take two to three weeks of testing and iterating on the level, based on feedback. (Once a level is finished, don't touch it! Even if it's a minor change, it isn't worth the chance that you could break something else and ruin all the effort that you placed into your level.)

7

On Unit Balancing

One of the weakest and ironically one of the most critical elements of a real-time strategy game is proper unit balancing. In the following discussion, Pardo explains its importance and offers some advice on ways to be sure that units have the proper "rock, paper, scissors" effect.

For game like *StarCraft*, unit balancing is the most important aspect of the multiplayer games. If this game isn't balanced for each race then there's no point in having different races, since everyone will only play one race. An entire book (or at least a chapter) could be written on this subject alone, so understand that these guidelines are not meant as a comprehensive list but rather as a starting point:

Early Game Unit Production Fairness

Every race needs to have the same opportunity to get early military units and/or defenses. If one race can get units substantially quicker than other races, you'll end up with one race winning a lot of games in two minutes.

Purity of Purpose

Every unit should have a primary purpose. For example, in *StarCraft*, the Zealot is tough ground attacker, the Queen is spell-caster so doesn't have an attack, etc. The units that don't have a "pure" purpose are always the toughest units to balance (Hydralisks, Marines, and so on).

No Invincible Unit Combos

It's extremely important that you find any unit combinations that are unbeatable by another player. It's acceptable if there is a powerful strategy, but it should never be unbeatable if a good player is preparing for it.

Avoid Redundant Units

In *StarCraft* we made a conscious effort not to have any unit duplicate another unit in the same race tech-tree. What I mean by this is that, while a Marine is the first troop you can build in the Terran tech-tree, it's still useful at the end of the game because no other Terran troop does the same job as the Marine.

Be aware of when new units become available. In each race's tech-tree, you must be aware of when a new powerful troop becomes available and make sure that the other races will have a counter to this new super unit at the same point in the game. Another *StarCraft* example: We found that Mutalisks were coming so early in the game that the other two races were not able to properly defend against them, so we increased the build time of the Spire (the building that allows Mutalisks to be built) to compensate.

Make Baby Steps

It's very important not to overdo a change. It's surprising to most people how one point of damage can make a huge difference in real game situations. Even if you feel that a larger change is warranted, it's always better to err on the side of a small change; otherwise you now have a balance problem in another area—and before you know it you have caused a chain reaction of changes that have unbalanced the game.

Evaluate All Effects of a Change

The obvious change is not always the right change. Whenever you're going to make a change to a unit, look at all places that this new change will impact. As a *StarCraft* example, we at one point changed the size of the Dragoon to medium, thus changing how much damage it took from large and small-sized troops. This had the positive effect of making Dragoons more susceptible to attacks from Vultures and Firebats (a previously underutilized troop) but also had the unintended effect of making them take less damage from Tanks. This in turn led to a new Dragoon rush strategy, and we had to undo the change.

Timothy J. Stellmach, Looking Glass Studios

As senior game designer at Looking Glass Studios, Tim Stellmach's latest and arguably most impressive work is *Thief: The Dark Project*. For this title, Stellmach was responsible for training and managing junior designers and overseeing the design of gameplay systems and missions. Who better to invite to talk about mission design? After all, *Gamecenter*, a popular Internet e-zine, awarded *Thief: The Dark Project* the "Best Story Line" award for 1998. That's right—an action game, of all things. And tightly woven in the story are the individual player missions, so let's begin.

Stellmach first defines scenario design and how he approaches it. In this segment, he also explains the differences between scenario design and puzzle design (discussed in Chapter 5):

In any mission-based game, scenario design involves a mission objective, a description of the space in which the mission occurs, some obstacles, and the tools for overcoming those obstacles. Note that the actual solutions to the

7

player's problems aren't on that list! That's the difference between a *scenario* and a *puzzle*. A puzzle has a solution designed into it, and that's really the only valid way of approaching the puzzle. One thing you see in a lot of games is missions designed as a set of puzzles the player has to "solve" in order to achieve the objective. There are games where that really is the point, of course, but you have to question that assumption. Can you design more than one solution? Could you enrich your game by making an environment in which the player can experiment and improvise?

The "campaign" in *Thief* is a work of fiction that holds the missions together and motivates them. Most action games involve a predetermined sequence of missions, so the campaign doesn't serve any interactive function. Instead it serves the interactivity in a support role. The fiction enhances the individual mission objectives by making them part of a story the player cares about. Success is its own reward, of course, but with a compelling fiction the player also feels like his success has achieved something meaningful.

Stellmach explains how to wrestle with mission design for a game and speaks on the common problems inherent in creating a successful game:

> Well, *design* in the first place implies setting goals, and planning and imple-
> menting solutions. People tend to forget what it means to do things "by
> design." It's important to stress the role of planning because in a creative
> business it's all too easy to get swept up in your ideas and just improvise as
> you go along. Generally, this leads to work that's sloppier and less focused
> than what you're really capable of. Think about what you're trying to do
> overall before you even start work on any individual part. Don't go off half-
> cocked.
>
> A corollary to this rule is to organize your work in iterations. Any job that's
> too big to understand all at once should be broken up into phases, each of
> which improves on the previous step. It's not actually possible to know
> exactly what you want to do from the beginning, so you have to be able to
> grip the problem as you go along, and adapt your plan. In designing a mis-
> sion, this means starting with a written plan, doing a general floor plan of the
> area first, and not working in details until they're necessary. The more
> detailed a construct is, the harder it is to rework, and everything you do will
> need to be reworked at some point. Plan ahead for prototypes and demos.
> Nothing is more useful in understanding the thing you're making than a
> working model.

That's all about getting work done in the first place—not wasting your time or straying off-track. To get good work done, I'd say the most important thing is just healthy amounts of playing time and willingness to adjust your work. This applies particularly to your communication with your play testers. There is no way for you to maintain your objectivity while working on a game day to day, for months at a time. When in doubt, the other guy is probably right, because you're too close to the thing to see it clearly. Build relationships with play testers who are good critics and good communicators.

Thief: The Dark Project was quite a unique action game in that the emphasis was not on annihilating everything in sight. Rather, its focus was on cunning stealth and subtle operation. Asked to comment on hurdles in light of the game's mission design, Tim replies:

The biggest obstacle was the amount of *Thief* that we were inventing ourselves. Nobody had done a first-person action-adventure game before where things like hiding in shadows and creeping around were so important. Or one where sound was really so basic to understanding the environment around you, rather than just being window dressing on a world that's essentially visual.

"I'd say the most important thing is just healthy amounts of playing time and willingness to adjust your work," says Stellmach. He also warns there's such a thing as getting "too close" to your work to make an accurate judgment. (Used with permission by Looking Glass Studios, Inc.)

It's hard to design missions around gameplay experiences you haven't really seen before. In production, it wasn't even really clear to us which parts of playing the thief character people would respond to. So there's all sorts of opportunities, not just to sneak around, but to pick pockets, ambush guards, defeat traps, and scout around eavesdropping and such. That led to a lot of richness in the game, but at times it was hard to get a grip on it all.

7

The key to dealing with this was a lot of game playing and critique up front to get a better understanding of the gameplay we wanted to see. Even many of the most original ideas have elements of a lot of previous work in them; there's no such thing as working in a creative vacuum. So there's elements of *System Shock*, *Prince of Persia*, *GoldenEye 007*, and a lot of other games in there. And we thought about similar-seeming games we didn't want to emulate, and what we wanted to do differently, and why. We asked a lot of sort of goal-level questions like "What are the tactical situations that make stealth necessary?" and "What are the emotional buttons those situations push, and how do we capitalize on that?"

In closing, Stellmach confirms this all boils down to the antecedent strategies: plan ahead, get the gameplay prototyped as early as possible, and get as much feedback from players as you can.

Greg Street, Ensemble Studios

Dr. Greg T. Street, game designer at Ensemble Studios, worked on the *Age of Empires: Rise of Rome* expansion pack and *Age of Empires II: The Age of Kings*. On these two products, his responsibilities included designing campaigns and random map types, helping contribute to unit and civilization balance, and providing historical background when needed. Street discusses the distinction between scenarios, campaigns, dynamic campaigns, and branching campaigns as they pertain to real-time strategy games. He alludes to his work for examples of each:

A *scenario* in an RTS game puts you in interesting situations where you must solve a certain mission rather than just build up and crush a generic computer opponent (although that often happens in scenarios). Scenarios rely on interesting maps, unusual victory conditions, unique art or sound additions, and attempting to tell a greater story.

A *campaign* is a string of scenarios in the way that a book is divided into chapters or a play into acts. In *Age of Kings*, one of the campaigns follows the battles of Joan of Arc. In one scenario, you must emancipate the city of Orleans being held by the wicked British. In future scenarios, you attack Chalons and Paris.

In a dynamic campaign, events in one scenario directly affect future scenarios, often by carrying over the health and status of your units to the next scenario (*Warhammer: Dark Omen* is a good example). Branching campaigns are those in which you have a choice of which scenario comes next in the story, either by directly choosing on the user interface or by your actions or degree of victory in a previous scenario. Personally, dynamic campaigns are not my favorite. Players often feel like they must not only win a scenario, but win by overwhelming odds in order to beat future scenarios. As a game designer, it's very hard to balance. Branching campaigns are a little easier to do successfully, but you're often committing to twice the number of scenarios in a campaign, many of which a particular player won't even see. In fact, one of the problems with branching campaigns is that players often choose to try both scenarios off a particular node, just to make sure they aren't "missing anything."

Game designers who would like to learn more about creating successful missions and campaigns should heed the following advice.

Make the scenario interesting. Why would a player want to go through your scenario instead of just playing versus other humans or on a randomly generated map?

Try to tell a story. Most players respond better to a scenario if they think that capturing the Assassin's mountain fortress will unite all the Saracens in a common front against the Crusaders than if they're just pitted against yet another bad guy. What are the two sides of the war? What is the historical significance of this battle? Will the outcome change anything? I've said this before (and you probably heard it before that), but "Red called you a monkey—go destroy his town" is not the stuff of epic literature.

For games such as Age of Empires Expansion: The Rise of Rome, historical accuracy was an important consideration, so Street researched the zeitgeist of the time. (Used with permission by Microsoft, Inc.)

Play test. Play test. Play test. Play through your level over and over, and then have friends, enemies, random Joes from the net, your parents, and your pets play through the scenario. You would be amazed at the goofy things people come up with that will break all your best-laid plans.

7

Are there any specific do's and don'ts Street can offer? Why do so many strategy games and sims have weak mission and campaign structure? Street offers us over a thousand words of advice in the following primer:

Plan Ahead

I always say that when designing a scenario, you should know exactly what's going to happen at any given time. Don't just plop enemy units down on the board and hope that they'll provide an interesting challenge. You should know that there will be a rush 5 minutes into the game, followed by a prolonged battle 20 minutes later, and that the entire scenario will take about 90 minutes for an experienced player.

The Fine Line Between Humor and Solemnity

Try to land on the continuum somewhere between cheesy melodrama and slapstick humor. If things are too sweeping, too desperate, too *clichéd*, then you can easily lose the mood and the player's desire to get through the campaign. (As a side note: FMV [full-motion video] and voice actors always tend to push you a notch or two closer to cheesy.) On the other extreme, backing so far away from an epic story that everything becomes one big joke won't push people onward either. A little tension break is good once in a while, but don't let the player feel that he or she is just a straight man for a bunch of zany events. *Warcraft 2* was quite humorous, but it never detracted from the grittiness of the story. If you have to make silly units because you're burned out on the story, consider making them cheats or Easter eggs.

Free Tools

Make whatever tools you use to develop scenarios available to the fans, preferably with the retail product. Having a well-documented editor is almost a must in the RTS franchise these days. The fans are very supportive of powerful editors.

Don't Sacrifice Quality for Quantity

People who play scenarios are very sensitive to repetition. If every mission feels the same, it's probably worth scrapping or merging a few. Alternatively, try to alternate scenarios where you basically build up to attack, fight a set-piece battle (a situation where you can't produce any additional units and must budget your starting resources), sneak a few units around a puzzle-type map, or have some other nontraditional victory condition (such as defending a weak unit, escort missions, etc.)

Use as many different victory conditions as possible. If the player just wanted to build up and crush the AI, he or she would use random maps. At Ensemble Studios, we strive to provide every scenario with a *hook*—something unique about the scenario that makes it fun. In the *Rise of Rome* expansion pack, one of the most popular scenarios that I made was the siege of Syracuse. The goal was to capture the Greek mathematician Archimedes in the center of the city, while avoiding the dreaded mirror towers that Archimedes designed to defend his city. (According to legend, the mirrors focused sunlight with enough intensity to ignite a trireme. There is some debate about whether this actually happened, although historians agree that the physics are believable.) The hooks for that scenario were being careful not to kill the weak Archimedes with indiscriminate catapult fire, and having your navy avoid the virtually unbeatable mirror towers protecting the Syracuse harbor.

One other caveat: Based on experience, prolonged sieges of an entrenched enemy sound really epic on paper, but the gameplay can be tedious as you slowly take out all of an enemy's defenses. The enemy should always be counterattacking. Don't let the player have more than a few seconds of peace, unless you are purposefully trying to prolong the tension.

More Bang for the Buck

Make it easy for fans to have access to additional scenarios not included in the main game. There are always retailers or periodicals eager to have some exclusive "bonus level." Make additional scenarios available on your company's Web site or encourage and facilitate the fan sites to trade user-submitted scenarios. Some of the *Age of Empires* fan sites literally have hundreds to thousands of scenarios.

Include Extra Touches

Use unique terrain, units, heroes, art, music, voiceover, or any other embellishment that encourages people to want to explore the map and play through just to see the next scenario. Including legendary heroes such as Alexander the Great and Hector of Troy in the *Age of Empires* campaigns and in the scenario editor was very popular with the fans.

Use Scripts But Don't Overdo Them

Do use scripts or triggers, but don't use scripting as a crutch. By scripting, I mean forcing an action as the result of a condition being met. Scripts or triggers can really enhance the single-player experience. An example would be

7

receiving reinforcements when you reached a certain area or defeated a certain enemy, possibly with a chat message or voiceover text.

However, if the human player feels that the computer opponents are merely responding to a specific set of actions (such as attacking every five minutes or attacking when the human player builds a certain type of building), the AI becomes very predictable and the human player feels that he or she has lost any chance to make real decisions. Blizzard's *StarCraft* did an excellent job of using triggers without overdoing them.

Try to Evoke Emotion

Try to evoke emotion in people playing through your scenarios or campaigns. I read once that good nonfiction conveys information but good fiction evokes emotion. Players should feel fear if they know they're up against a powerful enemy that can strike at any moment. Players can feel redemption or justice if they're beating off a predator from a victim or avenging a comrade's sacrifice. Even the map layout can convey emotion. Empty, barren battlefields speak of desolation, while cramped, jumbled surfaces can suggest paranoia.

Age of Empires II spans a thousand years, from the Dark Ages to the late Middle Ages. One of Street's objectives is to evoke emotions from the players. (Used with permission by Microsoft, Inc.)

On Difficulty, Hints, and Balance

Don't rely on a save-fail-retry mentality. It's very frustrating. Don't allow a player to stumble blindly into a battle from which he can't possibly survive, unless you're punishing him for making a bad choice. It should always be possible, if difficult, to win a scenario on the first try. If you plan an ambush, use some foreshadowing such as skeletons or crushed vehicles, or possibly burning buildings or fleeing refugees. If there is a right and a wrong path at a fork in the road, provide some hint for the right way to go, preferably "in story." Best of all, don't set up right-versus-wrong choices. If one path is more deadly, there should also be a reward hidden within. The classic trade-off is lengthy but less difficult, versus short but dangerous.

Don't Forget About the Single-Player Game

Multiplayer is very compelling in most RTS games, but I think designers sometimes forget the numbers of customers who don't yet have access to a reliable multiplayer connection (although that number is decreasing every day). When working on the *Age of Empires* franchise, scenarios were up against a strong multiplayer experience plus a random-map generator and tolerably good computer AI, so it would have been easy to neglect single-player campaigns. One of my responsibilities is to see that we don't!

The AI of the computer player can also prevent single-player scenarios from being very robust. Until very recently, it was typical in RTS games such as *Warcraft II* and *Age of Empires* for the AI not to build walls! Obviously that makes it pretty hard to defend.

Jon Zuk, Raven Software

Raven Software's Jon Zuk, the lead designer for the popular action/RPG *Heretic II* (published by Activision in late 1998) says there are different ways to create a mission or a goal for the game, and uses his last project as a prime example:

Heretic II has one large "mission" or goal that needs to be completed. Many games follow the idea of a large all-encompassing mission to win the game. Some games, however, use small individual missions. Take a racing game, for example. The user's goal is to win an individual race, but the other races don't really matter all that much. However, most games that have a large mission usually break that up into smaller, more manageable, and easier to remember goals. In *Heretic II*, the large goal is to cure the people of Parthoris of a plague. As you explore the first level, you meet a man who can give you a little information and a more immediate goal; meet the Celestial Watcher in the palace. Even though there's still that larger goal, a sub-goal has been introduced to steer the player in a direction.

"One thing I've noticed, though," continues Zuk, "is that in some games, there are too many sub-goals." He expands:

I can think of many recent role-playing games being guilty of this problem. What happens then is that the user loses touch with the larger overall goal and the focus of the game. It's easy to lose interest in a game when this happens. If you're going to have many missions reaching toward a large overall goal, make sure that they tie in together or at least keep the focus of the main goal.

7

In closing, Zuk warns, "Losing that focus can make the game no longer fun, which I think is the most important thing."

SECTION II

Production

CHAPTER 8

Programming

In this chapter, we get down to the meat and potatoes of game design—programming.

Programming, of course, refers to designing and writing a computer program, and, in our case, a game or game engine. It's the programmer's job to decide what the game needs to do, develop the logic of how to do it, and write instructions for the computer in a language that the computer can translate into its own language and execute (such as Microsoft Visual C++).

Another definition of programming is "the most fun you can have with your clothes on, although clothes are not mandatory." (Okay, that's debatable, but it *is* a real secondary definition at the FOLDOC Web site, the Free On-Line Dictionary of Computing at www.instantweb.com/~foldoc/contents.html!)

Call 'em what you want—code-crunchers, number-munchers, algorithm analysts—programmers are the talented folks who create the backbone of the game. As an analogy, think of the game as a building under construction. Programming represents the girders or the skeleton that forms the shape of the structure. All the beautiful art on the walls or incredible music pumping through the P.A. system will not substitute for poor engineering. A game, like a building, must be built on a solid and secure foundation.

There's a lot more to programming than graduating with a degree in computer science and hacking around with some code on your PC. Game programming takes cunning, patience, and an intangible *savoir faire* developed after years of practice, discipline, and a passion for the trade.

Over the next couple dozen pages, we'll hear from savvy programmers who want to share with us their years of experience on programming games, and how to overcome the tribulations inherent in this growing profession.

Kurt Arnlund, Accolade

Before leaving Activision to become lead programmer on Accolade's *Slave Zero*, Kurt Arnlund worked on such PC hits as *Mechwarrior 2: NetMech*, *Interstate '76* (all incarnations), and *Heavy Gear*. When it comes to programming a computer game, Arnlund says there are three key things a budding game programmer should bear in mind: the balance between time and ambition, the importance of specificity, and short versus fast routes to solve problems. He expands:

The Balance Between Time and Ambition

A game designer needs to walk the fine line between dreaming of this amazing game that goes so far beyond today's technology, and the time it takes to create amazing technologies. If you're too ambitious, you may be asking to create a game that can't be made in the industry standard timeline of a year. If you slip by six months because of a too-ambitious project, you run the risk of someone outdoing you before you can even come to market. On the other hand, if you scale your ambitions back too far, you run the risk of releasing a game that has been outpaced by your competitors long before you reach market.

Be Specific, Very Specific

As a game designer, it's your job to dream up coolness, then put it to paper in as exacting a way as possible. The programmer must then take this design document and make your dream a reality. A good programmer is going to go through your design and come across details that you hadn't anticipated. There are few things more frustrating as a programmer than realizing that the designer didn't put a lot of thought into creating a thorough design. This results in lost time and lost efficiency on the programmer's side because he may have already started coding your idea before the flaw is discovered. The more time you spend fleshing out every minute detail of your idea, the happier everyone will be. And as an added bonus, you'll get a killer game.

The Short Way vs. the Best Way

Game programmers are generally lazy individuals. That's right. It's true. Don't let anyone tell you otherwise. Since the dawn of computer games, game programmers have looked for shortcuts to coolness. We almost always try to take the shortest route from point A to point B. Sometimes when we look at a problem all we see is the shortest route to completion. What's the point of all this? Well, I'm going to let you in on a little secret. Sometimes the shortest route isn't always the best. As much as I hate to admit it, it's true. The more you, the game designer, know about programming, the more you're able to walk up to the programmers and say, "Hey, I think what you did is cool, but couldn't you have done it this way? That's what I really want." Better yet, if you really know what you're doing as a game designer, you can ask for a specific implementation right from the get-go.

You may be tempted to ask us programmers, "If you know that the shortcut isn't always the best, why don't you always do things the best way?" And my answer would be, "Because the best way isn't always the shortest." Actually, you should be quite happy that most game programmers think this way, because this means that things will get done on time. If we coded everything the most accurate way possible, we'd all end up with games that take three times as long and have one third as many features. Worse yet, we'd wind up with some over-budget, late, un-fun, technological showpiece like *Trespasser*.

Left, a pre-rendered screen shot from Activision's popular Interstate '76 combat racing game. (Used with permission by Activision, Inc.) Right, Arnlund's latest work, Accolade's Slave Zero. (Used with permission by Accolade. Inc.)

What about licensing an existing game engine, such as the *Quake II* or *Unreal* engine? Is it worth the greenback or should a programmer create his own?

> That's a tough call. I know a few programmers who wouldn't dream of working with a licensed engine because they think they'd lose working on all the cool engine details that they love so much. In the end, it probably doesn't matter too much. If you make an engine from scratch, you have to create and work on a whole lot of details that you don't need to work on if you license an engine. When you license an engine you can probably begin prototyping very quickly, but eventually you're faced with learning and possibly debugging all the details of the licensed technology if you want any hope of making the most use out of the technology. Because everyone codes differently, your licensed engine can range from indecipherable code to a beautiful masterpiece, but it'll most likely be somewhere in between.

Arnlund provides tips for newbie programmers who want to break into the industry:

> If you want to be a game programmer, a bachelors in computer science is a must. You don't have to go to fancy, expensive schools—just try to get a firm grasp of math and a bit of physics, and you'll be set.

> The best tip I can give to someone starting out is that if you really have a passion for games and you really want to be a game programmer or designer, then stick with it. Let everyone know that this is what you want to do. You never know who's going to be talking to a recruiter or who may know someone in the industry. Save up your money and attend a Game Developers Conference, or volunteer to work there and get a pass for free. Meet as many people in the industry as you can, and eventually you'll get lucky. I got lucky because a friend of mine who was seeking the same kind of work gave my name to a recruiter. Everyone in this industry has their story.

In closing, Arnlund suggests you set your goal, work hard, and hang in there. "Many people have gone from being testers to being designers or producers. Just stick with it and eventually it'll happen."

Jay Stelly, Valve Software

Jay Stelly is a senior software engineer at one of the hottest development houses in the gaming industry—Valve Software. This talented team of game designers, programmers, artists, animators, and sound engineers produced *Half-Life*, one of the most talked-about games of 1998.

Asked to address the many facets of game programming with which a software engineer must be concerned, Stelly answers the broad question with a short essay on frame-rate issues and memory limitations for 3D accelerator card support. The example is drawn from the *Half-Life* engine, a *Quake/Quake II* technology first licensed from id Software and modified greatly by Valve:

> Any game engine you can create or buy will have a set of technical constraints. You can choose some of these constraints, such as your target platform (CPU, memory, disk space, etc.), and target performance on that platform (frame rate, loading times, etc.); others are imposed by what hardware your audience owns. These choices do have consequences, of course. Let's look at an example.
>
> In *Half-Life*, we chose to support 3D accelerator cards for PCs. This allows people with additional 3D hardware to have higher image quality and frame rates. On the surface, this seems like an easy choice to make, but it comes with constraints of its own. One of the biggest challenges we faced was the fact that many of the 3D accelerators on the market only had access to 2MB of memory for storing textures. To make matters worse, the cost of swapping old textures with new textures was pretty high on many of these cards, so using more than 2MB caused a large frame-rate decrease. What this meant for *Half-Life* is that we had to limit any individual scene in the game to a maximum of about 2MB of visible textures.
>
> Think of programming time as a resource for overcoming constraints. You can only spend a certain amount of it. A good engineer can estimate the difficulty of a problem, and choose the correct set of approaches to consider as solutions to a big technical problem. Many of the defining decisions about a game are made as tradeoffs between different technical constraints. This was definitely the case with *Half-Life*.
>
> Early on, Valve recognized that managing texture memory for 3D hardware was going to be a big issue. Limiting ourselves to 2MB of textures per scene had tons of consequences. Not only did the environments themselves have textures, but each character in the game had its own textures. Also, each weapon the player could hold had its own textures, and the backgrounds in outdoor areas were made completely out of large textures. Because of the way our engine was designed, most of the lighting information in the world was also stored as textures. With that in mind, we spent programming time on managing this problem. We knew that there were too many consequences to limiting ourselves to 2MB per scene. It wouldn't provide us with enough

texture to reach the visual quality we were targeting. In fact, the problem was much larger than just a 2MB limit on some cards. As it turns out, almost all 3D cards on the market at the time *Half-Life* was released have dramatic performance differences that depend on how much texture memory you use, and whether your artwork is divided into textures with dimensions that are powers of two.

Jay Stelly: "One of the differences between an average engineer and a good one is the ability to think at a high enough level to choose the important problems to spend programming time on." (Used with permission by Sierra Studios)

In the end, we chose a set of technologies and work that allowed *Half-Life* to use more than 2MB of textures and still run well on 3D cards with that limitation. Our artists reworked character textures and user-interface element textures by combining multiple textures into single maps with power-of-two dimensions. We added a subsystem for managing paletted textures, which allowed us to store more textures in the same amount of memory. We changed portions of the renderer to try and draw all polygons with the same texture at the same time wherever possible (to minimize swapping textures). For cards that still didn't have enough memory, we added a feature to automatically scale textures down—which reduces image quality, but improves performance.

Another quality that separates an average engineer from a good one is being able to spend the right amount of time solving a particular problem. We could have spent a lot more or a lot less time on this problem. Choosing the correct criteria for evaluating the solutions to problems like these is very

8

important. Budgeting programming time is the balancing act that goes on when a game is produced. With good engineers, any piece of technology can be made better by working on it.

I feel that choosing the correct problems to solve and evaluating solutions well are two very important things that set *Half-Life* apart from other games.

What about the advantages and disadvantages to licensing a game engine versus creating one from scratch? How viable is it for newbie programmers to do it on their own? Stelly regards this as a very complex topic; to make this kind of decision, it's important to look at how game engines are developed.

The leading-edge engines for today's 3D action games are developed by teams of experienced programmers. Many of these programmers have built game engines before and have a good understanding of the challenges involved. Their engines represent many man-years of development effort. There are many games built on top of less complex (and less-often licensed) engines. As it turns out, most of these engines are built by teams of experienced programmers as well.

Even though it generally requires a team of experienced engineers, it's often cheaper to build an engine than to license one. [However,] several factors make licensing desirable, even though it can cost more. Because they have been used in one or more shipping products, licensed engines are often more stable. You're buying not only the engine's technology, but the time and testing that have gone into it. These engines also have a lower opportunity cost. If you have a team of experienced engineers, you can have them build your game instead of the engine, or build solutions to technical constraints of the engine. There are also marketing and hiring advantages to licensed engines. People who have purchased products using your engine have positive expectations about your game, and you may even be able to hire team members who are already familiar with the technology. Not to be overlooked is the ability to prototype game concepts immediately because you're working with a fully finished piece of technology.

Jay Stelly's most current work can be seen—and played—in the multiplayer *Team Fortress 2* by Valve and Sierra Studios.

Tip >> The World Wide Web has a number of handy resources for game programmers. Following is a short list of some of the more noteworthy sites to visit.
(Game design sites are listed in Chapter 24.)

- Game Programming MegaSite

  www.perplexed.com/GPMega

- Visual Basic Explorer

  www.vbexplorer.com

- Game Programming Galaxy

  www.geocities.com/SiliconValley/Vista/6774/

- Game Programming '99

  www.gameprog.com

- New Game Programmer's Guild

  http://pages.vossnet.de/mgricken/newgpg/

- Amit's Game Programming Information

  http://www-cs-students.stanford.edu/~amitp/gameprog.html

- GameProgrammer.com

  www.gameprogrammer.com

- Viper's C/C++ Page

  www.europa.com/~viper

- rec.games.programmer newsgroup

Charles Gough, Bungie Software

Charles "Chucky" Gough has been programming on and off since he was nine years
old, when his father showed him the basics of AppleSoft Basic on the old Apple IIe.
Although he didn't work on the celebrated *Myth II: Soulblighter*, developed and published by Bungie Software, gamers will get a chance to see Chucky's work on an unannounced action game that will "take the world by storm in the spring of 2000 and
move Bungie farther along the road of global domination."

Chucky offers his opinions for beginners on programming computer games:

1. Get your game up and running as quickly as possible. The sooner you have the
   basic engine and tools working, the longer you have to play and refine your game.
   It will also be easier for both your team and publishers to share your vision if they
   can see a working prototype.

8

2. You have to be willing to make compromises in your code to achieve goals. For example, you might have an incredible idea for a rendering algorithm that would outshine everything currently available, but if it runs so slow that it detracts from gameplay and takes so long to write that you lose your publisher, what have you achieved?

And a note to designers:

> The game has to be fun. For example, if you were making a role-playing game, it might be realistic to force the character to have to eat and sleep and defecate, but would it be fun? Sure, it might be funny the first time your character died of constipation because you weren't watching your crap meter, but it would get pretty annoying. From the beginning, making the game fun has to be the priority. The newest and best technology won't save a boring game.

Are there any good Bungie examples to support this advice?

> The *Myth* series is a good example of these rules applied to a genre that had seen only minor gameplay innovation. RTS [real-time strategy] games before *Myth* involved a lengthy buildup period before the action. And it was fun to watch your orcs smash the little humans, but other than the number and type of troops involved, you couldn't really affect the battle. The *Myth* team saw a lot of potential in the actual fight, and made the tactics of the battle the focus of the game. Jason Jones had a vision of what it would be like and decided to make a simple demo that involved a tiny 3D map, a dwarven grenadier, a troop of undead axemen, and the basics of a real physics engine. Originally he planned on having fully polygonal 3D characters and objects, but he felt that the frame rate would suffer and that it would take too long to develop. So he modified sprite code from *Marathon* and used that instead to quickly build his demo. This simple beginning was enough to get a cover of *Computer Game Strategy Plus*.

Understanding and adhering to tradeoffs (time vs. money vs. gameplay vs. technology) is a common theme in this chapter. Where does *Myth II: Soulblighter* fall into this common set of challenges?

> The biggest challenge was getting the game out the door less than a year after the original. We had a lot of things we wanted to change, improve, or add, but it quickly became apparent that there wasn't time to do it all. So we had no choice but to focus on those ideas that would have the most impact, like pathfinding, interface, and fire, while leaving out ideas like fully polygonal characters, non-bipedal units (cavalry and catapults), and burning trees.

When asked what reference material he finds beneficial to newbie game programmers, Chucky insists that, above all else, the most valuable resource is contact with experienced people and their code. "There's nothing more insightful than talking to someone who's written a few games, or looking at some real source code." Shy of that, Chucky suggests books as the next most useful resource, especially college textbooks, though it's "definitely hard to find good ones."

Michael D. McGrath, Dynamix/Sierra

Michael McGrath is an engineer/programmer at Dynamix who was responsible in part for the popular WWI combat flight sim *Red Baron 3D*, plus other past projects including *Netrek* (public domain) and *Extreme Warfare* (Trilobyte). Over the next couple of pages, McGrath offers some pointed advice on programming and game design, while touching on many of today's most common blunders in the gaming industry.

Design First, Program Later

Sitting down and writing a game, ad hoc, is one of the best ways to never finish your game. Most educated engineers can, in fact, write small projects in just this fashion, but written code ends up being a nightmare to use as "design notes" if you can't finish your work over a relatively short span of time. A good designer understands every aspect of his or her product long before it ever starts being written—because engineering and other design choices depend heavily on the job at hand. I've heard or been a part of too many projects that never got finished or went way over schedule—not because the engineers working on [the project] didn't know what they were doing, but because the lead engineers and designers clearly had no idea what *exactly* they were making until the project was nearly ready to ship. It *is* possible to design projects thoroughly beforehand, and if you don't, you pay the price.

Unfortunately, the games industry itself has its share of folks who don't understand this essential game-design philosophy. Take a good look at who you're working with before you start a project, and make sure they share the same philosophy with you. Unfortunately, many of the budding programming geniuses in the industry, who skipped out on the rest of college to write games, entirely lack the software engineering skills necessary to pull off a large game project efficiently. These people usually end up learning the hard way that programming is only a tool used by engineers to create things.

8

Engineering skill is the real necessity. Practically *everyone* in this industry is at least a competent programmer. Which brings me to subpoint 1 of tip A: Finish college, if you haven't already.

Learn to *think* before you *act*.

Know Your Audience, and Your Enemy

If you don't play games, you shouldn't be writing them. For that matter, if you don't play games, you shouldn't have anything to do with the games industry—except, perhaps, in a distant support role. Knowing how the industry works, how the audience thinks, and what the competition is doing is critically important to creating high-quality, successful games. It's also important to know your limitations as a game designer—and the kinds of games you sit down and play in an "addictive" fashion are *exactly* the kind of games you'd be good at helping create.

Don't pretend that you can design first-person shooters [if] you've been playing flight sims all your life, and recently got into your first shooter and loved it. To create and work on any game, you need to know every last incarnation of that genre, and be able to appreciate everything each instance has to offer. Once you can reminisce about the "good ol' days" with people who have adored that particular genre since day one, then and only then are you ready to bring your masterpiece to the masses. Otherwise you're on course to become another "clone," and to be lost in the overwhelming sea of fish who get eaten by the shark who *did* do his/her homework.

This issue is *very* important for everyone in the industry, but more so to programmers in particular. The programmers breathe the essence of life into any game—no beautiful texture, 3D model, or epic storyline will ever make a game great without a program to give it to the user—the gamer—in the right way. In order to understand the "how's" of presenting a great story, you have to experience the works of the past—both the flops and the smashes. There's no substitute, and never will be. Period.

Conveniently, programmers and others who work on games they're interested in also tend to work faster, harder, and better. If there's a team of people to be had on a project, I would consider this kind of enthusiasm to be right up there, equal with sheer talent and people skills. Put simply, it makes for a (substantially) higher quality product in the end.

Engineering Isn't Everything

Just because you can write blindingly fast code, 1,000 lines per day, and you *like* games, that doesn't mean you can do it all yourself. Writing computer games is all about telling and "living" a story—and although the engineers write the storyteller, you're still going to need a good story to tell. Everything [including] vivid artwork, an epic story, accurate physics engines, great multiplayer versus co-op teamplay, and moving music can go into making a great game experience. And in order to accomplish the task of creating a game, you need to understand each and every one of these things, from at least an appreciative perspective.

On top of understanding these things and their presentation, you need to understand their representation in the media you're using to tell the story. A 1-bit graphics pipeline will get you a great frame rate nowadays, but I doubt that anyone is going to really appreciate the visuals in your game if you decide to use such an engine. Part of understanding the "what's" behind telling a great story in this fashion come from experience—usually accrued from playing other games.

The last part comes from being able to work with and understand the people who help you (as any member of a game development team) tell these stories. You need to get good tools, you need to be able to teach others what they need to know to work with your technology, and, most of all, you need to have the patience and determination for doing all of the above. And to see it through to the end.

The games industry has no room for iron-fisted bosses, high-and-mighty anythings, or close-minded folks in any way, shape, or form. These kinds of people show up from time to time, and their game (and unfortunately their careers, and those [of the people] they work with) end up in the bargain bin... or, worse yet, never even make it out the door. If you ever find yourself working *for* someone, and not *with* them, you need to get away, because you're on the losing side in the (as of late) extremely competitive Deathmatch that is the games marketplace.

McGrath applies the aforementioned advice to Dynamix's *Red Baron II* and the problems that plagued the game. Says McGrath:

> *Red Baron II* was a good example of over-engineering and lack of forethought in engineering design. In *Red Baron 3D*, most of the programming work involved fixing bugs and understanding the workings of the code, so we

8

could add new features and technology. The original engineers no longer worked at Dynamix or had moved on to other projects when the conversion to *Red Baron 3D* began. The code was poorly documented, which caused us no end of trouble with the conversion—and, on top of that, we had no one to look to for assistance in understanding it. It would have been much simpler to convert (as a matter of fact, I believe the original team could have done it) if it had been designed well in the first place. But it was horrendously cryptic, being the work of many, many different people with no overriding design to guide them, in addition to being over-abstracted and over-engineered in places where the design *had* been thought through.

These two screens are from Red Baron 3D. Above, movable control surfaces indicate enemy maneuvering. Below, new cloud variations and layering effects create an awe-inspiring sky filled with dangers unknown. (Used with permission by Dynamix)

Red Baron II suffered the terrible misfortune of being developed first for DOS, then for Windows 95, then for DirectX, and then, finally, for hardware 3D. During its development, it was torn apart and rebuilt so many times that it became incredibly unwieldy in the end. The real problem was not the reconstruction itself, but rather that the engineering leads seemed to "over believe" in code reuse, and not in well-designed modularity. They would rip out [some] parts and keep others—tying them together with a mess of spaghetti that eventually rendered the code base very difficult to read and understand. If they had designed the pieces in a well-thought-out, modular fashion to begin with, they would have been able to finish the game far earlier than they did, despite the advancing technology that inspired the changes in the first place. That doesn't mean "if they had used C++," either—they did, actually. Object-oriented programming, with all its merits, can become a real nightmare when "abused" with poorly-thought-out design and corresponding makeshift engineering. Never ever let the "wow" factor of a programming language convince you that Ockham's Razor and legibility aren't important. Ever.

Note >> Thirteenth-century philosopher William of Ockham (also spelled *Occam* or *Occum*) coined this law of economy, known today as "Ockham's Razor"— the philosophical belief that the mind should not multiply entities beyond necessity.

In addition to chatting with others on Usenet and attending various conferences, McGrath suggests a few handy books that game programmers should consider:

- *Computer Graphics: Principles and Practice, Second Edition in C* by Foley, van Dam, Feiner, and Hughes (Addison-Wesley, 1996)

- The OpenGL programming guide (the "red book") and reference guide (the "blue book")

- The *Graphics Gems* series, edited by Andrew S. Glassner, James Arvo, David Kirk, Alan W. Paeth, and Paul S. Heckbert (Academic Press and AP Professional, 1993–1995)

- *Artificial Intelligence* by Patrick Henry Winston (Addison-Wesley, 1992)

McGrath is currently programming code for *Desert Fighters* and *Aces of the Pacific II*, while future plans include a rewrite of *Netrek* and a continuation to help create sci-fi flight/combat sims and conquest titles.

Allen Jackson, Origin Systems

Allen Jackson has been a software engineer at Origin for a number of years now and has had the privilege of working on many award-winning action and space simulations. These include *Crusader: No Remorse*, *Crusader: No Regret*, *Wing Commander Prophecy*, and *Wing Commander Prophecy: Secret Ops*. Primarily, Jackson works on the higher-level game code: interface design, Win32 GUI applications, game-defined objects, and networking.

Jackson shares with us here his three tips on programming code for games, and alludes to his most recent works for examples to support these suggested practices.

Keep the Engine Data-Driven

The engine that a programmer designs for a game should be as data-driven as possible. Instead of hard coding for every single type of situation in a game, the code should allow for a wide variety of elements to be assembled through data. The *Wing Commander: Prophecy* spaceships, for example, are mostly created in data. The programmers allow the different spaceships to have certain properties such as engines, guns, missiles, shields, and maximum acceleration. The designers then assemble a ship data file that describes the ship's art, properties, and statistics, which will later be read from the hard drive and then interpreted by the code. There are very few cases where the code looks for a specific ship to do a special effect, but even these cases should ideally be taken out of code so that multiple ships could share this property.

Another way of thinking about data-driven engines is as the trigger system in an action game that uses a map of some sort. *Crusader: No Remorse* featured a commando in the far future that ran along on an isometric map, shooting up the enemies. This map was full of objects that the Crusader could interact with, such as teleporters, doors, switches, and monitors. A trigger system allows a designer to choose a certain trigger (like a switch) and then attach an action such as "open door #21" when that trigger is activated. This relationship would be saved in the map file and interpreted by the code. If the trigger system is created properly, the trigger could activate many actions that the programmer didn't envision for the game at the beginning.

Missions should also be as data-driven as possible. The code shouldn't know what the specific missions are in a plot; rather, it should have a framework that allows a designer to create a large plot and smaller subplots that the players will interact with in the game. *Wing Commander: Prophecy*'s mission and plot designer allowed designers to have a "series" file that would contain the global plot flags, a series of missions, and the tree format that would link

all the missions together. The system is extremely flexible and robust, allowing for many types of tree branches and conditions to tell many types of
stories.

Experiment with Existing Engines

The strongest aspect a game programmer can have when working on any
application is class structure and hierarchy. If the interface of the low-level
code is written correctly, the latter stages of game programming will go more
smoothly. For example, if in the middle of game development the group
decides to switch the networking strategy for the game, the only modules that
should need to be rewritten would be in the low-level networking code. The
rest of the higher-level code shouldn't care what low-level code is running it.

There are many fine graphics engines out on the Internet. Download some of
them and try to create a simple application with them. Then try to examine
how the programmers put the architecture together. There are a wide variety
of ways to render a scene, for example. Some engines have the user create
the game objects, then have the objects inserted and deleted from the game
world to render them. Some engines want the objects to draw themselves,
using a screen class. Some engines want to draw the scene using a window-
ing technique, so that many independent scenes can be rendered all at once.
Some engines like to layer the objects onto the scene in a specific order to
make a crisper interface, such as displaying a main interface screen last so
it's always visible.

There are some game companies that have released their code from their
older games. While you may not be interested in using their archaic
ray-casting engine, you might want to investigate the main game loop,
the input control, in-game messaging, game object handler, debugging tools,
and the world-rendering system.

 Tip >> One of the latest examples of a developer/publisher offering the source
code for a game over the Internet is Raven Software and Activision. In
January 1999, they released the original *Heretic* and *Hexen* source code to
the public for free. Download them at www2.ravensoft.com/source.

Stay Away from Static Classes and Variables

Finally, Jackson warns about getting into the static class "memory trap," and provides a
sample of code as an alternative way to get around this common programming obstacle:

They sort of act like a global version of a variable that can be accessed by
most of the classes, but there can only be one instance of this variable. There
are some classes where there really should only be one instance of a class,

like ClassOperatingSystem, ClassGameSound, and ClassFileSystem. There are also some classes that look like there should only be one instance, but in other places multiple instances could be made. A classic example of this kind of static class is ClassGameWorld:

```
class ClassGameWorld
{
public:
    // static world data
    static void* m_GameWorldData;

    // static function members
    static bool Install( void );
    static bool Remove( void );
    static bool AddObject( GameObject& _obj );
};
```

Then the programmer could use the World::AddObject() function anywhere in his other modules, which is convenient but only allows for one game world. If the game design changed later, where having multiple game worlds would really help (such as for a massive multiplayer game), there would have to be a major revision of all the game code to accommodate this.

A better solution might be to create a non-static version of ClassGameWorld and then have a static templated list of game worlds somewhere else, such as ClassGame:

```
class ClassGame
{
private:
    static TemplateList<ClassGameWorld*> m_GameWorldList;

...

public:
    static ClassGameWorld& GetWorld( int _nWorld );
};
```

This would allow many instances of the same class available to the code, while retaining only one place to access all of the game world's data.

➤ In Chapter 3, Jackson also offers some tips on game design.

Ragnar Scheuermann, Wombat Games

At Origin Systems, Ragnar Scheuermann worked as a software engineer on *Ultima: Ascension* and *Ultima Online*. He later left Origin to be a principal software engineer, game designer, and VP at Wombat Games.

Scheuermann says his advice pertains to both novice programmers and game designers alike, and follows up his words with good examples based on his own experiences:

> First and foremost, make sure you know the game you want to make. From the very beginning, you should be able to describe what it's like to play the game, and how you interact with it. You should make sure everyone working with you knows and believes in the same vision of the game. And one last point—once everyone agrees on the vision of the game, don't change it.
>
> Second, you'll get a lot better ideas and an overall improvement in the work from people who love what they're working on. If you're just starting out, you're going to need all the motivation you can get in order to finish anything. I've also discovered that the coolest stuff in games is the "extra" that the programmers or designers put in or improve. Not because they have to, but because they want to.
>
> Finally, if you're just starting out, don't get in over your head. Feel free to make a lot of things in the design "optional," and just get the basics done first. Pick technology that fits the type of game you're doing. For example, if your game doesn't need 3D, and you don't like 3D, don't put it in your game just because everyone else does.

Scheuermann provides examples to help support and further expand on the preceding comments:

> *Ultima Ascension* is now five years in development. The primary reason for this is that the game's vision changed every year, forcing a large portion of the code to be thrown away. First, it was based off the *Ultima 8* engine, but with high-resolution graphics, and this engine later became *Crusader*. But then, just before I was hired, it was decided to make the game polygonal, which meant an entirely new engine, new tools, and training a programming team who had little experience with 3D.
>
> A year and a half later, the majority of the team was moved over to *Ultima Online* to help that project ship. During this time, one team member added 3D card support to the game. This had the side effect of inspiring the decision to change the camera perspective from primarily isometric to over-the-shoulder (*Tomb Raider*). This broke parts of the engine, forced the rebuilding of many areas to better suit the new camera angle, and paved the way for the next major change. Just before *Ultima Online* shipped, the *Ultima: Ascension* team was reassembled, with a new producer and a new designer. This

8

resulted in another shift away from the traditional *Ultima 7*-esque gameplay to more of a fast-paced action-oriented model. The phrase of the day: "Every 30 seconds must be fun." After a year, that producer was fired.

The game and management had changed so much by this point that, of the team that was in place when I was hired, six remained: producer Richard Garriot, programmers Herman Miller, Gary Scott Smith, and Chuck Zoch, and artists Scott Jones and Michael Morlan. The game has now changed direction again after another engine rewrite and the gameplay has regained some of its RPG roots. The problem with *Ultima: Ascension* wasn't that any of the designs were bad, but that the design kept changing.

Ultima Online suffered from a lack of clear vision as well, although not quite as badly. The vision of the game was never well described, and was different in the minds of different team members. Some people were making a virtual world simulation, some were making a quest-based adventure game, and then there was the pressure to be *Diablo*. However, the game suffered more because its requirements changed from an experimental test [of] 100 players per world to 2,500 per world. Unfortunately, the deadlines didn't change, forcing the code to evolve out of necessity rather than design. The end result of all this was a late, buggy game with no clear direction for players to follow; code that was extremely difficult to maintain; and all of the original programmers leaving.

For the game we're working on [a yet-to-be-disclosed massively multiplayer online role-playing game], we're trying really hard to give it a good start. We're making a virtual world whose principal inhabitants are players, and nothing is pre-scripted. When we've interviewed people, the most important questions have been whether or not they agree with this vision and want to work on this type of game.

Having worked through these problems in the past, Scheuermann has used this experience to his advantage while looking toward the future. He ends this discussion by reverting to the vision; he says they're "spending a lot of effort building up a good technological base we like before we build the game, rather than building it as we go to suit the needs of the day."

Matt Pritchard, Ensemble Studios

Matt Pritchard's title is Graphics Engine and Optimization Specialist at Ensemble Studios, where he helped program *Age of Empires*. Pritchard is currently absorbed with *Age of Empires II: The Age of Kings*, but he takes a moment out of his busy schedule to share a few words for aspiring programmers. What are the three crucial things program-mers need to remember?

1. You won't write an epic saga overnight; persistence and patience are your best tools.

2. Most things have already been done before; seek them out and learn what others can teach you.

3. Most projects are never finished; over-ambition and unrealistic evaluation of the tasks at hand doom them to being forgotten. Know yourself and your real limits, desires, and how far you will really take things.

What are the biggest challenges a game programmer must face? To Pritchard, there are two biggies:

- Keeping up with technology. The only cure for this is to focus on what's important and invest the time and resources to stay current in your learning.

- Discipline to manage the software development process; i.e., to get things done on time and as planned. This requires experience. Books on writing solid code and "code complete" are an aid in breaking the problems down. This is an ongoing bat-tle everyone seems to face.

To wrap up, Pritchard suggests game programmers should spend some time perusing the Usenet newsgroup rec.games.programmer to learn more about the art and science of cre-ating and modifying game code.

Chad Freeman, Dreamforge Intertainment

Chad Freeman is a lead programmer at Dreamforge Intertainment, the development stu-dio responsible for the delightfully creepy adventure game *Sanitarium*. Past games Freeman has worked on include *Anvil of Dawn* and *Warwind*.

In this segment, Freeman offers some free advice—and sample code—for game programmers:

> You may have heard that performance is the most important consideration when writing game code. Don't believe that for a minute! Only 10–20% of your code is going to be performance critical. The rest of your code needs to be flexible, because you'll either be making lots of changes to it, or ending up with an inferior game because your code is too brittle to allow modifications.

8

Don't be afraid to use something just because you didn't think of it. Many of the exciting things that have been done in 3D games are based on techniques that were first created for 3D rendering programs years ago. Spend a little time researching a technique that you would like to use in your game. This will give you more time to spend on the aspects of your game that are truly unique.

The most important thing you can do at first is complete something. Being able to complete a game is what will separate you from all of the people who start and give up. One of my fellow programmers likes to say, "You never finish a game, you just quit working on it." There's always something that can be done to improve your game, but at some point you have to say, "It's good enough," and let it go.

One specific technique I have found useful [with C++] is to use arrays instead of dynamic memory allocation wherever I can. You can implement any common data structure (lists, queues, stacks, heaps, trees) using arrays— just use an array index for your "pointers." This instantly eliminates memory leak problems with the data structure, and, just as importantly, forces you to think about worst-case scenarios for your game, among other benefits.

Following is an example of how an array versus pointer/dynamic memory implementation of a linked list would look, and a short example for efficiency versus flexibility.

Array example:

Using pointers and dynamic memory allocation, a linked list might look something like this:

```
Memory Address Contents

001 [ Pointer to first (010)]
002 [ Pointer to last (062)]

...

010 [ Pointer to unit graphic ]
011 [ Health ]
012 [ Pointer to next element (053) ]

...

053 [ Pointer to unit graphic ]
054 [ Health ]
```

```
055 [ Pointer to next element (098) ]

...

062 [ Pointer to unit graphic ]
063 [ Health ]
064 [ Pointer to NULL (end of list) ]

...

098 [ Pointer to unit graphic ]
099 [ Health ]
100 [ Pointer to next element (062) ]
```

If you forget to free one of these structures, that memory's gone until your game quits. Also, they're spread out over memory, so no matter how you run through the list you're generating cache misses.

Now, an array implementation might look like this:

```
List Header:

First [index to first unit - 001]
Last [index to last unit - 003]

List:

Array index contents Index to next element

001 Unit 1 info 002
002 Unit 4 info 004
003 Unit 2 info -1
004 Unit 3 info 003
```

You can't lose any memory with an array, as you always have the whole array allocated—no more, no less. Also, if your function to add a unit to the list looks for the first empty spot in the array, you can run through the list from element 1 to the last element in order, preserving cache coherency.

When we used this technique in *Warwind*, we had multiple lists, all using a single array. General unit processing ran through the array top to bottom. When we needed to do processing for a specific player, we would run through the list of that player's units. When we needed to do processing for certain types of units, we ran through that list, etc.

A note on flexibility:

This is something you'll struggle with every time you make a game. You're basically trying to predict the future as you write code. You'll inevitably

8

make an assumption that will turn out to be invalid later on. But there are good and bad assumptions to make. In *Warwind*, we made the assumption that every machine would have an exact representation of the game state every frame. This was a bad assumption to make because, on the Internet, where latency is high and lost packets common, syncing every frame slows the game to a crawl.

For more about Dreamforge Intertainment, its employees, and games, see www.dreamforge.com.

Stuart Denman, Surreal Software

Stuart Denman is the vice president and technical director at Surreal Software, the hot development house responsible for Psygnosis' action/adventure game *Drakan*.

Denman is no stranger to programming, and he says one of the single most important considerations when creating action games is watching the frame-rate speed. The three following memory strainers will ultimately affect frame rates unless you work on them religiously:

Polygon Counts and Minimum Specifications

Designers must have minimum-spec machines available to test levels on, so that they can be sure that the game will run smoothly, even on low-end machines. A level that runs at 30 fps [frames per second] on a Pentium II 400MHz can run at 8 fps on a Pentium 166 with the same polygon counts. It's a balancing issue between look (high-polygon counts) and feel (frame rate). Designers should *not* count on frame-rate optimizations later in the project.

Artificial Intelligence

Like polygon counts, AI contributes to CPU drain. Placing 30 enemies within the same area not only increases the polygon counts, but also increases the amount of AI computation required to maintain all those creatures. A limit on number of creatures should be established by the programmers once the AI programming is far enough along.

Lighting

In *Drakan*, point lights are dynamically computed on objects and landscape areas that change. This means that any moving light source or moving object will have to be recomputed. Large numbers of lights and large drop-off radii will contribute to slower performance.

A game's frame-rate speed is one of the most critical factors to watch in game programming, says Demnan. As seen here in Psygnosis' Drakan, enhanced lighting is one of the memory drainers. (Used with permission by Psygnosis, Inc.)

Other frame-rate issues of concern for programmers, says Denman, are making sure that models have lower levels of detail (to keep polygon counts low when objects are far away), and, as in *Drakan*, making sure that databases and parameters are organized efficiently. Explains Denman:

> Databases include sound, behavior, model, texture, and scripting resources. Clean organization of these [elements] is critical to allow the team to work effectively with the levels. In *Drakan*, any object in the game has parameters that define how it behaves. They're also the mapping between resources in the database and the code, so it's critical that parameters are kept in their proper settings.

Denman discusses the pros and cons of working with an existing game engine versus creating your own:

> As far as licensing goes, it really depends on what you want to do. If you want to create new technologies not available currently, then licensing is not the answer. If you just want to create an original game with advances in gameplay and features, licensing an engine is a very good option. Licensing saves years of work, and can allow more time to make a better game.

> Surreal was lucky because we got initial funding for a project with only a small demo. Most development groups won't get this. I realize now (although I didn't at the time) that it's very hard to break into this industry if you've never worked in it. You need to prove yourself with either reputation or a knockout demo. Aspiring entrepreneurs can always come out of nowhere and create demos that rival that of professionals; so as long as that's still possible, there's hope.

In programming, data is often stored in arrays—that is, strings of data. It's a frequent occurrence to access areas of memory outside of these arrays, which can produce an illegal operation in Windows—the General Protection Fault (GPF). For example, if the array has a length of five elements, and the program tries to access element 8, you'll get a GPF. To prevent these bugs, the following code warns the programmer when this problem has occurred so the bug can be fixed.

Every programmer must do this: Create a template for arrays, don't use C–style arrays unless absolutely necessary. The template definition would look like this:

```
template <class Entry> class Array
{
private:
   Entry *pEntry;
   int iSize;
```

The template then has inline members to append (allocate) and delete entries in the array, and members like this to access the array:

```
public:
   // Allows access to an array entry...
   Entry &operator [](const int iIndex) const
   {
      Assert(iIndex >= 0 && iIndex < iSize);
      return pEntry[iIndex];
   }
```

The Assert function is important because it raises a debugging error if the expression in the Assert is FALSE. This bit of code has saved us *so* many bugs, I can't imagine living without it. Our Assert macro looks like this:

```
// Debug case:
#if defined(_DEBUG)

extern BOOL MyAssertFunc(BOOL, int, char *);

#define NatBreak() {_asm { int 3 } }

// Asserts that exp is true.
#define Assert(exp) \

   if (MyAssertFunc((int)(exp),__LINE__,__FILE__)) \
      NatBreak();

// Non-debug case:
#else

#define Assert(exp)

#endif // _DEBUG
```

In the release build, all Assert macros get compiled out. In the debug build, the function MyAssertFunc is included in a library. The function evaluates the first argument and brings up a message box with the line and file where the assertion happens (the last two arguments). The programmer can then choose to continue executing, or break. If the programmer chooses to break, the function returns TRUE and the int 3 instruction causes the debugger to break on the Assert macro line.

➤ To read more about Deman's *Drakan* project, drop into www.psygnosis.com/drakan/.

Richard Moe, Humongous Entertainment

Richard Moe serves as both a project lead and software engineer (among other duties) at Humongous Entertainment. All Humongous games work in a proprietary language called SCUMM, which was developed by company cofounder Ron Gilbert. Some of the titles Moe has worked on here as designer and programmer are (in chronological order) *Junior Field Trips: Let's Explore the Airport*, *Pajama Sam in There's No Need to Hide When It's Dark Outside*, *Backyard Baseball*, and most recently, *Putt-Putt Enters the Race*.

Moe says each game brings its own set of challenges to a game designer and programmer. The following examples are from Moe's past experiences:

For creating children's games, the most challenging aspect is balancing the difficulty level so the game can be as fun and easy to play for a four-year-old as it is for an eight-year-old. Obviously, the skill sets for these age ranges are vastly different. For example, in *Pajama Sam* we have a simple game of tic-tac-toe called "Cheese and Crackers" that can be played on one of three board sizes: 3×3, 5×5, or 7×7. The 3×3 board is simple tic-tac-toe—three in a row wins. The 5×5 and 7×7 boards need four and five in a row to win, respectively. It's plain to see that the first of the three is the easiest—fewer permutations—and the other two are successively harder. However, by providing all three, we've given a fun challenge to all ability levels. Moreover, the computer opponent (the AI code) tries to match the ability of the opponent. If the player wins, the computer plays smarter the next time. Similarly, if the computer wins, it next plays a little dumber.

That tangent aside, I'd say the biggest issues for the designer in regard to programming are knowing the target audience and knowing current technology. The first point is related to the previous paragraph—if you're designing a kid's game, you've got to know what kids like. If you're designing a historical strategic war game, you need to figure out what war-game players like.

Obviously, a good programmer needs to keep abreast of the current technology. There is no such thing as a "Renaissance man" in the field of computer game programming. Specialization is imperative. A good game programmer focuses on the areas that he or she is good at, and leaves the rest for someone else. I couldn't write a blit routine [copying a large array of bits from one part of a computer's memory to another part] if my life depended on it, but there are people here who can, so I let them do their thing and provide me a library to use.

Must a programmer be well versed in other areas of game design?

Budgets being what they are, oftentimes a game programmer needs to wear many different hats on a project, since the experts aren't always available to all the projects that need them. Other times, the specific problem is unique to the game and the engine being used. I can't get a good C++ programmer to write a routine for me to use in my SCUMM game. That's when the programmer gets to wing it, and it happens more often than not. I recently had this problem when working on *Putt-Putt Enters the Race*. At the end of the game, the player got to race Putt-Putt around a pseudo-3D course. To get this to work effectively, I had to keep track of things in a 3D world. I have had absolutely no experience in 3D transformation, and no other programmers were available to help me. So basically I had to learn it and implement it myself. Luckily, I had a few experts' brains to pick, and thankfully, the results were good. It's no *Gran Turismo*, mind you, but then again, per the aforementioned point, I knew my audience (kids 3–8) didn't care about realistic physics models and real-time 3D rendering. Instead, I put in some funny-looking ducks that would quack and fly away if you drove too close to them.

And what's the best way to learn programming? "Plug your nose and jump right into the deep end," says Moe. "Start simple—a *Minesweeper* game, a *Tetris*–style game, or a *Space Invaders* clone. Soon, you'll be making the next third-person 3D real-time action/shooter strategy game."

Kurt Pfeifer, Cavedog

Humongous Entertainment's sister company, Cavedog Entertainment, was accountable for the mega-hit PC strategy game *Total Annihilation* (*TA*). Kurt Pfeifer worked on *TA*, the Sega Saturn port of *Duke Nukem 3D*, *Microsoft Soccer*, *Powerslave*, *DinoPark Tycoon*, and *Magic School Bus Across the Solar System*. Currently, he serves as the lead programmer on *Good & Evil*. Pfeifer offers a few indispensable pointers for those looking to create code for today's games.

Make a Clear Design for Your Game Up Front

If you want to complete your game anywhere near your scheduled delivery date, lay out what it's going to look and feel like up front. Game creation is a very inexact science, and usually is ad-libbed more than any other kind of programming. But if you can get a ballpark idea of what you're shooting for, it eliminates an amazing amount of guesswork and delays later on. Even just laying out storyboards to provide a visual reference is helpful, as any game has to be optimized for exactly what needs to be seen (for example, first-person point of view versus overhead, 2D versus 3D).

Pfeifer offers the following as an example:

One of the clearest designs you can program from is when you're porting an existing game to another platform. When we undertook the ports of *Duke Nukem 3D* and *Quake* to the Sega Saturn (when I worked at Lobotomy), we obviously had a clear design of what the game would need to be like. Instead of a design on paper that could possibly be modified or misinterpreted, we had the exact blueprint in front of us in the form of the PC game that had already hit the market. Every graphic, every sound, every nuance of the control system was laid out for us; we just had to squish it down to fit in the Saturn. We only had six months to complete the task (later upped to nine to allow for net link programming), so efficiency was crucial. This total understanding of the "big picture" of the design for the game allowed us to split up the tasks efficiently and plan our schedule effectively.

Get as Many People as You Can Afford

Easier said than done, as there are few schools out there to train people in game programming, and you need to find people with previous experience (of which there aren't many) or who know general programming and are eager to dive into gaming. Even the simplest programming tasks can add up to monumental ones, and if you're shorthanded all of the deadlines will start to slip.

Allow Time for Research and Development

[Allocating time for R&D] unfortunately is not done often enough due to a tight deadline. If you want to do something really unique, you have to sink in some time up front to research which off-the-shelf packages will fit some or all of your needs (3D modeling tools, paint programs, sound editors), and which tools you'll need to do in-house (often including map editors, scripting languages, and animation tools). This time can also be used for artists to create simulated movies or mock-up stills of what the game will look and move

8

like, using existing 3D animating and 2D paint tools. This way you can see if everybody agrees on it up front, instead of finding out a year or two down the road that the publisher or designer had something else in mind.

Pfeifer believes that the biggest obstacles are ones most people don't consider when laying out a project: keeping interest alive and not getting overwhelmed.

> More than once I've been on a project where the designer loses interest after the first half of the project, when it's past the honeymoon stage and into the ugly detail decisions. In that case, I've played designer as well, and since I'm stretched thinner, the project is not programmed as effectively as it should've been. Getting overwhelmed is easier than ever now in game creation, with games (and their budgets) becoming bigger, and feature lists increasing dramatically every year.

In conclusion, Pfeifer says, "Just managing a project can become an immense task, but not an impossible one if it's planned out ahead and tasks are divided up properly."

Jamie Fristrom, Treyarch Invention

Jamie Fristrom is a senior programmer at California's Treyarch Invention. He was instrumental in coding the celebrated action games *Die by the Sword* and *Limb from Limb* for Interplay in 1998. Fristrom shares a few thoughts with us on game programming and the modularity of design:

> There's an art, I think, to writing code that strikes some balance or creates some synergy between being easy to read, maintain, and evolve, and being able to get something to show, something up and running—quick—so you can see how well it works as a game.

> A programmer should consider himself as someone meant to facilitate the game/level designer, rather than thinking of himself as the game designer. The programmer should make it easy for the game designer to design. You'll get more *game* that way.

> The biggest obstacles are features you decide you need later that you never planned for: In our case, the ability to pick up limbs and hit people with them was a good example. The best way to deal with that is probably to rewrite the infrastructure to handle the new features, but for that particular feature we just sucked in our gut and kludged it on. It caused a lot of pain later, a lot of long hours fixing the bugs we introduced.

This leads Fristrom to his last piece of advice: "Bugs are bad. Kill bugs before they start to breed."

Michael Saladino, Presto Studios

After working at Mobeus Designs creating 3D graphics engines, Michael Saladino left to work at Volition (the creators of *Descent*), where he was promoted to lead programmer. Now he's an engine programmer at Presto Studios. Following is a list of Saladino's truisms, with explanation and support for each.

Never Underestimate Assembly Language

With each generation of Intel processors to come and go, a new round of discussion on the future importance of assembly language is launched around newsgroups and development house water coolers. Even though it's true that entire games for the PC being written in assembly language is a dead idea, it doesn't mean that assembly language can't often be an extremely useful programming tool. Tight loops that consume vast percentages of a game's total execution will always exist in one form or another. It used to be blit copying, then it was innermost texture-mapping loops. What's next? How about realtime tessellation of splines-based characters? A section of code that loops hundreds, thousands, or even hundreds of thousands of times per frame can often be sped up by assembly language.

I haven't seen a compiler yet that can understand the subtle nuances of a piece of code as well as an experienced programmer.

As a corollary to this rule, also remember not to rely entirely on assembly language to save the day. A slow algorithm will run slowly in assembly and in C. So remember to always start by trying to optimize the algorithm. Once you're secure that you've found a highly optimal solution (or you're down to the last five months of development and your producer won't let you rewrite your polygon-clipping algorithm for the fifth time), then you can focus on assembly in order to squeeze out the last bit of performance. And if you don't think it's worth it, what will you think when you realize that your game's direct competition had programmers that did think it was worth it, and their game runs just enough faster so that they could put in killer particle effects?

We Will Optimize No Code Before Its Time

There is no need to optimize a section of code before you're sure that it's causing a significant slowdown. If you do, you can often waste time doing so, and slow down future code development when others need to interpret your assembly code. Here are some classic examples:

Optimizing Initialization Code

What's the point? It's run once at the beginning of the program. Granted, if your game startup takes 30 seconds because of some massive texture pre-processing, then something should be done (most likely making this stage a separate step in your level processing), but in 99.9% of the cases, if it's run once, it's not something to worry about.

Optimizing Before You Profile

With my experience in programming going all the way back to the age of seven working on an Apple II+, I still often make mistakes over what is and what is not slowing down my code. Luckily, profilers (especially Intel's Vtune) have become commonplace as a programmer's tool. It can tell you quickly and easily what functions or even what lines are causing your code to run like molasses. And by doing this, you're sure to never waste time optimizing something that's already fast enough.

Optimizing Before It's Too Slow

I've often seen programmers converting perfectly readable C code into very obtuse (although often very clever) assembly language code when the program is already running at a constant 120 fps [frames per second]. I understand the desire to make your code as fast as possible, but this is too much. There is definitely something to be said for keeping your code readable by others, especially in a modern-day developing house where sometimes dozens of people will have to look at your code at one point or another. In most cases, introducing assembly code into a game during the first half of the project is a bad idea. It makes updates and additions that much harder.

Love Your Code, But Don't *Love* Your Code

I've seen more time wasted at development houses over this issue than I care to estimate. Programmers who are so attached to their code that they're blind to any problems it might have. Writing code is fun, but try to remember that it's just code. If someone spots a problem in it, it's not a problem with you. Don't take it personally. Love the fact that someone has just spotted a way to make your code run faster. And from now on, that little trick he showed you is yours too.

Also, don't get defensive over style issues. If I hear one more argument over whether to use tabs or spaces, I think I'm going to slit my wrists. I don't care where you put your spaces or brackets—just focus on the code. I think every office should make one of two decisions. Either everyone writes in their own style and no one is allowed to complain, or everyone must follow an exact standard.

Programmers as a whole need to separate their own individuality from that of their code.

Todd Johnson, Oddworld Inhabitants

Software engineer Todd Johnson worked on products including Genesis' *Sylvester n' Tweety in Cagey Capers*, *Demolition Man*, and *Izzy's Olympic Quest*, and PSX's *Oddworld: Abe's Oddysee* and *Oddworld: Abe's Exoddus*. As a programmer, Johnson says, the most important consideration is to recognize the limitation of the target system. He explains:

> I come from a console background, where we always struggle with a small amount of RAM. For example, *Oddworld: Abe's Exoddus* had to constantly swap animations, backgrounds, and even code into and out of RAM. On a PC, though, you might run into performance problems. Either way, some aspect of the target system will affect how the game is put together.

"Second, consider the player," says Johnson, because "after all, he is the one shelling out cash for the game."

> This generally means not to get too complicated. When we first started working on the emotions of the Mudokons in *Oddworld: Abe's Exoddus*, they each had their own personality and would react in different ways. From the user's point of view, though, it seemed entirely random because they all looked the same. We kept the emotions but scrapped the idea of personalities.

And last, "think reusability," suggests Johnson:

> It takes a while to code a design, so if the game is loaded with unique features it won't get done for years. The other extreme is complete monotony, so the trick is to balance the two. By adding simple parameters such as speed or timing to existing characters and mechanics, you can get a lot of mileage out of them.

What does Johnson see as the biggest obstacle for a game programmer?

> The biggest obstacle in game production is the communication gap. You have programmers, artists, and designers on a project, and each group has its own identity and realm of experience. It's much easier to communicate within the group than outside it, but that's the key to a successful project. Communication with someone from a wildly different perspective is one of those

things that simply isn't taught in schools. That's at least part of the reason it's such a big problem—not only at game companies, but for any business.

Gonzo Suarez, Pyro Studios

Along with friend and business partner Ignacio Pèrez, Gonzo Suarez cofounded Pyro Studios in January of 1997. It was here in Spain that *Commandos: Behind Enemy Lines* was born, later to become an international hit for Eidos Interactive.

Suarez provides a number of helpful tips for novice programmers who may be starting to code their first game:

> Before anything else, ask yourself, "What do I want to play in this game?" The question seems obvious, but it contains a good 90% of the issues that will come up during the actual development. Curiously enough, most of the time this question is answered with blazing speed (I would be thrilled to have such a quick answer myself), but it usually brings up immediate concerns. Usually the answer is along the lines of, "It's an action game with strategy elements and a feeling of adventure, and it displays 30,000 polygons.'" Answering the question "What are you playing?," with an "It's a…" sentence is strange enough, but to mention the number of polygons is worthy of a Kafka novel.
>
> To hope that the answer will survive all through the project is a luxury that only experience can sustain (not only knowing the issues involved in a video game, but also understanding their impact during development). Most of the time, any lack of clarity when faced with the question will be justified by "open design" and "appeal to everyone," but to me this road leads to suicide.
>
> As an example, *Quake II* and *Half-Life* could be considered games of a very similar nature. However, the emphasis placed on where, how, and when one shoots in *Half-Life* contrasts with the quick environment of moving targets and precise aim of *Quake II*; the powerful feel of weapons in the id Software game is opposite to the opportunities that *Half-Life* allows for stealth and sniper shots. All that makes their network gameplay completely different.
>
> During game development, one finds dilemmas where a sacrifice has to be made between conflicting options, all of which are attractive and can be given reasons for their validity. In other words, we all want the most beautiful car with the most powerful engine, best mileage, and lowest price, but the order in which we place these options can lead us anywhere from a BMW to a muscle car or [one that's] utilitarian.

After close to 15 years of programming and game design experience, Suarez says he heeds the following rules:

The Game

The main elements that build the gameplay logic are sacred over any other element. For example, the game logic criteria dictated that the graphics in *Age of Empires* would comply with the underlying grid world. In other words, game entities occupy one or several squares—they can never be shared with other entities, or placed in the middle of two squares. Distances and bearings in the game logic are measured based on the grid. Therefore the graphics must follow the same rules (more or less dissimulated). Despite this sacrifice in the graphical department, we have an outstanding game that couldn't have achieved such success without being faithful to these priorities.

A different example in game logic is *Commandos*. The logic game world is divided into irregular sectors, with any entity moving in continuous three dimensions and having volumetric information attached. This logic is what allowed the game graphics to be irregular and distinct (with the merits of a great art team exploiting it).

Commandos is not built on a grid or tile system, like Ensemble Studios' Age of Empires or Blizzard's StarCraft. Instead, the engine behind Commandos allows for asymmetric locations that are therefore more distinct. (Used with permission by Pyro Studios, Inc.)

Logical Interface

The issues of communicating game logic elements from user to machine, as well as from the machine back to the user, would be the second most important element. A good example is the mouse pointer through which the user accesses the game world.

Anything that involves gameplay must be communicated to the user (more or less explicitly) in the *most effective* way; also, any actions the user may want to communicate (perform) in the game must be made simple well beyond intuition. In other words, a) if something can't be perceived by the user, it better not exist at all; and b) if something can't be made to happen by the user, it better not be offered as an option (much less a seemingly *attractive* option).

Feel and Alienation

These [factors] encompass both the elements through which the game feeds back the user with sensations (visual as well as auditory), and the ability of the game to involve the player to the point that the player will believe himself to be inside the game (a 220-pound world-saving hero, for example).

Even though this seems to be the point most valued by players, I would keep it in third place in this scale of priorities. Otherwise, the outcome will be five minutes of awe, and then hours of disorientation. This is typically shown when the developer has created an amazing engine with this or that feature, so attractive that the developer forces it to be present in the game even though it doesn't blend well with the game logic.

Good examples of this include several cases (some of which could never be completed) where the programmer was so proud of the realistic and detailed physics engine, where everything rotated and collided just like in real life, that when these features were forced into the game they resulted in uncontrollable characters, and besides the first five minutes of curiosity playing with it, the rest was a plain nightmare. Going to the extreme, imagine a chess game in first-person 3D with each piece having a distinct face, battling in a beautiful valley where the ground has amazing grass animations, where the board squares can barely be distinguished. [You score] "10" in look and suspension of disbelief, but I don't know who could design an interface to play such a monster.

Features

Features like technology, licenses, and other side elements that are important for glorifying the product during marketing—for example, displaying 40,000 polygons in real time—should be the last concern of the programmer. This should always be the slave of slaves, the last one to dictate criteria for a video game. In all my video game development experience, I have never seen a game made of features; however, this is the most common element on which people base their ideas about video games.

In a game design document, it's disorienting to find pages full of pseudo-scientific affirmations and no game ideas. I say "pseudoscientific" because, despite the underlying promises of exactitude, they're always vague in deep nature. What does it mean to say "moving 40,000 polygons"? Or "motion capture"? Or "artificial intelligence"? Even though we believe we know what we're talking about, reality always has the last word. I remember when we pitched the *HeadHunter* project, my partner Javier Arevalo developed a technology prototype containing a host of jaw-dropping 3D features that have become commonplace ever since (flares, colored lighting, particle effects…). The people we met used to say "Looks great! Now you just have to put the game together with all this stuff!" Piece of cake, *just* the game.

Suarez concludes by drawing on an analogy: "It's great to embellish a game with features just like it is to add spoilers, alloy wheels, and such to a car, but if the car doesn't fit its purpose well, all these accessories mean *nothing*."

CHAPTER 9

Artificial Intelligence (AI)

Artificial intelligence, or simply *AI*, may best be described as an attempt to model aspects of human thought and/or behavior on computers. In computer or console gaming, it boils down to making players feel like they're playing against real, intelligent opponents. Unfortunately, this has been one of the most difficult challenges of game programming, so this chapter will be solely dedicated to AI, instead of being lumped with the rest of the topics covered in the programming chapter (Chapter 8).

Another reason for giving AI its own chapter is that single-player gaming should not be neglected. With the growth of multiplayer gaming, many gamers fear a developer's time, money, and effort will be spent on tweaking the multiplayer code rather than improving the AI. After all, if the AI is predictable or dumb, many gamers will flock online to play against real people instead. The key is to make a game that offers both a hearty multiplayer component *and* realistic AI for those who can't afford to go online or prefer the solo gaming experience.

With a panel of AI specialists, each working in different genres, this chapter discusses different kinds of AI and how a game designer should approach this tricky matter.

Brian Reynolds, Firaxis Games

As one of Sid Meier's "star" pupils, Brian Reynolds went on to help create such PC strategy hits as *Colonization* and *Civilization II*. He now serves as vice president of software development at Firaxis Games. Reynolds' latest efforts can be seen in *Alpha Centauri*, Firaxis Games' first release. "Contrary to popular belief, you don't need any black magic to write AI for computer games," says Reynolds. "You don't need any patented algorithms, you don't need the latest papers on neural nets. All you need is a little creativity and a lot of persistence." The following sections describe some of his favorite techniques.

The Iterative Design Process

First of all, with AI, as with game design, use the "iterative design process." Start by just making a simple routine that moves the enemy pieces—even if your algorithm is nothing more complex than "switch(rnd(4))". Then *play the game* against your AI and watch it make its moves. Watch until it does something dumb (shouldn't take too long at first); then think about a) what did the computer do that was stupid—e.g., moved its tanks slowly through the woods, or built only artillery units and nothing else; b) what would you have done instead (moved your tanks along the road; built a healthy mix of infantry, artillery, armor, and air); and c) what piece of information led you to (or helped you to) make that decision (road squares cost less to enter; you already had an artillery unit, but no infantry). Then just go back and revise your algorithm to incorporate this data.

Now play your game again and watch the AI; wait until it does something *else* stupid, and repeat this process. Repeat it over and over and over again, and your AI will get better and better. It's the poor man's version of the proverbial "AI which learns from its mistakes." Through your playing and revising, the AI is essentially building up "experience" and getting better and better at the game.

To illustrate his point, Reynolds shares with us an anecdote from when he was a young programmer working on his first game as a designer (*Colonization*). He recalls:

I was a little intimidated when it came time to start working on some AI. I mean, I had a game that you could play, move the pieces around, but the AI didn't know how to do any of that. Where was I to start? I can still remember Sid Meier's advice to me: Start by teaching it how to play one turn. Then teach it how to play two turns, and *then* worry about teaching it how to play 10 turns.

Reynolds says to play your game and watch the AI. When it does something stupid, figure out what you wanted it to do, then go back and revise your algorithm. Repeat this process as often as necessary. (Used with permission by Firaxis Games, Inc.)

9

Start Simple

Start with simple building blocks. For instance, in a strategy game, a useful algorithm to have is a routine that tells a unit how to get from point A to point B, called a *pathfinding* or *go-to* algorithm. A go-to routine is a nice, compartmentalized project to start out with—just teaching a unit how to get from here to there, and worrying later about how to decide where "there" ought to be. I'm not saying it's easy to write a great go-to routine, but it's easy to start with a simple, adequate routine and work your way up to something more complex. Once you've got a go-to routine, you can have another routine that decides where on the map the pieces ought to move, and it doesn't need to worry about how they're going to go about getting there.

 >> *Pathfinding* refers to a unit or units moving from point A to point B, and what path is taken to get there. Ever noticed how, in older real-time strategy games, units at times will get "stuck" in some places, while at other times they take a longer or illogical route to their destination?

Doubling or Splitting Your Values

Another excellent trick I learned from Sid Meier when I was getting started (and which, like almost all of our tricks, applies equally well to game design and AI) is this: If you have a value or an effect, and you think you need to adjust it, then either *double* it or *halve* it. For example, if you think tanks are too cheap to build, double the cost. Spare yourself the frustration of increasing it from 10 to 11 and wondering whether you can tell the difference or not. Make it 20, even if that seems initially ridiculous, and try the game out that way. This will give you a clear-cut difference in effect and show you what the game is like with tanks that are definitely more expensive. If they feel too expensive, then you can cut back to 15 to fine-tune. If you think your computer AI is making too many infantry units, halve the likelihood that they will build them. I can remember countless times when I've doubled or halved something, thinking it would be too drastic a change, but wound up doubling or halving *again* before I really achieved the effect I wanted. All of this once again depends on using the iterative process.

Reynolds leaves off with this simple piece of advice: "Try stuff out, see how it works, revise, repeat."

Mario Grimani, Ensemble Studios

Prior to moving to Ensemble Studios, Mario Grimani worked at 7th Level on *Dominion: Storm Over Gift 3*, among other PC titles. Currently, he is the resident AI specialist for the upcoming *Age of Empires II: The Age of Kings*.

What are the most important things to remember as an AI specialist? Grimani responds:

- Always remember that the amount of work in AI is not always directly proportional to how it's perceived by the user.

- Develop your AI through an iterative process. Implement a rough working system, test it, and improve the part that behaves the worst.

- Make your design flexible. Since you're most likely developing AI for the game that's in the making, you have to be able to modify it as the game progresses.

  AI for *Age of Empires II: The Age of Kings* allows for controlling the computer player's behavior through an external, easy-to-use language. Computer players can play against humans or against each other. This gives us flexibility in modifying AI behavior during the game design process. It also makes it possible for AI features to be added late in the development cycle.

Mario Grimani advises making your game's AI modular, because it's likely you'll go back and make modifications during the game's development cycle. (Used with permission by Microsoft)

Grimani discusses the different kinds of AI and some of the problems in programming it:

> In game terms, AI is used loosely to describe solutions for a wide variety of problems that can range from simulating human behavior for characters in role-playing games to pathfinding in real-time strategy games (RTS).

> The main AI problems encountered in RTS games are unit pathing, unit AI other than pathing, group AI, and computer opponent AI. Computer opponent AI in itself has many parts: strategic AI, tactical AI, building placement, threat evaluation, terrain analysis, and many more.

> Some AI problems are more challenging than others. Any problem that has clear mathematical representation will be easier to solve than a problem based on concepts and abstractions. Unfortunately, the human mind is more likely to detect flaws in solutions to problems based on abstractions.

As an example, Grimani explains a common hurdle while working on RTS games:

> It's fairly trivial for a human player to determine whether a certain area is easily defendable. For a computer player, this is quite a task. On the other hand, the computer player can keep track of all individual units and their statistics much better than a human player.

So does Grimani think the growth in Web-based or LAN-based gaming will reduce the need for better AI? He responds:

> Multiplayer gaming is growing at a fast pace. This is mainly due to the fact that fast Internet connections are becoming available to more and more people. This doesn't mean that multiplayer gaming will replace AI. These are really two different gaming experiences. I personally enjoy multiplayer games and I've been playing them for a couple of years. Still, this hasn't taken away from my interest in single-player games.

Grimani and the rest of the team at Ensemble Studios are readying *Age of Empires II: The Age of Kings* for a fall or winter 1999 release.

Toby Simpson, CyberLife Technology

Toby Simpson is the creative director for all *Creatures* products at CyberLife Technology, based in Cambridge, England. As producer of *Creatures 1*, *2*, and soon-to-be *3*, he has worked on quite a different kind of AI than other genres, since the whole emphasis of the *Creatures* series is on sustaining and teaching these virtual pets.

Ever wanted to know how those cute Norns in *Creatures* acted so lifelike, each with different personality types and seemingly "human" emotions and desires? The following is a short essay Simpson wrote for this book on artificial intelligence. In it, he discusses his four commandments for successfully giving life to inanimate objects:

> The most important aspect is to get out of the frame of mind that one "codes some AI." AI, implemented as a black-box add-on, is normally highly superficial and full of inconsistencies and faults. Building adaptive systems into entertainment products requires a whole new approach to the problem. However, if I were to distill this into things to remember, I'd probably come up with the following:

Model, Not Emulate

A model and a simulation are both types of simulation, but have dramatically different approaches to the same problem. Emulations attempt merely to *appear* like something else, whereas models attempt to *be* that something. A model tries to capture the fundamental structure and mechanisms underlying a system. Both models and emulations have the same ultimate aim, but models have some distinct advantages:

- There is little or no scope in emulated systems for intelligence or autonomy—as there is no logical relationship between the parameters of a system and the outward behavior.

- Models provide "order for free," as they're not abstract representations of a system; i.e., models are built from the inside out. Emulations are built from the outside in, and will never be a faithful simulation.

- Models are expandable, components can be exchanged, and they can be broken down and rebuilt in new ways—not true with an emulation.

Think Structure, Not Behavior

Try to get out of the mindset of looking at problems from the top down. Put in place the structure that allows the behaviors you require to *emerge*. You do *not* have to fully understand how a system works in order to get its functionality! By thinking of a computer as a container of machines rather than a data-processing device, you've already made a leap in the right direction. Many people are now constructing game engines that build in "autonomous agents" (although *agent* is a flaky word that's often misused) right from the start—an expansion of the object-oriented design paradigm—and therefore they're shifting focus away from code and onto data. This shift in thinking is taking place everywhere as people realize that creating complex virtual worlds in which entertainment can take place is practically impossible without a change of approach.

Nature Is a Great Place to Look for Help

By far the most incredible computing device on the face of this planet is a biological brain. Its ability to adapt to its own unique problem set (by making it up as it goes along), generalize, and learn directly the difference between positive and negative actions has never been reproduced inside a computer. Furthermore, when broken down, human systems are remarkably simple—10 trillion simple cells built from 100,000 genes. We understand the cells, and yet we don't understand why when they're arranged in a certain way we get a conscious, thinking human being. This is complexity management on scales never seen before—10 trillion simple "agents" that cooperate, allowing consciousness to *emerge*. There is no cell in charge. No "master program." There's a lot we can learn from this! Bear in mind that if we can model a bridge or a tank, we can model biological building blocks and then build artificial organisms from those building blocks. If you want plausible artificial actors inside self-consistent virtual worlds, then biological processes and structures may be the only way of managing that complexity. I don't have Mother Nature's 3.7 billion-year research and development program handy to reinvent a wheel that works fine already.

Creatures 1 and 2 are modeled after real biological principles. These cute Norns can learn and think for themselves, and even communicate with you as to their needs and wants. (Used with permission by CyberLife Technologies, Inc.)

Think, and Be Professional

You *cannot* develop professional software without professional software development practices! No amount of neat and groovy technology is going to save your soul if your processes stink or are missing entirely. Be professional! If you aren't part of a defined QMS (quality management system), define your own. Think about planning, module testing, effective design, and proper documentation. *Stick to your processes, and don't cut corners—it will come back to haunt you!*

There is quite a bit more to read on Toby Simpson's cyberbiology and AI practices as they pertain to the *Creatures* line of products, so be sure to visit the following Web sites: www.cyberlife.co.uk, www.creatures.co.uk, www.creatures2.com, and www.cyberbiology.org.

Scott Orr, EA Sports

As executive producer at EA Sports, Scott Orr not only helped the *Madden* football series come to fruition eight years ago, but he also oversaw the development of other well-known EA Sports franchises, such as *NHL Hockey*, *Andretti Racing*, *NASCAR Racing*, *NCAA College Football*, *March Madness*, and *Knockout Kings*. In preparation for this chapter of the book, Orr's name was brought up many times as the "AI guru."

Realism

"The first thing to consider is that the AI needs to be realistic," reminds Orr.

By this I mean that computer players need to move and react as closely as possible to their real-life counterparts. That's why all the players in EA Sports games have ratings ranging from their field intelligence to their speed/quickness to their throwing/catching ability. We also work with pro players and coaches who help us capture reality. I can't tell you how many times John Madden has looked at a play we've implemented in our game and literally gone to the whiteboard to diagram how it should really look.

It's this level of detail that sets EA Sports games apart from the competition, believes Orr. Okay, well, what if a gamer doesn't have the money or connection to get hands-on advice from the likes of John Madden or today's pro football players? His next two points don't require any six-figure budgets.

Realism vs. Fun

"The second point you need to keep in mind is that there needs to be a balance between making the game realistic and making it fun to play," says Orr.

Computer AI has progressed to such a level that we could make the computer virtually unbeatable. Obviously, this would make the game challenging but not a lot of fun to play, and we would lose our customers. A lot of designers resort to little cheats to keep the computer competitive. This can range from knowing what play the human player has called to moving the computer's players faster than the human's players. An EA Sports game would never take that "cheat" approach, however.

Simplified AI Programming

The final thing to consider when you design computer AI is to keep it simple from a coding standpoint. Orr says, "The more calculations you use, the bigger stress you put on the processor." What kind of effect will that have on gameplay?

> This can slow down your frame rate and compromise gameplay. Use lookup tables to keep rule-based data and speed up your processing. You'll get more bang for the buck this way, and smarter AI as a result.

Is sports game AI any harder to code than other genres? Orr answers, "Sports games are both harder and easier than other games from an AI standpoint." Here's why:

> Since we're designing products based on known rules and player behaviors, in some ways it's easier to define what needs to be created. On the other hand, designing how the AI works is harder than other types of games because customers' expectations are higher, since they know the real sport. You can't drop a computer player behavior simply because you can't get it to work correctly. If it's in the [real] game, it has to be in your game; otherwise, gamers will feel like something is missing. As we work with more powerful processors, the sophistication of the AI will improve. The things the computer players do now versus what they did just five years ago—from how smart they are about play calling to how well they work off of what their teammates are doing during a given play—is truly amazing. This is only going to get better as we design for more powerful hardware and build on the experience we get by the time we send another game to market.

Orr was reminded that this book is meant for budding game designers who may want to program AI in a shareware, freeware, or even retail title. When asked for any AI advice in light of C++, Orr offers the following:

> All I can say is that practice makes perfect. Try different approaches and then test them. Eventually, you'll come up with something that works—or works better than what you started with. Try to develop a library of common routines. By building a library of routines (hopefully they're efficient, with low overhead), you can build on your past work more quickly. [And] don't forget

the power of using lookup tables to reduce the number of calculations you
need to make to keep the frame rate up and gameplay fast.

Marc Aubanel

Also at EA Sports is Marc Aubanel, producer of the best-selling and internationally recognized *FIFA* series of soccer games (and the *World Cup* incarnations).

Aubanel says AI in team-based sports games can get quite tricky, since the program is
dealing with a number of characters at the same time (a soccer game has 22 players on
the field). "Humans have incredible natural intuition, a sense of how something should
act," says Aubanel. "The computer has no intuition whatsoever, so it has to be taught
how to simulate intuition." According to Aubanel, the hardest sports game to code AI for
is baseball, for a few reasons.

> First, the user likely has a subconscious expectation of what the player
> should be doing, and if the AI differs from this expectation, the AI will be
> considered *bad*. For instance, if a ball is hit to left field by the player, the
> outfielder has to make a split decision on what to do with the ball, if caught.
> Throw to home? To second? To third? Not throw at all? The second issue is
> the programming required to make these kinds of split decisions. Many fac-
> tors have to be taken into account, such as how many people are on bases,
> how many outs there are, and so forth.

"With soccer," says Aubanel, "it's all about form, space, and working toward a single
goal." Although he admits that this game, too, has its own set of AI barriers, soccer intelligence is generally easier to model than baseball games.

In discussing how the AI is programmed in the *FIFA* series, such as *FIFA '99*, Aubanel
says one practice during bug testing is to have the player take shots on an AI goalie, and
report any scored balls that should have been saves, or saved balls that should have gone
in the net. After careful deliberation, a realistic middle ground is nailed down.

Another practice is to try to teach the AI players in the game their sense of space on the
field. According to Aubanel, this is quite a difficult task:

> It's not hard to position the soccer players in the ways they should be posi-
> tioned on the field, but it's very hard for them to "recognize" why they are
> placed there, when to hold position, what tactical strategy to employ, and,
> generally speaking, how to give the players an understanding of "space."

Aubanel says in the event of a red card, where one team has a player off on a penalty,
another AI challenge is to have the other players compensate. "They must scale their
positions accordingly, to make up for the absence," says Aubanel.

The best way to create AI for a game is to do so in a testing environment:

> When we work on the AI in *FIFA*, we don't have any nice graphics or audio or anything. We want to strip it down to stick figures on a flat green field. This way, there's no confusion. Then we have multicolored arrows and lines coming out from players to illustrate their AI for everything—for passes, pathing, etc.—so it's all possible to debug. If we didn't do this, only the programmer would be able to know if there was a bug in the AI. This way, everyone on the design team can see and understand any potential issues. It's an effective test environment, so we can tune it and tune it a lot.

"Don't confuse reality with fun," says Aubanel.

> [The best AI looks real,] but it's not—all for the sake of the game. We break more rules about physical reality than adhere to them. For example, it takes roughly 18 seconds for a real soccer player to run across the length of a soccer field, but in *FIFA*, it's about half of that—because 18 seconds in a game is a long time.

➤ Marc Aubanel also discusses user interfaces in sports games in Chapter 12.

These four images illustrate how Aubanel and the rest of his team test the AI for the FIFA series. Take note of each of the player commands, such as seek ball, attack, defend, and pass. The numbers represent the player's position on the grid (field). (Used with permission by Electronic Arts, Inc.)

Jay Wilson, Monolith Productions

As lead level designer for *Blood* and *Blood: Plasma Pak* and project lead on *Blood 2: The Chosen*, Jay Wilson believes AI is one of the most important areas of 3D action game design.

He maintains that there are considerable advances in AI in the gaming industry—with games such as *Half-Life*, *Unreal*, and *StarCraft* as excellent examples—but agrees with the intro to this chapter that not everyone wants to play games online. He cites his father as an example of someone who plays games to relax and not compete (as found in most multiplayer games).

When it comes to creating AI for first-person perspective shooters, Wilson says the characters in the game aren't necessarily emulating real people, but rather multi-player Deathmatch opponents. Explains Wilson:

> The shooters today with strong AI play like bots and not like real people. That isn't particularly hard to do. What I'd like to see when I'm playing these games is for the AI to act like humans do: run for cover, drop weapons, shoot and miss the target, and so on.

Jay Wilson will also serve as project lead on the first *Blood 2* official add-on pack, to be released later in 1999.

➤ Web surfers should definitely check out this stellar site dedicated to computer game artificial intelligence: www.cris.com/~swoodcoc/ai.html. The Game AI Page contains a discussion of AI in light of a number of new and classic PC games, and contains a meaty links section directing the visitor to many related areas of interest on the Internet.

Although it's much more difficult to program, Wilson says he wants enemies in action shooters to start acting more "human," complete with faults, instead of as perfect Deathmatch bots. This screen grab is from Blood 2, with an enemy hiding behind a post. (Used with permission by Monolith Productions, Inc.)

CHAPTER 10

Game Art

Computer and console game graphics are among the most important facets of game design; they eat up the biggest piece of the game-budget pie, contribute more to a game's immersion factor, and, from a marketing standpoint, are crucial selling points (think of all the prerelease screen shots in magazines or on the Internet, and on the outside of the box at retail).

Generally speaking, there are two kinds of art in gaming: concept and in-game. In most cases, concept artists work with the game designers to help flesh out the graphical vision of the product by sketching characters and backgrounds, and perhaps some 3D modeling as well. In-game artists may work on character art ("painting" textures on 2D sprites or 3D polygons, for example) and background art (game locations). Then there are animators, of course (covered in the next chapter), and in some companies "art technicians," who work specifically on the programming side of placing the graphics in the game engine.

This chapter hosts a diverse collection of game artists who would like to share their advice and expertise with others on creating art for games, what tools to use, and the best ways to get into the industry as an artist. All genres are covered, but their order of appearance is purely random.

Mark Bernal, Bungie Software

All the eye candy you see in games such as *Marathon 2*, *Myth: The Fallen Lords*, and *Myth 2: Soulblighter* is due to Mark Bernal and his talented team of 12 artists at Bungie Software (including the West Coast office). Bernal currently serves as lead artist and art director for these award-winning PC and Mac titles.

Bernal starts off by discussing what he believes are the most important things to keep in mind as a new game artist.

Know Your Boundaries

"Understand the restrictions of the game engine in respect to sprite and texture resolutions, color palettes, and their importance relative to other sprites and textures," explains Bernal. As examples, he offers the following:

> 3D FX cards cannot support textures larger than 256×256 pixel textures. Some games use one 256-color palette for the whole game; others use a 256-color palette for each individual character. Another example relates to time management; that is, deciding which of the game elements should be higher resolution than others, based on their importance and placement in the game world.

Don't Rely on Software

Bernal insists you must have very good artistic skills and organizational skills, above all else:

> Knowing how to use different software applications such as [Adobe's] Photoshop and [Autodesk's] 3D Studio MAX is not enough to become a computer game artist. Computer software plug-ins are not going to create the artwork for you. The numbers of resources (sprites, models, sounds, etc.) we have in our games has been growing larger and larger every title, so you need to be able to organize the art you create and the way you manage your production time.

Teamwork

"There are several people working on a computer game, and each relies on the others," says Bernal, "so you can't work in a bubble." He expands:

> Good communication between all the members of a team will make game development progress much smoother. Level designers need artists to create environments that depict the layouts that they have designed. Programmers

need artwork to be created a certain way, or else the artwork might make the game crash. And so on.

Bernal offers a short primer on the differences in painting 2D versus 3D objects:

> Currently, most games represent objects in two ways: 2D sprite objects or 3D polygon objects. 2D sprites (characters, buildings, and so on) can be created either by painting them in a drawing program or by creating a 3D object in a 3D program and then rendering it (the rendered image is used as a 2D sprite). 3D polygon objects (characters, buildings, etc.) are created in a 3D program and then all the data that describes the object is exported out of the 3D program and imported into the game. The actual textures that are applied to the 3D polygon object are painted in Photoshop or some other painting application.

10

On the left is the wire-frame model of the Myrkridia monster in Myth II: Soulblighter. It was created in Alias' Power Animator. On the right is a rendered version of the same character. While in 3D now, it will become a 2D sprite when put into the game. (Used with permission by Bungie Software Products Corp.)

When painting characters as sprites, you have to paint every view of every animation for the character. When creating 3D characters, you build and paint the character once, and then create its various animations. It's quicker to build a 3D model and animate it than it is to draw every frame of a 2D sprite. What often happens, though, is that the time saved with 3D models is used to test and tweak the model's animations, textures, and the overall structure of the model.

How challenging is it to paint backgrounds in a 3D environment, such as in *Myth: The Fallen Lords* or *Myth II: Soulblighter*?

Painting a texture is no problem if you have good artistic skills, though there's a tradeoff between detail and resolution. For example, often you might want to draw every rock of a paved road, but the resolution of the landscape texture isn't high enough to accommodate that type of detail (small rocks would be represented by a pixel or less, thus becoming blurred with the ground around them and possibly a waste of time).

This in-game screen shot from Myth II: Soulblighter illustrates the amount of detail given to the environment. While not presented here in color, the grass and path each contain a mixture of textures to add additional realism. (Used with permission by Bungie Software Products Prod.)

The landscape needs to convey information to the game player and at the same time maintain the same style as the rest of the game textures. Tops of cliffs need to look different from sides of cliffs, to convey impassable terrain. Paths and roads should guide players as to which way they should or could travel. Texture colors for all objects should complement each other and indicate the light source in the world.

To accomplish the stunning visuals as seen in a Bungie game, Bernal lists the tools they use to create all the artwork in their PC and Mac games ("[…]along with our internal tools, 'Fear, Loathing, and Vegas'"):

- Photoshop (Adobe)
- PowerAnimator and StudioPaint (SGI)
- 3D Studio MAX 2.5 and Character Studio (Autodesk - Kinetix)
- MeshPaint 3D (a 3D Studio MAX plug-in from Positron Publishing)

While not required, Bernal says it also may help if an artist is familiar with any of these software applications:

- LightWave (NewTek)
- trueSpace (Caligari)

- StudioPro (Strata)
- Infini-D (MetaCreations)
- Maya (SGI)
- SOFTIMAGE (Softimage Inc.)
- Electric Image (Electric Image Inc.)
- form*Z (auto*des*sys, Inc.,)
- DeBabelizer (Equilibrium)
- Premiere, After Effects, and Illustrator (Adobe)
- Painter (created by Fractal Design, now owned by MetaCreations)
- FreeHand (Macromedia)

So what's next for Bernal and the art team at Bungie? While the West Coast studio is working on *Oni*, a futuristic, animé-inspired 3D action game, Bernal is secretly readying for another game scheduled for 1999. Could it be *Myth III*?

Joshua Staub, Cyan

Joshua Staub is the CG (computer graphics) art director at Cyan, the famous development studio responsible for the best-selling computer game of all time, *Myst*. Staub also worked on the follow-up product, *Riven: The Sequel to Myst*. According to Staub, new game artists should adhere to the following rules:

World Consistency

I suppose in the earliest stages of the artistic "design" process, the most important thing to remember is what you might call "world consistency." For example, after creating your environment, make sure your design for the characters fits the environment they live in. What types of clothes would they really wear in such an environment? What type of materials would be readily available in the environment for someone to make their homes with? Wood? Stone? Metal? Carry that through everything that gets designed. Expand the design to include a culture and history for your world.

Create Your Own Ambient Lighting

As far as aesthetics go, the simplest thing that you can do in a scene to achieve realism is to turn ambient lighting off. I can't stress this enough. Basically, turning ambient light off makes your entire scene black, until you add lights to it. Most programs default to having ambient light set to a brightness of 5 or 10 (sometimes it's a scene preference, sometimes it's actually set on an object's material), so that nothing in the scene ever gets completely black. Even if an object is in complete darkness, it "glows" a bit, which detracts from the realism in a scene. [Turning ambient light off] allows you to have ultimate control over the lighting in a scene; all of your shadows will be black until you add light to "fill" them. It means creating your own ambient or bounce light, which is much better than letting the software do it for you. In fact, having a bit of complete darkness in the corners of a room generally isn't a bad thing; it's a way of adding contrast, intrigue, and mood.

Texturing

Finally, the most important thing to grasp is texturing. On virtually any model, for every minute I spend actually modeling I spend at least three creating its texture, for several reasons. For starters, using a texture to create the look of geometry is far more efficient than using actual geometry. If you can achieve the same beveled edge, bumpy feel, intricate pattern, etc. using a texture, you put a lot less stress on your computer when it tries to render it. This is vitally important for pre-rendered games (like *Myst* and *Riven*) but even more important for real-time games, where you have so much less geometry to work with. And it looks better! The best way to get a realistic-looking texture is to go and find one in the real world. Take your camera everywhere you go; take pictures of every interesting piece of wood, stone, rusted metal, architectural detail, etc., and use it for the basis of your textures. At Cyan, we have our coveted Raw Texture Library filled with hundreds of patterns and materials that we use to create textures every day, and it continues to grow.

After turning to this massive texture library, what does an artist at Cyan do from there? What tools are used?

There has never been a better time to enter the world of computer graphics, and 3D graphics in particular. Game companies, movie studios, ad agencies, etc. are looking to improve their content with realistic-looking (but computer-generated) scenes, creatures, etc., and best of all, creating it is now affordable. Just before production of *Riven* began, we tested various hardware/software packages and realized that (at the time) the only way to get the speed and quality we needed was to trade up from our trusty Macs to robust Silicon Graphics workstations and the best 3D/animation/rendering package we could find: SOFTIMAGE. Frankly, the costs were staggering. Today, with personal computers approaching speeds up to 450 MHz and programs like

Kinetix' 3D Studio MAX and Strata's StudioPro you can "play with the big boys" for a reasonable investment of around $5,000. Add Photoshop (the industry standard for photo and texture manipulation) and perhaps Painter and you're well on your way to creating fantastic, realistic images.

The texture for the leather of this chair, left, was actually based on a picture of someone's hand, because they didn't have a good reference photo of real leather. Neat, huh? Right is an early version of the "Firemarble Press" as seen at the end of Riven. The gears didn't make it to the final version, but note the rustic detail to give the impression of the machine's age. (Used with permission by Cyan, Inc.)

Note >> If you're short on cash as a budding game artist, rule out SOFTIMAGE as a software tool. The latest version of SOFTIMAGE 3D (v.3.8) retails for roughly $10,000 to $15,000 U.S. It requires a Silicon Graphics workstation or a fast Pentium PC running Windows NT. The SOFTIMAGE official Web site has an impressive gallery of images used with this software tool, plus an archive of techniques and a list of events to attend (www.softimage.com).

Bryce Cochrane, EA Sports

At a ripe old age of 28, Bryce Cochrane is lead artist for the award-winning *NHL series* (PC, PlayStation, and Nintendo 64 platforms) at Electronic Arts in Canada. Here are his two (Canadian) cents on starting as an artist at a game company:

You Are Not Alone

"The most important thing to remember is that you're part of a team," says Cochrane, "and teams don't always get along." He continues:

You'll be working with programmers, producers, managers, and a whole bunch of other people, and all these people have to do one thing—make a game. Be prepared to fight for the ideas that you think are good; and remember that you have to work with these people every day, so keep it professional.

Keep Your Chops Up

Cochrane says to make sure your classical arts skills (drawing, painting, sculpting, etc.) don't fall behind:

When I look at someone's portfolio, I'm most impressed with an artist who has drawing and painting skills—not just Photoshop touch-ups and 3D model tweaks. I feel I can teach any talented artist how to use a piece of software in just a couple of days, but it would take me years to train him or her to be an artist.

Be Prepared for Criticism—From Everyone

When it comes to criticism, Cochrane says, people can be cruel, so take it constructively and move on:

Be prepared for it at your workplace from fellow artists and programmers. But the really tough critics are the general public and video game reviewers—they don't care if you only had a day to do a player model, or if the computer kept crashing. They only care about the bottom line—does it look good? I've had reviewers say a game that I've done "didn't get released, it escaped," or this game "was as fun as beating a dead horse." Just learn from your mistakes.

Cochrane says he uses a number of standard art apps and proprietary software:

EA has a lot of internal tools for getting the art from the computer and into the game, but most of the art is done in a few programs. For 3D, it's Maya/Alias, Power Animator and 3D Studio MAX. These are some of the higher-end programs, but you have to remember that I'm only using 1,000-100 polys [polygons] to make player models; you don't need top of the line software to do this. Any 3D package can handle 1,000 polys; just keep it simple, because you're making games and not a movie. For 2D art, Photoshop, Illustrator, After Effects, Painter; and the same stuff applies to 2D art as to 3D art. Keep it simple—and don't waste time working in the highest resolution, because in video games it's more important to have things look good with as little as possible.

EA Sports' Bryce Cochrane says to keep things simple, and don't waste your time working in the highest resolution. Why? Because detailed player jerseys like these are 600 pixels wide by 800 long, but when that texture makes it to the game, it's only going to be 120 by 160 pixels. (Used with permission by EA Sports)

10

Nicholas J. Corea, Electronic Arts

Nick Corea is a computer graphic artist at Electronic Arts who has added his golden touch to many award-winning Jane's Combat Simulations titles, such as *US Navy Fighters '97* and *WWII Fighters*, where he served as lead artist on both. He joins us here to talk about game artistry, essential tools, and the best way to break into the industry.

Expect the Unexpected

Computer art is usually produced for new technology. This means that although you think you know how to do something, and how long it will take, things will come up that you didn't expect. For example, say you have to make 6 sports cars for the next 3D racing game. You made 10 cars for the previous version and they took you 15 days each (5 days for the 3D model, 8 days for texture, and 2 days for integration and fixes). Your boss gives you more polygons, more articulation, and more texture. You really know what you're doing this time and you can make these new ones even better. You plan on taking 15 days for each of these.

Later you find, surprisingly, that "more polygons" didn't make it easier to define the forms—it made perfecting the shapes more precise and less forgiving (4 additional days/car). "More articulation" added doors to the car. Getting the doors to sit in their frames correctly became a tedious integration task (8 days burned). Eventually, you added a "closed door" object that disappears as the door opens, and an "opening door" object that disappears when the door is closed (2 additional days/car). Also, the shocks compress on this new version. As they do, the coarse z-buffer of the in-game 3D system causes the tire and fender to flash and trade in an ugly way.

More work with the programmers, who suggest a new and *very* specific grouping hierarchy that has to be applied to all cars, including those completed (10 days burned). "More texture" meant that the car's textures had to be broken into two pages. A car is now 500 pixels long and 256×256 is max texture size. The "texture page Tetris game" (cutting up and reorganizing the texture bits to fit efficiently on the texture page) becomes more difficult (2 additional days/car). Also, your boss doesn't want both sides of the car to share the same texture. "It looks fine when the car's in good shape, but if both sides are damaged," he says, "they shouldn't look the same." There's no room on the texture page for this new extra side, so you have to shrink and re-Tetris the textures of 3 previously completed cars to make room (7 days burned). Then this extra side is added to the task list (1 additional day/car). You thank your boss for telling you so late.

In the above example, a 90-day task on the schedule became more than 150 days. That's three unplanned man-months! Believe it or not, this happens a lot. Some of these items could have been foreseen and some could not have been planned for. (Items like the "more polygons = more time" and "more texture = splitting pages" should have been known.)

When scheduling computer art, try to think about all of the possible problems. Create a detailed task list of every aspect you can think of. (Remember integration time). Then add 20–40% to cover the unexpected. The more unknown the task, the more percentage reserved for surprises.

It's Okay to Compromise Your Artistic Vision

Corea warns, "None of you want to hear this, but computer games are produced to make money." Okay, we know that, but what is he getting at *exactly*?

> The game business is a lot like the film business. Art films don't usually make a lot of money. Game productions have deadlines and they have to sell well. Features and cost outweigh art and expression.

He offers the following scenarios to illustrate his point:

> You are creating the enemies for a first-person shooter, to compete with *Quake XI*. The plan is for 20 different enemies to populate 10 levels. They're already designed and sketched out in color. The schedule shows you get one 256×256 texture page and 250 polygons at 10 days each. You break it down to 4 days for the 3D model, 5 days for the texture, and 1 day for integration.

Your first beast becomes a masterpiece of flesh and scales, carrying a big iron club. Everyone in the group is totally impressed. The detail is awesome, right down to his sweaty brow. It took you 3 extra days, but man, it was worth it. The second villain is even more impressive. You can't wait to see the screenshots in CGW [*Computer Gaming World* magazine]. By now you're over a week behind plan, and your boss is "giving you the business." You promise to pull your production back on schedule. The third bandit on your list is a turtle with a missile launcher. Trying to make him look as good as the first two is tough. You're able to do him in 11 days, but you had to stay late twice. The programmers have the game running and they call every-one into a meeting to see how it's all looking. When your baddies are onscreen, they look great, but no one can see the amazing extra detail that you put into them. And the game is one enemy short.

Get the Work Done as Fast as Possible Within the Allotted Time

In fact, try to get stuff done early. Everybody else on the team will appreciate it—your art director, programmer, producer, and game designer. You can always put more into the work if needed. Don't think of it as "selling out." The best game artists do amazing work in a short time. They know when and how to make compromises. Their artwork might not be perfect, but it's within the constraints of production and the medium. That becomes the chal-lenge: How good can the piece be, given a limited amount of time and effort? It's a skill that will take you far. Any company can spend tons of money for the most beautiful art ever produced, but can they make that money back?

Nick Corea advises that game artists must learn to work well within time and money confinements and within the limitations of the medium. (Used with permission by Jane's Combat Simulations, Inc.)

Chances are, many gamers who have launched *Jane's WWII Fighters* have stopped to admire the graphic detail at some point. Corea discusses the 2D and 3D tools he used to create the art for the game.

2D Tools

According to Corea, Adobe Photoshop is the industry standard image-creation tool for its power and versatility. Says Corea:

> Get to know as much about its tool set as possible. The more used to the tools you are, the more you can be creative with them. (Don't spend too much time on effects filters; too many artists depend on them.) Photoshop was used in *WWII Fighters* to produce the textures and just about every other piece of art. Photoshop knowledge is a must for your résumé.
>
> [Equilibrium's] DeBabelizer is a common image-processing tool. Game developers use it to process large numbers of images at a time. Its batch capabilities are unmatched. It includes alternate color-reduction methods and filters. A collection of images can be reduced to a "super palette" and then all of the images mapped to that palette. The list of useful features goes on and on. Also a good one to have on your résumé. In *WWII Fighters*, Debab was used to process object and terrain textures.
>
> [MetaCreations'] (Fractal Design) Painter is a wonderful painting tool. It mimics real-world paint, ink, watercolor, paper, chalk, light, etc. Fun to play with, and amaze your friends. Clever artists will find ways to make textures fast and with a very natural feel. Drawing tablet is a must. Many folks paint in FD Painter and then move the results to Photoshop for pixel cleanup and/or processing. Nice one to know.
>
> Microsoft Paint (free with Windows 95/98) is a perfectly fine tool for getting to know pixel art. It has nowhere near the tool set of Photoshop, but it's fine if you want to get to know about painting with light. Try loading icon and game art, and modifying it. Many artists in the business started with DPaint or Mac Paint, similar in simplicity. If you're talented, it will show.

3D Tools

Corea believes 3D Studio MAX is a great tool for modeling, lighting, and animation:

> It isn't the best at any one thing, but it is very good at just about everything. 3D Studio MAX is currently used by many game companies for high-end cinematics, in-game 3D shapes, or pre-rendered sprite-style graphics. It's an expensive package, but if an older version of the tool can be "discovered," it

would be perfect to learn 3D on. There are several third-party books on using the tool. 3D Studio MAX was used in *WWII Fighters* to build the in-game shapes.

LightWave 3D is another terrific tool. A different "theory" of modeling, but very powerful, and versatile. Some artists swear by its abilities as a renderer and modeling tool. Used on *WWII Fighters* to produce the museum models and images.

Launching Your Career

In this final section, Corea gives us the skinny on how artists should break into the gaming industry. There's some shrewd advice here, so be sure to take heed:

> When learning to produce game art, select a subject matter that you really love. The processes that you learn might be *very* tedious, and you'll need that energy to help you complete the work. You'll also have a tendency to add more detail to the piece if you really care about it.

> If you're learning 3D modeling, natural forms are very difficult. You might want to stay away from the human form or animals, to start out. Imitating what you see on TV or film (a vehicle from *Star Trek*, for example) is a fine exercise, but don't focus on one subject for all of your work. Art directors see many demo reels and portfolios, and many young artists choose these same topics. Since many TV shows and films are made using computer graphics, however, they are a terrific place to get texture, modeling, effects, and lighting hints.

> Examples of computer art are not the only things an art director wants to see. They'll want to see pencil sketches, photography, painting, sculpting—anything that shows artistic ability. Important things are lighting, composition, color, form, storytelling, sculpting, detail, wrist (rendering), problem solving, and confidence.

> Show an example or two of process. If you've painted a mural, for example, include sketches, color comps, and a picture of the final piece on the wall. On your reel, don't show the same animation over and over. If it's very short, show it twice, with a nice little pause in between. If the AD wants to see it again, he'll rewind. Also, show only your best work. If you have 20 pieces, and you aren't too proud of three of them, you're better off leaving them out. A few bad pieces can put a bad taste in an art director's mouth. And watch the length. If it's long, the AD will get bored, and that's the worst. Make it short and beautiful. Leave 'em hungry for more.

10

Hugh Riley, Bethesda Softworks

Hugh Riley, a senior artist at Bethesda, has worked on dozens of games over the past 12 years, on most home computer formats—both as a freelancer and more recently in-house. Riley says there are three things a new game artist must consider, from a practical standpoint:

- **Economy.** Memory will always be limited, particularly on the consoles, so you'd better be good at low-polygon-count models, low-frame animations, and making small textures look impressive.

- **Technical understanding.** You'll be expected to bring your creative ideas to the process, but your work will follow a design brief and be limited by programming constraints. If your art is incompatible with the design or the program, your time will be wasted.

- **Quality**. Given the limitations of [the items above], your artwork should be the best you've ever seen.

 Note >> To expand on the first point Riley makes, the more polygons a character has, the more real-time memory it takes up. What effect does this have in the game? The more characters onscreen at the same time, the slower the frame rate will be; so Riley is suggesting you reduce the polygon count, where possible, for greater memory management.

Riley explains that the player character in Bethesda's latest game, *Redguard*, is more detailed than most of the NPCs in the game because he's "on-camera" all the time. Cyrus, the protagonist, is made up of about 550 polygons, compared to 350 for guards and about 380 for Lord Richton, the villain in *Redguard*.

Riley offers this advice on reducing your polygon count:

> The models were each a single mesh. In the game, *faces* [any of the mesh surfaces] that were required to flex were triangular, but those that were static, such as those in the head, were optimized into rectangles.

> For example, to save memory, there was only one guard model in *Redguard*, but there were three different textures. The three women in dresses in the game—the whore, the gardener, and the silversmith—shared the same model. Seventeen of the men on the island shared one model—all the pirates shared another.

Next, Riley discusses the best way to get into a game company as an artist and what to expect once inside:

> To get into a software house without experience on a published game, you will need a show reel. There are many sites on the Internet that give advice about how to present your work.

These four images illustrate how the malevolent Lord Richton was conceived and modeled for Redguard. The first image, upper left, is a loose sketch, later to be detailed, upper right. The wireframe image, lower left, shows the mesh of Lord Richton before it's painted and rendered into the final character, as seen in the game, lower right. (Used with permission by Bethesda Softworks © 1999 Bethesda Softworks)

Having knowledge of a 3D application, particularly 3D Studio MAX and/or SOFTIMAGE, is essential. Familiarity with Photoshop and other 2D applications is equally important. This is the catch-22. There's no way a beginner will be taken on without proven ability in one or more of these packages, but they're very expensive and have a steep learning curve. College seems the preferred route for those who don't have access to this software.

If you have enough talent to get a job, you'll be expected to work long hours and learn rapidly—but you'll be doing something you love.

And the benefits? Riley says, "Apart from the reward of having their work appreciated by the masses, most people in this business are at least comfortably well off, and some become superstars."

Ted Backman, Valve Software

Ted Backman is an artist and animator at Valve software. For the last two years, he's been working tirelessly on *Half-Life*, Valve's debut release. And what a "premier" title that was!

"As home PCs become more powerful, computer game art is becoming less archaic and process-oriented," says Backman. Fortunately, technological advancements in the industry are doing away with once-common constraints, such as having a limited amount of information to work with. Says Backman, "Frequently they were held to a small color set or a very low resolution image space (usually both)." On *Half-Life*, those things were not a concern. With the power and speed of Valve's graphics engine, Backman could concentrate on traditional problems in art, "without having to worry about painting with only 16 or 32 colors in an image."

So, as the medium comes into its own, the problems of old resurface, namely: a) using good reference material, b) incorporating valid criticism, and c) having the patience to see a piece of work through to its proper state of completion. Let Backman walk you through each of these three crucial areas and take note of examples from his own personal experiences while working on *Half-Life*.

Good Reference Material

Using good reference material is something that many an artist forgets. I can look back on the creation of *Half-Life* and see times when I should have gone to the library instead of banging my head against an artistic problem for hours on end. A good artist knows that he or she cannot rely on invention and fantasy alone. You must continually draw upon real-world things. For example, when creating the skin for the *bullsquid*, I looked at many things for inspiration. I looked at the markings on sea slugs, the patterns on jungle cats, and many other unusual sources. When you create an image, you're communicating in a visual language; the vocabulary of that language is the shared set of images and experiences that all people know. So if you neglect to include pieces of our shared visual experience, you really aren't communicating at all. In the case of the bullsquid, the coloration should cue most people that this is a poisonous animal. Yellow and black markings are nature's way of saying "stay away."

Backman decorated this bullsquid with yellow and black markings to hint that this predatory animal is dangerous—a common color association for humans. (Used with permission by Sierra Studios)

Accept Criticism

Criticism is an inseparable part of traditional art. From time to time, you must let a trusted friend look at your unfinished work and help you to see problems that you may not have noticed. Very frequently a piece of work will have a handful of features or areas that are the focus of the piece. In developing these focal areas, an artist can lose perspective on the piece as a whole. The role of the critic, then, is to help the artist see what he or she has been neglecting. Use trusted criticism early and often in the creative process; you will have a better finished piece because of it.

Perseverance

Finally, having the perseverance to work a given piece of art to its proper state of completion is the most important aspect of working on game art—or any kind of art. You must have the patience to keep working on something, not in a linear start-to-finish mentality, but in a free, explorative manner. When you begin to design a character, for instance, you must make many preliminary drawings so you can capture a range of good ideas. From these you must sort and rework, always keeping yourself open to a change in direction. Many people make the mistake of thinking of the final outcome when they first begin to draw. I can't say enough that you must keep yourself open to new ideas. Make many drawings, throw them away, keep working; you'll arrive at your inspiration when it's ready to come to you. Don't be heavy-handed.

Half-Life had rich, imaginative characters. How were these created? What tools were used in the process?

10

To create a new monster or character in *Half-Life*, I would use a range of software, from a 2D package like Photoshop or Painter to the 3D editing environment (3D Studio MAX). The process in terms of the tools goes like this: scan pencil sketches into Painter and continue to work the image with surface quality and coloration in mind, with last-minute adjustments for form also taking place here. Use that color illustration as the basis for your model. Print it out if you can, and keep it close to your monitor.

Next, you must begin to make the shapes that will eventually become your character. I start with a plug-in for [3D Studio] MAX called Clay Studio Pro [Digimation]. With this plug-in, I can create rough musculature for the parts of the character. I always build the character in pieces or subassemblies. For a human, I'll make a leg separately from the torso, mirror it for the other leg, then continue that kind of process for the arms. Make sure you're looking at external references at this point. Once all the pieces are formed, I'll begin to weld them together and adjust proportions. Usually at this point I have a higher resolution than I'd like, so I'll divide the model along any kind of symmetry it might have and begin to eliminate any unimportant faces.

Half-Life enthusiasts should get a kick out of these behind-the-scenes drawings and explanations of a few memorable enemies: the barnicle, hound-eye, and big mama. (Used with permission by Sierra Studios)

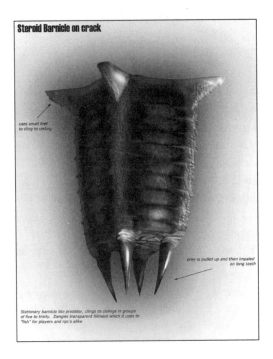

Steroid Barnicle on crack

uses small feet
to cling to cieling

prey is pulled up and then impaled
on long teeth

Stationary barnicle like predator, clings to cielings in groups
of five to thirty. Dangles transparent filiment which it uses to
"fish" for players and npc's alike

10

Once you have an efficient model, you can begin to paint the skin for it. I'll use the Windows Print Screen function quite a bit in this phase. I'll select a set of faces in [3D Studio] MAX, apply a mapping plane to them, and then essentially take a screenshot of that selection set and mapping plane and use that as a template in Painter.

Backman says in the future he hopes to be able to "create intriguing game worlds, compelling characters, and engaging scenarios in many game genres." If *Half-Life* is any indication, we should be seeing a lot more from Backman over the next few years.

Marc Hudgins, Yosemite Entertainment

Marc Hudgins is an art director and game designer at Yosemite Entertainment (Sierra On-Line's Oakhurst, California, studios). We've heard from him in this book in the storyboarding chapter (Chapter 4), but he's here to shed some light on art and gaming.

Limitations of Technology

Hudgins advises budding game artists to be aware of the limitations and possibilities presented by current technology. He urges artists to keep abreast of advances in hardware and software, and always look for new technologies on the horizon. Asked if he can provide an example to support this guidance, Hudgins offers the following:

> When we started B5 [*Babylon 5*], we were looking at using a software-rendering engine in addition to taking advantage of the first generation of 3D accelerators. Because of some delays in working out the license, and the

rapid development of 3D cards, we found ourselves abandoning the software solution. When we were stuck with a software renderer, we needed to keep our polygon limits extremely low due to the heavy load the renderer put on the processor. Once we knew we were free of that burden, we could double the size of our ships. This isn't the most colorful example, but it demonstrates the need to keep your art development process flexible enough to keep up with the rapid changes in technology. The other aspect of this issue is keeping up with the latest tools and the ability to see where you can create synergy between the tools and the game technology.

Consult with the Artists

If you're the game designer on a project, it's key to communicate with the art team at an early stage in the design process to identify potential trouble areas, as well as areas that could be enhanced by art, says Hudgins. As an example, Hudgins recalls:

> A troubled area of a game that was enhanced by art was *King's Quest 7*. We had several realms; each of these was composed of multiple rooms or screens. We found that the needs of the design created non-intuitive solutions to puzzles because of the *disconnectedness* between these rooms. By rearranging the visual composition of the rooms and creating new visual relationships between their elements, we were able to strengthen gameplay. Sometimes game designers don't have the strongest visual sense; although they do their best to solve problems, they can often come up short or with an inelegant solution. The artist can interpret the design and often simplify the scenario.

On Software Tools

> The main gun of any digital artist is Photoshop; get it, learn it, live it. Beyond Photoshop, there are a few more or less ubiquitous tools: 3D Studio MAX seems to be everywhere in game development; a base knowledge of [Macromedia] Director is always a plus as well. Beyond that, the tool set gets pretty varied. The biggest problem is getting over the cost barrier. Employers often insist on having experience with a specific tool. They usually want someone who can hit the ground running. Unfortunately, that means getting access to some pricey software. In the absence of the ability to beg or borrow the high-end stuff, I would recommend trying stuff like [Jasc Software's] Paint Shop Pro or one of several cheaper 3D tools, so you can at least begin to master the basic concepts.

10

Hudgins is using Newtek's LightWave 3D for their upcoming Babylon 5 game, along with Photoshop and their own proprietary Direct3D engine. (Courtesy of Yosemite Entertainment, Inc. Babylon 5, characters, names, and all related indicia are trademarks of Time Warner Entertainment Co. L.P. © 1998 Time Warner Entertainment Co.)

The number one tool I insist on is a solid foundation in traditional art skills—figure drawing, in particular. An artist who can competently solve the problems involved in drawing the human figure can do almost anything. Game artists are called upon to perform tasks from many disciplines, so a good sense of design, color, and composition is also a major asset.

Hudgins leaves off with a collection of do's and don'ts that pertain to a lead game designer, as well as game artists:

- *Do* talk to your entire team frequently.
- *Do* solicit advice and suggestions from the development team.
- *Do* admit to yourself from time to time that you don't have all the answers.
- *Don't* assume that something is possible without asking the experts first.
- *Don't* become rigid in your thinking. Be open to change (when appropriate).
- *Don't* remove yourself from the development process.

➤ Marc Hudgins has his own Web site that serves as an online art gallery. Many images are never-produced preliminary game-design sketches and storyboards. Be sure to drop in and look around at www.marchdesign.com.

Mike Nicholson, Dreamforge Intertainment

You can thank Dreamforge's senior artist and designer Mike Nicholson for your nightmares—he was one of the driving forces behind the beautiful (and disturbing) PC game

Sanitarium. Nicholson directs his advice to game designers and how they should approach the subject of art.

Focus

You MUST have a focused idea in your mind on how the game will look. It's *very* easy to see other styles in various media and become influenced by them throughout the development cycle of a game. If you don't have a definite vision and you switch art styles in the middle of the game, the game will become muddled, and conflicting styles will destroy the overall look you wanted in the first place.

Tough Love

If you employ an art staff (which is almost mandatory nowadays), it can be difficult to reject artwork—no matter how well done—simply because it doesn't fit within the established look of the game. As you can well imagine, this can lead to heated discussions, and if diplomacy is not applied, to disaster! Very early on, it's *crucial* to get the art staff on the same page, and be willing to except rejection if their style conflicts with the game's look and feel. If, as a designer, you are not artistic, then bring in photos, movies, books, or anything that can convey to the art team what look or feel you want the game to have.

Originality vs. Execution

And a word to artists:

Somewhere out there, your artistic vision has already been done before, is being done right now, and will be duplicated after *you* are done! As hard as that is to accept, it's sadly true. The reason I bring this up is merely to point out that this is not uncommon, and that you should stick to your guns. With so many games in development at one time, it's a fair guess that someone else is thinking up the same "brilliant" idea as you! It all boils down to execution. If you maintain a consistent look and feel to your game, then you'll succeed in your goal. We felt that, although 3D engines are the rage, we needed a more 2D, traditional approach to the game to pack in the detail level we wanted.

With Sanitarium, Nicholson and company's main goal in the look of the game was to convey a "Twilight Zone" type of atmosphere, with stylized cinematics. (Used with permission by Dreamforge Intertainment, Inc.)

10

Know Your Limitations

"The best suggestion I can give is to know your limitations early on, and work within them," offers Nicholson.

Careful planning will reduce headaches that can arise from poor palette choices. For example, if you know your main character has to be incorporated into a palette range of 256 colors that must also include background art, set aside a certain range just for the character (say 36) and then reduce the palette of your backgrounds separately. That way, if you find later on that changes need to be made to either the background or the character, they won't have a crippling domino effect on the rest of your artwork.

Sanitarium was our best example of good, complex palette work. Luckily, I had the good fortune to work with two extremely talented individuals on the project: Keith Lash and Jason Alexander. Those two guys had the less-than-glamorous task of *palettizing* entire levels of *Sanitarium* into one 256-color range. That included MAX (the main character), all NPCs for the level, their animations, inventory objects, and the sprawling background images. It was tough, but they tweaked the palette until all the individual components worked well with each other, with as little dithering as possible.

Along with most of the other artists that comprise this chapter, Nicholson maintains that Adobe's Photoshop is the best overall art program out there, and it was heavily used during *Sanitarium*'s development. Nicholson believes that the newest version of Photoshop "also has great palette abilities, but we prefer to use [Equilibrium's] DeBabelizer Pro for the bulk of our paletting work."

Louis Castle, Westwood Studios

For the past 13 years, Louis Castle has worked as a designer, executive producer, programmer, artist, and art director in the gaming industry. He is also one of the cofounders of Westwood Studios, one of the hottest PC development houses in the world. When asked what makes the artwork in *Blade Runner*, *Lands of Lore III*, and the *Command & Conquer* series stand out, Castle responds:

> At Westwood, the artists work with the game designers to make sure the art is appropriate for the game, but the overall look of the game really comes from the artists themselves. You want your artists to feel an ownership of the visual presentation, so try not to dictate things in too great detail. Try to keep lead artists and designer/artists from over-directing your talent. If they tell them *exactly* what to do, you'll never get those moments of raw creativity that every artist should be capable of.

But there must be some focused form to start, no? Doesn't a game's visuals require some consistency?

> We use concept drawings and storyboards a great deal. The art staff often wants to create their own designs, but in general I have found that having specialists in design and storyboarding tends to work better. A concept artist can *own* the look of a product and maintain consistency, but things get a bit divergent when too many people are doing concept work. If you're doing a large production, you may have to separate out logical sections and have multiple concept artists.

> Once the concepts are done and edited, the execution takes place. Again, each artist is encouraged to put [his or her] own ideas into every moment. We have a very flat management structure, so the more competitive members of the staff really only have quality to compete over. I think that helps keep people focused on their work.

> My best piece of advice would be to very clearly define your art pipeline and the scope of your product in advance. This includes any technical limitations. You can always choose to let an artist run with an idea once you have a plan, but don't expect someone else to do the hard work of deciding what your game is about, or the scope of the product.

All Westwood Studios games begin with concept sketches and storyboards, but artists are encouraged to interpret the designer's vision. These drawings are Command & Conquer: Tiberian Sun units for both the GDI, above, and NOD, below. (Used with permission by Westwood Studios)

JUMP JET INFANTRY

Joel Thomas, Ritual Entertainment

Joel F. Thomas is the concept artist at Dallas' Ritual Studios, the savvy developers responsible for Activision's 3D shooter *Sin* and an official *Quake* add-on pack, *Scourge of Armagon*.

Learning software tools often takes precedence over raw art ability in the gaming industry. Thomas explains why this *shouldn't* be the case:

> One of the most important things for a new game artist to know is how to draw. The better the artist's drawing ability, the better the 3D model will be. It will also give the modeler a chance to spend his time making the model as good as it can be, as opposed to spending time deciphering an amateurish drawing.

Joel Thomas shows us the evolution of the sinister Elexis Sinclair, from colorless sketch to comic-book style drawing to 3D rendered image. (Used with permission by Ritual Entertainment, Inc.)

Okay, assuming an individual has some genuine artistic talent, what should he or she concentrate on?

They should also realize how important it is to *know* reality. The world around you is an excellent tool for creating fantastic creatures, weapons, or items. A lot of artists, especially first timers, are afraid to use a reference source, thinking it will make them look less creative. Of course, the exact opposite is true—the less you look at the world around you for reference, the less inspired your concept will be.

Also, it's very important to have some understanding of basic human anatomy. Muscle placement, as well as proportion, is vital in pulling off a realistic character. In all bipedal creatures, regardless of size or sex, the muscles and their placement are unchanging. The artist's aesthetic treatment of them is what brings variety and flair.

An awful lot of aspiring artists learn to draw from comic books. While this has some minor benefits, it can limit your visual effectiveness. Learn the anatomy first and then look to your references. That's how to do it properly.

10

Thomas discusses what he believes to be a good artist's ultimate downfall:

The most important thing to remember is this. Never, *ever* believe your own press. You may be good, but there is *always* someone better and faster. The way to hold your own in a progressive and often cutthroat field is by getting to know who's out there. Learn from the competition. Never think you're such a badass that there is nothing that you can't learn. Life loves to kick those people in the gonads. Hard. Learn from your competition. Honor those you admire and help those coming up. Not only will you learn a great deal, but you'll also create some invaluable allies.

You might think that Thomas, as a concept artist, doesn't use a computer as much as a CG artist would. This isn't entirely true, though. He explains:

Well, first I start with the basics. Sketches. I do all my sketch work in pen and ink. I don't like to use pencils because I feel it makes the mind sloppy. With a pencil, you can lay down lines and erase them over and over until you have a starting point. With a pen, you have to think about what you're doing. The line means more, and you have to think on the run. When I finish with the ink sketch, I'll use a whiteout pen and remove the excess lines to clean it up, or I'll scan it in and start to work toward a final version in Photoshop.

The other way I'll start a drawing is right in Photoshop. I use a Wacom pad with a pen stylus and start drawing. I find that to be a little more liberating because I'm able to resize and move portions of the sketch on the fly. This adds to the spontaneity of the design. From there, I'll finish it up and send it off to the modeler. On *Heavy Metal: F.A.K.K. 2* [Ritual's next game, aside from a *Sin* add-on pack], I'm doing more digital paintings and fully finished images. This is to help everyone involved feel the story and get to know the characters as I see them.

Joel Thomas is working on the Eon and Peon mutant duo from Sin. Above, how the characters look in Photoshop; below, charting the various forms, from concept to fully rendered.

CONCEPT ART   FINAL COMP   IN GAME MODEL   HI POLY MODEL

Kevin Cloud, id Software

Kevin Cloud is an artist and part owner at id Software, who started way back during the development of the classic *Wolfenstein 3D*. Since then, he has worked on such hit games as *Doom*, *Doom II*, *Quake*, *Quake II*, and the upcoming *Quake III: Arena*. Cloud takes some time out of his busy schedule (touching up baddies from *Quake III*, no doubt) to offer his expertise on creating art for games.

What's been most difficult for me is following good advice. Because everyone is different, with different talents and different circumstances, each individual must find his or her own way. But if you want to make sure you're going in the right direction, watch what other successful artists have done. So I guess my first bit of advice is to be a student of life. Always maintain your interest in the world around you and be open to understanding and learning from the successes and failures of other artists.

The golden rule for being successful at anything is to do something you enjoy. I know its a cliché, but that's because it's true. And this is a rule everyone tends to forget and relearn. Computer game artists need to like computer games, enjoy working with a team, and being part of a process. As a computer game artist, you'll be subject to creating things that other people design, making art that follows bizarre restrictions, and working under criticism from others. But if you love making worlds for people to play, you'll enjoy doing it all. Certainly tons of game artists are ambivalent about games. But from my experience these people are rarely happy doing their jobs. And trust me, you can't be successful unless you're happy. Happiness is a requirement for success.

10

The next stage, says Cloud, may sound fairly obvious, but it tends to be overlooked quite a bit in today's gaming industry. Cloud admits even *he* has learned this way:

Next, learn to be an artist, not just a computer artist. I graduated with a degree in political science. And although I took several art classes, I wish I would have taken more. I'm proud of my ability to learn new tools and take advantage of what's available to make the best art I can in the quickest possible time. But I've had to pick up on many fundamental skills as I've gone along. If I started out today with the skills I had in '85 when I started at my first job, I probably wouldn't be hired. The day of the hacker/computer artist is over. Either by reading books or going to school, learning the fundamentals of art is imperative. Color theory, animation, the human form, painting, drawing techniques, composition, and so on aren't skills you pick up on your own.

So what's someone to do outside of school? What are the tools to learn first, and best?

Get set up at home with your own system. You can't learn to be a computer artist unless you spend time on the computer. Buy an old system and find public domain or used software on the Internet. Take the bus or bike to the university, but get a computer. You don't need the best software or system to get started, but you do need something. There are so many good programs out there, but you won't make a mistake by learning two programs— Photoshop and 3D Studio. If you can't find an old copy of one of those, then get any 32-bit art program and polygon modeling tool you can afford. Other alternatives to having a system at home are using a friend's system, using the school's, or getting a job (any job) at a place that has computers. Some suggestions are a copy/fax place, a service bureau, or a small computer store.

Although I applied for the position of artist at my first computer company, Softdisk, they said they didn't need an artist. Instead I took the job of answering technical support calls. It took time to convince Softdisk they needed an artist, but in the meantime I got a chance to talk to their programmers and use their computers and software to learn.

Cloud says once you've got some schooling and real-world experience behind you, the next step is to focus on being a better artist. He expands:

Avoid the millions of distractions that come your way. This is a lesson I have to learn over and over again. Although I never stop doing art, I often get sidetracked on other projects, and about a year later my head explodes. I have to learn once again that I'm an artist because that's what I like doing.

Throughout your career, remain focused on being a better artist. Seek out more art resources—books, good Web sites, art collections on disk. There are tons of biographies about artists featuring their art and stories about their lives. Every artist should spend some time following the lives of their favorite artists and emulating their styles. You'll learn so much just by trying to match the style of a great artist, and in the end you'll gain the flexibility to create your own style. Look for discussion groups on the Web, and don't be afraid to ask questions. And ask the advice and comments of your coworkers. Surround yourself with positive people who are interested in becoming better artists. Focus on improving your art skills, and opportunities will be out there for you.

Finally, the extra piece of advice is don't be afraid to move, take risks, and strive to be great. If possible, finish the project you're on—but if a better opportunity comes along, take it. Try to surround yourself with positive and talented people. Working with the best will always bring out the best in you. And keep in mind that your future is in your hands. Don't settle for being just one of the many. Do something different to set yourself apart. Develop a style or technique that is your own.

The last words from Cloud are to "try to make a difference on any project you're on, so that people will know that your hands have been on that game." Amen to that.

Brad Crow, Ensemble Studios

Our third Texan artist in a row (purely coincidental!) creates breathtaking images for a different genre altogether. Brad Crow is the lead artist at Ensemble Studios, a hot young design company currently creating strategy games for Microsoft. Past products include the best-selling and award-winning *Age of Empires* and *Age of Empires Expansion: The Rise of Rome*.

Interestingly, almost all artists in this chapter are offering very similar pieces of advice for newcomer game artists, regardless of the game genre. Crow is no exception. He suggests artists adhere to the following principles:

- **Have a clear vision for how you want your game to look.** This allows you to make a lot of progress in the early stages of production.
- **Be flexible with your vision once production is underway.** Allow the look of the game to grow and evolve to something different from your original vision. Constantly reevaluate your vision and allow new techniques, technological advances, and, most importantly, the artistic strengths of individuals on your team to influence and improve your original vision.
- **Look for and evaluate artistic criticism from anyone.** You want your game to be played by many people—no sense in limiting your market by following a style of artwork that only a small percentage of potential players like. If someone has a problem with how a part of your game looks, evaluate those concerns for any validity; many others may share the same view.

Currently Ensemble Studios is primarily a 3D Studio MAX house. On *Age of Empires*, most of the game was completed in 3D Studio, Release 4, before the very end of the project, when 3D Studio MAX was released. For the upcoming *Age of Empires II: The Rise of Rome*, due out sometime toward the end of 1999, Crow and company are using 3D Studio MAX for the art and animation.

Joe Koberstein, Raven Software

Joe Koberstein has been in the industry for five years (eons, for the gaming biz!) and is currently employed at Raven Software as an artist. The last product shipped out of their Madison, Wisconsin, studios was the well-received *Heretic II*, published by Activision.

On advice for newbies, Koberstein is straight and to the point:

- The computer is just a tool, like a pencil or brush.
- Learn to draw—it's the foundation to great art (computer or not).
- Don't take your work too personally; you're not a fine artist. Your vision may not coincide with the director's, but the people who are going to succeed in this industry are the people who are able to adapt. This industry changes on almost an hourly basis; this is very exciting, but can also be very intimidating. Just keep your ego in check and choose your battles carefully.

Koberstein agrees with most of the game artists in this chapter on what tools to use when creating a hit game:

> Photoshop and 3D Studio MAX have become the standard in paint programs and they're great tools to learn. The learning curves are a little high, but these programs are very powerful and offer a lot. Advice to anyone learning Photoshop: Use layers. They allow you to take chances you normally may not take in traditional art. Advice for 3D Studio MAX: Read the tutorial and start small. Don't attempt to make the *Star Wars* trilogy for your first project.

> Creating breathtaking images on the computer or on canvas, it all comes down to practice, and lots of it.

"Concept art is crucial to game development, whether it be story-boards, thumbnails on a napkin, or a fully rendered 3D environment. Continuity is crucial," says Koberstein. This is a preliminary sketch of Heretic II's Corvus. (Used with permission by Activision)

Mike Nichols, Surreal Software

Scheduled to be published by Psygnosis in mid-1999, *Drakan* is one of the most highly anticipated action/adventure hybrids of the year. Mike Nichols is the VP, founder, and creative director at Surreal Software, the developers for the game. Nichols offers budding game designers and artists his views on the three most significant considerations of game art. He decrees:

Composition

When it comes to painting the landscape, the designer, just as an artist, needs to be aware of the composition. Make sure all your tiles are placed correctly. You wouldn't want a solid dirt texture next to a solid grass texture without some sort of transition.

Aesthetics

It's important that a designer have some aesthetic sense. A mountain isn't just a textured, cone-shaped object. This is where you really need to be an observer of shape. Even before a single texture is painted, a shape should convey its meaning and emotion. In *Drakan*, the landscape is every bit as important as the characters. Some might even say it's the lead character.

Sweat the Details

Attention to detail. It makes all the difference in the world, and the player appreciates it. Personally, I'm more interested in games that *involve* me in the world, not just put me in it.

As a reference point, Nichols discusses *Drakan* in light of the aforementioned points:

Drakan includes some of the most expansive landscapes ever seen in a video game. Its release will certainly mark another chapter in gaming development. When designers approach a level, they need to have a clear understanding of the flow. How does it start and carry the player through the level to the end? Make it "feel" correct. The shape of the level has everything to do with how the player will explore it.

In *Drakan*, the designer must shape the polygons to reflect a "natural" scene. An artist will create a set of tiles that the designer uses to paint on the landscape. These tiles are a series of pictures that, when put together, can create the illusion of an expansive landscape. *Tile* also refers to the method of how these bitmaps are created. They're drawn to tile or mesh with each other without a seam. We use this tile method because we don't have the memory to create the HUGE bitmaps it would require to texture our vast landscapes.

To achieve these detailed and expansive landscapes, a number of tools are used by the Surreal art team:

For 3D Art: 3D Studio MAX and SOFTIMAGE

"MAX is a solid choice for creating games for several reasons," says Nichols.

It covers all the functions you need in a single package and it's cheap. Unfortunately, one of the drawbacks of a product like this is you get what you pay for, and not everything works the way you'd like—and that can get frustrating the more you use the program.

10

It's also an easy tool to learn on. For a beginning 3D student, it's a snap to get into and start learning your way around the world of 3D.

SOFTIMAGE, on the other hand, is a much more robust tool. It's our #1 choice for character animation. It offers advanced animators the control they need to take their animations to the next level.

For 2D Art: Photoshop

"It's a standard," agrees Nichols, but "a good standard. Photoshop is one of those tools no 2D artist can do without. It has an easy interface and powerful tools to help you create beautiful textures." He continues:

By no means are [these programs] the end-all of computer artistic creation. There are many software packages that are worthy of note. It really comes down to what's familiar and has the ability to grow as you do. A tool that can't do what's in your head is worthless.

For anyone creating art—or wanting to create art—on the computer, it's important to stay true to your vision and not let the software dictate how your creations look. Take control of your software; don't let your software control you! It's always worth the extra investment in time it takes to really get on the screen what's inside your head. Many times I see artists let the program dictate what their artwork looks like, and it's a good explanation why a lot of artwork out there looks the same—and why many who are not artistic think they can be.

In the next segment, Nichols covers what he believes is "one of the most important skills you can have as an artist… the one you learn first and never master."

Understanding Shapes

I don't mean having the ability to draw any shape in the world. I mean having the understanding and the observation skills required to create meaningful and expressive shapes. Master artists spend their lives trying to conquer just one aspect of shape—the human figure, still lifes, landscapes, etc.—and not one will ever tell you they have truly mastered it.

So relax and enjoy what you create, and, as my art teacher used to say, "Always look around for inspiration, whether it be in a colleague's work, nature, or a bottle."

Creating 2D textures for landscape tiles can be tricky, says Nichols. "You need to create a texture that has no seams when placed side by side over a large section of landscape. In order to create a non-repeating pattern, you need to keep the texture fairly generic." (Used with permission by Surreal Software, Inc.)

10

Tony Lupidi, EA Sports

Tony Lupidi is an art director for Scoreboard Productions, an in-house division of Electronic Arts that concentrates on the *March Madness* basketball simulation series for EA Sports, as well as other titles such as *Knockout Kings*, *NASCAR Revolution*, and *Hot Wheels*. Lupidi has worked on art and animation for a number of games, TV programs, and movies, so he has some lessons to share with newbies to the industry:

> Never become so enamored with the latest whizbang technology as to allow it to overwhelm the fundamentals of your craft. For example, just because the latest 3D cards can do real-time bump mapping with reflect maps doesn't mean all worlds must now be shiny and bumpy. The basics of design and composition apply to game art as much as any other genre of art.

> Use pencil and paper sketches to do your conceptual designs. Don't design directly on the computer. It's much faster and more efficient to do loose sketches for conceptual work. There's less of a tendency to become emotionally attached to a sketch, and this makes it easier to develop your design.

> Create the best art possible within the performance limits of your game engine. *People will never see your work if the game is too sluggish to be fun to play.* The art should enhance the player's experience, not hinder it. Game art is inevitably a compromise between quality and performance. Games ship all the time with this problem.

Lupidi comments on creating art for sports games, and how it may differ from other genres:

Sports games are a type of simulation, and as such usually try to mimic the broadcast television experience. Everyone knows what a televised basketball game looks like, and [you] have a set of expectations as to how the game should look. Since no one has ever seen 16-armed purple aliens, as an artist you can have more "wiggle room" in your interpretation when making a non-sports title.

I liken developing sports games to automobile design. Like cars, sports games usually come out annually, since they're tied to the sports season. Like cars, these games undergo incremental technical/artistic improvements each year. People appreciate a continuity of design from year to year, and a nice, polished, clean design and great performance will satisfy your customer.

Does Lupidi use the same tools as other artists in the gaming industry? More or less, confirms Lupidi:

Our current platform for developing games is Windows 98/NT 4.0, and our software tool set consists of 3D Studio MAX 2.5 for 3D modeling/anima-tion/texturing; Character Studio 2.x with the Promotion plug-in, Photoshop 5.0, and [Adobe] Illustrator 8.0. And a whole bunch of internally developed tools.

And for people looking to break into the biz? Any secrets or strategies?

For someone just getting into the [industry], the *Doom/Quake/Quake II* engines are very extensible and modifiable, and are an excellent way to get your feet wet. You can create/replace everything in the games—worlds, tex-tures, models, sounds, etc. The tool sets to create whole new games based on these engines are available for free (or very little) on the Internet. The other nice thing about this is that there are many very helpful people willing to give advice to newcomers. Many people who work professionally in the industry got their start doing this. Some of the tools people use are Paint Shop Pro [www.jasc.com], Worldcraft [www.worldcraft.com], and QPed [planetquake.com/qped] to manipulate Quake archive files.

In closing, Lupidi predicts "we are right on the verge of the emergence of a new, inter-active form of mass media." Some of the technologies driving this new media are real-time 3D display hardware as a consumer technology (à la Voodoo or TNT cards), broad-band networks (cable modems for the masses), and continued development of faster and cheaper computers. Can you say, "There's never been a more exciting time to come aboard"?

Toby Simpson, CyberLife Technologies

As creative director for the various *Creatures* life simulations, Simpson discusses his approach to computer game art and how it may differ from that of other disciplines:

> In order to achieve self-consistency, *Creatures* products are theme based rather than story based. We define history and geography first, so that it's possible to create self-consistent stories out of that theme. This makes it easier to be creative within the correct scope, as it's akin to having a style guide to stories. This is the sort of approach Tolkien used to create his Middle Earth stories—design the world first that you're going to set your stories in, as it saves a hell of a lot of time!
>
> Initially, we work out where any given product fits into the theme. This automatically defines the geography, and we then follow the *Creatures* style to sketch scenes within the new world. Eventually, we'll have designed the entire environment and its contents (both living and non-living) on good old-fashioned paper. This then gets scanned into the computer and placed in the product so that development can take place, while the artists gradually fill in the drawing with rendered or hand-retouched computer artwork.

The art team at CyberLife Technologies is currently in the process of sketching new virtual worlds for the third product in the highly successful *Creatures* series.

10

CHAPTER **11**

Animation

Working hand-in-hand with art is animation, since objects rarely remain static throughout a game. Quite simply, the purpose of animation in games, movies, or television programs is to simulate life through frames of movement. Animation in games is even more challenging, because it must synchronize with the program's artificial intelligence to mimic life (or machinery) *and* must be easily controlled by the player at the same time.

 Note >> There is also pre-rendered animation that is not interactive, such as the Silicon Graphics (SG) intro movies and cut-scenes that are popular in PC and console games today.

This chapter focuses on both classical 2D animation (sprite-based) and 3D modeling and rendering, using traditional keyframing, motion capture, and other proprietary and alternative animation techniques. We will hear from—and soak up some pointers from—a number of animators in the industry, representing companies such as Electronic Arts, Sierra, Valve Software, Treyarch Invention, Ubi Soft, and Ensemble Studios.

Ted Backman, Valve Software

Ted Backman, an artist and animator at Valve Software in Kirkland, Washington, offers his *savoir faire* on game animation and alludes to his work on the mega-successful and critically celebrated game, *Half-Life*.

➤ For Backman's views and advice on game art, see Chapter 10.

Backman believes the three most important things a new game designer should pay attention to are how the animation affects behavior (artificial intelligence), using reference material, and being especially careful with timing. The following is an elaboration on these precepts.

Animation and AI

Character animation in *Half-Life* is one portion of the character's outward expression of its artificial intelligence (AI); the character may also display its AI through sound cues and visual effects. What I mean by this is that the nature of the character animations can drastically change creature behavior— things like how fast they run, how often they attack, how quickly they recover from taking damage are all controlled by the length of the associated animation. You can do great harm to the behavior of the creature if you aren't careful in planning the relative speeds of the above-mentioned actions. It's very important to create an ongoing dialogue with the engineer responsible for creating the AI.

Use Reference Material

Motion, especially human motion, is a familiar thing to all people. If you create an animation of a human and are not extraordinarily careful to re-create all the subtle gestures and weight shift, it will stand out. People can spot bad human motion very easily. The only way to make believable human motion is to look at how people move on video and in pictures.

Backman says one especially useful source is a book by Eadweard Muybridge, *The Human Figure in Motion* (1989, Dover Pub.).

As seen here in 3D Studio MAX, Backman referred to a side view of a person running from an Eadweard Muybridge book to help create natural and believable human motion. (Used with permission by Valve Software)

Watch Your Timing

Another thing I see all too often is for someone to make an animation start to finish and then never go back over the motion to add subtlety and good timing. I spend more time working on timing and subtle motion than any other part of the animation process. Some general rules I like to follow: a) animate from the center of mass out; b) start with broad motions, then add smaller motions; c) slide keys around until the timing is correct.

11

But how does Backman achieve the fluid animation in games such as *Half-Life* and make it look so lifelike without using motion-capture technology? And what's the advantage to using a skeletal animation system? He answers:

The main difference between *Half-Life* and its competitors was the amount of data available to the animation engine. In most cases, artists will set up a bone system in a character they want to animate. The difference with *Half-Life* is that the engine actually looks at the position of the bones every frame, instead of the position of all the points on the mesh every frame. Since there's much less data to describe each frame of animation, you can have more animation for the same memory cost. This means you can animate at 30 frames per second as opposed to the traditional 10 frames per second. This yields a smoother and more realistic final animation.

Backman offers a few tips for newbie game animators, and discusses what software tools he uses:

> There are really no tricks to creating good animation, though; you just have to be patient and observant. Don't settle for something that looks *okay*; keep working until you're absolutely satisfied. Having a solid process helps—this means having a clear idea of what you want when you start, acting out the motion in front of a mirror, looking at video. And keep working on something, even though your deadline is in one week. The only way to get good motion is to work very hard at it; there are no shortcuts.

> The only real tip I can offer is to look at whatever you wish to animate, figure out where its center of mass is, and map out where that center of mass will move in relation to the feet. This is really how all motion occurs.

> The tools I use to animate are fairly standard: 3D Studio MAX [Autodesk] and Character Studio [an Autodesk/Kinetix plug-in for the 3D Studio MAX modeling package]. There is little out there in the way of plug-ins or great tools to simplify the process.

Backman is currently working on the art and animation for Valve Software's upcoming *Team Fortress 2*.

Peter Akemann, Treyarch Invention

Peter T. Akemann, Ph.D., is a managing member of Treyarch Invention and project lead on the critically acclaimed *Die by the Sword* by Interplay. He created the VSIM system that drives most of the animation in *Die by the Sword* and *Limb from Limb*. The fluid and lifelike animation in these products garnered attention from the gaming community.

Is there a difference to working on game animation instead of television or movie animation? What's best remembered by a junior game animator? Akemann offers three pieces of advice in this area: responsiveness (to control) is more important than smoothness; response (to action) is at least as important as the action itself; and 80% of the appreciation will be for 20% of your effort (most likely the easy 20%!), so accept this in advance and don't sweat it when it happens.

When asked how the VSIM technology works and why it's advantageous for games, Akemann responds:

> VSIM was a new take on the animation process, wherein we used a mathematical model to simulate the character motion, rather than pre-scripting it via a key-framed or motion-captured sequence. It was something less than a full physical simulation, but at the same time it was better because it focused

on the game it was created for (*Die by the Sword*) and was more amenable to artist tweaks than a complete simulation would have been.

Most animators are familiar with IK (inverse kinematics) from animation tools such as 3D Studio MAX, etc. Here they use an algorithm to orient a jointed body in a natural way to achieve a desired end result (e.g., the foot on the ground, the hand on the object being reached for, and so on). VSIM takes this a step further by not only generating an end result, but the motion required to get there. It's largely a combination of IK targeting and a muscle/joint physical simulation underneath.

It's the inevitable progress of every technology that automation always increases. However, far from putting animators out of work, these technologies should allow them to achieve even better results with greater ease than was previously possible.

Treyarch Invention's Akemann says, "Our hope for VSIM and related technologies is that they can be made general enough to add to every animator's toolbox, providing a powerful new tool for the animation process." These shots are from their popular action game Die by the Sword. (Used with permission by Interplay Productions)

11

According to Akemann, the animation was mostly created in their in-house Move Editor, a kind of virtual motion-capture studio for VSIM characters. "That and loads of text files with parameters. Not really the ideal path," admits Akemann. Traditional key-framed animations (for the non-interactive movie segments) were created in 3D Studio (not MAX) by Interplay's Mike McCarthy. "I think [3D Studio] is a good tool for an intro-level animator, and you can probably get it *really* cheap, since it's old," suggests Akemann.

Akemann closes by saying, "The best piece of advice I can offer is, when you're thinking about animation, try to envision the mathematical structures implicit in the motion. That was definitely the root of the inspiration for VSIM and *Die by the Sword.*"

Note >> *Rotoscoping* is another form of 2D/3D animating, but it isn't often used in games. In this process, actors are filmed and then animated over top. *The Last Express* from Brøderbund was one such PC game to use this technique.

Brøderbund's adventure game The Last Express featured rotoscoping animation, the technique by which actors are filmed and then animated over the film. (Used with permission from The Learning Company, Inc. All rights reserved.)

Jean-François Malouin, Ubi Soft

As art director at Ubi Soft's Canadian headquarters in Montreal, Jean-François Malouin has worked on the *Playmobil* lineup for kids, and an undisclosed new project. Similar to the response from Peter Akemann at Treyarch Invention, Malouin reminds readers about the key difference in creating animation for games, as opposed to other entertainment media such as TV and movies:

> In the video game industry, an animator has to be conscious of the fact that a player will control the character he's animating (if it's the main character) or at least interact with it (if it's a secondary character).

Since every game has its own pace, its own way of interacting with the environment, and its own character design, the animator doesn't really have a specific recipe to follow. Some games will allow animation with more frames for greater realism, but usually games need animations with very few frames that allow a better reaction time by the enemies in the game, or better control over the main character. Personally, I think that game developers—especially in 3D—are not paying enough attention to that.

Fun over Realism

Nintendo's *Mario 64* is cited by Malouin as having good animation, yet not necessarily adhering to the rules of nature:

> The appeal of *Mario 64* is largely due to the control of the main character. It's even fun just to run around without actually playing the game! If the basic principles of animation had always been followed to animate Mario, the game wouldn't have been as good. For example, Mario can bounce unrealistically far or jump extremely high. The animators did it so Mario would be a very lively and dynamic character, and we understand everything he does.

> Malouin says that, although this doesn't necessarily hold true for all game styles, animators should aim for a drastic change in the pose of the character, for a dramatic effect.

A bad "receiving hit" animation, right, and a good one. The bad one is not extreme enough because it takes more time to understand it and the message is less clear. (Used with permission by Ubi Soft, Inc.)

good

wrong

Understand the Character's Actions

"Since he doesn't have a lot of frames to illustrate a certain movement, the animator has to concentrate on the message he wants to give," advises Malouin.

> The player has to know what's happening to the main character because he *is* the main character. The player also has to know what people/ creatures/objects around him are doing. If you hit a bad guy, it has to show

right away; if there are questions about it, it's no good. If there are strong currents in the water, illustrate it—otherwise the player will expect to swim in a lake and will be frustrated to miss whatever move he wanted to do. Both these aspects are very important because the interaction between the player and the machine depends on them.

Once you're conscious that what you do as an animator will influence the player's mood, I guess the most important thing is to stay deeply interested in your game. Teams that love their game usually produce better products, because they're motivated.

What tools do Malouin and his team use to create animation in Ubi Soft games? Aside from some proprietary in-house software, they use the standard 3D Studio MAX and 3D Studio (www.autodesk.com). Malouin urges animators who are really serious about their work to practice lots of classical 2D animation as well, whether on paper or computer.

Scott Easley, Oddworld Inhabitants

Scott Easley is the senior animator for Oddworld Inhabitants, and has been there since its inception as a world-class development studio. Outside of Oddworld Inhabitants, Easley won two Emmys for the animation and also writing of a television commercial in 1994, and he also did the first computer-rendered poster for Marvel Comics in 1995.

Easley believes gameplay takes precedence over everything—including animation. He explains:

The game designer should create the best game he can, without the bias of including animation or graphics because it looks cool. It should be the last thing on his mind, as opposed to the engaging gameplay. We make stuff look sexy, but it should be restricted to when useful, not gratuitous. Imagery is all about conveying a clear story, as in movies or commercials—or gameplay, in video games. If I see one more chrome gargoyle on a demo tape, I'm going to throw the TV out the window. Tell me a story with animated blocks—and no spinning camera.

Conveying the message is premier, and in most cases, people get drunk on the imagery possibilities.

When asked what makes the animation in *Oddworld: Abe's Oddysee* and *Oddworld: Abe's Exoddus* look so good, and whether he can share any tricks or techniques, Easley replies:

There's no secret, pill, or "Do It" button. It's simply studying motion as best you can with the same basics afforded the Disney folk or Max Fleischer.

Look at the Eadweard Muybridge photographs and copy them, verbatim, into a skeleton you've made to have the same proportions in your software. Make the skin of your character out of boxes. Stay away from anything other than a boring block model so you can concentrate on motion alone. Study it from every angle, make it work from every angle. If you haven't spent an exhausting week on a 12-frame walk, you don't care as much as the guy who will get hired. Period.

Study motion, as we all do, every day. Look at the silent body-language conversation between two people whom you see across the street or through a window. Are they in love, in hate, indifferent? Do extremes at first—the grasp of subtlety will come with time.

What are the tools Easley uses to create breathtaking animation? Is there any motion capture in the *Abe's* games?

I can't stress enough that while motion capture has its place for football or sports games, I believe it atrophies the natural abilities of the animator. It's a quick way to impress friends and family, but you really didn't animate it— you *maybe* modified existing data.

 Note >> Game animators on the Internet should get to know the following Usenet newsgroups: comp.graphics.animation and rec.arts.animation. Newsgroups serve as interactive bulletin boards for like-minded people.

11

Vance Cook, Sierra Sports

Having developed golf simulators for close to a decade, Vance Cook has not only witnessed the evolution of sports game animation, but has been a significant participator in it. In fact, Cook worked on the coveted *Links* golf series at Access Software before leaving to start his own company, Headgate, Inc. (later to be sold to Sierra, where Cook is today).

Right off the bat, Cook explains why character animation is a challenge to achieve:

Human motion is one of the most difficult things to do because everyone knows exactly what normal movement looks like and they can pick out even the smallest problems. Our golfer characters can move in hundreds of different motions, but the golf swings were by far the most difficult. I believe that the golf swing is one of the most scrutinized motions in sports.

Therefore, Cook and company used motion capture in *PGA Championship Golf*. But that's not an easy task in itself:

We went into the studio with a couple of actors, talented motion-capture directors, and a script of several hundred motions. We left a week later worn out. After the studio session, the work was just beginning. Many weeks of editing were still ahead of us.

Note >> Motion capture (or *mo-cap*) is the process by which the movement of a real object (usually a person) is captured and mapped onto a computer-generated object.

Vance Cook says he wouldn't recommend trying to mimic human motion without motion capture. If cost is a factor, libraries of motion are becoming more cost effective. Notice the female golfer's underlying polygon mesh and her appearance with texture skins, above. The image below is a rendering of the same character's swing from PGA Championship Golf: 1999 Edition. (Used with permission by Sierra Sports)

We spent quite a bit of time heading down a non-motion-capture path before giving up. We attempted to mathematically represent a golf swing. We were able to basically put a body through its motions, but soon learned that basic motions are nowhere close to looking realistic without all of the numerous subtle motions one makes.

When it comes to striving for realism, is there such as thing as going too far? Cook responds:

I think it's possible to make a game too realistic. Many games are attempting to simulate real-world challenges. I think you've become too realistic when you start modeling the bad aspects of a real-world challenge. In golf, when we start making you book tee times and find your lost ball in the woods, we may have gone too far. I think it's hard, though, to make a game too realistic-looking. There are certainly some stylistic reasons to not look realistic, but most of us are chasing the realism dream in our games.

 Note >> Acclaim's next wrestling game, *WWF: Attitude* (due out in May 1999) is rumored to contain a whopping 400 motion-captured moves! Acclaim has a motion-capture studio in their Glencove, New York, studios.

Unfortunately, many novice game animators don't have the opportunity (or budget) to learn how to use mo-cap because of the limited number of available studios and its enormous expense.

Evan Hirsch, EA Sports

Evan Hirsch is the mo-cap guru at Electronic Arts in Burnaby, British Columbia (outside of Vancouver). This location houses EA's only motion-capture studio.

"First of all," begins Hirsch, "motion capture is just another medium; it's not a substitute for good animation, nor is it a substitute for a good game." Hirsch explains the two different kind of motion capture and which one EA Sports relies on:

Optical motion capture uses triangular calculations in the form of markers we place on a human body. Each marker becomes the third point.

Magnetic motion capture is easier to set up, but the subject must wear wires, a harness. Obviously, this isn't too safe for stunts.

EA uses optical motion capture because it gives us better data. Roughly 20 to 30 markers.

So does Hirsch prefer motion-capture technology over more traditional animation for the same reasons as Vance Cook?

The benefits are as follows. For one, it's an easier and quicker way to get animation into a Silicon Graphics machine (these workstations are used for all of EA's animation editing). Second is the human subtleties it picks up—the natural *warmth* of human motion and expression. It keeps this flavor in the game. For example, in games like *FIFA*, subtleties such as shaking or wincing.

Markers are taped on a character's joints and other key areas. With optical motion capture, the points between the markers are inferred by the computer; with magnetic motion capture, you get position and rotational information directly from the input device itself.

Hirsch reminds gamers that mo-cap doesn't do it all for you:

> You have to be a good animator, too. Motion capture is just a tool, and what you do with that data is everything. Because mo-cap is so expensive, you have to do your pre-production: have your move lists, directions, details, and lots of rehearsal.

Gamers are the ultimate judge. Boot up a recent copy of *Triple Play Baseball*, *NHL Hockey*, *Madden NFL*, *FIFA*, or *NBA Live* and notice how lifelike and fluid the animation is.

Brad Crow, Ensemble Studios

We heard from this savvy lead artist in Chapter 10, where he offers techniques on game art. Here, Ensemble Studios' Brad Crow gives budding animators a piece of advice. According to Crow, the most important aspect of character animation is one's attention to detail—or lack of it:

> It's the most subtle motions or gestures that bring character animation to life. We're all experts on how the human figure moves because we experience

movement and study it every day of our lives. So it makes perfect sense when somebody looks at digital character animation and can determine that "something isn't right" with the movement. The hard part is figuring out what small detail we left out of the animation that gave it away.

Currently, Ensemble Studios uses 3D Studio MAX as their primary animation tool. In fact, *Age of Empires* was completed in 3D Studio, Release 4, and it wasn't until the very end of the game's development cycle that 3D Studio MAX was released.

Ensemble Studios' Brad Crow offers these rare screens for Age of Empires fans. Above, a horse animated in 3D Studio MAX. Below, the same unit in transition from sketch to wireframe to final rendered image. (Used with permission by Ensemble Studios, Inc.)

11

Crow says he achieved the fluid movement of the humans, animals, and weapons in *Age of Empires* and *Age of Empires Expansion: The Rise of Rome* by studying movies and books, and he "actually acted out movements sometimes, in order to catch all the details."

Note >> *Stop-motion animation* is the cinematic process by which an object is brought to life by filming one frame of film per increment. This classic animation technique isn't found often in games, but a perfect example is DreamWorks Interactive's *The Neverhood Chronicles*.

The Neverhood Chronicles is a perfect example of stop-motion animation. These clay figures were moved and photographed incrementally to simulate movement. (Used with permission by DreamWorks Interactive. Inc.)

CHAPTER **12**

The All-Important User Interface (UI) and Game Control

While it's likely that you'll find some conflicting advice in areas of this book on art techniques, level design suggestions, or the best way to animate a character, it's universally recognized that a bad *user interface (UI)* in a game can be its own demise, regardless of how good the content is.

While compiling this book, a number of designers were asked if there was any truth to the gaming industry adage that a user interface can make or break a game. For the most part, the designers agreed that it can indeed *break* a game. They were also clear that if the game itself isn't good, the UI certainly can't save it. Nonetheless, it's one of the most significant areas of game design that's often overlooked.

Keep in mind that there are two distinct areas of a game's interface. The first is the menu screen, or *shell interface*, used mainly to set up video or sound options, configure controls, launch a multiplayer game, access saved games, exit to a desktop, and so on. The second is the *in-game user interface*—that is, what the player sees on the screen while playing.

Control is another important aspect to game design, and many lump this area into user interface because they're closely related. Far too often, the player pays $50 for a game and can't control the character or machine (or "camera" angle of the action, in some games). In other cases, the control layout is fine, but the objects onscreen don't respond quickly or smoothly enough.

Many gamers would agree that the sports game genre seems to have the most difficulty when it comes to a good in-game UI. Part of the reason, with team-based sports games such as football, soccer, basketball, or hockey, is that the gamer must have all the players accessible at all times, and must choose which player(s) to control. To complicate the issue even more, in some cases it's also necessary to give commands to other team members. I'll cover team-based sports games in a moment, but first let's look at sports games where there's only one character to control—such as in golf, skiing, or boxing. These sports games have their own sets of UI challenges.

Vance Cook, Sierra Sports

Vance Cook, lead designer on Sierra Sports' *PGA Championship Golf 1999 Edition*, answers the question, "How important is a good UI in a sports game such as golf?"

> A good user interface is important in all software products, not just games. A great game must achieve a high level of quality in all areas: shell interface, in-game interface, graphics, playability, game balancing, storyline, etc. If any one of the pieces is weak, the game will be weak. It's not very useful to discuss which is the most important. With that said, you definitely don't want to get your in-game interface wrong. That's where the rubber hits the road. That's where the customer connects to your game.

When discussing the different kinds of UI, Cook recommends adhering to the following guidelines.

Shell Interface

Cook suggests managing the choices for the customer in the menu or shell screens of the game (not gameplay). This is done to prevent the player from being overwhelmed with too many choices. "Present only the relevant information for a given context, and hide everything else. If making a certain choice removes the possibility of other choices, make it obvious that those choices are no longer available by graying them out or hiding them," says Cook.

In-Game Interface

"Different games must use different philosophies, but many games are faced with the challenge of needing to maximize the viewing window while still allowing the user to perform many interface actions," believes Cook. When creating a new game, developers are often faced with the battle between hiding interface choices to keep the viewing screen clean, and making them easily accessible:

> It's easy to hide interface choices if you don't care about how many steps the customer must take to perform an action. It's also easy to make interface actions very accessible if you don't care about how much screen real estate you take up. Game developers are always coming up with creative ways to balance these two requirements. You first have to determine the proper balance between screen real estate and accessibility for your particular game. Categorize your interface actions into two groups: items that require frequent access, and items that require infrequent access. Items requiring frequent access must be only one or two steps away. (A step could be a mouse click, a mouse drag, or a keystroke.) Items requiring infrequent access can easily be hidden behind an Options button or icon.

PGA Championship Golf 1999 Edition is used as an example of how the in-game user interface can be split up for functionality versus aesthetics. According to Cook, there are four main areas to the UI:

1. The aiming and swinging interface is located right by the golfer and requires only one step.

2. The shot information is grouped together in the lower-right corner of the screen. The user can see all of the necessary information without taking any steps. The user also has the option to click on existing pieces of information for more detail if he or she wishes. For example, the most important distance is the distance between the ball and the hole. The distance readout is always displayed. Sometimes it's nice to know what the elevation difference is between the ball and the hole. This information is accessible by clicking on the distance readout.

3. Frequent interface actions are grouped together in the lower-left corner of the screen. These actions are things like selecting a club or setting up a creative shot. These actions are one or two steps and located close to the golfer for easy access.

4. Less frequent actions such as finding the flag are available by first selecting the Options button in the lower-left corner of the screen. Only choices that are currently available show up when you click Options. An extra step of clicking Options is required for all of these actions, but it's worth it because the Options button takes up very little real estate and these actions are not frequently needed.

12

All the pertinent information the golfer must know before taking a swing is accessible to the right of the player... nothing more, nothing less, and just the right size. (Used with permission by Sierra Sports, Inc.)

Game Control Interface

Cook says game control is unique to every product; therefore, it's difficult to give advice on it as general rules:

> But this is often where the real magic of a game is created. Depending on the game and game genre, there are currently a few choices available for game control: mouse, keyboard, joystick, gamepad, steering wheel. Others are available, but most developers stick with these basics in order to make the game playable by most people. You have to look at these choices and decide which device or combination of devices is most similar to the real-world challenge you're trying to create. In most games, these devices are not even close.
>
> In the case of golf, none of them are close, but we've chosen to go with a mouse swing because it has the most parallels to a real swing. Customers can control the path and speed of the golf club. This gives us the ability to simulate very soft and very hard shots. It also gives us the ability to introduce side spin (hooks and slices) when the mouse slides sideways out of the straight path. Finally, it allows us to simulate missed hits when they don't return the mouse to the place where it started.

One of the key points Cook makes is that game control is one of the most important aspects of the immersion factor:

> You must make your customers feel connected to the game. The control devices must become an extension of themselves, and with time become intuitive. Anything you do to remind them they're playing a game will detract from the enjoyment of the experience.

Golf games exemplify this statement, says Cook, and he offers his own game as a reference point:

> My competitors may not agree with me here, but I believe that a delay between when you've performed a swing action and when the golfer starts swinging greatly detracts from the experience. In *PGA Championship Golf*, the golfer moves at the same time you're swinging and he or she moves in the same path that you move your mouse. If you slide to the right or left, the golfer will move the club outside or inside of the swing plane.

Tip >> As Cook touches on, UI and game control may be a personal thing, so many developers of PC and console games are now allowing players to customize these settings to their liking. For instance, in many 3D shooters and simulations, it's possible to select or deselect what information is given onscreen with the tap of a key or click/drag of a mouse. Similarly, most games, in all genres, allow players to remap keys/buttons to their liking, or assign hotkeys or macros. Give players the option to make the game their own.

In closing, Cook reminds readers that, above all else, "You must attempt to immerse customers into the experience—make them forget who they are and make them believe they're the character onscreen."

12

Vance Cook's advice on menu or shell UI is applicable to all other game genres as well. Note the simplistic design for the Options screen in Interplay's Baldur's Gate, an award-winning RPG developed by BioWare. (Used with permission by Interplay Productions)

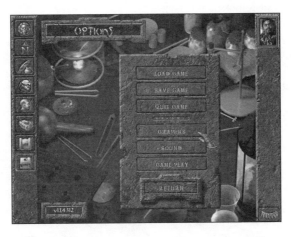

Scott Orr, EA Sports

Having designed, produced, and executive produced at EA Sports for a number of years, Scott Orr understands the necessity of extremely good UI. Some of the award-winning titles and series under his belt include *Madden Football*, *NHL Hockey*, *Andretti Racing*, *NASCAR Racing*, and *NCAA College Football*.

According to Orr, the key word in interface design is *simplicity*. He elaborates:

> Gamers are notorious for not reading manuals. If they can't quickly and easily get into a game, they'll become frustrated and look to other games for satisfaction. If they can't immediately play a game and have some measure of success, they'll put it down and look elsewhere. As a result, designers should spend a considerable amount of time working on the menu interface as well as the game controller interface. This is not as easy as it seems, given the incredible number of options most sports games have on the 32-bit and PC systems.

It's one thing to say designers *should* spend time working on a simplified UI, and it's another thing to make the time and effort to do it. Are there any examples at EA Sports? Orr responds:

> My goal in the *Madden 2000* product is to literally be able to pick a team and kick off with no more than two button presses in Arcade mode, and to greatly reduce the number of menus gamers need to navigate in Sim mode. Our designers have spent a lot of time trying to simplify the menu interface without sacrificing the number of options available to our customers. It's an ongoing process, and one that benefits from focus group testing and feedback from our customers and reviewers.

EA Sports redesigned the UI in Madden NFL '99 to provide a one-button interface option for novice users to start playing instantly, with almost no learning curve. (Used with permission by EA Sports)

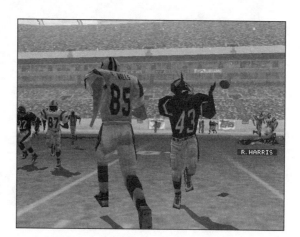

When it comes to controlling the game, Orr says the very same principles apply as with creating a good UI—it all boils down to player intuition and simplicity:

> Look at arcade games for inspiration, since they're usually the best examples of game interfaces [that are] easy to understand and play. Look at other products in the same sport to see if there are de facto standards to adhere to. For example, if the top-selling game in a particular sport uses the X button as the Action button, you should probably use it too, since gamers are already used to it that way. That familiarity makes it easier for them to play the game and get hooked by it sooner.

"Finally, create a controller interface that works with your AI," concludes Orr. Instead of using three different buttons to accomplish three different moves, Orr says to map them to one button and use the AI to trigger the right move based on the context of the action (which Orr and the folks at EA Sports refer to as *context-sensitive artificial intelligence*). "That way, you get all the benefits of the multiple moves while keeping your controller interface simple. Of course, this only works if your computer AI is topnotch—but when it works, it works great."

Marc Aubanel, EA Sports

Marc Aubanel is the producer of the celebrated *FIFA* and *World Cup* soccer series for the PC, PlayStation, and Nintendo 64 platforms. He works at the new Electronic Arts Canada studio in Burnaby, British Columbia.

Most of Aubanel's suggestions pertain to soccer games, because this is what he spends all of his time on, and he leans more toward the control aspect of UI. Keep in mind that in most cases his advice could be applied to other team-based sports games, and the challenges faced when designing a good UI for them.

Camera vs. Character Control

At EA Sports, Aubanel says, they have always opted for camera-relative control, as opposed to character-relative. That is, if the player presses on the down button on the controller, the player onscreen moves toward the bottom of the screen. If the game was created to move relative to the character, and the down button or arrow was pressed, the character onscreen would move downscreen according to the character's perspective.

According to Aubanel, the camera-relative option is much more intuitive to the player, unless the game opts for a first-person perspective view of the action, so it's as if the gamer is looking out of the character's eyes (as with many shooters). "In *FIFA* and other soccer games, you don't see the world through the player's eyes, so, in my opinion, it's a

12

Chapter 12

mistake to go with character-relative control in a third-person camera game." The only exception is when the player has the ball and is targeting the object (such as the net in soccer); then it switches to character-relative targeting so the player can aim where he or she wants the ball to go.

Keeping it Simple

Another challenge when working on UI for soccer games is allowing the player to have quite a bit of control while at the same time keeping the control method simple and intuitive. Aubanel explains:

> The goal here is to try to get the kind of complexity you want in a soccer game—like "deeking out" opponents or changing speeds on the fly as in real soccer games—while at the same time maintaining simplified control.
>
> The way we get around that is to *contextualize* what's happening onscreen; therefore the program determines the desired or logical act in question. For instance, if you want to get the ball from someone and you choose to be a bit rough in getting it, you can push or elbow him if close enough; but if five feet away the player may slide down to steal the ball. It's the same button command, but it's contextually sensitive. It's the same when you're scoring on the net. If you kick the ball toward an open net, it may look different than if you're farther away or if the goalie is in the net. This is to make it more realistic. Other examples are some of the special moves, such as the "air play" moves. The program will figure out which header or chest play move to perform. Instead of "diving headers" or "volleys," the player may "bicycle kick" the ball [backward] if he's 180 to the net. So this aids in the challenge to have many moves, but with few buttons.

The players in EA Sports' FIFA '99 are contextually sensitive, so they may act differently depending on the situation or context. However, the player doesn't have to learn additional controls. (Used with permission by Electronic Arts, Inc.)

In the following sections, Aubanel provides two pieces of solid advice for game designers who may be working on UI and control:

Follow Your Assumptions, and Test Them

"Focus on whatever your assumptions are when it comes to a user interface, and take into account other people's preferences," recommends Aubanel. "The only way to do this is to study other people playing them, with as many testers as possible. For the *FIFA* games, it's not unlikely that we'll get 60 testers to play the game and tell us what they prefer, and I remember I had to put my opinions aside in one instance because the majority had spoken. While I say 'go with your assumptions,' it's also important to remember the game isn't just for you, so ensure that you're testing."

Experiment with Ideas, and Test Them

"Here's another fine line," says Aubanel. "Don't feel like you have to stick with what others have done before you [in that type of sports game], but don't go crazy by adding too many new things, either." Aubanel says to experiment, but test out these changes with a large testing group. When it comes to game control and soccer games, Aubanel admits they have a long way to go in this area.

Giving the Best of Both Worlds

The last piece of advice from Aubanel is very specific to soccer games and other team-based sports games. For non-control UI issues, Aubanel says that the farther the camera is from the gameplay, the easier it is to play, since you can see everyone on both teams. But with more players on the screen at the same time, it can be a frame-rate issue, so you have to find that balance.

Aubanel says that many players like to play the game with the close camera option to appreciate the art and animation, but it isn't the best way to play the game, since not all characters are in sight. Therefore, to give the game the best of both worlds, *FIFA* games and other EA Sports titles often show close-ups and other scripted segments up-close for dramatic effect when the ball is out of play (after a goal is scored, penalties, and so forth).

➤ Be sure to also flip to Chapter 9, where Marc Aubanel discusses artificial intelligence issues and solutions in sports games.

Richard "Lord British" Garriott, Origin Systems

Lord British is one of the pioneers of the computer gaming industry, best known for his mega-successful *Ultima* role-playing game series. To date, there have been over a dozen sequels, plus countless other products including children's cartoons, comic books, novels, and songs. *Ultima: Ascension* is the ninth installment in the prestigious series (not including the second *Ultima VII* game), due out sometime in 1999.

When asked his opinion on how a good UI should be implemented, Lord British declared that everyone has a different religion on this subject, but that he adheres to two main principles when creating games.

Familiarity

"The more familiar the UI is to the player, the better," says Lord British. When elaborating on this "first hurdle," he says that this doesn't always mean it's the better interface, but the more familiar:

> Right now, the Windows 95 interface is familiar to many gamers, with the left and right mouse-click functionality. I'm not necessarily endorsing it, but more people can relate to it. If the game has a UI that resembles or borrows from Windows 95, the gamer will be better off because of its familiarity.

The Backhoe Operator Syndrome

The second principle stems from the familiarity factor and should be something every game designer strives for—making the UI so intuitive to the gamer that he or she becomes one with the onscreen avatar. Lord British calls this one "the backhoe operator syndrome." After familiarity, the key is to make the UI (from a dexterity standpoint) almost nonexistent, so the player no longer considers it an interface at all. Lord British elucidates:

> You know those backhoes on construction sites—those machines that dig dirt? After a period of time, the operator of the backhoe no longer thinks about how to tip the bucket and scoop up the dirt—he just does it.

Lord British explains that a good UI is the same thing. The player should *be* the avatar onscreen and not *control* it. Hey, after all, Origin Systems' motto is "We create worlds."

To achieve this level of immersion, Lord British insists that game designers should create as simple a UI as possible, without forfeiting the player's options. He explains that he learned this the hard way throughout the evolution of the *Ultima* series, and recalls how the simplicity factor has come full circle:

> With *Ultima 1* on the Apple II, there were only a half dozen commands, such as north, south, east, and west movement, and hotkey letters that started with the first letter of that function, such as *s* for save and *l* for load. Then things got more complicated as the series matured. By *Ultima VI*, every letter meant

something—with no exception—so I had to stretch it. For instance, I had to use the *z* key to bring up stats because the *s* key was allocated for the save function. The problem was that I needed to add more commands, so I collapsed the keys into meta-commands, such as the word *use* to unlock a door or light a torch. Therefore, this noun/verb interface evolved, expanding into five graphical icons in *Ultima VII*, but it was still a two-step effort because you had to click on "talk to" and then click on a character, for example. Because the gamer had to do these two things, it was still difficult to get that "backhoe" effect. In *Ultima VIII* and *IX* [*Ascension*], it's one direct command and all mouse-driven. The program now determines what the player wants to do. For example, if there's an NPC [non-player character] on the screen and you want to talk to him, all you have to do is talk to him. If your sword is drawn, he'll fight. The UI is now contextually sensitive, with visual clues to confirm that this is indeed what the player wants to do before doing it.

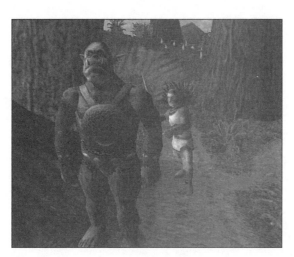

Lord British has streamlined the UI in Ultima: Ascension to make the game more intuitive to the player. (Used with permission by Origin Systems, Inc.)

12

In Lord British's opinion, the UI we use today could have been done 20 years ago, but we needed to go through this stage of reorganization.

Ragnar Scheuermann, Wombat Games

At Origin Systems, Ragnar Scheuermann served as a software engineer on *Ultima Ascension* and *Ultima Online*, but left to become a designer, programmer, and VP at the newly formed Wombat Games, Inc.

Scheuermann agrees with Lord British: "When in doubt, do it the way Windows does it, since that's what most people will be used to." But there's a lot more to be said about good versus bad UI. Says Scheuermann, "This is something I've seen few games of late get right." To sum it up in one sentence, Scheuermann says the goal of the UI is to make performing all possible actions within the game easy, for both the newbie and the expert player.

> Unfortunately, many games only manage to cater to one of these groups, either leaving the newbies bewildered or forcing the expert players to navigate through countless menus and beautifully slow opening animated windows to get to the functions they need.

> Always be sure to emphasize function over form. In many classic games, this was taken to the extreme by having only keyboard commands for everything, and no menu. But recently I've noticed more and more of the screen real estate taken up by pretty but useless pictures.

Scheuermann provides examples of RPGs with poor screen real estate, in his opinion:

> There's games with extremely thick borders around windows and buttons (*Ultima Online*), inventory and status screens that occupy half the screen (*Diablo*), or slowly opening menus requiring mouse clicks and no hotkeys (*Return to Krondor*).

> Always make sure the function is there first, and that the art or animation doesn't detract from it.

The easiest method to help out newbies is to provide access to all game commands via some sort of menu, offers Scheuermann. "If your menu is iconic, make sure you have tool-tips or a status bar describing what you're hovering over. Ideally, provide a method (such as right-clicking, or hovering over something and pressing F1) to bring up more descriptive help on an item."

It's the newbies you must be concerned about and not the veteran gamers. "Providing support for advanced players is even easier. First step, assign hotkeys to everything trivial to the program. The second step is to make those hotkeys programmable," says Scheuermann. "*Quake* does this beautifully by putting all of its standard interface keys in a script that's customizable by advanced players, and even allowing for some fairly complex macros."

Wrapping up, Scheuermann's last piece of advice is to try to follow some standard practices to make the game feel more intuitive to the new user. Examples? Esc key to abort, Enter to accept, cursor keys to scroll through menus and items once selected.

We'll see Scheuermann's practices in action with Wombat's first game, a yet-to-be-disclosed massively multiplayer online role-playing game.

Tom Hall, ION Storm

Game designer and ION Storm cofounder and vice president Tom Hall has been preparing the PC gaming world for his ambitious 3D role-playing game, *Anachronox* (pronounced uh-NAH-kruh-nox). He has also worked on some of our industry's beloved classics, such as *Doom* and *Wolfenstein 3D*, at id Software.

It comes as no surprise when he points out—as do the other designers in this chapter—that a good UI is critical, and must be both easy to use and intuitive. "If you ship a demo and it's hard to control, people will get frustrated and go, '&#*@ this!' and never play it again, no matter how cool the content is," says Hall.

So what about examples of games with good or bad UI, and why?

> Games I've worked on with great interfaces are *Commander Keen in "Goodbye, Galaxy!,"* *Wolfenstein 3D*, and *Doom*. They're simple and elegant. You don't have to search around for keys, or memorize the manual. You just go and do. I like all the LucasArts adventure interfaces. It's very clear how to do things.
>
> I don't want to go off on competitors' games, so two games that I've done that shipped with bad interfaces were *Keen Dreams*, whose menu was a horrible, non-intuitive nightmare, and *Rise of the Triad*, whose version 1.0 controls were unwieldy. By the time version 1.1 fixed them, we'd lost all those people who said, "&#*@ this!" You only get one chance at converting a player to your side; don't blow it. Have fans of your genre play it and be brutal.
>
> Your mom should be able to play the game intuitively, even if she doesn't like it.

12

Anachronox contains over 100 levels and over 150 monsters. And you can bet Tom Hall won't let a lousy UI ruin all that hard work! (Used with permission by ION Storm, Inc.)

Ron Gilbert, Humongous Entertainment

Tom Hall cites LucasArts adventure games as excellent examples of easy-to-use inter-faces. Having conceived the idea for the *Monkey Island* series, one of LucasArts' most popular franchises, Ron Gilbert can take much of Hall's compliment, along with other adventure game designers at LucasArts, particularly Tim Schafer.

Gilbert left LucasArts to start Humongous Entertainment, a software company that quickly became one of the leading developers for kids' games.

In Gilbert's opinion, a good UI is critical: "Nothing gets me more frustrated than a game with a bad user interface." But a good interface design isn't as easy to create as one may think. Explains Gilbert, "There's a fine line here. The UI has to be simple and intuitive for the gamer, but at the same time you want to give the gamer a lot of choices, a lot of power. Very seldom these days is a UI so wrong, but there are a few games that have a poor user interface." As examples, he points to *Diablo* as having a very good interface, along with Cavedog's upcoming *Total Annihilation: Kingdoms*, a fantasy real-time strat-egy game Gilbert is also working on (Cavedog and Humongous Entertainment are sister companies).

In Gilbert's opinion, Blizzard's Diablo has a good user interface because it's simple to learn yet multifunc-tional. (Used with per-mission by Blizzard Entertainment, Inc.)

Alex Garden, Relic Entertainment

"Depending on how you look at it, every game ever made, every piece of it, is just a glorified UI," says Alex Garden, CEO and lead designer of Sierra Studios' upcoming *Homeworld*. "The whole purpose of the game/UI is to help convey an idea to the player in the least obtrusive way possible." Since every game is essentially UI, what then are good or bad examples, and why? Answers Garden:

> Take *Quake*, for example. Running through the world quickly becomes sec-ond nature to the player. The elements of the game don't take away from the game experience in any way, because each one is concise and easy to under-stand. There are a plethora of great ideas out there that fall short of the mark,

because elements of the game/UI are too cumbersome to be "transparent" to the interactive experience. One poor example is *Star Wars: Rebellion*. *Rebellion* is a fantastic idea, but it's so buried under menus, screens, conflicting input systems, and information that it's almost impossible to play!

The best UI is no UI. That's my motto. If you don't *have* to have a menu pop up, then don't. Wherever possible, use natural, real-life-based interaction to convey information. For instance, if you have a choice between popping up a window with some text on it or speaking the text out loud, it's always best to speak the text out loud, and provide a backup written transcript for the player to review.

Relic's Alex Garden says "The best UI is no UI." Here's some proof from his upcoming game, Homeworld. (Used with permission by Sierra Studios)

➤ For a great read, Garden recommends finding the chapter on UI in *Computer Graphics: Principles and Practice, Second Edition in* C by Foley, van Dam, Feiner, and Hughes (Addison-Wesley, 1996).

Mark Green, Psygnosis

Before moving over to become production and design liaison for Psygnosis' Leeds studio in the U.K., Mark Green was the lead designer on *Global Domination* for the PC and Sony PlayStation. In the following short piece on control and UI, Green discusses the importance of this area, the differences between control and the UI, and their relationship to one another:

> Both control in a game and user interface are vital to a good game. Without either of them, even a brilliant game will become decidedly frustrating. Who wants to play a game that relies on speed and accuracy of response and has a

12

sluggish control mechanism? And who has the patience to soldier on through a confusing and unintuitive user interface that makes it difficult for the player to understand what's happening?

These two items are among many reasons why there are getting to be more and more designers in the game industry. A programmer codes and an artist models, but neither is necessarily aware of all the design features required in a game. That comes down to the designer.

Global Domination borrowed from James Bond's Never Say Never Again, the board game Risk, and the arcade classic Missile Command. Poor UI would have sunk this 3D title. (Used with permission by Psygnosis, Inc.)

Control of a game is how a computer interprets your instructions to do things. (You press a button to move your character and the computer doesn't immediately respond, resulting in your untimely death at the hands of a giant wolf).

A user interface is the way the player tells the computer what to do, and the computer tells the player what's happening. If the user interface isn't intuitive, then it's wrong. You can't rely on the user learning how to use your super new command system unless it follows some pretty standard rules of intuition.

Assorted Advice from the Pros

Other game designers offered the following opinions of UI, mirroring much of the sentiment given by the rest of the designers in this chapter.

Sid Meier, Firaxis Games

When creating his latest game, *Alpha Centauri*, the UI was an important consideration to Sid Meier, and he tried to cater the UI design to both newbies to the turn-based strategy genre, as well as to gaming veterans:

> I wanted the game interface to be easy to use, with everything accessible with the mouse, but I also wanted keyboard shortcuts. In *Alpha Centauri*, we realized people wanted to learn more about the information onscreen—units, terrain, buildings—so if you right-click on a given area, it will tell you more information, in depth.

Right-clicking on an area in Alpha Centuri will bring up additional information screens. This was a UI decision so the gamer doesn't have to leave the environment to learn more about the game. (Used with permission by Firaxis Games, Inc.)

12

Matt Householder, Blizzard North

Following are a few quick UI pointers for new game designers from the producer of Blizzard's *Diablo II*:

- Don't frustrate the player's desire for perfect control within the game world.
- Any sense by the player of lack of control (however brief) can be fatal.
- The user interface must be intuitive and consistent.

  This makes it easy for new players to learn and encourages experienced players to become experts.

Jay Wilson, Monolith

Both the in-game UI and the interface during the menu screens are extremely important, according to Monolith's Jay Wilson. And customizability is also critical. Says Wilson:

If I can't play a game the way I want, I just won't play. I'm not going to mention which game it was, but I waited a year and a half for it to come out because it looked incredible. And when it did, there was no mouse support at all. You have to make the way the game looks and controls familiar to the player.

Although most game companies don't do this, Wilson insists a menu screen should always have a Help box to click on that will explain all the options in the game.

CHAPTER 13

Sound Engineering

Not too long ago, sound effects in PC games meant the odd *bleep* or *chirp* from an internal speaker. Fast forward to 1999 when, during a heated game of *Half-Life*, you can literally hear a slimy alien creep up from over your left shoulder…

As audio software and hardware continues to evolve for the PC, sound is becoming an incredibly significant part of the gaming experience. And consider for a moment the rate at which this new technology is not only accessible, but affordable. In less than two years, we've witnessed the emergence of Dolby Surround Sound, Dolby Digital (AC-3), Dolby Surround Pro Logic, Microsoft DirectSound and DirectSound 3D, Creative Lab's Environmental Audio, Aureal's A3D, surround-sound speakers, multiple-channel surround-sound speakers, DVD players, powerful subwoofers, USB connections for a cleaner channel, and digital inputs for all kinds of supported musical gear. Point made?

With this new technology comes a new breed of audio specialists, determined to breathe new life into the interactive entertainment industry. This chapter delivers advice from a number of well-known and respected sources in the gaming industry on getting into sound design as a profession, ways of achieving the effects heard in popular games, which archived sound packages are worth getting, and how sound design fits into the grand scheme of game design.

Matthew Lee Johnston, Microsoft

Matthew Johnston, audio lead at Microsoft, has worked on a number of well-received and best-selling gaming and multimedia titles. Some of his most impressive works include *Flight Simulator 95* and *98*, *Microsoft Golf 2.0*, *3.0*, *98*, and *99*, and *Monster Truck Madness 1* and *2*. When asked what pieces of advice he could give budding sound engineers on succeeding in the gaming industry, he responds as follows.

Understand the World of the Developer

According to Johnston, most sound designers currently working on games come from traditional post-production backgrounds, including many failed careers as live sound operators or recording bands down at the local rock star sweatshop. "I can't tell you how many times I've sat in a game developers conference discussion and listened to guys whine incessantly about how the developers never listen to them, don't understand them, or treat them like s——," says Johnston. He amplifies:

> This treatment, while it may not be entirely justified, is understandable. Waxing ecstatic about design concepts without being able to provide the developer with concrete examples of how it can be implemented is negligent, and can be offensive to someone who has spent the last year thinking about everything but the audio. Educate yourself on basic programming concepts, understand the relationship between the game engine and the sound engine, and be a diplomat when it comes to working with the development team; they're holding your design in their hands and can make or break your ideas.

Make Yourself Useful

"Rarely does anyone design game audio that has any use," Johnston believes. What does this mean, exactly? Surely he's not insulting the efforts made by fellow sound engineers? Of course not. He explains:

> Someone has brought you in at the last possible moment, and they hand you a list of individual sound effects that already map to some specific graphic element on the screen. This is a lot like scoring a film, and comes from a lack of awareness on how much of a part sound plays in the overall human experience. What people don't understand is that you're not making a movie,

but you are attempting to re-create an interactive environment that contains visual and aural elements that combine to create an "experience" that's totally defined by the player's actions. Think of your sound design as going way beyond "making sounds for the graphics," and come up with ways that the sound can be a critical element of gameplay. The gaming industry is way behind on this concept, and you will start to see games coming out that use sound as important parts of the gameplay more often. Get ahead of the game, and start thinking this way now.

Johnston cites an example of a game he's worked on where sound effects play a very significant role in the player's actions. In Microsoft's *CART Precision Racing*, using engine sounds for other cars will warn the player of what's coming up behind, and using stereo panning localizes the predator to a particular side of the vehicle.

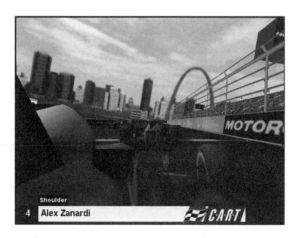

In Microsoft's CART Precision Racing, it's best to keep your eyes directly on the road and not on other cars. Spatialized audio cues are provided by Johnston so you know when another driver is sneaking up from behind, and on what side. (Used with permission by Microsoft Corp.)

Break the Mold

In the following passage, Johnston addresses respect, professionalism, and proving your competence:

> Nothing pisses me off more than being called a "musician" or "sound guy" after spending the last ten years of my life developing expertise in audio system design. Content creation is only part of the tune. Earning respect in this industry is already difficult because audio is such a subliminal partner in a multimedia presentation. Most people are not aware of how much effect the sound has on a person's perception, emotion, and immersion in a game product. If you couple this lack of awareness with a tight budget and the misperception that you're just a bong-smoking hipster with a guitar, you've got problems. Be a professional, cover your ass by knowing all there is to know

13

about the environment that your sounds will be such an integral part of, and for gods' sake, stop using the word "dude." Take on the role of the educator, and get used to having to prove yourself and your ideas to someone who thinks you are "a nice thing to have around, but not critical." You will eventually win them over with tight, thorough, and well-substantiated attempts to bring them out of the video coma and into a new aural enlightenment. Make the words "proof of concept" your new mantra.

Is it possible that audio can even influence visual perception? Indeed it can, says Johnston. He cites a classic example stemming from MIT research that proves the power of audio over the visual. In a nutshell, the MIT media lab showed two groups two video clips: one with bad audio content, and one with really great audio content. The overwhelming feedback received indicated the clip with the better audio track "looked better" to the subjects. Studies such as this one strongly suggest humans don't necessarily differentiate the sound content from the visual content. Because our visual senses are less subliminal and more conscious, all of the accolades go to the video.

Note >> In a related study at the University of Toronto, two groups of psychology students were shown the same video segment of a car accident. One video contained the original audio from the recorded fender bender. The second group was exposed to a "treated" audio track with an additional sound of tires screeching and a louder *slam* for the collision. Ninety percent of the second group felt the oncoming car was "speeding," compared to only twenty percent in the first group.

At last check, Johnston was busy tweaking sound effects for Microsoft's highly anticipated *Flight Sim 2000* and the latest in the *Madness* series, *Midtown Madness*, due to be released sometime in 1999.

Pictured here is Matt Johnston recording golf sounds for Microsoft Golf 1998 Edition on Rialto Beach on the Olympic Peninsula in Washington State. He is holding a Neumann "Head" Binaural Microphone to capture nature noise as background sounds in the game. (Used with permission by Matthew Johnston)

Tim Larkin

Hands down, one of the best-sounding computer games in the history of the interactive entertainment industry is Red Orb/Cyan's *Riven: The Sequel to Myst*. Responsible for the majority of this exceptional audio design and editing was Tim Larkin, now with Sierra Studios' Yosemite Entertainment.

Along with Matt Johnston, Larkin believes game designers, generally speaking, don't realize the grave importance of sound in a game. "The tongue-in-cheek expression we use is that it's '50% of the experience, 10% of the bandwidth,'" jokes Larkin. In other words, he believes sound to be on par with the visual stimuli given during a game, but sound designers are usually not allotted more than a tenth of the CPU's power.

Larkin does believe this will change over time, and the ball has already started rolling. "Think about it—CD-ROM technology is only five years old, so multimedia is really only in its infancy. Compare that to the movie or TV industry, which has matured over time." Larkin says developers and publishers are starting to acknowledge the importance of audio in games, and even attributes the advancements in graphics. "Fortunately, graphic technology is getting better, so people will naturally want better sound, for balance."

There are two disciplines Larkin lives by as a sound engineer, and he passes on the following mandates to newcomers to the profession.

Get Creative

Larkin says he's all for purchasing library CDs (and he particularly likes the *Hollywood Edge* ones) but the key is *not* to use the stock sounds as is. This is a big no-no, according to Larkin. "Sound designers ought to get in the habit of creating something unique, by using a sound and by editing, processing, and blending it together with others."

For example, the trams in *Riven* (used to travel to the five islands) were created by a number of combined and edited sounds. First off, it started with a stock sound of the BART (Bay Area Rapid Transit), a fairly smooth-sounding electric train. After toying with the sound, a process wind effect was used over top, and then a rumble to simulate turbulence.

13

In total, the tram's audio effect took a full 24 tracks to get the right sound. (Used with permission by Cyan, Inc.)

Start Off with a Good Sound

Larkin points out it doesn't cost very much money to get your gear in order as an audio engineer, so there's very little excuse not to use high-quality sound in games—aside from dealing with bandwidth issues with the programmers! "Approach designing or editing sound for a game as if you were creating audio for a feature film," says Larkin. "You can buy a couple of stock CDs for $50 each to start, and the software is only a couple of hundred dollars now."

 Macintosh software packages such as Macromedia's Deck II and Digidesign's Pro Tools were used for all the sounds heard in *Riven*. Macromedia's Deck II was bought by BIAS (Berkley Integrated Audio Software) and is now known as BIAS Deck 2.6. For info on this product, see www. bias-inc.com. For Pro Tools info, drop by www.digidesign.com.

Larkin admits he often creates music and sound in games not for the gamers themselves, but for his peers. "I do it for other sound designers—people who would critique my work." He's currently working on Sierra's upcoming *Middle Earth*, based on the works of legendary fantasy writer J.R.R. Tolkien.

Chris Rippy, Ensemble Studios

Serving as sound director at Ensemble Studios, Chris Rippy has worked on the award-winning *Age of Empires*, *Age of Empires Expansion: The Rise of Rome*, and *Age of Empires 2: The Age of Kings*. Much of his helpful advice for new sound designers circles around the basics: understanding you're part of a bigger picture, knowing the advantages and limitations of your software and hardware, and gathering plenty of hands-on experience.

There are definitely a number of things to keep in mind when doing sound for games. I think the most important rule, and this goes for musicians, sound guys, artists, etc., is that the game is much more important than any one sound or "thing" that you're working on. In other words, if the sound gets in the way of the gaming experience, it's got to go. Secondly, it's very important to know your equipment inside and out. You'll make much better sounds, and make them much more efficiently, if you take the time to learn your software, your DAT, your mics, and anything else you might need. Finally, listen to everything. Listen to music, listen to water, listen to car doors, listen to feet, listen to cows breathing. The more you listen to the world around you, the better your sounds will be.

Rippy draws from his own experiences at Ensemble Studios to support his recommendations. First, there were several times where Rippy had to bite his lip and accept that the gameplay had priority over sounds he considered to be pretty cool:

> In *Age of Empires*, and in most games, we had to keep the size of the sound to a minimum (this is due to technical constraints, such as RAM availability and the speed at which the computer can play the sound). This immediately limits the length of the sounds that I can use, as well as the resolution of the sounds, so some of my ideas were quickly squashed. Other times, I've had sounds that I've liked a lot while developing them, only to have them annoy me (and my office pals) when placed in the game and played repetitively. Again, the game came first, and the sounds were pulled.

The second rule is contingent on how much time and effort is given to the sound engineer's tools. Recalls Rippy, "I know that when I first started using sound-editing tools like Sound Forge, I had a very narrow view of what they could do. But after spending many, many hours in them, I've learned my way around them, learned all of their tools, and learned their hotkeys. This just helps get things done faster, and your sounds will sound better."

The third and final piece of advice is more a way of life than a specific practice. For example, Rippy explains how the sound was achieved for the catapults in *Age of Empires*:

13

> That sound is pieced together from several different sources, most of which I don't recall. The recoil sound of the catapult arm slapping the crossbar is something I do remember, though. I made that sound by bending a wooden ruler on the edge of my desk, then I released one end so it would slap the desk repeatedly. I then manipulated it in the computer, and *ta da*—a catapult. If I hadn't remembered making that sound in elementary school, we might have had a really quiet catapult!

Now, every time you play Age of Empires, you'll remember that the catapult sound stemmed from Chris Rippy's delinquent class behavior!

Geoff Kirk, Humongous Entertainment

As sound designer and sound effects programmer, Geoff Kirk has waxed his talents on all of Humongous Entertainment's mega-successful kids' lines, such as the *Pajama Sam* series, the *Putt-Putt* series, the *Freddi Fish* series, and more. Kirk's work focuses on cartoon adventure games, and, naturally, his advice on sound effects and music follows suit. "I would recommend watching cartoons," says Kirk. He elaborates:

> The greatest preparation for what I'm doing today was the time spent when I was very young watching cartoons, especially the old Warner Brothers' Bugs Bunny. They used music as a sound effect in a way that's still rather revolutionary. The background music on those old cartoons is also very cool and ahead of its time.

If you're looking for TV cartoons' influence in some of Kirk's work, look no further than the first *Pajama Sam*, dubbed *Pajama Sam in There's No Need to Hide When It's Dark Outside*:

> Some things just seem funny to me and I'll try them and see how they work. For instance, there was a bush in the first *Pajama Sam* game that, when clicked on, slapped its leaves together. After I looked at this for a while, it seemed to me it would be funny if it had a seal's bark/fin-slapping sound, since it sort of looked like a seal to me.

Kirk also attributes his wacky effects in Humongous titles as merely "messing around" with various sounds. That is, recording something and then changing the pitch by an extreme amount, and then mixing it with something else. "Animal growls and roars are quite commonly used in this fashion these days," says Kirk.

Pajama Sam was designed to be like an interactive cartoon, so the sound effects created by Geoff Kirk borrowed from good ol' Saturday morning inspiration.

 Tip >> Suggestions from Westwood Studios' sound designers also encourage experimentation and the use of unusual sounds. They claim it's often better to use something that doesn't sound "real," but rather sounds like an exaggeration of what's real. Real audio tracks tend to lack the impact of beefed-up sounds—a trend you can attribute to the movie and TV industry.

However, not all sounds are created out of this kind of experimentation:

> Some [effects] are based on the art that's drawn. For instance, if there's an elaborate background scene with many machines and so on, then we'll add a lot of background sound of printing presses or sorting machines mixed together. If they don't already have the room ambience of a large room or [manufacturing] plant, then [we'll try to simulate that] with the use of reverbs or delays.

Kirk recommends that sound engineers spend time learning the ins and outs of reputable sound-editing programs, such as Syntrillium Software's Cool Edit Pro (www.syntrillium.com) or Sonic Foundry's Sound Forge (www.sonicfoundry.com), and perhaps learning to program a synthesizer of some kind.

13

Kelly Bailey, Valve Software

Half-Life was nominated for the "Best Sound in a Game" award in Gamespot's "Best of 1998" feature (www.gamespot.com/features/awards1998). The reason? For a development company's debut title, *Half-Life* enjoyed some of the best sound design and sound programming the business has seen (or heard, for that matter). This is all thanks to Kelly Bailey, who was also responsible for the music in the game. So what's the secret to creating such incredible sound?

Work with the Other Engineers

According to Bailey, working very closely with the engineers who are placing the sounds in the game is critical:

> Working directly with the engineers who were adding the sound code to monsters, characters, and weapons turned out to be a very positive advantage. I was often able to construct a set of sounds, give it to the engineer (okay, who was sometimes me!) and hear the result directly in the game within a few minutes. This let me quickly determine whether or not the sounds were working for the weapon or monster, and provide quick feedback on volume levels, pitch, frequency of playback, etc. Having that fast turnaround time on hearing sounds in the game was a great benefit, and saved me a ton of time.

Get Creative and Use Different Sources

The second pointer is using a creative mix of recorded and synthesized sounds, to bring sounds to life in the game environment. Says Bailey:

> I found that some recorded sounds, such as footsteps or bouncing shell casings, translated very well directly in the game. But often I found that I needed to augment certain sounds or portions of sounds to liven them up in the game environment. For instance, direct, cleanly recorded gunfire or explosions often translated as a quick sharp "pop" on anything but the most high-end playback system. In order to give the gunfire a more visceral quality, I would often mix in low frequency synth information, or mix several attack transients together, or compress and distort to increase apparent loudness by broadening their frequency spectrums.
>
> Overall, I found I needed to do a lot of mixing and massaging of the original recordings to give them a more aggressive or exciting quality. Playing back sound effects on a wide variety of PC speaker systems, with and without sub-woofers, was also very important to achieving equalization that translated well to a wide audience. Mixing and constructing sounds on just one set of speakers or headphones can lead to nasty surprises; you don't want the guy down the hall to start raging about his distorting subwoofer.

Test the Sounds—Repeatedly

The third piece of advice from Bailey is "letting sounds sit in the game for a period of play-testing time before calling them 'final.'" Here's an example:

While playing a complete game for 20 or more hours, a player may listen to a particular sound effect thousands of times. It was really important to me to make sure we didn't include sounds that became accidentally grating or annoying after repeat listening. To help with this, many of our sounds are actually mixed and modified pseudo-randomly on playback. For instance, we may slightly change the pitch of a sound each time it's played, or swap in a slightly different version of the sound effect, or mix together two component sounds in different ways to come up with a single sound. Although a lot of this work is done with code, I reworked the effects for most of the frequently played sounds (such as gunfire) up to five times before settling on a final version. It helped to quickly get a sound into the game and have people live with it for a number of days. After a week of listening to a sound coming out of other offices down the hall, you develop a surprising awareness of what's working and what isn't.

Also, try to pay attention to sounds that get people excited while they're playing the game. It's easy to get too used to your own sounds, so relying on the consensus of other people around you can really point out trouble sounds, and also help guide you toward the kinds of sounds people want to hear more of.

Kevin Schilder, Raven Software

Kevin Schilder is the manager of the audio department at Raven Software in Madison, Wisconsin. He is half of a team that concentrates solely on sound design, music composition, and audio production for their games. Past credits include *Heretic I* and *II*, *Hexen I* and *II*, and *Mageslayer*, to name a few.

With over 30 years experience under his belt, Schilder closes off this chapter with the following three commandments for becoming a successful sound designer at a game company:

13

Think Creatively

When I first began using sampled sound effects, I realized the title on the CD often didn't correspond to the way I used it. If I need to make the sound of a large door closing, I may find that the recording of an actual door doesn't work as well as the sound of an explosion with some creative processing. You have to envision the sound you're looking for and then consider all possibilities for creating that sound.

Exaggerate for Effect

In the action games I've worked on, the sound effects must be bigger than life. It isn't enough to make a flaming arrow sound like a real arrow firing with a campfire sound attached. That thing has to sound like a cruise missile and shake your speakers!

Watch Your Processing

Process sounds carefully. I have heard some people make nice sound effects but have them clip off too soon at the end. A little mistake takes away the realism.

CHAPTER **14**

Music and Games

No other segment of the entertainment industry welcomes as many different talents and specialties as does the gaming industry. Where else can writers, programmers, artists, animators, sound engineers, and musicians all work together as a team for one single product? This is one of the key reasons why this young industry is so exciting. And the opportunities are virtually endless!

Fortunately, developers of PCs and console gaming titles are slowly recognizing the importance of a good musical soundtrack, and more effort and financial resources than ever before are being poured into music. Sure, it's still a tiny piece of the overall pie when compared to the money spent on graphics (and licensing, where applicable), but it's a growing field, and the top musicians in the gaming industry are able to make a good living. Sure beats playing seedy bars or giving it up for a day job, no?

Let's take a look at the top musicians in the business and what advice they can give to those looking to break into the gaming industry.

Chance Thomas, Yosemite Entertainment

Chance Thomas is a senior music producer at Sierra's Yosemite Entertainment studio in Oakhurst, California. Along with creating orchestral scores, rock singles, and independently released game soundtrack CDs, he's also lobbying for game music to be considered as a new category at the Grammy Awards.

The ideal way to preface Thomas' advice is to read from the liner notes of Sierra's *Quest for Glory V* soundtrack. He writes:

> Music is mysterious, elusive, familiar, capricious.… It's like a language we knew before our birth, its intimacy both surprising and obvious in turn. Writing music seems to be a tussled balance of discovery and ingenuity, of sheer will and catalyzed coincidence. The composer forages, struggles, demands, coaxes, curses, and finally relents. And often in the quiet humility of surrender, the muse comes out of her hiding place, satisfied that our best efforts have sufficiently softened the soul. She speaks to us from the inside out, triggering emotions so subtle and profound, as her voice finds an inevitable path to the surface.

First on Thomas' list for budding game musicians, and for new game designers who may be looking for musicians, is placing a priority on the *quality* of the game music. Says Thomas:

> Get the highest quality music you can. Our ears are trained to expect sonic excellence through our exposure to films, television shows, and our favorite albums. If the player ever has to make a mental downshift, "Oh well, this is just game music…" then an entire level of impact has just been obliterated. Music loses impact as it loses credibility.

If time permits and it's financially feasible, Thomas also recommends using real instruments, rather than synthesized ones:

> No amount of technology can ever overcome poor source material. There's no "emotion fader" on a mixing console. That's why more and more of us are proponents of hiring real, living, feeling, passionate professional musicians to play as much music as we can possibly afford. There's nothing like capturing a brilliant performance of red-hot musicians pouring their feelings into fine acoustic instruments to give you emotionally stirring source material to work with.

Because we're used to hearing professionally recorded music with film and TV sound-tracks, says Chance Thomas, if the music in a game is recorded in poor quality, its impact will be lessened con-siderably. (Used with permission by Chance Thomas)

Thomas' recorded works are filled with this approach. As an example, he used a 36-piece orchestra and then a 32-piece orchestra for various sections of the *Quest for Glory V* soundtrack: "We recorded two passes on every track—recording multiple takes in each instance until we got the magic one—to create the sound of a 72- and 64-piece orchestra, respectively. I wish you could listen to the difference between the synthesized version and the live version of each. No comparison."

Okay, so *most* game musicians don't have a full orchestra accessible to them. Understood. "The point is, if you want to make a BIG emotional impact, you'd better pay BIG attention to your music," asserts Thomas. "George Lucas said 'Sound is half the movie-going experience.' Please keep that in mind as you consider the role of music in your games."

So when exactly should a game musician get involved in the development cycle? As early as possible, says Thomas:

> There is an amazing synergy that's only possible with early and ongoing involvement. I've written pieces of music early in development that inspired entirely new sections of a game. Having music in place can assist voice actors in delivering a more powerful and dynamic performance. Not to men-tion the raw enthusiasm that a great tune or score can generate with the cre-ative people on a team.

14

Quest for Glory V was Sierra's first live orchestral score. "Firsts" like this help to draw attention to a product; by the time this game was on retail shelves, there were over 40 different articles focusing on the music alone. (Used with permission by Chance Thomas)

Music is the language of emotion. It speaks to us in ways that words and images can never express. Thomas proposes to ask yourself, "What do I want a player to *feel* in this game? And if the composer is worth his salt, the score will induce that emotion."

George "The Fat Man" Sanger

George Alistair Sanger, a.k.a. The Fat Man, has been composing music for games since 1983. Along with Team Fat, his legendary team of three other cowboy composers, he is internationally recognized for having created music for more than 130 games, including *Wing Commander I* and *II*, *The 7th Guest I* and *II*, *NASCAR Racing*, *Putt-Putt Saves the Zoo*, *Tanarus*, and *ATF*.

Throughout our lengthy telephone interview on creating game music for a living, the conversation continuously boils down to one factor: passion. To The Fat Man, whatever makes you get up in the middle of the night and say "Yes!" is what you should be doing for a living.

> If you don't like a lot of games and a lot of music, get out. In fact, you have to love games—not just *love* games, but LOVE games. You don't go to try to make it in Hollywood if you don't watch movies, do you? When something is really speaking to you, do it—whether it be making scads of money or making music for games. Love it even if you fail. Whenever you're making a game or music for a game, do it because you love it, not for someone else. Just forget whoever else may like it. Also, don't make decisions entirely on intellect. Balance that with info from your heart, and if it adds richness to your life, you're in the right business. You must follow your heart, your passion, your bliss.

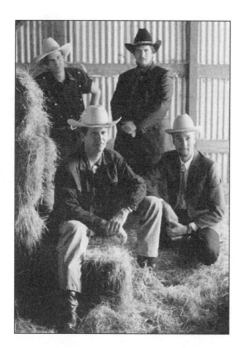

Team Fat: Clockwise from top left are "Ramrod" Joe McDermott, David Govett, "Professor" K. Weston Phelan and George "The Fat Man" Sanger. (Photo courtesy of Spanki Avallone, Avallone Media)

Like Chance Thomas, The Fat Man recognizes that music is usually not a priority to larger developers, and believes the amount a company is willing to invest in the music is directly proportional to the quality and "wow" factor. "If you put 1% of your resources (i.e., money and time) in a game's music soundtrack, it will be good. At 3%, it's almost guaranteed… to get results where people will walk away and say the music is 'awesome,'" says The Fat Man.

But how should a game designer go about finding music for his/her game? The Fat Man urges you to work with people you know and trust at first, and be up-front about the project:

> If you are looking for people to create music for your game, be entirely honest with anyone you deal with, and give them whatever money you can afford—or a percentage of the game's revenue. Just give them something to start… even if it's just lunch. Go to your friends and find out if they are as motivated as you are.

Obviously, you can't have it all if you're just starting out. The Fat Man reminds new game designers that, "[…]as with most specialists in their respective fields, if they have no experience, it will be less money, but more hassle. On the flip side, the more experience [you] have, the more money it will cost you, but with less hassle."

14

Assuming you're the musician here, and not a game designer looking for a musician, what kind of equipment do you need? According to The Fat Man, whatever recording gear you have right now, and a good PC, is all you need to start off. "Just find a way of getting music into the PC via a [Sound Blaster] AWE 64 or Live! card or any other cards that have a good input, and a stereo one if possible. Then you'll need a CD burner or DAT (digital audio tape) to record WAV files." Once the music is recorded, it can be submitted to a game company for evaluation.

 Tip >> The Fat Man hosts an annual Game Music Demo Marathon at the Game Developers Conference (GDC) in the early spring of each year. Ninety-second demos are accepted in the following formats (in order of preference):

- CD-ROM (PC format, 44.1 16-bit stereo .WAV)
- Audio CD
- DAT
- Standard audiocassette

If you want to get into the industry, this is a great way to start. The Fat Man's official Web site (www.fatman.com) has the complete rules, entry information, and CDs from past years.

The Fat Man also hosts an annual convention, known as "Project Bar-B-Q," dedicated to improving the production quality of music on computer and computer products. Information on attending can be found at his Web site.

In conclusion, The Fat Man reminds us that music is a contributing piece of the overall gaming experience, and as with many other art forms—poetry, music, visual arts—it's all about going beyond the power of words to express something in your heart. Yes, even if it's as simple as, "It's fun to kill stuff," The Fat Man concedes with a smile.

> Gaming is souls recognizing each other without relying on language. A relationship between the designer and the gamer. It's a deep connection that is beyond description.

Tommy Tallarico

Tommy Tallarico has worked on more than 140 games during his illustrious career. Some of the more well-known games (selling in excess of 25 million copies combined) include *Prince of Persia*, *The Terminator*, *Cool Spot*, *Aladdin*, *Earthworm Jim 1* and *2*, *MDK*, *Wild 9*, and *Test Drive 4* and *5*.

Tallarico coments on how important music is to the overall gaming experience:

> I truly believe music is 25% of the gaming experience. For the most part there are four parts of a game: *art*, which provides you with your graphics,

visuals, animations, etc.; *programming*, which is the way the game moves, interfaces, acts, etc.; *design*, which is the level layout, fun factor, presentation, etc. And *audio*, which can set a mood, accent a motion, and pretty much set the emotion for the scene/level. For example, you could have a scene where a character runs up to a huge cliff and slowly looks over it to reveal miles and miles of scenery. Depending on what the audio is doing is how the player is going to react to that circumstance. If the music is haunting or scary, it may seem like you're getting chased and you're trapped; if it's beautiful and epic, it will give you the sense of beauty and accomplishment. Oh yeah, and if it's country music, you'll want to turn the game off and shoot yourself in the head.

When asked what is the key to creating a successful video game soundtrack, Tallarico says what has worked for him is trying to create something different, and he provides a number of examples:

All the soundtracks I've won awards on had one thing in common. It was the first time anyone had heard music like that in games before. For example, in *Global Gladiators* I used samples triggered in the music (drums, guitar hits, orchestra hits, voice, etc.) to create a song. No one had really done that before to any extent on the Sega Genesis. They mostly used samples for speech. On *Terminator* for the Sega-CD, it was the first time anyone had heard live guitars and real rock music in a game. In *Skeleton Warriors*, it was huge 95-piece orchestral stuff. *Treasures of the Deep* had tons of acoustic guitars and things. In the *Wild 9* soundtrack, I took the beats and rhythms from techno and/or industrial music, but combined it with orchestras and guitars. The beats are great for flow, but the orchestra and guitars are perfect for power and melody. It's like creating a new style of music! Uniqueness is the key to writing great music for games, and I think the secret is to do something that no one has done yet—and probably the most fun part of what I do.

Chance Thomas mentioned that it can be quite helpful for both the musician and the game designer to get involved in creating music early on in the development cycle. But Tallarico says what commonly happens with him is that he gets the game much later on down the road. It's much later in the game's cycle before he plays the game (with no sound). Then he waits for the inspiration to hit him. He continues, "Then I go into my studio (upstairs) and figure out the notes on the keyboard that were dancing around in my head seconds before." If the game or level isn't complete, Tallarico may work off a storyboard.

14

This sketch pad from Tommy Tallarico shows the varied music styles planned for the different themes of Cool Spot 3: pirate world, horror world, sci-fi world, adventure world, and so on. (Used with permission by Tommy Tallarico)

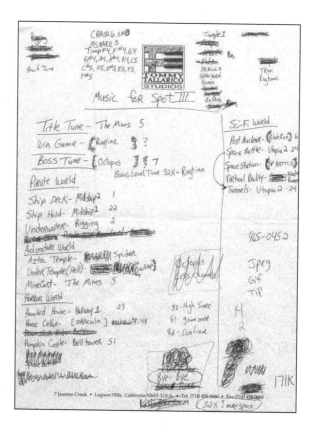

As far as style of music is concerned, every company is different. There have been instances when developers have approached Tallarico with a clear vision (e.g. "Can we have the rhythm section of Prodigy, the sounds of The Chemical Brothers, the feel of Nine Inch Nails? Oh yeah, and the guitar sound of Waylon Jennings?"), but most of the time they leave it up to him to see what fits.

For example, in *Earthworm Jim*, Tallarico would play the game with no sound. In the first bonus level, Jim and Psycrow would be racing each other on rockets, and every time he played this portion of the game, it always looked like they were riding horses. "I kept hearing a country banjo-type thing, so I went with it," says Tallarico. In other levels, he would watch the way Jim moved or ran, and he would come up with rhythms based around that. And the environment itself plays a role, too: "For example, ambient or slower-type music always works well in darker areas."

The last portion of the interview focuses on what a budding game musician should be using for equipment and how exactly to break into the industry.

On key gear:

> Any kind of sampler is good (Roland, Akai, etc.) because it provides the stand-alone musician with lots of diverse and acoustic sounds. With a CD-ROM hooked up to your sampler, you have an almost unlimited supply of hundreds of thousands of new and unique sounds. For a sound designer or sound effects guy, you should have a fast Mac with some good sound-editing software like Sound Edit Pro, Alchemy, Digital Performer, etc. For the PC diehard, Sound Forge is the way to go.

On getting in the door:

> The best thing to do is put together a demo tape with three or four of your best two- or three-minute tunes and send it to every publisher and developer in the industry. You can easily find lists of names and addresses on the Internet. The most effective way, however, is to go to either the Game Developers Conference or the Electronic Entertainment Exposition (E3). There is where you will personally meet designers, producers, VPs, and so forth. I've found it's always better to talk to someone in person than to just send out tapes.

Look for Tommy Tallarico's music on the upcoming *Tomorrow Never Dies*, *Messiah*, and *Pac-Man 3-D* game soundtracks.

Tommy "The King" Tallarico says it's key for musicians to make it to events such as E3 or GDC to strut your stuff. Thank you, thank you very much. (Used with permission by Tommy Tallarico)

14

Bobby Prince

You may not have heard his name, but if you're a 3D shooter fanatic, chances are you've hummed his music in the shower many times. Bobby Prince is a composer and sound designer who has worked on such groundbreaking titles as *Wolfenstein 3D*, *Doom*, *Doom II*, and *Duke Nukem 3D*. He's best known for his melodic MIDI tunes. In fact, you can hear many of these instant classics at his Web site, www.bpmusic.com.

Prince usually gets involved early on in the development cycle. "In *Commander Keen*, my first game, the music was written long before the game was playable. I saw static art-work of the game's characters and had been told about what the game was expected to include. This was mostly true of all the games I have worked on up to *Duke Nukem 3D*."

Prince had the opportunity to plug in music and sound effects for the first time and try them out within a working game environment. "Even *Doom* required that I ask a pro-grammer to recompile the game with prospective music/sound effects. This took a good bit of time and didn't allow quick-and-dirty tweaks," Prince recalls.

Prince believes it's possible to write appropriate music without seeing the game first if there's a good explanation of the characters and story of a game. Besides, it has been Prince's experience thus far that the story and characters will change several times before the project is finalized. "This is a great part of the fun and excitement in the game indus-try. It's a lot like early Hollywood—that is, tools of the trade are still being standardized and the middlemen still don't have a handle on things."

Dozens of Bobby Prince's MIDI songs are available at his Web site. Note that the b and p in his logo are half notes. (Used with permission by Bobby Prince)

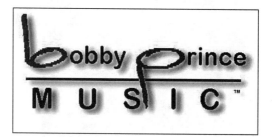

Bobby Prince is kind enough to share his top three pieces of advice for musicians look-ing to excel in the gaming industry:

1. "Computer chops" on the part of the musician are at least a big plus. For the most part, composing music for games is not a cut-and-dried, "deliver the music in X format and collect a check" business. This is especially true of MIDI music. Many times, I have had to debug code by writing sequences that tested the MIDI

playback engine. On one occasion, the engine was removing note information and leaving less important data.

2. Communication. Be prepared to tutor non-musicians in all aspects of computer sound. Producers and programmers are generally a smart bunch, but, like the general public, they lack an understanding of the basics. There are those who will request digital music (audio CD or "Redbook") when the game leaves insufficient room on the game CD for it. It's also important to learn what non-musicians' music terminology actually means. I have had several occasions where I was requested to change the volume of the music, when it was actually the tone (equalization) that needed changing. I have also had cases where instrument names were confused.

3. Don't wait for a gig to start writing music. Luck is usually being ready for an opportunity when it hits. Before the opportunity hit me, I spent many, many nights writing music and learning the tools.

So what kind of tools are we looking at here? According to Prince, MIDI music players can successfully record music with the following equipment: a decent computer, basic sequencing software, a wavetable soundcard with the MIDI kit, a MIDI keyboard, speakers, and headphones. For digital audio, add digital recording/editing/effect software and some type of digital recording device for mastering (DAT, CD recorder, etc.). Any other equipment is nice and probably makes things easier, but it isn't required.

Michael Land, LucasArts

As sound department manager and a member of the music team at one of the hottest developers/publishers in the gaming business, Michael Land has composed music for a number of hit titles over the years: the *Monkey Island* series, *X-Wing*, *TIE Fighter*, *The Dig*, and *Day of the Tentacle*, to name a few. Asked what three most critical things a game musician should remember, the following words are Land's insightful response:

Play the Game

This one is fairly obvious, but it's easy to cut corners on it if you're in a hurry and you think of the "cue list" as your blueprint. Remember that whoever came up with that list was probably not a composer. While cue lists with descriptions are a great way to start, there's no substitute for actually playing the game yourself. Even looking over someone else's shoulder, while much better than not seeing the game at all, is not nearly as effective as actually getting in there and feeling the flow of the interactivity. Not only might you see ways to improve the cue list to better reflect the game's interactive structure, but more importantly, that experience of feeling the game yourself gives

14

you an intangible edge in sensing what kind of music to write to enhance the player's experience. And as your music starts getting coded into the game, go back and play it again and see how it's working. You can often learn more about how to improve the music in that one moment than you could ever figure out by working on the music alone.

The Audience Is a "Player," Not a "Listener" or "Viewer"

You're writing music to accompany an interactive experience, so no matter how good the music is, you have to make sure it translates well to the non-linear world of interactivity. Things like repetition, loop structures, transitions, and other issues unique to interactive music can either be seen as hassles or opportunities. Your music will end up working much better if you approach these "problems" as an artistic challenge, where the goal is not simply to deal with them, but to unlock their potential to leverage the unique power of interactivity. Start by diagramming out how every piece connects to every other piece. Then, as you write each piece, make sure to keep in mind how it will flow in and out of the neighboring pieces.

Know Your Delivery Technology

Make sure you have a good grasp of what the game's music and sound engine can and can't do, and find out what you'll be allowed to ship in terms of data format, resolution, disk space, etc. There are lots of variables in the technical domain, and most of them have some impact on your artistic options. Not all of these variables are cast in stone at the beginning of a project, so the sooner and deeper you get involved in the technical questions, the more influence you can have on how things turn out. The most obvious question is hard to miss (i.e., will the music be MIDI, Redbook, DLS, streamed audio, etc.?). But within each of these options is an entire tree of sub-questions that get increasingly more detailed (okay, maybe not for Redbook). The more you examine that tree, the more you'll be able to use the cool features and avoid the "gotchas" for whatever technology you'll be using.

Asked to discuss the inspiration behind some of his classic LucasArts soundtracks, and why LucasArts puts such an emphasis on music compared to many other game companies, Land responds:

The inspiration for the classic LucasArts soundtracks comes from several sources. Not in any particular order, these include the great stories and wonderful characters in the games, affinity for classic films and film music, the creative and thought-provoking insights of LucasArts game designers, deep love of many styles of music, and the collaborative and competitive aspects of three composers working closely together for almost 10 years.

Kelly Bailey, Valve Software

Kelly Bailey was responsible for all the music and sound effects in the mega-hit *Half-Life*. He also wrote the code to allow characters to speak, and he implemented the software system that provides reverb and echo effects.

In the following paragraphs, Bailey takes some time to explain what he feels is critical for budding game musicians to remember, and draws from his own personal experiences while working on *Half-Life*.

What's the Mood?

The first rule, says Bailey, is to create the music to match the mood of the game design:

> One of the challenges I faced in constructing the *Half-Life* soundtrack was to make music that consistently reinforced the central mood of the game. *Half-Life* has a strong action/horror theme, and it was important to me to try to convey this in the music. I found that it was really important to continually keep in mind the kind of music I was trying to make, and be very intentional about musical choices. Limiting my choices to action and horror moods definitely helped me move forward in the studio, and not get too lost in the jungle of sound selection and construction. Sometimes, after letting a finished track sit for a week or so, I would return to it and discover that it just didn't quite fit with the mood of the game. I would either rework it or discard the track and move on to a new track. It's hard to decide to discard a track just because it doesn't quite fit with the mood [of the] game, but for me, trying to be my own best critic helped a great deal in keeping a consistent feel to the *Half-Life* tracks.
>
> I also found that composing for a game meant that, in our case, the tracks needed to stay between 30 seconds and 2 minutes in length due to space limitations on the CD. This was a constant challenge, and required a good deal of discipline and planning to accomplish.

14

For Valve Software's Kelly Bailey, the first rule is to write music that tightly fits the mood of the game. Half-Life was filled with primarily two themes: action and horror. (Used with permission by Sierra Studios)

A Comfortable Workplace

Number two on the list is to "have a great place to write, create, and experiment with soundscapes and ideas—and be able to return to the work after letting it sit for a while," says Bailey.

> It was important to me to be able to work on the soundtrack in a very comfortable environment. I updated my soundproof recording studio at home and populated it with a collection of analog and digital synths, samplers, a good-quality computer hard disk recorder, a very clean 8-bus mixer, some pro-level balanced outboard effects processors, and a number of "real" instruments such as guitar, drums, flute, and bass. Being able to work on music any hour of the day or night allowed me to stay productive in the studio, whether I was trying to construct an experimental soundscape late at night, or cleaning up and mixing down tracks earlier in the day. Later in the project, under fairly critical time pressure, having a studio at home that enabled me to keep flexible hours was a lifesaver.

Working Under Pressure

The third and final piece of advice from Bailey is to learn quickly how to produce under time and quality pressure:

> Being able to produce music under time pressure was surprisingly important. I had originally planned on having several months to finalize the last 10 tracks—but I was wrong! I ended up working up to 18 hours each day doing game design during the final 5 months of the project, and had to finish the music in my "off hours." By having a studio at home that I was very familiar with, and being disciplined about sticking to my creative process, I managed to get through it. Near the end of the project, I worked on many tracks

simultaneously, which really helped keep my hours in the studio productive. If I was stuck, or just "too close" to a track, I could switch quickly to a different track and keep moving forward. It was also super important to be able to let tracks sit for several days before returning to work on them. This let me keep checking with fresh ears to make sure I was staying close to that action/horror theme.

Bailey is currently writing more music and creating new sound effects for Valve's *Team Fortress 2*.

Haiko Ruttmann, Blue Byte Software

Continuing our roundtable discussion on game music is Blue Byte's hardworking Haiko Ruttmann. This resident of Germany is responsible for composing and recording every Blue Byte PC game soundtrack, as well as creating sound effects and producing voiceover recordings.

Ruttmann's advice for newbies is straightforward and practical. He warns, "If you want to start developing music for computer games, you will need more than one favorite kind of music. There might be a game that will require R&B or another one that will need an orchestral soundtrack."

Logically, as much information about the game as possible should be known before a musician can start composing the soundtrack. Says Ruttmann, "You have to look to the concept, the idea of the game. Is it a run-and-jump game or a strategic game? Is it science fiction, horror, or sports-related? If you have the information, listen to other soundtracks (film or game), watch TV, go to the theater or read books, talk to people, and play your instrument(s)."

Settlers III featured a number of cultural themes throughout the game, such as Roman, Asian, and Egyptian worlds. Naturally, the music reflects the cultures of each. (Used with permission by Blue Byte Software)

14

The next step, according to Ruttmann, is to create demo files of your work and talk about them with your project manager. "Typically, I start to compose music by playing chords on my piano or keyboard, just to get the score into the computer. On the sequencer I can arrange the melodies—themes with different instruments and effects—by adding strings, brass, woodwinds, etc. For *Incubation*, I mixed natural sounds, animals, and some technical effects with orchestral themes, and voilà!"

Ellen Meijers-Gabriel, Oddworld Inhabitants

As composer/sound designer at Oddworld Inhabitants, Ellen Meijers-Gabriel has written music and designed sound effects for both of the development studios' products: *Oddworld: Abe's Oddysee* and *Oddworld: Abe's Exoddus*. Meijers-Gabriel says there are a number of important rules to keep in mind for game musicians:

> First is to have a solid setup and to know how to use your equipment when starting out. Know your tools and the limits of the platforms you're dealing with, so you don't have to make major changes to your setup during projects. It's also good to be organized and to archive your work.

> Try to get as much information as possible about the game that you're about to work on. If you're working on the music while the game is being developed, you can start with storyboard images and watch videos of the game as it comes along. Eventually, when the game is close to finishing, you'll be able to play the game yourself, but by that time your work should be close to finishing as well. If you start writing the music after the game has been finished, you'll have the advantage of being able to see the complete product that you're writing the music for, but in this case it's likely that you'll have less time to work with. One of the advantages of working simultaneously with the development of the game is that you'll get the chance to try things out and sometimes even to change the outcome of the game.

> In writing the music, try to be inventive, break boundaries. Instead of thinking about the individual pieces, I like to think of the game as an interactive piece of music rather than just a series of linear songs. The type of music you write for a game depends on the people behind the creation of the game, and on the game itself. After having spoken to the people who created the game, you should have a good idea of the style of music they're interested in for that specific game. After that, you'll write something in that style while trying to match the action in the game as much as possible.

When the music you've created represents the feeling of each level and character in the game, and it enhances the experience of playing the game, you know you've done a good job.

➤ Andrew Barnabas runs a resourceful mailing list on the Internet. He says the following about this organization: "The VGM (Video Game Musician) mailing list is open to anyone who works professionally within the audio side of the games industry. Currently we're just over 100 members, covering the majority of the big software companies and a hefty wad of freelancers. The aim was to get musicians to communicate with each other (rather than being the hermits that I was used to). It was just a stupid idea I came up with because I was fed up with fielding questions from other musos (being the sociable type, I just phoned all these people up), and tried to get them all to talk to each other. We also have a Web-based FTP area on the free drive for musicians to upload music.

"The topics we cover vary from discussions concerning the upcoming developments in interactive audio [to] differing surround formats and musical styles to 'Why can't I link up two O2Rs, and tell me a PC audio card that can sync to a 44.1k word clock!' Over the last few months, it has attracted a great deal of interest from hardware manufacturers and non-game software developers (Microsoft, Creative Labs, Cirrus Logic, Dolby) and has gotten the blessing and interest from various meetings at the CGDC and Fat Man's BBQ. I also know of people who have gotten work directly from the list!

"Currently it's based here where I work (Sony Computer Entertainment, Cambridge, UK— we just did *Medievil*, if you saw that). If anyone is interested in joining, they should send me a mail here at work at barney@scee.sony.co.uk, or, if that fails, try my home email address—bar.ney@dial.pipex.com. My only stipulation for joining is that members (assuming they meet the criteria) write a paragraph or two about themselves, covering what they do, what they do it with, and who they do it for."

14

SECTION III

Post-Production

CHAPTER **15**

Testing

It has been mentioned innumerable times throughout this book that play testing a game is an extremely critical process that must be performed thoroughly before a product's release. So why then are there so many bugs in computer games? Why does it seem there are multiple patches for each game these days? Are designers getting lazy in this department, or are they taking advantage of the Internet as an effective distribution method for patches?

Well, there's a number of reasons for this. First and foremost, developing a computer game is not like developing a game for a console platform, where the end user is playing the game on a fixed piece of hardware. That is, all the millions of PlayStations, Dreamcasts, and Nintendo 64s are built the same (though the software may vary for a geographic area, such as North America, Asia, or Europe).

With computers, very rarely do you find two gamers with the same setup. If you think about it for a moment, there are literally thousands of combinations of software and hardware, making it extremely difficult for a game to work smoothly on all systems. Thus, designing a game for a PC is like trying to hit a moving target.

Secondly, game companies are big business. If a product misses its shipment date, it loses money (especially during the profitable holiday season), and since many large game publishers are public, they must disclose quarterly fiscal results. One bad quarter may have an extremely adverse effect on the company's stock value. For this reason, on top of marketing commitments with various publications and distribution commitments with various retailers, many games are prematurely shipped out the door with the attitude of "We'll have a patch up on the Internet within a couple of weeks." What game publishers are starting to understand is that a gamer who is dissatisfied with a company's product may not purchase from them again.

Note >> According to *PC Data* video game report coordinator Matt Gravett, over 30% of console games and over 25% of computer games are sold during the month of December each year. The unfortunate reality is that many computer gaming publishers will prematurely ship their games to be on store shelves during this time.

It seems there are many ways for companies to test for bugs and compatibility issues for games, as we'll see in this chapter, but generally speaking there are two kinds of game testing:

- Although it varies from company to company, *beta testing* is an incremental procedure handled internally at the development studio or publishing house, and in some cases distributed to volunteer consumers in the gaming community in exchange for feedback. It usually begins semi-formally when the game is in late alpha/early beta stage, hence the name.

- *Quality assurance (QA) testing* is typically performed by outsiders in a proper testing environment and is usually administered toward the end of the game's development cycle. Bug reports and any other queries/beefs or comments are submitted for evaluation prior to the game's release. Then, after a game has shipped, technical support staff begins submitting user complaints (plus, developers read newsgroup postings and Web site forums), and a list of fixes will be collected and organized for the first patch. Keep in mind that in some cases the patches are fully justified, such as when a new 3D video or audio card is introduced after the game has been released.

This chapter concentrates on how to properly test your game throughout its development, with suggestions from a number of reputable companies: Acclaim Entertainment, Electronic Arts, Psygnosis, Interplay, Firaxis, Origin Systems, Humongous Entertainment, and Blue Byte.

Carol Caracciolo, Acclaim Entertainment

15

Carol Caracciolo is the quality assurance manager at Acclaim Entertainment in Glencove, New York. She has worked on many products, such as *Mortal Kombat II*, *Turok: Dinosaur Hunter*, *Quarterback Club*, *All-Star Baseball*, *NBA Jam*, *WWF: Raw*, *WWF: Warzone*, *Alien Trilogy*, *Revolution X*, and many more. She is currently maintaining a staff of approximately 75 employees over two full-time shifts, seven days a week!

Caracciolo says the most important rules to live by when testing a game are as follows: a) never let anyone talk you out of writing up your bug; b) always research before reporting; and c) verify, verify, verify.

But how hard is it to find someone whose job is to find *problems* in software? Are these gamers hard to find? Says Caracciolo:

> Finding testers is an easy process. You'll find that people who love games are driven in their passion; most times, they'll find you. The problem is sorting through the mountain of people who "love games" and finding the few who love them enough to spend 8 hours a day, 5 days a week for 4–6 months testing a game.

Caracciolo comments on how many people are needed during the quality assurance stage of a game, and how she ensures that her employees are reporting bugs properly:

> I find that a mixture of two temps to one full-timer is a good mix during crunch time. With a full-time staff of 20, I'll maintain up to 30 or 40 temps when the titles are coming in fast and furious.

> Ensuring quality testing with a group this large can be difficult; however, I have assembled a management staff of outstanding supervisors and lead analysts who guide them through the entire process and do some hand-holding for a probationary period. Over the years, we have culled all of the very best methods for approaching testing, with test plans and researching and reporting bugs. Spot checking bug sheets and databases always keeps everyone on target. We also require everyone to attend "re-training" classes periodically to keep fresh.

Are there any specific examples Caracciolo can pool from? She answers:

> The most recent product that changed our testing methodology was *Bust-A-Move*. This seems like a fairly innocuous title that could easily skate through the testing process. However, the amount of options in selecting a path

seemed endless. This forced us to take a hard look at how we approached the testing process and committed us to extensive pre-planning in the form of a test plan. This is essential not only for tracking a project through test, but is invaluable for projecting testing needs in terms of personnel and equipment.

Sean House, Electronic Arts

Asked whether how they test games at EA Sports is any different from the "norm," Sean House, associate producer at Electronic Arts, responds that it is, and for good reason:

> The only real way to test the sports games is at the end (the last three months or so). This is because the schedule is generally accelerated (development to ship date is one year). The programming team is generally working their asses off trying to get the features implemented that they signed up to implement; therefore, any bugs that testing may uncover during development will not get any attention. There isn't really any time to debug until the feature is nearly finished, or the programmer's list is nearly finished.

EA's Sean House says the testing process is a little different at EA because their development cycles are accelerated; they have only one year after the last version to get the new game out the door. This is a screen shot from Madden NFL '99. (Used with permission by Electronic Arts)

House recognizes that this isn't an ordinary situation and believes that ideally, incremental testing is the way to go:

> This allows testers the ability to spend many months testing a product, even if this means constantly switching areas of the game to be tested. The testers usually are able to work on one area for a while, then move on to something else, then back to the original area. This reduces burnout and increases productivity among the test staff, because it keeps the tasks fresh. This also can

make the debugging process much more efficient because usually many features are intertwined. A bug in one area can cause several in another; flushing out each feature as you go will lead to easier debugging down the road.

The differences between beta testing and quality assurance testing are explored by House as it pertains to EA Sports:

> In my experience, QA is done by a group of people at the company that get the product after the regular product-testing guys. They're the last line of defense before the product hits the market. The game that comes to them should arrive "bug free." They are to take the attitude of an end user and give feedback on functionality of the game, as well as find any bugs that may have gotten through. They're also in charge of verifying legal issues with the product (legal screens, license info, etc.). These guys are generally the same people who will handle customer support on the product, so they have a definite stake in the quality of the product. The worse it is, the more work they have to do in supporting it.
>
> Beta testing is when you release a product that's in beta form (nearly complete, very few bugs remaining) to the public or select members of the public, and they play the game, giving feedback on issues or bugs that they find while playing the game. This is done to dramatically increase the number of eyes on the product in a short period of time, in an effort to quickly clear up any last-minute problems. We don't use beta testing on any of the products I've worked on here at EA. We do, however, use regular product testing, and this generally starts a month or so before the alpha stage (all major features are in the game, although buggy) and continues throughout the remaining development life of the product (ship).
>
> Both product testing and QA are important to the success of any software product, in my opinion. The two groups tend to balance each other out. Often, especially near the end of a project, many of the testers become fairly burned out (from working 16-hour days for too long), and it's easy to miss some obvious things. QA is there and fresh to find these issues. Also, their strength is in representing the end user, and because they're fresh and haven't been associated with the product until the end, they're able to give a good, objective view of the product.

House says he can recall a good example from his professional past on the importance of both kinds of testing. Here is the anecdote in its entirety:

> Five years ago, I was working as a product tester at Media Vision in Fremont, California. We were working on a few different multimedia titles.

We had one product that was slated for release and needed to be final on the 26th of December. The product was almost done on the 23rd, and none of us wanted to work on the 25th, so we worked straight through from the 23rd through 6 a.m. Christmas day. Well, needless to say, we were all very burnt, and were getting pretty sloppy. The product was a floppy product. We got the last version of it at 3 a.m. on the 25th, and I was told to make copies and give them to everyone. There was one last bug that we needed to verify whether it was fixed or not, so I did it quickly once before distributing the disks to the others. It required that you enter your name and company info during installation. When prompted for the name/company during installation, I entered "coitus interruptus" (just a funny name). I got it all installed and the bug was fixed, so I then gave the other disks to the other testers. We all tested it for a while and then I gave my disks to our boss, who would take it to be mastered. We didn't have a QA department for software at this company, so he would just take it directly to the mastering people. We made it! We got it finished. We were all pretty happy.

About three weeks later, after the product was in the store and everything, a few calls started coming in. People were unable to register their product for some reason. They said it kept coming up with the words "Coitus Interruptus." Well, needless to say, all the disks in circulation had to be recalled. It cost over $225,000. My boss took the brunt of the blame. Of course I felt really horrible, but I learned a valuable lesson: A last line of defense is a good thing. Had there been a QA department there, they would have caught our (my) slip-up in our extreme fatigue. A fresh crew of QA guys would have spotted it right away. Also, my boss probably should've given the product a once-over with the master disks, but that's another story.

House concludes by saying there have been numerous other instances in which the importance of testing and QA have been shown, and he can't imagine a development process without the two services.

Mark Green, Psygnosis

From the Psygnosis office in the U.K., Mark Green discusses his approach to proper testing and the chronological routines Psygnosis follows for every game shipped. He also covers when, how, and why they should be executed.

The back-end phase is the last six months or so of a project that really tells the men from the mice. It's this phase of development that makes or breaks a game. You can have everything done perfectly up until this point. But if you mess this one up, then you may as well never have bothered!

15

If you're bright, you'll have been liaising with your QA department all the way through the project. Usually the lads and lasses in QA are the closest link you have to the real gaming world. They're all diehard gamers, and if something isn't quite right then they'll let you know.

I know what you're going to say now—"But I know what a good game is. I can tell you what's wrong with a game. Why do you need testers to point out the obvious?" Well, the problem is this: Developers get so close to a product that they can barely see the wood for the trees. Half end up thinking that their game is fantastic when it actually stinks, and the other half think their game stinks when it's actually rather good. There really is no substitute for a neutral opinion. More and more now, we're actually getting magazine reviewers—truly objective people—to take a look at a game well before launch so that we can get extra feedback. It's things like this that make the difference between an okay game and a brilliant game.

When you get to six months from launch, you enter what we call the *alpha* phase. This is supposed to be "feature lock" on the game. At this point you should have everything in the game that you want in—it doesn't have to look good, it doesn't have to work 100%, and it doesn't matter if it crashes every now and again. The important thing is that you don't add anything more after this point. During alpha, your job (and that of QA) is to test the game and make it look good, play well, and stop crashing. Alpha normally lasts for about six weeks.

The next phase is *beta*. By now you should have a game and it's down to the hardest part of all: The Bug Hunt. People (those darned producer types) put a time scale to this, but essentially it comes down to "How long is a piece of string?" If your coders are really good and use a good coding standard, then your problems are slightly less; but whatever happens, this is the hardest time of all. And just to make matters worse, Marketing will want members of the development team to go to shows, talk to magazines, and generally spend time away from creating the game. Beta should normally last about four weeks.

Now, the last section is *submission*. This comes in two varieties (if you're developing for a platform): internal and external. First of all, your in-house QA department gives a final thorough work over, allowing you to change things that are a problem. Then you send it off to the relevant manufacturer. They spend another couple of weeks, not only checking for bugs but also checking the game against their own company guidelines to make sure the game is up to scratch. If you fail this, then it comes back to you and has to go through the whole submission process again! [In our setup,] each sub-mission takes two weeks, so failing can make this phase stretch out far longer than expected.

And finally, there's *master* [a.k.a. *gold*]. This is where you breathe a sigh of relief and suddenly regain the social life that you sacrificed for the last two years of development. A month after this, your game hits the shop shelves and you hope and pray that your game makes it to that golden number one slot.

The latest game Mark Green designed and produced was *Global Domination*.

Chip Bumgardner, Interplay Productions

Chip Bumgardner has produced a multitude of games, including *Chessmates*, *Lost Vikings 2*, *Earth 2140*, *Dragon Dice*, *Max 2*, and the *Caesar's Palace* series, to name a few. He also helped with level design for the controversial *Redneck Rampage*. Bumgardner says the testing phase of a game starts a lot earlier than you would think. He continues:

> In fact, the team that's developing a title usually tests throughout the life of development. It makes it *much* easier to catch bugs early and also to see where some things don't work (as well as get an idea of what you will need to add to balance gameplay).

Bumgardner admits that much of the testing goes on during the final weeks (or months) of the project, to make sure that everything that *should* work, *does*.

Chris Taylor, Interplay Productions

Chris Taylor has served as lead designer on the popular *Fallout* and *Stonekeep*, and as a campaign designer on *Max 2*. "Many people have different ideas about game testing," says Taylor. But he believes there to be basically three different stages: team testing, beta testing, and QA testing. He expands:

> The team should constantly be playing the game and testing it. They are the only people who really know the game and what it should be doing. Beta testing is having other people look at the game. They can find problems and can help with compatibility testing. Quality assurance is a more formal beta test, I guess. Very detailed bug reports and compatibility tests. Sometimes QA can help with the actual game design; sometimes they're too busy just finding bugs to really help there. I think all companies and products have different testing needs and ideas.

15

Chris Taylor's current project is Star Trek: Starfleet Command. Although they've done considerable testing already, the product still wasn't ready to ship at last check, emphasizing that early testing is critical. (Used with permission by Interplay Productions)

Wolfgang Walk, Blue Byte

Wolfgang Walk was the project manager for *Incubation* at Blue Byte Software in Germany, where he continues to work as a writer and designer. He seems to be in agreement with the other game designers on this subject:

> Testing is everything. Not only to fix all the bugs, but to fix all those minor design flaws that you can't avoid during the early development, when everything exists just in your head and on some paper, but you can't play anything. Testing tells you if the game is fun or not, and what you have to change to erase the frustrating and boring stuff that will show up during development.

> And then, of course, finding bugs. Suffice it to say that even if you had 100 testers they would never find all the bugs that the 50,000 testers will find as soon as they've bought the game. It's just a matter of chance. Games are so complex today that it's nearly impossible to publish a game that's 100% bug free. Journalists and gamers often forget about that.

"One exception," says Walk, "is that of course there is no excuse for games with obvious major bugs that appear after two minutes of average playing."

Richard Garriott, Origin Systems

The one and only Richard "Lord British" Garriott, conceiver of the legendary *Ultima* series at Origin Systems, says a lot of effort is poured into game testing there, especially for online games, as experienced with the popular *Ultima Online*. Says Garriott, "A successful online game must have good engineering from the start; you have to have good code. And once you have good code, the QA testers can do their job well."

Unfortunately, there was no way to thoroughly test a breakthrough, massively multi-player game like *Ultima Online* early on in the process, as evidenced by a few unhappy players after the game's initial launch. But many more servers around the world have been added for less Internet congestion, while a handful of full-time engineers are handling the bandwidth issues back in Texas as well.

Lord British says that testing is important not to just make sure that there aren't bugs in the game; the game must also be played on all types of systems with multiple configurations. (Used with permission by Origin Systems, Inc.)

Garriott says when they test their games internally, they attempt to play the game as a player would, and go through a checklist procedure. This includes all of the game's features and combinations of features, and can become quite the tedious task. He explains:

> For example, if a magic system has 50 spells, a tester must test each of the spells and the spell combinations, on all monster types, NPCs (non-player characters), and items, on every map. This is a huge matrix—in fact, we have binders full of these [checklists]. And you have to do this with every version of the game [every "build" throughout the game development process].

On top of all this, Garriott reminds us that this all has to be done on all machine types and configurations. Sounds like fun, huh?

Sid Meier, Firaxis Games

The honorable Mr. Sid Meier has appeared many times throughout this book to lend his thoughts on game design. When it comes to proper testing, he mirrors the sentiment offered by Richard Garriott.

> First is bug testing, which should be done by as many people [as possible] on many different machines. Also, it's important for the tester to use a method of reproducing and documenting the bug.

After all, finding a bug isn't worth its weight unless it can be captured and reported; therefore, Meier uses various techniques, such as an autosave feature in the game that will bookmark the game every 10 seconds or so. This way, a previous game can be loaded if a bug is found.

The second kind of testing done under Meier's supervision is to find out if the game is too hard or too easy:

> Designers have no way of telling because they're too close to the project to get an objective look at the game. The key is to give the game to people and watch what they're doing, and to see where they get stuck.

Meier also believes that the first half hour of gameplay is critical, and an important determinant of whether the gamer will keep playing the game.

Ron Gilbert, Humongous Entertainment

The omnipotent Ron Gilbert is responsible for many best-selling LucasArts, Humongous Entertainment, and Cavedog Entertainment games. When the topic of testing comes up, Gilbert reminds us that "adventure games are different." What does he mean by this?

> Adventure game testing is more just looking for bugs than anything else. You don't have balancing issues as in real-time strategy games, or the kind of testing needed in multiplayer games. In adventure games, there's a set path, set objects—not a whole lot of permutations.

Gilbert says when it comes to testing games like Cavedog Entertainment's *Total Annihilation: Kingdoms*, they spend days play testing it to make sure that all units are balanced properly. And after a multiplayer skirmish, they all get together to talk about the experience. Is this common? Says Gilbert:

> It's the only way to go for a game like this. For bugs, testers should fill out forms and documents, but when you're testing gameplay, it's best to talk about it.

Gilbert offers an example of a gameplay issue found while testing. "If archers are building up too quickly and you're able to swarm an enemy base, we adjust the building of those units by slowing it down, and then we play it again. We do this until everything is balanced out."

Gilbert says they do no outside testing at Humongous and sister company Cavedog, as all QA testing is done internally by the respective teams. But, in closing, he reminds us that "there is no set nomenclature for things."

One of Cavedog's testing rituals is to conduct post-gaming powwow sessions with the development team to iron out balancing issues. (Used with permission by Cavedog Entertainment, Inc.)

CHAPTER 16

Marketing and Public Relations

The unfortunate reality is that no matter how good a game is, if no one knows about it, it just won't sell. In this day and age, hype, exposure, and distribution muscle are needed to sell games—or at least one of the three. (Let's face it—the mega-successful *Deer Hunter* had no hype or magazine exposure, but it was found in every Wal-Mart, with a $19.99 price tag!)

Public relations representatives (reps) and marketing reps have the same goal—to get the product known—but how they go about it varies greatly. Loosely speaking, public relations (PR) reps work with the press to get media exposure, while marketing reps tend to deal more directly to the consumer through advertising, packaging, and promotions; and in some cases they deal with retailers regarding distribution channels and presentation issues.

Doug Lombardi, a marketing representative at Sierra Studios, elaborates on the job requirements for each of these two important positions:

> Two key areas that every game publisher must address in garnering critical mind share for a product are marketing and public relations.

> Generally speaking, public relations representatives handle all communications with the press, which subsequently gets the information to the end user via previews, features, news stories, etc. Specifically, the PR duties include setting up press tours, promotional events, and editorial visits to the studio or development house. Additionally, the PR reps manage the creation of releases about the product, developer, and company—while also responding to all inquiries from the press for interviews, artwork, etc.

> The marketing folks, on the other hand, manage the creation of more direct communications to the consumer, such as advertisements, packaging, and so on. In most cases, the marketing manager works very closely with a creative agency to produce the product's visual identity as well as the aforementioned promotional materials. And in some cases, the marketing manager pursues third-party (or co-op) promotions and agreements, in which a software publishing house, for example, partners with a technology company to co-promote both companies' products.

Many gaming developers and publishers opt to hire an outside PR agency or marketing firm to handle their business. There are pros and cons for hiring an agency, as discussed over the next few pages.

The goal of this chapter is to shed some light on these two roles by delivering helpful advice from seasoned industry professionals. They'll cover the best ways to conduct successful public relations and savvy marketing for your game.

Public Relations

Bill Linn, Linn PR

Linn Public Relations, Inc. was founded by Bill Linn, a longtime game industry public relations veteran. His clients include well-known gaming companies such as Sierra, THQ, Brøderbund, and the 3DO Company, to name a few.

Linn maintains that game developers have greater pull in the media than publishers, and they should know this. Argues Linn:

> We believe that bringing a journalist to the heart and soul of the product is the key to great coverage. Oftentimes the publisher overlooks this. I lead

with this because there are several things the developer can do to ensure breakout press coverage, at little or no expense.

Following are but a few of Linn's golden rules on what separates the good PR reps from the inadequate.

Relationships

Linn believes that the best articles come from knowing the editors. Just how do you build that relationship?

> Developers who don't have PR people should go out of their way to give the "right" information to the "right" editor at the "right" time. I emphasize that because developers can over-communicate and irritate editors. For example, a developer reads in a magazine about another company doing a similar product. Find out who the editor is and shoot him an email. It might say, "I saw your article on (*game name goes here*) and wanted to let you know about our product. *Blah blah blah.*" End the *brief* email with an invitation to see the game in person. Don't panic if he or she doesn't reply. The next time you have a major milestone, send the editor a little note saying, "Hey, we just did x, y, or z; is this something you might be interested in seeing?" Casual, down to earth, and honest is the key. Editors hate arrogance, big claims, and pushy people.

Sell the Vision

Although he admits it's a slightly different approach to what most PR reps do, Linn encourages developers to sell more than just the game's feature set. He explains:

> Early on, you must sell the vision of your game. What inspired you? What games influenced your design? How does your background play into the design? What team did you assemble to create it? Those are questions for which journalists want the answers. If you hit them with adjectives and unsubstantiated claims, you bore the crap out of them. A good way to [provide the details they want] is to create an outline—your game is the story. Make the outline chronological, from the time you began to the current date. Pick out the highlights that will be interesting to the journalist and then use them to map out a presentation.

Teamplay

Along with selling the vision of the game, Linn recommends pitching your entire development team:

> Often we make sure that the journalist gets to meet the lead artists, the lead programmer, and even a tester. Everyone on the team contributes to selling

the game. Make sure you use them. Before you do this, however, be sure to train them on working with the media, prepare an outline for a press visit, and practice a lot before anyone comes to your company.

To learn more about Bill Linn's philosophies, background, and services, visit www.linnpr.com.

Genevieve Ostergard, Sierra Studios

As senior PR manager for Sierra Studios, Genevieve Ostergard works with both the gaming press and more consumer-based publications for the titles she represents. Before settling down with Sierra Studios, she worked at an outside agency and internally for some of the largest PC gaming publishers in the world, namely Microsoft and Interplay.

Ostergard confirms good relationships are key to a successful public relations career:

> Public relations is all about relationships. If you're doing your own PR, get to know the gaming editors by meeting them face to face. Good ways of doing that are at trade shows, industry gatherings, or meeting with the editors in their offices. Similarly, know their publications and which editors are assigned which beat.

Other than securing trusted bonds with journalists and editors, Ostergard offers a few random pointers to bear in mind as a new PR rep:

- **Press releases:** Write well and to the point. Don't over-hype. Get a book on writing for the news or public-relations writing to get the gist of good writing techniques.

➤ Ostergard suggests that budding PR reps consider the following books as recommended reading: *The Associated Press Stylebook and Libel Manual*, Norm Goldstein, editor, et al (Perseus, 1998); *Writing Broadcast News: Shorter, Sharper, Stronger*, by Mervin Block (Bonus Books, 1997); and the Publicity Handbook by David R. Yale (NTC, 1992).

- **Know your strategy.** Come up with a plan. Don't just throw information to the world and hope someone comes knocking on your door.

- **Be responsive.** Call back or leave alternate ways of reaching you. This will help create a trusting relationship between you and the journalist.

- **Be creative.** Mailers, freebies, and giveaways are always good, but try an event and invite the press. Keep in mind that even though a party is fun, there's nothing newsworthy about it. But a party with a celebrity or special guest is sure to bring attention to your game and journalists in attendance.

- **Keep a very good database.** If you make a promise to follow up with someone, make sure you do it.

16

Scoring the front cover of a popular gaming publication for your product is as good as it gets. Of course, it helps to have a great game to pitch. Genevieve Ostergard arranged this Half-Life cover story with PC Accelerator magazine. (Used with permission by Sierra Studios and Imagine Media, Inc.)

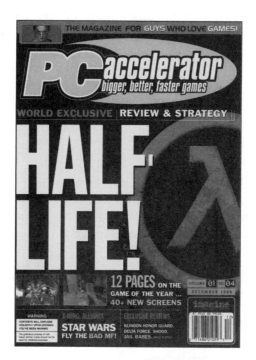

Michael Meyers, Acclaim Entertainment

Mike Meyers is the director of product public relations at Acclaim Entertainment. He is instrumental in the promotion of their console game products and worked on many campaigns such as *Turok: Dinosaur Hunter*, *Turok 2: Seeds of Evil*, *NFL Quarterback Club '98* and *'99*, *South Park*, *WWF: Warzone*, and many others. Meyers offers three crucial considerations for newbie PR reps:

Know Your Media

Don't pitch any publication, television show, radio program, or Internet site unless you're very familiar with their style, editorial schedule, tendencies, etc. If you know a journalist's work, you'll have a better chance of the journalist wanting to become familiar with your product.

Relationships Are Essential

Game developers and gaming journalists have something in common—they're both passionate about games. One of the best things about my job is that I get to talk gaming with journalists who have the same passion about the subject. If journalists recognize your passion for gaming, they'll find you much more believable when you tell them your game is the best _____ for _____ platform.

Don't Operate in a Vacuum

One of the biggest mistakes developers and/or PR representatives can make is presenting their product without thoroughly researching the competition. A journalist will want to know how your game differs from something else within the same genre. If you don't know how your game exceeds the competition, the journalist won't be able to tell his/her readers.

In the following anecdote, Meyers applies these three pieces of advice to a project he worked on recently:

One of the largest PR efforts I've had the pleasure of being associated with was our launch of *Turok: Dinosaur Hunter* for the Nintendo 64. *Turok* was one of the first third-party titles available for the N64. More importantly, it was the first title of Acclaim's big turnaround effort—the survival of Acclaim was tied to its success.

Everyone on the Acclaim PR team as well as at our agency (TSI) had a role in the *Turok* effort. I was in charge of what we deemed the "*Turok* Internet Assault." The Internet Assault was a grassroots PR effort to get every amateur and professional N64 site to dedicate a large portion of their front page to *Turok*. The Assault took place over an eight-week period leading up to the launch of the game. Every Monday we would distribute exclusive screenshots and QuickTime movies to the largest "professional" sites. Each of these large sites was given 3–4 days exclusivity, and then all materials were placed on a server where anyone could download them and use them on their site.

Within weeks of the launch of this Internet effort, the Web was filled with images and buzz about Acclaim's upcoming game. Since consumers who read dedicated N64 Web sites are more likely to own an N64 (or plan on buying one soon), we provided our most valuable potential customers with all the information they needed to make an informed buying decision.

Keep in mind that many of Meyers' games were bestsellers in 1998: *South Park*, *Turok 2: Seeds of Evil*, and *WWF: Warzone* on the Nintendo 64 and Sony PlayStation.

➤ The Public Relations Society of America (PRSA) is a great place to start for those interested in learning more about the trade. The URL is simply www.prsa.com.

Adam Kahn, Acclaim Entertainment

Also at Acclaim Entertainment, but responsible for the PC gaming lineup, is Adam Kahn. Just before moving to Acclaim's East Coast offices at the end of 1998, Kahn worked at Shandwick International, a PR firm, on the Microsoft games account. Over the next page or so, Kahn discusses his approach to gaming PR and what newcomers to the professional could gain from this advice.

Kahn on Strategy, Smarts, and Focus

I think there are a few key things that game designers should know about PR in the games industry. First of all, they should know that it's not rocket science. PR for games is about being strategic, smart, and focused, but it's certainly nothing to get intimidated about. That being said, it's also important for them to understand that PR is best undertaken by someone who can *be* strategic, smart, and focused. I've worked with a lot of small development companies, and seen a lot of people who think they're strategic, smart, and focused, but they're really not. There are a lot of examples out there that show it's very difficult to be a full-time game developer and a PR/marketing guru. They're wildly disparate job functions and probably cater to completely different personality styles. Developers would do well to leave the PR to someone who knows/enjoys PR and stay focused on developing a great game.

Here's what I mean by strategic, smart, and focused.

Being strategic means seeing PR from a very high altitude. It means looking at a PR campaign from beginning to end, very early on, and deciding when you want coverage, where you want coverage, and what types of coverage you want. I've seen a lot of developers get very tactical in their PR. They get whipped up on a title and start thinking that they need coverage *right now* in a certain magazine, or they see John Romero in *Rolling Stone* and think that should be them. It just can't work that way. If you're strategic, you've planned ahead and, barring any major shifts in the marketplace, you can sail right through those issues without worrying. Being strategic means making tough decisions very early on. Let's say you have two titles that are shipping within a few months of each other. Which one is your focus title? There are companies out there who say that every title they release gets the same marketing and PR budget, but that just can't work in the long run. Certain titles will benefit from bigger budgets, and others won't. Strategic thinkers look at these situations, step back from company politics, and make decisions.

Being smart means knowing who you're dealing with, specifically in the press. There are a lot of games out there, and editors and freelancers are under a lot of pressure to get their jobs done. Anything you can do to make their job easier will be rewarded in the long run. If writers call you and ask for screenshots, you get the screenshots to them as soon as possible. There are no ifs, ands, or buts about it. You just do it. Being smart also means that there isn't anyone small enough to ignore. Editors at the smallest gaming

16

Web sites can become editor-in-chief at major gaming publications—it's happened before—and blowing someone off is the easiest way to kill a relationship. Pay attention to everyone.

Being focused is kind of the opposite of being strategic. You can't stay in the clouds all the time, so it pays to spend time focusing on tactical things like events, creative execution, and timing. Take pride in pulling off a great event that uses editors' time effectively. Be creative. But never waste writers' time. That goes back to being smart. You want editors to open your email every time you send them something. The fastest way to get into their "ignore" box is to waste their time.

Does someone need a lot of money to deal successfully with the press? Kahn talks about how someone with little or no budget can get their game exposure in the media:

It really doesn't cost that much to do PR, especially if you've been in the industry for a while and know the right people to contact. If you don't know the right people it's a lot harder, but you can do a lot of the grunt work just through research in magazines and on the Web. If you haven't been around very long, you're probably going to need to visit gaming publications and get in front of editors. This is the most efficient way to get noticed, and since the U.S. gaming press is mostly in San Francisco, it's easy to take a few days and see nearly everyone.

Of course, it's probably a good idea to hire a small PR agency that specializes in gaming. They've spent years developing relationships, and you can leverage those relationships financed by all the fees that other companies have paid them. Using an outside PR firm allows you to focus on game development, which is probably what you're best at since you're a developer.

And finally, Kahn says that, assuming you've spent some time getting to know the various editors at gaming magazines, getting reviews shouldn't be hard at all. Get them final code on time and they'll do a review.

Note >> When it comes to PR, should game developers or publishers do it themselves by bringing people in internally, or should they hire an outside agency? There are advantages and disadvantages to both scenarios. On one hand, internal PR has a chance to get closer to the development of the product—not to mention that they only work for that particular company, so their vision is arguably more focused. An agency, on the other hand, usually costs less than internal positions and likely has an experienced staff and a database full of great contacts in the media, and many of these PR reps already have a relationship with members of the press. However, an agency typically has multiple clients and may not give your account the attention it deserves.

Marketing

Brandon Smith, Cavedog Entertainment

Having worked as communications manager on the breakthrough title *Total Annihilation* (and its expansion packs*)*, you can bet Brandon Smith played a role in the game's international success. Says Smith, "I think one of the most important things for any marketer to keep in mind as they develop strategies for marketing their products is to *know* their audience." He expands on this advice:

> And I mean really *know* them. Know what they eat, where they hang out, what they do in their spare time (besides play games)—you name it, you should know it. I can't stress and/or express this enough. If you don't know these things, a marketer's life can become very difficult and a product's life can become very short.
>
> However, with this knowledge firmly in place, what you need to do on the marketing front becomes much easier and more intuitive. You'll quickly discern what things incent your audience to make purchases and how best you can fit into that picture. For example, knowing that your particular audience has a preference for football over baseball could lead to an effective promotional campaign with the NFL. Or maybe your audience rents games from a retail chain at phenomenal rates; the result might be a special tie-in to offer dollars off a purchase of your game if they rent at least three titles from that retailer.

Asked how a company can market a product on a shoestring budget, Smith responds by saying this gets tougher and tougher each year, as our industry gets more and more competitive. "Truth be told, you really *must* partner with a strong publisher or distributor to do your title justice." So what's a small developer to do? Smith responds with a few ideas:

> I think there are a few things that companies can do to help themselves out when they don't have an EA or GT Interactive providing the retail muscle most products need these days (and FYI, these points are true of all companies, regardless of stature):

- **You have to make a good product!** There are no ifs, ands, or buts about it. No amount of marketing power will save a poor software title. I'm sure there are exceptions to the rule, but I would never want to bet money on that horse.

- **Focus your limited marketing funds on press relations.** It's tremendously more efficient, with the potential of a much greater return. It's one thing to say that you

16

have the hottest new game technology in an advertisement, but if an editor at Next Generation says the same thing it will have a much larger impact—guaranteed. Marketing and advertising are key to a well-rounded campaign, but can be extremely expensive (and if you have to shave dollars, I'd do it here). Positive press coverage of your title can create tremendous word-of-mouth and eventually demand for your title. It will also help accomplish the last point.

- **Build up grassroots support for the game with consumers early.** This will help on a number of fronts. One of the most important (and expensive) aspects of marketing is convincing the retail channel to carry the game (hence the need for a strong publisher or distributor)—if they don't carry it, you can't sell it. This usually involves demonstrating to retail that the game will be supported with a MASSIVE marketing campaign. Unfortunately, this is quite expensive, and if you don't have the money the odds are already stacking up against you. This is effectively a traditional *push* strategy, where you're telling the retailer they must carry it because of what you're doing to support the title.

Smith elaborates on this last point, the grassroots aspect of a marketing campaign:

> [This] can help (keyword *help*, since it's no guarantee) accomplish the same goal, but by using a different means. Rather than you convincing the retailer to carry the product, you allow the consumer to do so. By incenting and evangelizing consumers about the product, you can effectively get them to work to your goal of securing shelf space and selling units. With a combination of fans contacting their local software retailers and you informing them of the already huge consumer demand for the title (using press clippings, etc.) you can engage in a *pull* strategy, where retailers feel that they'll lose out on sales if they don't carry the title. You can end up at the same place, but just use a different route to get there. Of course, the best route would involve a solid combination of push and pull.

> These are all simplistically detailed points, but still cover some key areas. How exactly individual companies go about doing these things is what will separate those that succeed from those that don't.

Can he offer any direct examples of faultless game marketing?

> I really respected Sony's campaign to launch the PlayStation some years ago. They did everything right (of course they had a virtually bottomless budget). They knew the audience so well that they "out-cooled" the coolest company

at the time—SEGA—and stole their user base. They had a great piece of hardware.

At the same time it suddenly became okay for a 20+ year old to own the system, thanks to a clever ad campaign. This meant older consumers with larger disposable incomes were purchasing a traditionally younger platform. The product's ads were so effective that potential consumers were recording those on television and tearing them out of magazines because the company had hidden codes for the upcoming games in them. Thus ads were being viewed again and again, and being heavily discussed at work, home, and online. Great grassroots stuff.

They launched the PlayStation Underground—a club where consumers could get demos of the latest games… again, very grassroots focused.

I believe it to be one of the most effective consumer product launches of all time (not just in the game industry—*all* consumer products).

Smith is currently weaving his magic on the marketing for *Total Annihilation: Kingdoms*.

Vince Desiderio, Running With Scissors

Joining us on our panel of marketing reps is Vince "Desi" Desiderio, CEO of the Running With Scissors development studio in Tucson, Arizona. Their first highly controversial title was *Postal*, an action game where the player assumes the role of a disgruntled postal worker who takes it out on his town… with weapons. It may be argued that the exposure and marketing decisions surrounding *Postal* are largely responsible for its success. Desi touches on its infamous coverage:

> *Postal* won numerous awards and accolades. My favorites are being called the "#1 worst thing in American society" by U.S. Senator Joseph Leiberman of Connecticut (#2 was Marilyn Manson and #3 was Calvin Klein underwear ads); the other is "Best Packaging" by SPA—so ironic since it was taken off the shelves of the major retailers after the first month.

According to Desi, most games are designed without ever considering marketing. With that in mind, he outlines the most important marketing tips for new game designers.

- **Game type/game system and audience.** For example, are you trying to reach the RPG crowd or the casual gamer? In other words, what kind of game is it: action, sports, puzzle? For what age group? What system—PC or console?

- **Your name.** Running With Scissors is a company name that tells you right up front we're not about education. *Postal* is simple and clean, like *Doom* and *Quake*. Names can be more than one word, but it has to say something—make you think of what it could be, make you want to play.

- **The story—a good story leads to more.** Who's the lead character? Who or what are the enemy characters? Licensing potential (novel, game book, cartoon, action figures), add-ons, sequels.

Desi gives us a brief account of the history of Running With Scissors and how they took advantage of their controversial debut in light of the marketing of the product:

> We started a new game development company and we wanted to be known for making outrageous games, hence "Running With Scissors." When asked, "What is RWS? What does it mean?" I say, "We're everything your mother told you not to do."

> We had one and only one chance to make a hit (we self-funded development and early marketing) so we needed to make a game that would be instantly recognizable and shocking; hence *Postal* was born. We needed an anonymous vehicle to get the word out, so we created *The Gimp* (which currently, one year later, still has an active mailing list of about 10,000 subscribers).

Note >> The Gimp is Running With Scissors' mascot and something of an alter ego for the staff. From a marketing perspective, Desi thought it would be good to have a vehicle to release info and to form a network around. Currently, The Gimp continues to write a weekly newsletter. "In short," says Desi, "The Gimp has been a very real part of the marketing effort of our company."

> We used press releases combined with setting up the RWS site to break the news to the world that *Postal* was coming. This immediately generated a response from the U.S. Postal Service in the form of an original letter from the Postmaster General himself. What did I do? I took his letter and used it for my next press release. The rest was history; not only was the game media drooling for more, but mainstream media was calling from as far away as Australia. We made the front page of the *Wall Street Journal* (plus two more stories), the *Sunday London Times*, over 50 TV appearances across all major networks, over 100 radio shows, debated the governor of Arkansas live on CNN, and on and on.

Although the game has been out for some time now, Desi says their risqué rap and cunning marketing skills have kept Postal in the media, even in 1999 in a recent Reader's Digest story. Above, a bloody screen shot from Postal; below, a concept drawing of the main, uh, hero. (Used with permission by Running With Scissors, Inc.)

16

So what's the bottom line here? What can be learned from all of this? Answers Desi:

> Marketing is responsible for creating awareness, whether this is through ads in print or online, radio or TV, press releases or news articles, and especially word of mouth. The real question becomes how the marketing effort gets that word of mouth with no dollars. The answer is to create news—the most economical method is by using online press releases, but a key factor that's all too often missed by even many of the major publishers and developers is the follow-up support. All the news that was created by the announcement of *Postal* and the hype that went with it would have died out except for the fact that we continuously added to and built upon what we had established. This was done by many hours of personal involvement—answering thousands of emails, creating The Gimp, and constantly releasing new information about the game. I asked myself why it is that people still ask about *Postal* (and actually the more important question, "What is Running With Scissors doing next?"), and the terribly obvious answer is because we created a following, a need, a desire!

For those of you who have asked yourself the same question, their next title is dubbed *Flesh & Wire*.

Doug Lombardi, Sierra Studios

Along with giving us a more thorough explanation on the differences between public relations and marketing, Sierra Studios' Doug Lombardi is here to discuss the necessity and timeliness of Internet gaming demos.

> From a purely marketing perspective, a public demo is one of the most powerful weapons for promoting a new product. This is especially true if said product has not captured a considerable amount of the gaming community's attention.
>
> Sometimes a great title just isn't picked up by the gaming media, for whatever reason. In this case, releasing a killer demo—a few weeks before the product is published—gives gamers a chance to check it out, and the game can achieve critical mind share via word of mouth, the most effective form of advertising known to man. Any research done on the subject shows that most gamers prefer to try before they buy, and many gamers simply will not buy a game unless they have a chance to play it first. Given the short lifecycle of a software title in this day and age, it's now critical that some sort of compelling public sampling is made available in a timely fashion. A compelling demo gives players a look at the game's strongest features, and when done

right can leave players thinking, "Wow, this is as good as they said it was. I must have it."

But is it possible a demo could backfire? Lombardi says it depends:

> The other side of the coin is when demos were simply not ready for prime time, and there are dozens of examples of those—*or* those that gave away the farm, leaving the players feeling like they'd gotten their fill.

> With reference to timing, releasing the demo before the full title hits store shelves can be effective, but also dangerous. Certainly, in the case of several classics, the demo helped make them—and arguably *made* them—a smash. But there are several examples of publishers/developers that released their demos way too soon, sometimes months before the full product's feature set was finally complete.

> More and more these days, we're seeing the demo released just after the product is released. A risky option with a title that has received only limited buzz. But if the title has the hype, releasing a solid sampling within 90 days of the product's release can certainly help give the title a boost at retail. That is, so long as the demo rocks and leaves you wanting more.

Wolfgang Walk, Blue Byte

Project manager Wolfgang Walk explains why, from a marketing standpoint, a release of a demo is important for developers to consider in 1999:

> From the customer's point of view, a demo is the best way to test a game and decide if it's worth buying, before throwing away $40 to $50 on a piece of crap. This is the most important target of a demo, even for the developer. You want your customers being happy with your game. Giving them a demo gives you the possibility to say, "Hey, at least we told you so!"

On the other hand, Walk says a demo of a weak game doesn't guarantee that the full game will be a hit. "The buzz on the Internet is good for marketing, though I don't think that many games—those that aren't as good as other games, or have less marketing power behind them—become winners because of the demo."

And finally, Walk also believes a great demo doesn't mean a successful game, either. Are there any specific examples from the Blue Byte camp?

> *Incubation* created some interest with the demo, and a few hundred people maybe bought the game afterwards who had never heard of *Incubation* before, but it was far away from becoming a hit. It was [selected as] the best

turn-based strategy game in the U.S. in 1997 by *PC Gamer*, so quality probably wasn't the reason for so little interest. Well, as the project manager, I
must say lack of quality could *not* be the reason. There are still fan sites for
Incubation and newly created levels appear around the world quite often.

Blue Byte's Wolfgang Walk says a demo is ideal if the game is worth it, but warns it doesn't necessarily contribute to a game's retail success. Such was the unfortunate case with the critically acclaimed, yet poor-selling Incubation. (Used with permission by Blue Byte, Inc.)

Liz Bell, THQ

THQ's Liz Bell comments on the option of free demos for PC games as an effective
marketing strategy.

> Demos should only be released on high-quality games that the publisher
> expects to be reviewed positively. They should be a clear representation of a
> piece of the final product, but should only include enough of the game to get
> the consumer excited. Withhold levels, weapons, characters, and the multi-
> player option so the consumer longs for the complete experience. The ideal
> schedule would include a covermount [typically, the cardboard artwork on a
> magazine's demo disc] exclusive with a magazine eight weeks before ship,
> hitting online, and the rest of the covermounts four weeks out, and educating
> your smaller retail chain managers with the demo at ship. If the lead time on
> the demo is only four weeks, online exclusives are also very effective.

CHAPTER **17**

Gaming Web Site Design

In less than five years, the Internet evolved from being a virtually unheard-of medium to one of the most exciting innovations of the 20th century, from a couple thousand university students and government officials to over 50 million surfers, and growing exponentially.

The birth of the World Wide Web, in particular, was an integral component to the commercialization of the Internet in the mid-1990s. With the graphical and easy-to-use interfaces of Mosaic and Netscape, it was now easier than ever to navigate around this information highway to access the millions of documents and databases, not to mention that it added multimedia— pictures, sound, music, animation, and video—to all this text.

The Web is also one of the most important inventions for the gaming industry. People can play their favorite games against one another (or many others) from anywhere in the world. No longer do gamers have to wait a couple of weeks for a patch to arrive on a floppy disk. Gamers can "try before you buy" with an endless number of commercial game demos. Budding programmers, artists, game designers, and musicians can showcase their own creations internationally, from the comfort and convenience of home.

Electronic magazines (*e-zines*) cater to the gaming community by the dozens. Game developers and publishers offer free, downloadable add-ins to their existing titles (or the opportunity for gamers to make their own modifications). Fan sites give dedicated gamers their own soapbox to millions of other like-minded individuals. Gamers can purchase games online and have them delivered right to their door. Free cheat codes, strategy guides, and walkthroughs make it harder to justify spending $15 on a hint book (plus all the interactive chat groups and bulletin boards gamers can partake in). Gaming journalists can work anywhere in the world for any magazine, newspaper, or Web site, since stories and images can be submitted electronically. And the list goes on and on and on (and on).

This chapter looks at the necessity of creating and maintaining an excellent Web site to accompany the release of a game, whether this is for your own shareware or freeware title or you want to work for a developer or publisher to help promote their games. Throughout the following pages, we'll hear from Webmasters as well as marketing representatives on using this new medium to your advantage—what's best to include on a Web site in this day and age, and a handful of tips on what separates great Web sites from lackluster ones.

Daniel Bray, Cubik Media and Marketing

Daniel Bray is a creative director at Cubik Media and Marketing, a company dedicated to designing and building Web sites. One of their biggest clients is Eidos Interactive, Inc. Bray was asked why a computer game publisher (or developer, for that matter) should create a Web site to correspond with the release of a game. What should be offered there? How important is the use of multimedia (plug-ins, etc.) versus load time? He responds:

> Cool Web sites go hand in hand with cool games. Gamers are very tech savvy. They're on the Web; they use the Web as their first point for getting info on new games. Downloading demos is the number one reason why gamers come to gaming sites. A demo should always immediately precede the release of a game. Also, screenshots are crucial. They give the gamer an idea of how the game looks.

> Multimedia is very important. It brings the site to life, it makes it exciting. Yes, load time is an issue, but it will decrease in importance as technology races forward.

In short, Bray admits, "We love plug-ins!"

Bray predicts that gaming Web sites will soon become the number one way gamers get information on games. With that in mind, he says to add as much multimedia as possible to create a "buzz" about it. (Used with permission by Eidos Interactive, Inc.)

Sacha Fernandes, Eidos Interactive

While Cubik's Daniel Bray and company create the Web site layout for Eidos Interactive, Sacha Fernandes is the in-house online marketing manager, in charge of managing the interactive marketing and the Web site itself. Here's what she has to say about the importance of a good gaming Web site:

> With emerging trends in technology and the huge Internet revolution, the World Wide Web is a valuable tool that most businesses are not taking for granted. In the short history of online marketing, the Web has become a marketing vehicle of enormous proportions. Gamers are a tech savvy audience, and they spend quite a substantial number of hours—long hours—surfing the Web for hints, tips, chat sessions, etc.

More and more people are turning to the Web for information, travel arrangements, shopping needs, and entertainment, including online gaming networks. It's important to have a site up live corresponding to a product launch; in fact, gamers are looking for information months before a game is scheduled to launch. Having a Web site enables the publisher/developer to communicate with its consumer and therefore becomes an effective marketing tool. Often in this industry, products slip, and the Web becomes a viable source of the latest information. The goal is to keep people coming back and have your site become a community of sorts, gaining valuable cross-sell opportunities [corporate branding, building equity in other product brands, etc.].

On what should be included on game-related Web sites, Fernandes offers the following:

Product information, including storyline and cool features. Remember, this is a marketing tool. Therefore, [include] all information pertinent to selling the game to the consumer within an aesthetically pleasing layout.

With the slew of Web sites out there, you're competing for attention and need to have compelling stuff on your site to be able to stand out. In order to first sustain that traffic base and then increase it through word of mouth, you have to go above and beyond in terms of the quality of your Web site and the programming tools used. Dynamic [Shockwave] Flash, Java-enabled sites, etc. capture attention—more so than a basic Web site.

Generally, we find our traffic base to own fairly good systems, browsers, and modems (more often than not, they have T1s, ISDNs, or DSLs), so file size is not a big issue. We find that it's the content rather than load time that determines the download numbers. Demos can be as large as 50MB and the download numbers are huge. That's directly related to the hype revolved around that title. If it's a great game, people are going to find a way to get the demo or plug-in.

Regarding downloads, installation instructions and approximate download times given various modem speeds are an optional courtesy.

We've covered content, but how important is good navigation? Fernandes responds by asserting that "navigation is key." She continues, "This comes into play more with e-commerce sites, but even otherwise, fluid, efficient navigation is a must. If it's too complicated or someone's spending a lot of time and getting nowhere, chances of them returning are slim—you failed to make it a pleasant experience."

While wrapping up, Fernandes discusses an extra bonus Eidos Interactive has added to their site for their consumers—Eidos TV.

We launched Eidos TV (eTV) in April 1998, using Flash technology. In addition to just having product information on our wealth of Eidos games, we host fan clubs, newsletters, our strategy War Room, etc. All of this serves as an added value to our consumer and makes it all a pleasing, interactive, and fun environment for them to hang out in—and, more importantly, come back to.

At eTV, visitors can interact with original art and music inspired by the games (as seen here with this Lara Croft music video), plus enjoy online games, artwork, stories, links to fan sites, and more. (Used with permission by Eidos Interactive, Inc.)

17

➤ Be sure to drop by and check out Eidos Interactive and Eidos TV at www.eidos.com.

Matthew D'Andria, CyberNation

CyberNation creates Web sites for some of the more popular gaming destinations on the Internet, including Capcom, Activision, Konami, and Cendant Software. Chief creative officer Matthew D'Andria joins us here to discuss the importance of a stellar Web site and what makes it stand out among the online crowd:

The Web provides a powerful platform from which to build brand recognition for any new game title. The gaming audience is one of the largest and most Internet-savvy groups online, and they tend to take full advantage of whatever the Web has to offer, including chat, online gameplay, multimedia content, and online commerce.

A good game site will offer cool, exclusive content at its site as a value-add beyond what's available in the manual or other media. This way, game companies can count on a steady stream of return traffic from the game's most dedicated followers (and its best market for tie-ins and merchandise). Online commerce has extremely low overhead and offers worldwide distribution. CyberNation has built a number of successful online stores, including those for Capcom and Activision. It's always great to build an online community through chat, bulletin boards, or mailing lists for large game series such as *Resident Evil*.

But what about multimedia? What about those who have slow Internet connections? D'Andria says they've seen that most gamers have powerful computers, lots of memory, and fairly fast Internet connections. He continues:

> Therefore, we can create sites that require a little more bandwidth than we do for most of our other non-gaming clients. Wherever possible, we try to implement multimedia and an enhanced user experience without the use of plug-ins. We have built several online games without the use of plug-ins, including the first playable demo of a console game, *Super Puzzle Fighter*.

As illustrated here with three separate clients, game Web sites may feature key game information (Konami, top), the option to purchase products online (Activision, bottom), or online games (Capcom, opposite page). (Used with permission by CyberNation)

Many game designers who are just starting out can't afford to hire CyberNation, so D'Andria offers some advice on creating content for the Web and getting the word out:

> You don't necessarily need a lot of money to design a good site—just good people. The best way to make a site successful is to offer something that can't be found anywhere else. Content is key. With very little money you can build a small site. Be sure to get the site listed on all the major search engines and portals—which is usually free. Also start emailing and calling the people in charge of other successful game sites, and try to work out deals to exchange links. Word of mouth is always the best advertising for a Web site, no matter what your budget is.

➤ All of CyberNation's work for their gaming clients can be accessed at their home page, www.cnation.com.

Chris Sivertsen, EA Sports

Chris Sivertsen, an Internet marketing specialist at EA Sports, says a Web site is an ideal medium to promote and market a video/PC game for numerous reasons:

- **Budget.** A site can scale to a wide spectrum of budgets. Whether you have a startup or *Star Wars* title to push, you can find an equitable way to present the information. Games are full of many wonderful digital assets (text, art, sounds, and so on) that you can feature within different levels of packaging. More budget, more sophisticated packaging.

- **Choices.** Gamers are online and they're accustomed to having numerous sources of info at their fingertips. You can provide much deeper info than any other medium allows. You can also update this information frequently and add new features to

17

encourage consumers to return again and again. Where else will consumers learn about your game? You can also leverage proprietary content like "making of" stories, where you can share and educate consumers as to the painstaking efforts that went into the environments you created, or how 1,500 different sounds bring things to life on your screen.

- **Call to action.** A dynamic Web site can offer numerous actionable next steps for your consumers. On your site you can sell your game, sell related merchandise, register consumers to receive updates on your products via email, publicize tournament or other fan sites, run contests, ask for user submissions such as replays or screen shots, etc. This is your chance to make contact with your consumers and tell them you want them to become more involved with your product/company.

"We try to keep all of the critical info on the site just a few clicks away at all times," says Sivertsen. Above, check out the official EA Sports Web site. Below, the NHL Hockey page. (Used with permission by Electronic Arts, Inc.)

Sivertsen addresses what newbie designers should consider when creating a Web site for their game, in terms of content and navigation:

> A downloadable game demo is almost mandatory for a credible PC game launch. Research consistently rates product trial as the top factor in motivating game purchases. Consumers want to try before they buy, and you must respect that. Your competition is probably doing it.

> I'm a big fan of keeping site navigation simple. You should group related content and not make people work to find what's important or new on the site. You should spoon feed that info to them.

Barry Dorf, EA Sports

17

As assistant producer at Electronic Arts, Barry Dorf has worked on the *Madden Football* series and was responsible for running the popular *Fantasy Football* game on the EA Sports Web site. Dorf was asked why a game publisher should ponder creating new pages for each new game that's released, what should be offered there, and whether load times are ever a consideration at EA Sports:

> Free advertising, baby! We have this huge Web site for EA. We're one of the top 100 sites on the Internet. It would be stupid for us not to put out a Web site that corresponds to the release of a new game. To take it a step further, there should be a Web site up at least six months before [the game's] release.

> The site should have all the marketing hype you can fit on one page. The site should be updated often, and it should try to drive interest. When I worked on *Madden Football*, we never had the chance to get a demo ready before we shipped. A retail product differs from a Web-based product. It was important to us, but not more important then shipping a quality game. So as soon as we shipped, it was the first priority to get that demo up and show off our game. When we worked on the EA Sports Edge *Fantasy Football Analyzer*, we were able to put the whole product up for free. We gave it away for a few weeks and generated interest. The site had walkthroughs, sports content, and the analyzer. It was a new medium for EA and we were not sure how to sell it.

> Plug-ins, load times, and browser compatibility were all new questions. We didn't want to require plug-ins, but we had strict browser requirements. We thought that people would be willing to download a 4.0 version of Netscape or Explorer, because it's free. We were wrong. We also required a long initial load of all the stats. Once the load was done, people would be able to move

around the site and get all the info they needed with no load times. If you had a 56K modem, this turned out to be about a 2–3 minute download. I thought it was worth it; there was so much info there, a one-time download was great. We figured it would be the longest load time the product would see. With the improving technology and modem speeds, if that was our biggest problem, we were in good shape.

Dorf insists that posting a free game is a great way to get some recognition for your site. "The way things travel on the Internet, there's a good chance that a really good Web site will be seen by the executives. Then who knows what can happen from there?" (Used with permission by Electronic Arts, Inc.)

Dorf comments on the necessity of easy navigation:

Navigation and interface is the key to any Web site. People like to surf but they want to be able to find the things they want fast. If you're on a football Web site, you want to be able to find the standings, stats, and transactions with one click. If you have too many sub-menus, people will get bored or sick of the load times between screens.

Michael McCart, Ensemble Studios

In this chapter, we've talked with people who either work at large publishing houses such as Eidos Interactive or Electronic Arts, or Web site design companies such as Cubik Media or CyberNation. However, this last entry will be from the development studio side of the industry.

Michael "Archangel" McCart is the Webmaster at Ensemble Studios, and he offers some insight on gaming Web site design. *Note:* His story is particularly inspiring since he was hired by Ensemble Studios because of his work on an *Age of Empires* fan site!

McCart discusses the indispensability of a good gaming Web site:

> We believe a developer should have a Web site as soon as possible, to state the company vision and its people. As early game development starts, some of the initial graphics for the game and a small fact sheet should be published on your Web site. The reason for these initial graphics and fact sheets is that they act like a teaser for the press, and help you on the road to a strong Internet fan base.
>
> As the game develops screenshots, more detailed information and designer comments should be added to your Web site. This practice develops a strong fan base and also gives the press somewhere to go for prerelease information.
>
> With the release of the game, more updated press, screenshots, files, etc., should be added to the game the site is covering. All this should be possible without the game part of your company Web site getting larger than 8–12 pages.

Should a gaming Web site be flashy and full of bells and whistles?

> As for multimedia (plug-ins, etc.) we shy away from those. At most, just a simple MIDI song from the game will be added to the main page on the different gaming Web sites we publish. The number one reason for this is that the number of images and screenshots we display on our gaming Web pages—for people to enjoy and get a visual feel for the game—increases load time.

What if you've spent all your money developing your game and have very little left to promote it online?

> If you have very little budget for this, your best bet is to get hosted by one of the larger gaming news sites [McCart's *Age of Empires Heaven* page was hosted by GameStats (www.gamestats.com)]. Most of the time, this type of site will offer you unlimited bandwidth (bandwidth usage = Big $$$) which your shareware or freeware program would eat up with a fair amount of downloads off the Internet.
>
> Some of your other choices could be some of the large ISP networks that offer free home pages.
>
> If you're just offering a shareware/freeware program on your Web site, include detailed program information (installing, what it is, etc.) and something about the company and its people. Most people who download shareware and freeware programs don't read the included *readme* file, so try to include as much as possible on your Web site.

17

On good versus bad navigation, McCart proposes the following:

> For the most part, that's in the eye of the user, but I [prefer] a simple top
> (header), and a main menu with major topics listed, with a sidebar dividing
> up the subtopics. Trim down the use of Java applets and scripts; these some-
> times have trouble with the older browsers.

Ensemble Studios'
McCart says to keep
the information easily
accessible, with a
main header and a
sidebar to divide up
the subtopics. (Used
with permission by
Ensemble Studios,
Inc.)

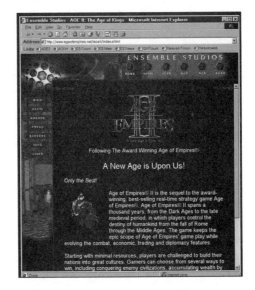

➤ McCart has published a long list of do's and don'ts for people who want to create and
maintain their own gaming fan sites. He invites all those who are interested to read
these suggestions at his home page, www.electrosonic.net/resources/angel.html. And be
sure to see his work on the official Ensemble Studios Web site at
www.ensemblestudios.com.

Technical Support and Customer Service

Once a game is released via traditional retail channels or over the Internet, it's the company's responsibility to then support the title for their consumers. All this work done *after* the product ships is an essential and important part of the game's cycle. Furthermore, if and how the consumer's needs are met becomes a critical determinant on whether he or she will deal with the company again in the future.

There are two main areas of support in the gaming industry. *Technical support* provides troubleshooting help for installing, setting up, and running software or hardware. Common issues for the PC gaming industry are driver conflicts, setup for 3D accelerator support, multiplayer gaming, joystick configurations, and more general DirectX problems. *Customer service*, on the other hand, focuses on help with orders (purchases or returns), warranty issues, billing inquiries, account information (if it's an online game or network), and other non-technical problems. Both tech support and customer service provide consumers with avenues for satisfaction with their purchase.

Most gaming companies prefer to handle technical support and customer service internally, but in some cases they hire outside agencies to control the traffic. And it's a common practice for publishers to take care of the technical support and customer service issues, instead of the development studio. For example, Interplay will deal with any technical support calls, emails, and faxes relating to *Baldur's Gate*, rather than BioWare, the developers of the game.

This short chapter looks at the recommended ways of running a smooth technical support or customer service operation, whether this is to be done for your own shareware or freeware title or for those who want to get into this side of the gaming industry at a publishing company.

Michael Kelly, Eidos Interactive

Eidos Interactive's customer support manager, Michael Kelly, was asked how important this part of a game's cycle is, and why. Do game companies pay enough attention to it? Kelly responds:

> This is something that cannot be quantified. While customer service and technical support can and do lead to the overall happiness that the customer feels toward the company and the product that they've acquired, it doesn't express itself in any measurable manner. You rarely hear stories of how wonderful someone's experience with either of these departments has been. On the contrary, all I've ever read are bad experiences. Especially in the U.S., customers expect a high level of service for their dollar. Even if this level is not a reasonable expectation. I feel that the industry (computer game publishing) doesn't put high importance on either customer service or tech support, but the consumer seems to.

Asked what key points to consider if you're going to run your own customer service department—that is, the do's and don'ts of this field—Kelly responds:

- **Access.** The customer must have some sort of access to support.
- **Timeliness.** The customer should have some reply within a reasonable amount of time.
- **Accuracy.** The customer deserves and expects that the information given is accurate and useful to [solving] the problem.

Kelly insists that the end user *must* be given an answer to his or her query, and by useful means. He expands:

I firmly believe that fax and email are very poor tools to use for technical support. There are just too many variables in computers for these media to be useful or productive in solving a customer's problem. However, it's quite satisfactory for providing user information that doesn't require a reply [from the consumer]—for example, where to send their disk for replacement.

In wrapping up, Kelly reminds companies to release patches as soon as they're available to ensure consumer satisfaction with the product.

Mark Linn, Interplay

Mark Linn is the lead technician at Interplay's Irvine, California, headquarters, and has been part of the technical support team for close to three years. He explains that at Interplay his technicians are trained to handle customer service calls, so they can resolve issues on the spot. "One-call resolution is best for the consumer and for us," explains Linn. He admits that phone calls are more effective than email or faxed queries, and it's also faster for both parties—therefore less expensive for Interplay and more timely for consumers.

Because this book caters to budding game designers who may want to start their own company or who aim to get a job at an existing developer or publisher, we asked Linn for the best advice he can give on running a smooth technical support operation. His answers are as follows:

18

A Good Database

According to Linn, setting up a database and good call-tracking is the most important first step. For larger companies, all technicians should be networked together in case customers don't get the same person on the phone each time. At Interplay, all calls are logged on a Microsoft Access database that records information about the user, their system, what happened during the last call, if the game in question has any known bugs (and how to get around them), and so forth. Linn admits that they tend to get calls from the same people repeatedly, so they call up the file by the customer's phone number. "Most of the people who call technical support are new computer users who are unfamiliar with the computer or older operating systems such as DOS," explains Linn.

Because they maintain a clean and organized database, they can often get to the root of the problem faster; therefore, it also reduces the hold time for customers calling in. "It's on their dime, so we try to make it quick and painless for them."

Some slightly older Interplay games, such as Redneck Rampage or Carmageddon, were written in DOS, but meant to work in a Windows 95/98 environment. Often there are driver conflicts, and the system may need to shut down and restart in DOS for it to work properly, says Linn. Pictured here is Redneck Rampage. (Used with permission by Interplay Productions)

Proper Training

Linn emphasizes *proper* training, since most of their applicants are familiar with computers, but it must be on operating systems that are relevant to gaming and the games themselves. Says Linn:

> We won't even give them an interview before they pass a test to make sure they understand computers the way we need them to (for example, operating systems such as Windows 95/98 and DOS). Then, for the first few days of training, we sit them down and make them play the games. The more familiar they are with the games, the more they'll be able to assist the callers.

Be a Good Listener

Linn says it's crucial that his staff be good listeners and possess good customer service skills. Moreover, they must not take things personally. "Callers may be irate—and they don't think of it as 'something is wrong with *their* computer,' but more like 'something is wrong with *your* product.'"

If these three rules are adhered to, any technical support operation should run smoothly and efficiently, says Linn.

Tom Bazzano, 3DO

Customer support supervisor Tom Bazzano takes some time out on his day off from the 3DO Company to offer his expertise on the proper way to handle technical support and customer service. First off, how important are these two areas at a game company, and why?

> Tech support should hold a much more important role in the development cycle of a game, although for the majority of titles/publishers in the industry today, it's usually an afterthought. If your customer support group is allowed to work with a development and test team during the alpha and beta phases of a product's development, they can provide valuable feedback to the development team on issues that could incur serious support costs. The reality of the situation is that many support groups don't get a copy of a game that they'll need to support until after the game ships to stores!

> Some of the most frustrating things for a customer support group are the small annoyances in a game's install or interface that consistently generate customer calls. These types of contacts are *usually* quick phone/email contacts, but they're also completely avoidable by getting your support group involved during the development phase. The CS [customer service] reps can tell QA [quality assurance testers] or development exactly how the customers are going to react to a questionable feature or situation that is occurring in a game that's in development. They'll also be able to pinpoint features in a product that will cause customer frustration.

> Our support organization is involved with nearly every aspect of product development. Our CS reps review all of the printed materials that are packaged with every product we make. They scrutinize the box, manual, artwork, system requirements, Web pages, strategy guides, keyboard overlays, quick reference cards, installation instructions—as well as the actual software itself. There isn't another group in our company that will be as diligent as the support reps in finding problems or inconsistencies in these types of materials. It's always going to be in their best interest to find problems during the development cycle, because when typos or errors slip by the production groups and product development, it's Customer Support that will have to answer the calls about it.

With this in mind, Bazzano says if tech support and customer service employees/departments adhere to the following rules, they should be able to satisfy their customers:

18

Good Follow-Through

Your support group has to have good follow-through on all customer issues. You need solid tools to make this happen, and you need to think hard about department policies. Without consistency and the proper tools to do the job, you'll have poor follow-through. The absolute last comment you want to hear from a customer is that they have been promised a callback the last X times they have called, and have never heard from anyone in your group.

Share Information

It's critical that your customer support staff share information with each other in order to provide the best support possible. It's also critical for a CS group to get this information out to customers in as many ways as possible. For example, during the launch of *Might and Magic 6*, our CS group was holding meetings at noon and at the end of the day to discuss new customer issues and to see if any of the reps had found workarounds. When one was found and confirmed, we would immediately publish it to all members of the group via email, and post on our FAQ on the *Might and Magic* 6 Web site. This ensured that at least some customers could get their problems solved outside of normal business hours, and noticeably reduced the number of calls on those topics.

Treat Your Customers Well

When dealing with customers, don't make it seem like an effort. Try to be upbeat and happy when talking to them on the phone. Use their first name and build up a rapport with them. Don't intentionally lie or deceive your customers; tell them the truth. A customer can deal with the fact that there is a problem with a product they purchased, as long as they are dealt with fairly and they have faith that the company will do right by them and patch it or remedy the situation. Forcing your employees to intentionally lie, deceive, or "state the company line" in order to save face will only frustrate your customers and demoralize your support reps!

Some busy technical support and customer services offices rely on automated phone systems (for example, "press one for game x, two for game y," and so on); others rely strictly on Web feedback (email queries and discussion forums); and a handful of publishers still depend on the old-fashioned telephone and snail mail. What does 3DO use, and prefer? Answers Bazzano:

> You should make an attempt to have your tech support group reachable by any and all mediums. Give your customers as many options as possible.

Following are some thoughts, both pro and con, for each of the methods of reaching a tech support group.

The phone is the fastest way to resolve tech support issues. When a phone rep is on a call, he or she is in a one-on-one situation with the customer. Because of this, the phone will also have higher CPT (cost per touch), as there is little opportunity to practice the concept of "one to many."

Email, fax, or a tech support message board are the second-best methods. They have reasonably fast turnaround times, and you can employ the use of FAQs or scripts to increase efficiency. The downside to email and message boards is that a single issue can drag on for weeks, whereas the same issue on a phone call, with the customer at the computer, could be resolved in under 20 minutes.

Snail mail should really be a last resort for tech support issues. If someone is trying to resolve an actual technical problem via snail mail, your best bet is to get them on the phone or some other more expedient medium.

But what if the publisher or small developer has very few resources (time and employees) to set aside for support? Can a game company survive with little or poor support? Bazzano replies:

18

No, this is just not a sane way to do business. Smaller companies need to scale their level of service accordingly. They should start by handling customer contacts via email, normal postal mail, or even fax. This will allow you to answer a large number of customer questions using scripts.

Once again, this is where the one-to-many philosophy will come into play. You should look at ways to get the largest amount of information to your customers with the least amount of labor. The most obvious is via the World Wide Web; posting a support site for your game should take minimal time, and could easily incorporate FAQs (frequently asked questions) and basic troubleshooting, as well as links to things such as Microsoft's DirectX page, or driver pages for various sound and video card manufacturers.

Another concept for the World Wide Web is that of a message board, where your customers can post questions and your designated support person (you did say they had no money) can post the answers. This will allow other customers to browse the board and find posts of people with similar problems. With this type of setup, you'll also find that many customers will help each other with workarounds that they've found on their own.

Speaking of Web sites, Bazzano comments on the timeliness of patches to repair/update games:

> The issue of when to release a patch should really be taken on a case-by-case basis. You NEVER want to prematurely rush a patch out the door. If you find that you have a problem with a title that's going to require a patch, and it's within the first week or two of a title's release, WAIT! Chances are there are other unanticipated problems that can be combined into a larger patch.

> You can find yourself in a situation that demands that you release an immediate patch, where you don't have the luxury of waiting to include other fixes. If there's a bug or issue with a game that prevents people from being able to play or install the product, you're going to need to fix it ASAP.

> Public demand can easily drive a company to release multiple patches in short order, but remember that this is an undesirable position to be in; you should seek creative solutions that appease your customer base and allow development to implement fixes for all known problems, rather than rushing out a patch every two weeks.

> One of the best ideas to handle such situations is getting your customer base involved in "testing" your patches for you by starting a "beta" program where the customers test early versions of the patch and return feedback about its performance and what hardware they tested it on. This will a) buy your development team time to address all the bugs they would like to fix, rather than just the ones people are most vocal about; and b) give your customers an active role in the patch's development and show them that the company is responding directly to their feedback.

Tom Bazzano invites newbie game designers to visit the 3DO Support page in order to get ideas on how to properly conduct their own technical support and customer service. (Used with permission by the 3DO Company)

Carin Lockrem, Purple Moon

Customer support manager Carin Lockrem makes sure that her employees are properly catering to Purple Moon's many customers. For the uninitiated, Purple Moon is a software studio dedicated to providing gaming software for girls ages 8 to 12. The *Rockett's Adventure* series is Purple Moon's current breadwinner.

Asked how important technical support or customer service is as part of a game's cycle, and why, Lockrem replies, "Extremely important," and expands on the sober answer:

> In the computer world, the type of technical/customer service support that a company provides contributes strongly to a customer's overall impression of that company, the quality of their products, and their willingness to stand behind what they're producing. Depending on a user's experience and technical knowledge, the level of support you're able to provide can make the difference between a favorable experience and one of "I never want to use this company's products again." You can make a customer's gaming or computer experience much more enjoyable if you take a few minutes to explain things to them in terms that are on their level of knowledge and understanding.

Based on Lockrem's long history in this field and this medium, she provides what she believes to be the best advice to pass on to others on this subject matter:

> Make sure that your technical support management is involved with the developer/publisher during the development of the product, not just at the final moment. Input from technical support can sometimes eliminate a compatibility problem with some systems, or at least can be addressed in readme notes, etc.

> Once beta stage is reached, make sure that technical support not only coordinates the beta testing, but that they're completely informed of areas that may have some minor issues that have been deferred, so that proper training and documentation has taken place prior to the general release of the product.

> Make sure that some type of database is established immediately in order to start compiling information on your customers.

When asked what form of correspondence she and her customers prefer, Lockrem says it's all of the above:

> I strongly believe that to best support your customer base, all forms of communication need to be in place, including email, phone, and fax. As the world depends more and more on computers for communication, it's imperative to be able to offer some online help regarding technical support issues,

18

along with the ability to email questions if not answered on the Web site. In addition, you need to have the ability to speak live with your customers.

If you reach a stage at which you feel you need to outsource any of your support systems, you need to personalize that training for your company and your product—buzzwords, etc. Bottom line: The more knowledge you can give to your support staff to handle customers, the better your products and your service level will be.

What if the publisher/developer has no money and it's a shareware/freeware game? Do the same principles apply as with larger companies? Lockrem responds:

Again, I think you should try and develop the same principles but customize them to the size of your company. You need to establish what your customer support criteria is going to be and what is acceptable; i.e., all calls/emails should be returned within a certain timeframe, or all support issues will be handled vie email and you can expect a response by a certain date. If you set your expectations and then publish them to your customer base via online, your product packaging, etc., your customers will appreciate the information and will respond in a positive manner.

Rodney Hodge, Imagic Online

As a game producer at Imagic Online, Rodney "Hatch" Hodge adds some different flavor to this chapter on support, since he works primarily with online games, such as the mega-popular *WarBirds*. Do the same standards apply? Is technical support as important for online games as for a boxed game? Hatch says even more so for multiplayer games.

In our business model, customer service is *very* important. Unlike the retail side of the business, where you make a product, ship it, support it for a time, then move on to the next product, we develop an ongoing relationship with our customers. We have an ever-increasing customer base that has been growing steadily since we opened our doors three years ago, including accountholders that have been with us since day one. Our yearly release schedule averages three releases and/or upgrades per game, as we're continually improving each with new graphics, features, and the like. This means that we have to satisfy new accountholders when they're just getting started, and also keep our longtime customers up and running with the problems that they invariably encounter with new releases, installing other software, hard drive crashes, and the like.

Hatch was asked if they handle their technical support queries by phone, email, and/or fax, and what works the best for them and their customers:

> I'm kind of old-fashioned in this area, and think a quick connection to a calm, instructive human voice is the best way to go. In most cases, in my experience, when a consumer calls you, he has already beaten his brains out trying to figure out the problem, and is usually at the end of his rope.
>
> The last thing I like doing when I'm in this state is sitting on hold waiting, or finding my way through a maze of pushbutton menu choices, when all I want is to tell someone about the problem I'm having and have them tell me what to do. Second best case is a quick email reply.
>
> We have our tech support Web pages split into help areas for each game. In each respective help area, you'll find a phone number and staffing information, FAQs and newsgroup support areas, and last but not least an email form to fill out and submit.
>
> One of the newest forms of help that I particularly like is the support newsgroup. The support newsgroup is very nice when you have an established player base, because it takes the least amount of input for the benefits it provides. This is an area where the customer can go to look for and/or post about the problem he's having. More times than not, another customer has already run into this problem and has posted about it, or will answer a post, explaining a fix to the problem. On top of that, a developer can go through this support newsgroup answering problems that have yet to be resolved by another player, and address a larger number of people with one post than he can effectively reach with one-on-one phone or email support. The developer can also use the support group as a good place to see what kinds of bugs or problems his customers are experiencing, and use this information to help find bugs or make design changes that improve the usability of his product.

18

Imagic Online can also boast one additional technical support angle not found in most gaming companies. Hatch divulges this unique practice:

> Another aspect of customer support, which I haven't even touched on, is the method of drawing from your customer base to help train the newcomers on the finer aspects of your products.
>
> These pages were all put together by players, for players, costing nothing more than free connect time for the people involved. They also staff a training arena five nights a week for 2½ hours every week.

The Imagic team—and especially the hard-core fans of WarBirds—have established this free training and technical support forum for newbie pilots. The goal is to help novice players get the most out of their multi-player experience. (Used with permission by Imagic Online, Inc.)

Hatch agrees it may be best to consider *only* email and FAQ files if money is tight, since it can get costly to run a support line and employ technicians to receive the call. "In that case," says Hatch, "just be sure to be prompt and professional." He continues, "The main objective here is to promote the image to your consumers that you care and want to help them, and will do so to the best of your ability."

SECTION IV

How to Make It Happen

CHAPTER 19

Doing It Yourself and the Shareware Revolution

Not all success stories in this book involve getting a job at a well-known development house or publishing company and climbing the ranks from within. Sure, it's probably beneficial to work around the likes of Sid Meier or Richard Garriott, but, similar to what's happening in the music industry with the emergence of many popular independent bands, some designers have chosen to simply sell their own creations over the Internet, and, in many cases, work from home.

You can create your own company, corporation, or other legal entity to manufacture, market, and distribute your game, but this chapter focuses on those game producers who distribute and sell their games over the World Wide Web as *shareware*. For the uninitiated, shareware games are free to download, but a small payment from the user is required to continue playing. This "try before you buy" software may be limited in time (for example, two hours of play) or in features (perhaps three out of ten levels are available), or the entire game can be given up front in good faith.

Is it really worth releasing your beloved game this way? What are the pros and cons for selling shareware, as opposed to working toward a packaged retail product? The following entries are from folks who made the decision to do it alone, and have succeeded. If this is the road you choose, take heed to this advice.

Jeff Vogel, Spiderweb Software, Inc.

Jeff Vogel is the president of Spiderweb Software, Inc., a small two-person operation in Seattle, Washington. With the help of a few freelancers, they produce and sell shareware fantasy games for the Macintosh and Windows, and likely are best known for their *Exile* role-playing game series. In fact, *Exile III: Ruined World* won the 1998 Shareware Game of the Year award from *Computer Gaming World*.

For Vogel, shareware is the best way to go:

> Someone just getting started in game development would be doing themselves a grotesque disservice to not consider shareware. Research the computer game industry, and you'll find a very bloody, competitive, corporate place. If you develop a game, you almost always have to make it recognizably part of an established genre, with the graphics done in just such a way, with all the buzzwords covered (polygons, Internet play, etc.), and even then you have to scramble like mad to get your game in the stores. With shareware, you can do your game exactly the way you want, how you want, keeping the hours you want.

But can you make a lot of money going the shareware route? "Well, no," says Vogel. "You won't get rich… but you can make a very, very good living." As with any part of the gaming industry, shareware is not a get-rich-quick scheme. As Vogel puts it, "You must first program a game good enough for people to give you money for it." Admittedly, this is no easy task in itself, and then Web surfers must notice the game, download it, and play it. "But if you can get these things, shareware is a terrific way to make a living in the computer game industry."

Just how much money can a shareware game yield? According to Vogel, his games that "look crude, have no Internet play, and have rough sounds" are making six figures a year. He explains why this is:

> Because, first, for all the graphical lack, they're extremely well-designed games. Second, I have worked hard at making sure that they get properly marketed and people hear about them. I send out a lot of press releases. I don't use magic spells to get people to buy my games. I work hard to develop them, and I work hard on our Web site and on Usenet to find and communicate with gaming magazines (online and otherwise).

Your game has to be fun. Not just "kind of fun." *Really* fun. Fun enough to get a person to pull a credit card out of his/her wallet and give you the number. This is shareware. People get to play the demo. You have nowhere to hide. Your game has to be very fun. It can look rough. It can have lame sounds. It can even have a few bugs. But if it doesn't grab people and shake the change out of their pockets, it will fail. Again, to succeed, you have to write a game that's good, no matter what.

Shareware games don't need to feature the latest and greatest in graphic or sound technology, or have multiplayer support, says Vogel. (Used with permission by Spiderweb Software)

Vogel has experienced over 100,000 downloads of Spiderweb Software games, and has received a number of calls to put his games on shareware CD compilations. However, he hasn't been approached by any major game publishers to re-release his games in retail. Not that he's interested anyway, but he qualifies it as follows:

> I just don't do anything they're interested in. I write old-school iconic games, like *Ultima IV* or *VI*. For one player. I have no interest in multiplayer, fancy cut-scenes, or the like. This is something no publisher will touch, and I can't blame them. If my games don't have these qualities, the stores won't put them on the shelves.

Along with many of the larger shareware repositories on the Web (see list, next page), Spiderweb Software games can be downloaded from their official Web site at www.spidweb.com. In addition, their Web site contains game news, screen shots, downloadable plug-in modules, contact information, and registration forms.

19

Make some room on your hard drive, because the following Web sites contain thousands upon thousands of PC and Mac shareware games, freeware, and commercial game demos:

- shareware.com
  www.shareware.com
- DOWNLOADS.COM
  www.downloads.com
- Happy Puppy
  www.happypuppy.com
- Games Domain
  www.gamesdomain.com
- Filez
  www.filez.com
- File Mine
  www.filemine.com
- File Pile
  www.filepile.com

- Jumbo
  www.jumbo.com
- TuCows
  www.tucows.com
- ZDNet Software Library
  www.hotfiles.com
- WinSite
  www.winsite.com
- 32bit.com
  www.32bit.com
- Softsite
  www.softsite.com
- Beyond.com
  www.beyond.com

Seth A. Robinson, Robinson Technologies

At 24, Seth Robinson is the CEO of Robinson Technologies, Inc. (www.rtsoft.com). You may have heard of this small Oregonian gaming company because his latest shareware game, *Dink Smallwood*, has been featured in a number of international publications. Much of their success is due to the Internet as an effective distribution medium, according to Robinson.

> Today, self-distributing through the shareware route makes much more sense than it did a number of years ago when there wasn't the [commercialization of the] Internet. With the Web, you can instantly put a demo of your product in 50,000 people's hands, and if you provide an easy way to buy the product that's quicker than driving down to the store, people will do it. Especially if the product is niche—it might not even exist in the stores.

> The best part is the cost! Generally the only investment is time and a small fee for Web access (which by now I'm sure *everybody* has). If your product sells badly, so what? Update it or start a new one.

Seth Robinson serves as lead designer/programmer Greg Smith does "a little of everything," and they generally hire artists on a project-by-project basis. Here's a shot from the celebrated Dink Smallwood. (Used with permission by Robinson Technologies, Inc.)

Robinson has covered *why* a game designer should take the shareware approach, but more important is *how* to go about doing it. When asked to supply some do's and don'ts for gamers looking to selling their goods online, Robinson gives us a number of pointers to bear in mind:

- Start saving email addresses of game-site editors. They don't always see your game—and then magically they'll announce it and put it up for download the first day it's out. It's up to you to have a "press" list to keep informed. This list will grow as you make friends in the industry and will prove invaluable later.

- We didn't make a fortune off Dink Smallwood, but it did open many doors for us. Being able to take a jewel case with a game you wrote to an interview proves many things to your possible future employer, not to mention the fact that you have "finished" something. A rare breed!

- People always say how hard the gaming industry is to break into and that you need experience to get in. The solution is simple: Work for free. Find a local gaming company and see if they offer internship. Greg [Smith] started here that way; now he has a salaried position.

- Don't even *think* about taking preorders for an unfinished game—especially if this is your first game—as we did, and I regretted it. The two months we were late were hellish…

- Don't be discouraged by low sales. The first year *LORD* was available, I sold only 7 copies. Over the next 7 years, I sold 30,000 more. The point is if your product is

19

high quality, word of mouth will do its thing. Just don't forget to update it regularly, especially your support Web page. Constant updating (at least monthly) tells the consumer that you still care about the product and won't leave them high and dry if there's a problem.

- Start small. Rate your project's difficulty from 1 to 10 and *never* start on a project that is more than 2 rating points higher than the last one you completed. Your first project? Pick a 1 or 2. That would be something like a random-quote generator or a simple screensaver.

- Use Microsoft Visual C++ and DirectX.

- Ask a friend to try your game, and watch him play it. Notice which parts he gets confused by and which keys he instinctively hits to abort menus, etc.

Wrapping up, Robinson comments on the ways to remind gamers to register their shareware product. There are many different schools of thought in this area, and Robinson believes it depends on the shareware type:

> For a utility that's used over a long period of time (macro program, paint program, etc.), showing the days left at each startup and disabling it after 30 days or so is a great way. For games, the 30-day or limited time is a bad idea. You want to provide them with the "not too hard" beginning of the game— and remember, if they don't finish the shareware portion, why would they buy the full version? So keep the shareware easy and fun and end it right about when things seem the most interesting. Think about what products *you* personally have registered; most likely they used a great registration scheme.

Robinson's words on shareware may be fitting for adventure/role-playing games such as *Dink Smallwood*, but what about classic card games? Do the same principles apply? What about the ways to remind gamers to register? Let's take a look at two other companies that make a living from creating and selling package-less Solitaire card games.

Jonas Stewart, Silver Creek Entertainment

"Well, let's start out with the fact that when you're a small fish in a big pond, you better give them your lunch money or get a shark cage," quips Jonas Stewart, vice president and "lead creative guy" at Silver Creek Entertainment (www.silvercrk.com). *Hardwood Solitaire* and *Hardwood Solitaire II* for the PC and Mac are their flagship products. Stewart is commenting on how difficult it is to get your product out in the stores, and how little the people who actually make the game take home at the end of the day. He expands:

If you want to sell in a store, you have to find a publisher (who takes their cut) and distributor (who then takes their cut), and hopefully they find you some shelf space at a superstore. You'll be lucky to get a couple dollars a game—and more than likely, even less than that. Now, if you aren't well known or your game isn't mainstream, you'll probably be lucky to get in the valueware $5 CDs. And after all those cuts… well, you do the math.

So what's a little game company to do? "Pull up a seat to the Web, my friend," says Stewart. "If you think you have a great game and know the world's gonna love it, and the publishers are not biting, the Web is the place to be."

In his opinion, the shareware model works great on the Internet because it allows game designers like Silver Creek to pop up a site and sell games just like anyone else. As Stewart puts it, "Basically, all you need to do is make your game, build your site, promote it, and if you have a game that people like… watch the orders come in."

Stewart believes that with shareware, everyone wins. The gamers get a good feel for what the full version of the game is like, and the designers benefit from greater consumer satisfaction. Since you have to deal with all of the customers directly by selling games yourself, it will be less hassle, and there should be fewer dissatisfied gamers because they had an opportunity to see what the game is all about before reaching for their credit card.

"With shareware," continues Stewart, "you can make as many or as few improvements as you like, and you decide if at some certain point you feel that you've added enough to warrant selling a new version of your game." He recalls the decision to sell *Hardwood Solitaire II*: "We had spent a lot of time, and more importantly had made enough improvements, to call it a new version of the game to sell."

19

In Hardwood Solitaire II, Klondike is free, but the other games and additional features are unlocked once the registration fee is collected. (Used with permission by Silver Creek Entertainment)

Getting gamers to reach into their pockets and spring for the full version is not an easy thing, warns Stewart. "They don't give it to you without a fight, so what seems to work best is to use the $^1/_3$ rule. That is, give them a third of the game for free, and if they want more fun and excitement they need to pay."

To collect the money sold from your games, Stewart says there are roughly three ways to do this: Get a merchant account and take orders on your Web site; use a service that collects them for you, and they'll take care of the processing and credit card orders (but will likely take around a 25% fee); or use "ad-ware," where the full game is given away to the consumer for free but you must sell advertisement space in your game. This last option is commonly found on Internet-only games.

➤ To learn more about shareware marketing and other handy advice, be sure to drop by and visit with the Association of Shareware Professionals (ASP). Their mission statement, FAQ, and membership information is available at www.asp-shareware.org.

Bryan Horling, Freeverse Software

Some shareware developers take a slightly more aggressive approach to reminding the user that the program needs to be paid for to continue playing. Such is the case with Freeverse Software (www.freeverse.com). If you've never heard of *Burning Monkey Solitaire*, chances are that you're not visiting the shareware archives regularly enough. Bryan Horling is an associate programmer on this popular PC and Mac game that adds animation, a whole host of options, and most importantly humor, to a collection of Solitaire card games.

The latest version of Burning Monkey Solitaire for the PC garnered more than 30,000 downloads in its first two weeks from one site. (Used with permission by Freeverse Software)

In *Burning Monkey Solitaire*, if the gamer doesn't register the program after 15 plays per game, it will be unavailable the 16th time the game is booted up. For instance, if you play *Klondike* the most, it will be deleted from the list of options. Then, after another 15 plays of, say, *Strict Klondike* or *Pyramid Solitaire*, they'll become unavailable as well. This continues until all of the games are inaccessible, unless a registration code is given. So why this approach? Horling says:

> Make sure you have something in the program that either cuts off some features or annoys [users] if they haven't paid their shareware fee. Given the opportunity, many users will use your software forever without paying, either through deliberate choice or ignorance. If you're just writing for the experience and knowledge that people like your stuff, this isn't a big deal, but if you hope to finance your next computer upgrade, it's more of an issue.

This method still beats selling the game up front through regular retail channels, believes Horling, and it boils down to "simplicity and control." Says Horling, "Shareware is a very simple model—you basically write it and release it. You control the distribution and collect all the profits." But how can a company that makes classic card games make any money? Freeverse's *Burning Monkey Solitaire* and Silver Creek Entertainment's *Hardwood Solitaire II* are both good examples of simply improving on a good thing. In other words, shareware game designers need not feel they must reinvent the wheel. It *is* possible to create a product, and demand for that product, by borrowing from the classics. Does Horling believe this to be true?

> Yes, absolutely. But check out your competition. Download all the relevant competitors and make sure you have more features, lower price, or a better implementation. On the whole, though, I do think it's a good idea. Improving lets you start with a presumably successful base and just work on making it better. This is much easier than starting from scratch and then trying to both teach users a new game and convince them that it's a good idea in the same breath.

19

Seumas McNally, Longbow Digital Arts

At the time of writing this book, the number one download on many shareware sites and gaming e-zines was *DX-Ball 2*, the sequel to Michael P. Welch's popular *Breakout* or *Arkanoid* clone. Seumas McNally is the programmer who's responsible for the game at Longbow Digital Arts (www.longbowdigitalarts.com). The fact that Seumas (along with the other three McNallys in the family software business) lives in central Ontario, Canada, and not Silicon Valley doesn't matter when you're a shareware purveyor.

Right now the World Wide Web is becoming a very viable medium for independent software sales and advertising. We're just starting to see computers and the Internet become almost ubiquitous in the middle class home, and the large credit card companies are finally opening up to Internet transactions with prime-time TV commercials extolling the benefits of shopping with a point and a click. Unfounded consumer fear regarding online transactions is diminishing, as more and more people realize how easy it is to shop on the Internet.

McNally recognizes that the Internet is an exciting and practical tool for shareware developers, but this technology isn't worth much if the game isn't up to par:

> What it all boils down to, of course, is having a kickass product. It's easy to be blinded by your own love for a game, especially if it's your first project. You have to look at a game objectively, taking into account all the other products in the genre, to get a good feel for how it will do. I've seen a lot of shareware games for Windows that perhaps shouldn't have even been released as freeware. But don't be discouraged, learn from your mistakes, and your next products will be better.

McNally says if a game is really not catching on, no matter how hard it's pushed and promoted, that probably means it's just not that good, or at least the learning curve is too steep for people to get into it. (Used with permission by Longbow Digital Arts)

McNally insists that once you have a good product, a lot of the marketing will take care of itself, with player word of mouth and online editorial coverage. After all, the overhead is minimal to run the operation yourself. Says McNally, "Two key things are having your own Web site with a domain name (only $100 a year or so, plus perhaps $20/month for Web storage and a few email accounts), and getting your software's demo or free version as widely known as possible."

>> To increase the awareness of your shareware product, it may be worth investing in AddWeb (www.cyberspacehq.com), a program that automatically submits your web site to hundreds of search engines and directories. A free demo is also offered.

We've looked at how role-playing games and card games typically "request" payment from the gamer. Where does an arcade game like *DX-Ball 2* fit in? "Giving people the whole product and asking them to pay if they use it, the most classic and altruistic form of shareware, doesn't work worth beans," says McNally. "You need to give them a little, just enough to get them hooked, and then gently suggest that they can instantly purchase even more of this fun goodness for only xx dollars online at _____." For *DX-Ball 2*, that "little bit of goodness" is 24 free levels out of a total of 150 in the full version.

In closing, McNally also suggests that it helps to include an offline ordering method (send a check or money order for xx dollars to the company address) to give people confidence that you're not just some fly-by-night Internet operation, and for the odd person who doesn't have a credit card.

Steve Moraff, MoraffWare

Steve Moraff was one of the first independent game developers to release "shareware" in the early 1980s, though he was not aware of the term *shareware* until a few years later. Some of his best-selling work includes *MoreJongg*, *SphereJongg*, and *RingJongg*, three variations of the classic Asian tile game Mahjongg available from his Florida company, MoraffWare (www.moraff.com).

When asked why a game developer would prefer to go the shareware route, as opposed to working at a development house, Moraff offers this straightforward guidance:

> The bottom line is that authors have to decide what kind of lifestyle they want. If they self-publish shareware, they have a real relationship with their users and they're their own boss, but they have to handle a lot of non-programming work to support their business. If they go with a publisher, they have to do what the publisher wants, and they're at the mercy of the random winds of the corrupt retail distribution system, but they don't have to deal with non-programming tasks as much.

Moraff and company offer full games up front to the user, but with fewer background images, music, and tile sets to choose from. The following are Moraff's opinions on finding the right way to encourage gamers to pay money:

> Shareware reminders generally have to be somewhat obnoxious to work. Making games stop functioning after a 30-day trial may be the most effective

19

way, but it really annoys users and cuts down on distribution. Annoying nag screens that have to be clicked off at the end of the game are what I use, and I find them to be the best balance between the need to get registrations and the need to maintain a desirable shareware game.

He concedes, though, "I do have a particularly annoying second nag screen that appears after about eight hours of use."

Steve Moraff's games, such MoreJongg, above, and Fancy Jiggler, below, add music, art, and stunning photographs to classic games. (Used with permission by Moraffware)

CHAPTER **20**

Breaking Into the Industry

As evidenced by the interviews published in this book, there are many ways
to break into the gaming industry. The two most common ways, however,
are to get a job at an existing development studio or publishing company, or
to create the game on your own terms and approach a publisher and/or distributor to pick up the title. Exactly what kind of company you launch on
your own is another consideration altogether, and there many varied ways to
do so.

The gaming industry is full of success stories from people who have chosen
either of these two popular avenues. The first half of this chapter focuses
on the best ways to present your idea for a game (or the game itself) to a
publisher, and the second half concentrates on getting a job at a game
company—and the best ways to get in the door. Keep in mind that other
chapters, such as those on art, animation, programming, and music, offer
advice specific for those fields.

Before diving into this chapter, here's a few inspiring and valuable words from Jim Charne, president and executive director of the Academy of Interactive Arts and Sciences (AIAS). He reminds budding game designers that PC and console gaming has gone from a hobby to a thriving industry over the last 10 years, and it's an exciting time to jump in. Advises Charne:

> This means there are long-term career opportunities for people who are serious, hardworking, and prepared. Like any career, it takes talent, hard work, perseverance, and luck to rise to the top. But there's no doubt the opportunities are there.

Charne also offers tips on ensuring your success:

> Get as much education as you can. As systems become more complex, training at the university level and even postgraduate work will serve you well. This is especially important in technical areas (advanced math is critical), but also applies to music, art, and design.

> Keep current in the literature of the field. Read the magazines, know the products. Don't just play the products—study them. Know what works and what doesn't. Form opinions and be able to express them intelligently. People respect that.

And finally, Charne encourages you to learn what's going on the world:

> Read the *New York Times* every day. Be able to discuss politics, religion, history, literature, music, current events. Your game must find an audience in the real world. Don't isolate yourself from it.

And on with the chapter we go...

Pitching Your Game to a Publisher

This is the preferred path, but it's hard to pull off. This strategy is the most ideal to a designer because the chances of getting your own game on store shelves are much greater, and of course faster, than working your way up internally at another company. Assuming this is the way you want to go, the following talented advisory board offers do's and don'ts of how, when, and why a game should be pitched to a publisher.

Mitzi McGilvray, Electronic Arts

Mitzi McGilvray is a supervising producer at Electronic Arts. Some of the well known franchises she's worked on include *NCAA Football*, *March Madness*, and *NHL Hockey*.

McGilvray admits she has received quite a few pitches on EA's behalf from budding game designers, so she's eager to discuss how a game or game idea should be presented for consideration to a publishing company.

Before we get into the content of the package, McGilvray urges game designers to protect themselves and their ideas:

> I don't recommend sending anything unsolicited without making some contact within a company. Some companies require that nondisclosure agreements be signed in advance; others may wait. Remember, you may think you have the most innovative, creative idea ever, but there's a high likelihood that it's been done before, is being done, or has been rejected. *Great ideas are easy to come by; great executions take hard work, talent, timing, and luck!*

McGilvray admits she's witnessed some pretty sloppy pitches from game designers, so she wants to set the record straight on the best way to impress a publisher. She insists a well-presented "package" is very important because "if you can't clearly communicate your ideas and present them in a way that the publisher gets excited about it, how do you think the consumer is going to like your work?"

Design Documents

A *design document* should be included with the package, and according to McGilvray, it should contain a way for production and marketing to understand and plan for what the game is intended to be, and a blueprint for programmers to create the code for the game. Most important of all, the design document should be a "living" document that can evolve as the game comes to life.

McGilvray indicates what she believes to be critical when writing a design document:

> Details, details, details. As you're creating the design document, imagine that you won't be around when the game is being programmed. Be sure to cover all of the details.

> Plan for flexibility. It's very likely that once you complete the design document you'll need to go back and modify it on a regular basis. Keep the design modular so updates can be made without impacting large portions of the game. Examples would be to allow the addition (or subtraction) of game features without blowing up the entire game. Also, have a few sacrificial features that you can eliminate if you run out of time.

> Listen, listen, listen. Get lots of feedback on your design by a good variety of skill sets before you start coding. You'll learn that you've probably left a lot

20

of holes in the design and that there may be more effective ways of communicating your ideas.

Be graphic! This may sound goofy, but pictures, flow charts, and diagrams really help out the artists and programmers when they're trying to figure it out.

Persistence vs. Annoyance

McGilvray says if you're ready to pitch your game—or even after you've made your presentation—*do* follow up, but *don't* annoy:

This is a very fine line. Publishers are usually very busy, so it's important that you "stay above the noise" by sending occasional emails or phone messages to see what's up. Don't be a pain, however.

And don't try to snow the publisher! Most publishers have been burned too many times and get very nervous when someone comes in and says that they can do the impossible.

The Ideal Pitch

Want to know what to do to maximize your chances? McGilvray lays out what she believes to be a solid package from a game designer:

Ideally a finished, polished product. But since this is the real world, publishers understand that most people don't have the funding to do this on their own.

Next best thing to a finished product is to get a prototype. This should be working code and graphics that captures a small portion of the look and feel of the product. In addition to the prototype, include a one-pager that describes what the product is to be and how it will play. Also, a great thing to include would be a sample "back of the box." This would include a few mocked-up screens as well as the top selling points and competitive features of the game.

Can't do a prototype? Then just send off the one-pager and the sample back of the box. Also, include a few paragraphs on what the game might be like to play. Include info on what the buttons will do and what will be fun.

Be prepared once you pitch a product to supply additional information, such as a more complete design document. If you're planning on developing the product yourself (with artists, programmers, audio technicians, etc.), many publishers will request budgets, timelines, documentation on ownership of the design, as well as information on the financial status of your company.

Mitzi McGilvray says she'd like to start a line of sports products at EA geared toward the "girl gamer." Have any ideas? Now you know how to pitch 'em.

Josh Resnick, Pandemic Studios

At Activision, Josh Resnick served as producer for *Mechwarrior 2* and director for *Dark Reign*, and oversaw the production of *Battlezone*. Last year, he left Activision to form and preside over Pandemic Studios, a new development house affiliate for Activision. Resnick says there are five key pointers on pitching a game idea to a publisher. But shouldn't gamers first try to make the game on their own and *then* try to sell it? Didn't EA's McGilvray says it's ideal if the game is already finished? While Resnick agrees it may be easier to get it picked up if it's already done or near-done, he urges gamers to "start getting experience on someone else's dime first," and comments that someone "would be absolutely crazy to do it all on their own." At the very least, there should be a working demo of the game engine, says Resnick. With that in mind, let's get right to his five commandments:

Get a Team

"It's getting more difficult for one guy with a concept to go to a publisher these days," admits Resnick. "Publishers are interested in *teams*, and everyone on the team should have a background." At the same time, Resnick understands the catch-22 here about publishers preferring designers with backgrounds. As with most (if not all) of the entertainment industries, such as film, music, or television, production companies/labels expect you to have experience, but it's often hard to get experience unless a company hires you! "Teams are absolutely critical in my opinion," repeats Resnick. "You won't get the best development deal in the world if it's just you cranking away on a game in your basement."

Be Realistic and Professional

"Don't walk into a publisher's office and pitch them on an idea that isn't realistic, such as expensive full-motion video or 100+ missions," warns Resnick. "Look at what others can do with a certain amount of money within a timeframe, because you have to look like you know what you're doing. It's critical to prove yourself realistic and professional." Show an accessible interface; show that the engine can compete against what's out there.

For instance, a *Battlezone* or *Dark Reign* style of game will cost roughly $1 million to $1.5 million. Says Resnick, "If that's the case, show you're willing to eat Cup-a-Noodles for a year! Publishers want to see commitment, and that you're willing to make it work—maybe even not take salary for a year."

20

What About a Licensed Property?

"One of the best bets is to ask yourself, 'How can I attach this to an licensed property?'" says Resnick. Publishers are focused on a licensed property because the consumer is already familiar with the game's universe, rules, and characters. Only franchises allow publishers to have stability in their portfolio and budget planning. Once they know that a particular title will be able to sell at least "x" number of units, they can then be much more accurate in their spending against that title and their revenue projections. "That's one of the differences between a game like *Dark Reign* and *GoldenEye 007*," comments Resnick. "But as luck and talent would have it, *Dark Reign* has now become a franchise, with its own consumer recognition."

Another reason why publishers are drawn to a popular franchise, says Resnick, is because they can own it outright—for a price, but it will be likely worth it.

➤ Chapters 2 and 3 discuss the pros and cons of working with a well-known franchise. Content in those chapters is contributed by folks who have worked on *Star Trek*, *Star Wars*, and *Dungeons & Dragons* PC games.

Depending on the franchise rights, publishers may also have to pay roughly 10% of the revenues to the owners.

But sometimes licensed properties don't work out. Explains Resnick:

> In hindsight, we shouldn't have spent the money to license the *Battlezone* property; as it turned out, we didn't need it and [the game] wasn't anywhere close to the original. It probably worked against us. This was because the gameplay was totally new, cutting edge, and not like the original arcade game. It caused confusion.

 Note >> *Battlezone* was one of the first games to mix real-time strategy and a first-person perspective view of the action. Other games that melded these genres include 3DO's *Uprising* and Microsoft's *Urban Assault*.

Protect Yourself

As a rule, Resnick advises, "You can never protect yourself enough," but fortunately, "publishers are not out to steal ideas." In fact, a mutual NDA (nondisclosure agreement) may be insisted upon by the publisher to say that it's the designer's game and/or game idea, says Resnick. These NDA forms can likely be picked up in a stationery or office supply store.

Before even approaching publishers, game designers with little cash can mail the game (or design document for the game) to themselves in an envelope—and then don't open it. Why, you ask? The stamp will be dated, proving when the idea was originally documented or programmed. Of course, this is a temporary measure. Resnick suggests that game designers who are worried about someone stealing their idea have a lawyer witness the idea during a meeting, with the lawyer taking notes to record the idea. "This may cost a couple hundred dollars," says Resnick, "but it may be worth it."

As a side note, Resnick advises that if game designers are lucky enough to sign on with a publisher, they should watch what they're signing:

> Don't sign your life away. [Contracts] can be very one-sided. Publishers will naturally try to grab everything they can. A *one-off* deal [an agreement with the company to publish just one game at a time] is great because you're not obligated to the publisher for 10 years or anything. And besides, if the game is successful, they will surely come back for more, or other publishers will.

Get in the Door

Resnick recommends that game designers take advantage of the fact that the PC and console gaming industries are still relatively young. He explains:

> Fortunately, it's not too hard yet to break into the gaming industry, like it is in the film industry. There's so many forums, expositions, trade shows—and no egos yet, so you can approach some of the biggest names in the business. And all the key people are still accessible and will answer email, too.

Perhaps the last of Resnick's advice is the most pointed—thousands of people out there are capable of making a great game, but only a few have the desire and *chutzpah* to sell themselves, their team, and/or their game to a well-known publisher. Just remember, the worst case scenario (if you protect your idea) is that they won't be interested. With nothing to lose and so much to gain, the only ones who lose out are the ones who don't do anything with their idea at all…

 Note >> "Dave" from the popular "Dave's Video Game Classics" Web site says downloading emulator source code is a good way to test out your game programming skills. Says Dave: "Open source code allows anyone interested in working on the project to get involved, and thus allows the project to develop more rapidly (assuming it gets popular enough, like MAME [Multiple Arcade Machine Emulator] did)." According to Dave, a few authors who started by resurrecting arcade games via emulators such as MAME have gone on to large development companies. "Dave's Video Game Classics" is at www.davesclassics.com.

20

Michael Rubinelli, THQ

As vice president of development at THQ, Inc., Michael Rubinelli manages the people who manage the game developers. Who better to ask about the best ways to approach a publishing company?

Rubinelli says there are three pieces to the puzzle, and, while you don't need all three to spark interest with a publisher, the more you have, the better:

- First on the list is a compelling design document. To reiterate, this is a comprehensive outline of all the game's features and story, with information for all members of the design team.
- Second, a 2D, colorized storyboard or character model collection is recommended. Rubinelli says it's important to have an artist give the publisher an idea of the visual tone or flavor of the game by submitting sketches, rendered characters, or background drawings.
- Third on the list is some form of demo technology—that is, a working prototype of the game's engine.

Rubinelli says it sure helps if you have a talented team already chosen to work on the game.

The last piece of advice from Rubinelli is to know the platform on which the game is going to be published. In other words, understand the strengths and limitations of the platform (for example, Sony PlayStation or Nintendo 64), and be sure the publishers know you're aware of the platform.

 Note >> Rubinelli says it can cost anywhere from $20,000 to $25,000 for a console development kit. This is something the publishers would likely have to purchase for the developers. Yes, this is on top of paying salaries for the developers.

When asked what kinds of games he looks to scoop up at THQ, Rubinelli admits that his answer would sound trite, but couldn't be closer to the truth:

I'm looking for a *hit* game. That is, I want to know what kind of game a designer has a real passion for. If the developers are working on something they really want to work on, it comes through in the game, and everyone wins, regardless of the game genre.

Rubinelli admits he thinks sports games are a little limited in scope, while action games have more flexibility to them, with more variations of gameplay.

Melanie Cambron, Virtual Search

As a full-time headhunter in the gaming industry, Melanie Cambron has learned a thing or two about what a publisher wants to see when someone is pitching a game.

➤ To read Cambron's article on ways to impress a publisher, turn to Chapter 21, "Game Agents and Headhunters."

Franz Lanzinger, Actual Entertainment

After independently developing games such as *Gubble 1* and *2* for close to 10 years, Actual Entertainment's Franz Lanzinger has a few words of wisdom he'd be happy to share with others. Though it may be more sobering than one would wish to hear, it's the truth, according to Lanzinger:

> My general advice to aspiring game developers is this: Don't quit your day job. It's about as tough to make money in the game business as it is to break into the movie business. Most people start by taking a job at a game company first, and then breaking away once they know something about the business.
>
> If you love games and simply have to work on games because anything else would suck in comparison, then yes, give it a try, but don't expect to get rich right away—if ever.
>
> Marketing and distributing your game on your own isn't for the faint of heart, or poor of pocket. Be prepared to lose whatever money and time you might be inclined to invest. Sometimes it's the only option to get your game out there, and it can be fun to try. Be aware, though, that most of these attempts, including ours at Actual Entertainment, turn into labors of love rather than big, successful companies.

Paul O'Connor, Oddworld Inhabitants

We heard from this veteran game and level designer in Chapter 6, but he offers a few words here on breaking into the business:

> My answer is to seek a well-rounded education. For every game you play, read three books. Take writing courses in college.
>
> Develop an ability to critically analyze all forms of entertainment—learn to break things down and determine what makes them tick. Game design is a collaborative art, so if you can't get along with others, seek other work. This task involves meetings and continual compromise. If you want to work alone in a garret, you're better off writing novels. As far as breaking in is concerned, most game designers seem to start as testers—it's a low-wage job with impossible hours, but it's your best opportunity to impress a company with your grasp of games and move up into a design position.

20

Getting a Job at a Gaming Company

While it may not be as glamorous, getting a job at a game developer or publishing company may be the most educational and advantageous plan in the long run. Consider the time spent with a hand-picked team of talented artists, animators, programmers, level designers, musicians, and so forth, where each member is responsible for his or her own part of the overall picture. Moreover, development tools are provided, so it costs much less to work at a development company rather than starting your own right away. And finally, this scenario allows the individual to understand the codependent relationship between a developer and publisher.

The following is a collection of advice on getting into your favorite development studio or publishing company.

Paul Jaquays, id Software

id Software's Paul Jaquays reminds game designers that it's not that easy to become a respected "pro" in this field.

> For every 10,000 kids who dream of working as a professional game maker, only a relative few will actually make it as a pro within the industry. And of those who do make it, even less will become "household names" even inside the industry.

So how do you know you're fit for the part? Jaquays begins as follows:

> Evaluate yourself and answer the following questions *honestly*:

- Do you have a driving urge to make things?
- Do you prefer making games to playing them?
- Do you like the challenge of solving problems on a daily basis?
- Are you willing to commit yourself to a career in which your working hours will be longer—sometimes *far* longer—than those of the average working guy or gal?
- Do you have creative ability in more than a single area?
- If you're already in a relationship with someone, does he or she understand how much of your life will be consumed by your job (and is he or she willing to accept that)?

Needless to say, the correct answer really needs to be "yes" to all questions.

As someone who works at one of the most prestigious gaming development houses in the world, Jaquays has often been asked what kind of background it takes to make it in the biz. The answer? "A varied one," says Jaquays. He expands:

A successful candidate needs to develop multiple talents and skill packages. Examples of talent areas include but are not limited to story creation, 2D texture art, 3D modeling, model skins, level design, game scenario script writing, dialogue writing, music, sound effects, programming, project management, and business. Focus on one skill in particular, but try to be a polymath with as many other useful skills as you can manage. The most valuable team members are those who can wear many hats and perform several functions on a project.

Raw skill is all fine and dandy, but Jaquays encourages schooling, where possible, to get training in your talented areas:

Employers really want creativity, but they really *need* people with the technical skills to put those talents to use. If you want to write, obviously you should take a creative writing class, but just as important, take a typing class. If you want to do game art, take all the art classes you can get—even if they have nothing to do with computers. If you want to build 3D game levels, take computer assisted drafting (CAD) classes. Want to make music? Join the band.

Going back to the point on "wearing many hats," Jaquays insists that even if you don't have skill in all aspects of game product creation, you should learn as much as you can about the areas that are not your forte. "You will need to understand your future teammates and what it is that they do."

If you can get an interview, Jaquays reminds you to be prepared: "Always have a printed résumé and a presentation package of your best work available to send out at a moment's notice." He also suggests having additional résumés handy, and mentions that it may be worthwhile to set up an account with a next-day delivery service so that you have shipping supplies on hand at all times.

Assuming someone has some raw talent and schooling to help sharpen their skills, when should they begin knocking down doors? Jaquays offers the following:

20

Don't expect a potential employer to immediately recognize your raw talents. Get experience first. Generally this means nonprofessional experience participating in non-commercial conversions or modifications of existing games. Treat the project like it's a commercial endeavor. Show that you can do work of professional caliber, and, most important, finish your contribution to the project on schedule.

Once you've made up your mind that this is what you'd like to do for a living, is it best to jump in feet first? Is your meal ticket written? Jaquays says it's not likely:

> Don't quit your day job. This is important. Chances are you'll spend a long time before getting your foot in the door. Even if you're living rent-free in your parents' home, you'll need to keep yourself in relatively up-to-date computer hardware.
>
> Everyone dreams of being a star. The truth is, most folks working in the business don't get their pictures in *Newsweek* or their pithy thoughts quoted in *Rolling Stone*. They don't drive expensive foreign sports cars or vacation frequently on tropical islands. You can dream, but don't expect to start at the top, or even somewhere in the middle. There are a lot of "overnight success stories" out there, but most of them paid their dues to get there, starting off at the bottom of the food chain. Now, just because I've said that, it doesn't mean that you shouldn't set your goals high. It doesn't hurt to apply to high-profile game development companies, but recognize that most of them are as successful as they are because they have already hired experienced people.

Instead, Jaquays recommends you consider temporary employment situations, since it's a chance to show someone what you really can do. Talented temporary staff often find their way into full-time situations with their employer, or even a recommendation to another development company. Need an example? Here's one right from the horse's mouth:

> My first job in the computer game business started with a nine-week contract at Coleco, trying to design a fantasy role-playing game that would work with a primitive bar code reader. By the time it ended, I was a creative director in charge of a staff of designers making games for the ColecoVision, Atari 2600, Intellivision, and ADAM computer.
>
> And don't limit your job choices to a single geographic area. Be prepared to move around as needed. Make sure that your spouse (or future spouse) understands this. Companies come and go in this business. Don't plan on being anyplace for long.

Many people are overwhelmed by the size of the growing gaming industry and feel they can't penetrate its borders. How can someone from the outside get in? Keep your eyes and ears open, says Jaquays, and get out to gaming events:

> There's a great deal of truth in the old saw, "It's not what you know, but who you know." Quite often, industry jobs are gained by someone referring

someone they know as a friend or acquaintance, or have met in person at least once before. I know that as an art director, I was usually more willing to assign illustration projects to people I had met than to unknowns who just sent me portfolios. Given this, you should try to go places where industry professionals get together. National or even regional LAN parties, professional game tournaments, and design seminars are all excellent places to meet people already working in the industry. Make an effort to introduce yourself, and if possible have them look over samples of your work.

And once you're in the door? What happens now? Jaquays says to "be nice to each other." Isn't that obvious?

I shouldn't have to explain that, but I will. The Internet has rapidly replaced the fan magazines and amateur press associations that were prevalent when I started my career. Fans of old used those venues to express their opinions on their hallowed topics, "flaming" any who disagreed with them. Interchanges of ideas took place over periods of months. Now, fans who have interests in things can communicate with each other instantly in chat rooms, message boards, and online forums. The relative anonymity of the net often lulls people into thinking that they can be rude to others whenever they feel like it. However, being disrespectful can catch up with a person. Trashing the comments, beliefs, or skills of someone online may feel good for the moment, but this is a small industry we work in (or hope to work in). Folks working in it tend to know lots of other folks working at other companies. And they talk to each other. Word gets around. It should go without saying that you ought to treat everyone working in the industry like they might possibly be your boss someday. That is to say, give them respect. Treat other would-be professionals with respect also. You never know when you might be on a development team together. Or even find yourself working for them.

When you finally get that job in the game industry, continue to treat everyone working in the industry like they may be your boss someday (two guys I hired to work at Coleco had previously hired me to do freelance work for the game companies they worked for). And remember to extend a helping hand to tomorrow's professionals.

20

But how do you really know if you're good enough to give it a shot? Who can you trust for honest advice?

Be wary of the flattery of your friends. Appreciate it, but recognize that your friends probably aren't qualified to give you the insight you need to grow and develop your skills (and friends often find it difficult to criticize). Seek out legitimate criticism of your work by people you recognize to be better at the task than you are. Accept criticism gracefully. Be especially appreciative if it's constructive criticism.

Finally, are there any downsides to making games for a living? There couldn't be, right? Jaquays warns:

> Be prepared to lose your game-playing hobby. This has been true for me, but it may not be true for you. When I started creating games professionally, the type of game I worked on no longer became fun to play for pure recreation. It started when I was first doing role-playing adventures. The more I wrote game scenarios for pay, the less I wanted to do it for fun. When I started making arcade game conversions for Coleco, I quickly lost interest in popping quarters into machines in arcades. (However, due to the kind of designers I was able to hire, we put together an incredible role-playing game group after hours.) When I went back to designing role-playing adventures once more, I stopped doing it for fun again. Now I really like making 3D FPS game settings, but I have a hard time playing them for fun. It's not that I don't like them; it's that I can't play without turning on my professional eye. Essentially, when playing I don't see the game, I see how it's made.

Kevin Cloud, id Software

Artist and part owner of id Software Kevin Cloud believes that you should get into the industry at any position to start. Says Cloud:

> A game designer shouldn't break into the business. Out of all of the positions in a game company, a designer requires the most experience. It isn't enough to have a good idea. Designers need to understand the process of creating a game. They need to understand what can be achieved, how many people are needed to get it done, and how long it will take. A game designer needs to break into the business as a writer, project manager, artist, programmer, level designer, or beta tester.

Concludes Cloud, "A designer needs to be anything but a designer when he starts."

Peter Molyneux, Lionhead Studios

The genius behind such beloved PC classics as *Populous*, *Syndicate*, *Dungeon Keeper*, and *Magic Carpet* offers the following advice on breaking into the gaming industry, and touches on a few do's and don'ts as well.

There are three main ways into the game industry. The first is education—get a related degree such as math, programming, or philosophy if you want to be a programmer, or a branch of the visual arts if you intend to work as an artist. To take this route in the U.K., you would need a very good degree from a very good university.

The second way would be to start at the bottom, say as a games tester or assistant, and work your way up.

The third way, and the hardest way these days, is to get together with some like-minded game freaks and start your own company.

My do's would be as follows—if you want to be successful at anything, you must be willing to make it the most important thing in your life. It's no good expecting to be a success if you want a 9-to-5 job. If you're sending stuff out to prospective employers, make it brief but exciting. This covers everything from CVs [curriculum vitae] to games design—detail can be long-winded and off-putting.

Finally, Molyneux urges you to "believe in yourself, because if you don't, no one else will."

Phil Steinmeyer, PopTop Software

President, lead designer, and lead programmer at the newly formed PopTop Software (responsible for the award-winning *Railroad Tycoon II*), Phil Steinmeyer offers some words of wisdom on breaking into the industry:

Don't Overshoot on Your First Game

The Internet is littered with abandoned projects by three or four guys with no game development experience who were going to create a better *Quake*, or the ultimate first-person RPG. If you're working in your spare time, with no prior experience, don't expect to outdo experienced, professional, large, well-financed teams. Shoot for something achievable. If you like level design, do a series of levels for your favorite first-person shooter or strategy game. If you're a programmer, do a clone of your favorite early '80s arcade game (*Pac Man*, *Space Invaders*, etc.). If you're an artist, do skins for *Quake*, or 3D character animations based on your favorite game. Above all else— *complete it*! That's the main reason for choosing something of modest size and scope—it's achievable. I'd rather see a finished *Pac Man* variant than a *Quake* killer that's 10% done, consisting of a few polygons slapped on the screen.

20

When Applying for a Job, Have Samples

With everyone hooked up to the Web these days, there's no excuse for not having electronic samples of your work available for any prospective employer—either attached to your application, or accessible at your Web site (include the URL with your application). For a level designer, this should be levels, well made, preferably to two or more different games (the more games you do levels for, the more likely the person you're applying to will be familiar with at least one of them and be able to fire it up and take a quick look at your level). For an artist, include as wide a variety of art types as possible—2D, 3D, hand drawn, animation, characters, mechanical objects, etc. For a programmer, a playable demo, with at least some art (you may have to hook up with a friend for the art).

Be Versatile

PopTop Software is a six-person company. We don't have separate full-time positions for every type of job we've got. One artist does sound as well. Another does video and art. Our chief scenario designer got the job in part because he's also a talented artist and a good writer—so for the long stretches of projects when the game is too rough to start level design, he can do other things.

Choosing a Game Theme

The first time you're in a position to design a real commercial game, be original (remember, newbies, I recommend something simple for your first effort—now I'm talking about *after* you've got that under your belt). Most likely this first game will have a modest budget, and your own skills as well as those of your team may still be a bit rough. Don't try to outgun the 50-person, $3 million budget AAA titles that overcrowd the first-person shooter and real-time strategy genres. Pick a niche where there's little competition, or where the existing competition is similarly modest in budget. Some examples are war games, puzzle games, retro 2D action games.

In conclusion, Steinmeyer reminds us that "it's far easier to shine with little competition, then move up to more ambitious projects."

Michael Rubinelli, THQ

In the first half of this chapter, Michael Rubinelli speaks to game designers who want to pitch games or game ideas directly to publishers. Now he offers some advice on getting a job within an existing company:

Instead of trying to get into a company as a game designer or producer, it's best to start at an entry-level position, since these titles [game designer or producer] are usually given to those who have been in the industry for a while. The people who get those positions have a history, so if you're just starting out it's best to start off in the testing department or perhaps customer service. The good news is that when a large company starts hiring, they often look internally first; they look to promote from within.

Rubinelli says many employers turn to the testing group when looking to promote an employee.

Josh Resnick, Activision

Resnick, whom we also hear from in the first half of this chapter, says a great way to get in the door to a company is to submit levels or maps. In fact, Activision has even paid a few *Dark Reign* map designers, when their content was used in some way. Says Resnick on using game editors, for all professions:

It's one of the best ways to get hired for a development team, period. A level designer can make a level using free utilities for action or strategy games, programmers can submit a MOD, artists can make skins. It's never been easier. And it also kisses the ass of publishers because these designers liked their games enough to take the time to create these add-ons.

In closing, Resnick reminds those who are looking for a job to get online. "Game developers and publishers are always looking for good people on the Internet."

 Tip >> Alex Garden, CEO and lead game designer at Relic Entertainment, offers this tidbit on getting a job at a game company: "A great way to get in the industry is to critique existing products, play the entire game, write a design document, point out how to improve the game, and send it to people who made the game—someone will take you seriously, and even if they don't hire you, you will get great practice."

Sid Meier, Firaxis Games

"Get involved as a play tester, and over time, demonstrate your knowledge, be active, and offer suggestions," says Meier, outlining the best traditional way to climb the ladder. "Another way is to write manuals for a company," says Meier. "That is, do something related to game design, and if you have talent, it will be recognized."

But what about doing it yourself instead of this traditional way of getting in the industry? Says Meier:

20

The second route is the quickest but requires luck and a lot of talent. If this is what you want to do, and you're a programmer or are working with one, put together a playable demo of your game and shop it around. We all know of the story with *SimCity*. Will Wright took it to eight publishers who all turned it down, except Maxis. Now publishers are a lot more sensitive, but you must put together a good prototype. And it doesn't need FMV [full-motion video] or polished graphics.

➤ Be sure to read Sid Meier's advice on general game design in Chapter 2.

Richard "Lord British" Garriott, Origin Systems

As one of the most-recognized and longest-running game designers in the industry, Origin Systems' Lord British has given quite a bit of advice over the years on how to get into the industry. He offers the following:

Find a way into the building of a game company. Get a job in customer service or quality assurance testing, because it's very hard to be a game designer right off the bat. Maybe 20 years ago, but not now... But, on the flip side, our industry is very young, and it may only take you three to five years to get to the top; there are huge opportunities.

Twenty years ago they didn't care if you had a degree, but now it's very important. Their fear is that you're a hacker and not an engineer. Hackers are good too, because they're good at finding problems, but the industry needs and wants more quality engineers. You're also going to need more than classical education. You're going to need demonstrable capabilities, example pieces of code. Good practice is to write *D & D* (*Dungeons & Dragons*) modules or interactive novels.

Everyone believes they're competent designers five years before they are.

➤ Looking for a job in the gaming industry? In Chapter 24, "Game Design Resources on the Internet," GameJobs.com's Rick Vandervoorn talks about their free service and how the Internet has changed the way game developers can seek employment.

Toby Gard, Confounding Factor

The gentleman who created the luscious Lara Croft for Core Design's *Tomb Raider* explains here how a game designer can get into this highly competitive industry. To Gard, the best way is to do an apprenticeship at a big company. He explains:

Reading books is one thing, but it's no substitute for the sheer weight of knowledge and understanding you get from actually working on a game. Besides, you probably don't want to leap into one of your own games as your first project, because you'll have to learn so much that you'll end up making a bit of a mess. Better to be part of a team and get your experience that way. Also if you've seen a game through to completion, people will take your game designs more seriously. So I wouldn't bother sending designs to people if you're just starting out; just get together a good art portfolio and start out that way. Resign yourself to learning the trade for a couple of years and then you'll have the experience to pull off one of your own designs afterwards.

Jane Jensen, Sierra On-Line

Jane Jensen is an award-winning writer and game designer at Sierra, where she conceived and directed the first three *Gabriel Knight* interactive mysteries: *Sins of the Fathers*, *The Beast Within*, and *Blood of the Sacred, Blood of the Damned*.

So, what does this highly respected game designer have to say about breaking into the biz?

It's quite difficult, so I usually recommend that they study some ancillary skill such as programming or art, and come into the business through that avenue. Very few companies will hire an inexperienced "game designer" off the street. Either they hire experienced people or they promote from within. Remember, most every programmer or artist working for a game company wants to be a game designer, and they, at least, have a chance to prove their creativity and motivation in-house. The other way in is to start your own little company with some friends and actually put together a prototype. If it's good enough you might be able to get hired into a company, or have a larger company fund your project to completion. But it does take a lot of work and time to make a great prototype—including fantastic art, etc., and it's not easy putting together these resources on your own.

Matt Pritchard, Ensemble Studios

20

Ensemble Studios' programmer Matt Pritchard shares his thoughts on the best ways to prepare for and get into the gaming industry. Before he breaks it into individual positions, Pritchard covers the basics first. In a nutshell? You need to a) love games, and b) be interested in more than just playing them. According to Pritchard, there are roughly four major categories of people involved in the direct creation of a game.

Programmers:

These people are proficient in computer programming languages such as C++ and Assembly. They usually have studied hard about such topics as software design, algorithms, data structures, and math.

Artists:

> These people are proficient in drawing the 2D and 3D images used in games. They have studied art and honed their artistic skills, which include texture and composition skills, as well as know how to use software such as Photoshop, 3D Studio MAX, and others.

Sound engineers and musicians:

> These people usually are musicians in their own right, and are responsible for creating the sound effects and musical soundtracks for games. They are both musically inclined and sophisticated users of the latest in sound editing and music composition software and equipment.

Finally, the game designers:

> These people understand the underlying game mechanics and theory. They usually have played a huge variety of games, including board games, war games, and pen-and-paper role-playing games. They're responsible for the myriad of statistics, properties, and rules that go into a game, and have to balance the details to make a game "fun." No specific course of study for designers, other than that they study everything: history, science, and the inner workings of hundred of games. Designers spend a great deal of their time creating the content that goes into a game—the levels, the puzzles, the scenarios, and so on.

Sinjin Bain, PyroTechnix

Sinjin Bain is cofounder and studio manager at PyroTechnix, a wholly owned subsidiary of Sierra On-Line. Much of 1998 was spent completing the RPG sequel *Return to Krondor*, based on the work of author Raymond E. Feist.

In the following passage, Bain offers some advice on getting into the gaming industry:

> This is a rapidly maturing business and there are many areas of computer gaming that the designer must understand. Perhaps the greatest challenge for the game designer of today is to develop an innate understanding of how technology and art integrate. The challenge to develop a compelling game has been and always will be the objective, but as we all know technology is changing at an ever-increasing pace. This really adds to the challenge of the designer in many ways. I can't emphasize enough the benefits of understanding the specifics of the hardware and software for whatever platform the game will be delivered on. The impact this area has on actual gameplay techniques, development cycle, budgets, and other areas is incalculable.

As an example, Bain refers to *Return to Krondor*, where their goal was to build and develop from the success of the popular *Betrayal at Krondor*. Recalls Bain:

> Our intent was to develop a "franchise" of games that compliment Ray Feist's literary franchise. *Return to Krondor* was developed in a totally different style than the first game, *Betrayal at Krondor*. We did this for two specific reasons: first, we wanted to broaden the market for the franchise past a pure RPG market, so this impacted the design process. Second, we wanted to elevate the look and feel of the game to present a game in the RPG/adventure genre that hadn't been seen yet. We accomplished this by taking advantage of the art talent at our disposal and using our True3D real-time technologies. We adopted some design decisions and chose to use 2D pre-rendered backgrounds combined with real-time 3D characters with motion-capture animation and RGB color lighting, thereby producing a truly unique look and feel for the game. While it's important to innovate and advance, it also must be acknowledged that good gameplay is timeless, and *Betrayal at Krondor* had many elements of great gameplay, especially the turn-based combat system, so we were intent on maintaining this aspect of the game. In essence, what we focused on was producing an innovative and accessible RPG/adventure game that took advantage of all the new technology of today, while maintaining the great gameplay elements of the first game. I think we succeeded on many levels, but as with all things there is always room for improvement. One of the areas we will focus on in the future is more attention to interface elements, for example.

CHAPTER **21**

Game Agents and Headhunters

Let's face it—not all game designers have the know-how or courage to successfully sell themselves or their games to a reputable publisher. And in many cases, game designers *prefer* to concentrate only on the game itself, and leave the number-crunching to others.

Following suit with other entertainment industries, such as film and music, agents and headhunters represent designers and publishers, respectively. While they work differently, their goal is one and the same—to unite talented game designers and their products with publishers and/or distributors.

This chapter is dedicated to both of these third parties by covering how they work—and more importantly, how you as a game designer can take advantage of the services they offer.

Susan Lewis, ThinkBIG

Susan Lewis is the founder and president of ThinkBIG, an agency created to represent and promote the interests of game developers and publishing companies. In particular, their focus is to aid game developers who are seeking world-wide publishing deals, as well as publishers who may want to expand their distribution into foreign territories.

Lewis comments on why a game designer should opt to sign on with an agent, as opposed to pitching a publisher directly, and what they should do to prepare for the relationship:

> A game studio tends to hire an agent, not a game designer. So the first advice is for the game designer to get a team together before approaching an agent. That said, the group needs a game design document—or at least a precursor to a full design doc—as well as a functional prototype of the game. This is not to say that, given a particularly intriguing group, exceptions aren't made. One recent client of mine was made up of two guys who were leads on one of the biggest PC games of the previous year. All I had was a two-page game design and two guys, and a bunch of commitments from their friends to join the team if I got them a deal. It was a laborious process with so little to go on. However, based on the résumés of these two guys, we landed a deal with a top publisher (the game comes out Q1, 2000). This was an unusual situation, however, and the exception to the rule as far as I'm concerned. If you don't have a fleshed-out concept and a prototype, you need a very impressive track record to get the attention of most agents.

How exactly does the process work? And how is the agency compensated?

> The process is somewhat similar to submitting to a publisher. I get solicited and unsolicited game designs and prototypes regularly. If my company is interested, I'll begin a dialogue with that developer and gain an understanding of the game design, the prototype, [and] get a feel for the staff and their capabilities and weaknesses. I was a recruiter for the game industry before becoming an agent, so I can be very helpful in filling in gaps in a team. If I like what I see, and feel it's *sellable*, I'll sign a contract with the developer, which appoints ThinkBIG as their exclusive worldwide agent. There is often a big difference between games I personally like and games I know I can sell. For instance, I love sprite-based real-time strategy games like *Warcraft* and *Command & Conquer*, but I will rarely if ever agree to represent one. The reason is that unless it's in one of these big brands, it's lucky to sell 20,000 units, and most of the publishers wouldn't even bother to look at it.

> After the contract is signed, I contact the appropriate publishers and arrange to meet with the executives, show them the prototype, and pitch the concept. When it gets to the contract stage, I work with the developer's attorney and the publisher's legal department to negotiate the deal terms and contract.

Following the signing of the contract, I stay peripherally involved in the project, checking up on the developer's progress, checking in with the producer, following up on late milestones or payments, and interfacing with the publisher if there's a problem.

I get paid based on what the developer receives from the publisher; that is, 10% of all up-front development advances and 10% of all back-end royalties and bonuses.

Lewis mentions in her bio that she has a working relationship with a number of publishers, such as Electronic Arts, Acclaim, Fox Interactive, Atari Games, and BMG Interactive. Naturally, readers will be curious about any success stories she can share.

I'm quite proud of the work I did for BMG Interactive with their N64 basketball game. BMG retained me to sell off U.S. or worldwide rights to some of their titles when they closed their U.S. division. The basketball game, developed by Z-Axis, was an NBA game with a nontransferable license. Well, NBA is one of the most difficult licenses to acquire, and virtually all of the publishers who have one have their own basketball game. Exhausting the options we had as an NBA game (plenty of publishers wanted the game but none could secure a license), it was decided that Z-Axis would do a quick conversion to college basketball. The new problem was that we were precariously close to "March madness," and Nintendo has a lengthy final approval process before a game can manufacture and ship. In the end, I contacted Fox Interactive, who had just announced their entry into sports products; they picked up the game, which released in the fall of 1998 at the start of the new season as *Fox Sports College Hoops*.

➤ For more information on ThinkBIG, visit their Web site at www.thinkbigco.com, or for answers to general queries, go directly to their FAQ (frequently asked questions) page at www.thinkbigco.com/faq.html.

Melanie Cambron, Virtual Search

As a self-proclaimed "game recruiting goddess" at Virtual Search, Melanie Cambron serves as a full-time headhunter for a number of such well-known clients as Electronic Arts, Microprose, Hasbro, Mattel, Accolade, and many more. Cambron outlines the best way for a game designer to begin a relationship with a recruiter:

Send a well-written, proofread résumé to one reputable recruiter. When you work with several, oftentimes efforts are duplicated and folks get annoyed. Be selective when choosing a recruiter. Showing up at a GDC [Game

21

Developers Conference] or IGDN [International Game Developers Network] doesn't hurt either.

Programmers need to have clean, well-commented code samples ready to show. Artists need to have a mind-blowing demo reel complete with music. Game designers should have design documentation to show—obviously, check on status of NDAs [non-disclosure agreements] before sending it around. After receiving your résumé, hiring managers will frequently request code samples/demo reel before ever chatting with a candidate.

So how does a headhunter get paid? Cambron responds as follows:

> My fees are paid by the hiring company [i.e., the developer/publisher]. Some clients retain my services, while others choose to pay on a contingency basis, meaning that the employer pays me a percentage of the new hire's first-year annual salary.

Other than the fact that it's free for game designers, Cambron comments on other benefits game designers have by working with a recruiter:

> Often brilliant people have no idea how to market themselves. I've seen so many résumés with atrocious mistakes! That old adage about first impressions is painfully true. Also, good recruiters have a wealth of contacts within well-established game companies and can often get your résumé to the hiring manager, who will actually sit up and take notice.

Cambron has provided us with a short article on breaking into the gaming industry. It was originally written for programmers, but can be applied to general game design as well:

The Résumé

Without omitting important information, try to be concise. Résumés should be no more than two pages—ideally, just one page. Translation: Don't list every grunt job you've ever had. Focus on what you've done that's applicable to the desired position in the game industry. If you have done some *gratis* game design/programming, by all means, list this on your résumé. ANY, repeat ANY computer skills that are not from the Land That Time Forgot should be one of the first things on the page. Those of you who actually received your degree, you should place your education info at the beginning of your résumé; therefore taking the spotlight off of your lack of experience. Most importantly, proofread your résumé before you send it in. It's amazing how many résumés are submitted with basic spelling and grammar mistakes, as well as seriously incorrect dates of employment and education. Your résumé is usually the first impression you make on a company or an agent. Yes, you may be a programmer, and you may feel your spelling ability simply isn't important to writing code, but companies are looking for well-rounded, intelligent people who care about everything they produce.

Résumés can be very personal things, but if you can, have a friend, family member, or trusted game agent read over your résumé before you send it out. You may have looked at it a thousand times, but many times a "fresh eye" will catch mistakes your tired brain simply missed. Finally, chill on the funky fonts and colors. Today, many companies scan résumés, so use a basic font (in black) on white paper. Furthermore, hiring managers want to find the important information easily, rather than meandering through a maze of wacky fonts and graphics. In addition to your résumé, it's *imperative* that you have code samples ready to send to potential employers upon request. These samples should be about three pages of very clean, well-commented code. Once again, have this proofread by a knowledgeable *amigo*.

The Game Demo

Game companies want to know not only that you can cut code, but that you have a passion for games. So dedicated are you to the making of games that you would program your own game just out of sheer love for the industry. It doesn't matter if the game is a pixelated mess, just show that you made the effort and you have the passion. This goes a long way. Ask around. You'll find that most folks in this biz are not here for the money.

Common Mistakes/Simple Tips

Oftentimes, extremely zealous individuals will spam their résumés to companies repeatedly. All this does is annoy. You end up looking "desperate or just plain stupid," to quote the hiring manager of a very large game developer. Be sure to keep an accurate record of where and when you have sent your résumé to avoid [duplication]. The other résumé turnoff is telling hiring managers or recruiters to "check out" your résumé on the Web. These folks receive such a voluminous amount of résumés that they don't have time to hunt down your info on the net. Make it easy on them; you'll get a much better response.

Moreover, only send your résumés to companies for whom you really want to work. If you have no intention of moving to Florida, don't send your résumé to Gainesville Games. Also, when working with an agent, be sure to share this information so they don't get rejected due to your previous résumé

21

submission, or having to reject the company's interest due to your location requirements. No one likes rejection.

Be prepared for that big interview. Regardless of whether it's a phone screen or you're actually sitting on the other side of the desk of the Vice President/Chief Technical Director of Everything, do your homework. Make sure you have thoroughly researched the company and are prepared to answer questions about your skills as well as your favorite games. With regard to fashion, being overdressed is always better than appearing as if you sauntered in for a sandwich. Pants/khakis and a button-down shirt are usually appropriate for game industry interviews. When in doubt, don the suit.

Most importantly, even if you think you have a brilliant idea for a game, get experience first. The game biz is much like the film industry—it's who you know. Each year, hundreds of companies come and go without ever getting a game on the shelf. Save yourself some heartache, time, and expense by starting your career with an established company. Learn from those who have been there, done that. Then, if you still feel a burning desire to do your own *thang*, good luck to you.

➤ To learn more about Virtual Search, drop into www.vsearch.com or call 1-800-779-3334.

➤ Another agency to consider is Game Agents at www.gameagents.com. To commemorate their launch in January 1999, they announced the successful negotiation of a licensing agreement between Aztech New Media and Monolith to develop an add-on pack for Monolith's runaway hit PC game, *Shogo: Mobile Armor Division*.

CHAPTER **22**

Divine Intervention— G.O.D.'s Way

As we've covered elsewhere in this book, there are many different kinds of development companies to form and varied deals to sign with publishers and/or distributors. There *is* another option, however. A new company, and a new *kind* of company, formed in mid-1998, known as Gathering of Developers, or simply G.O.D. In a nutshell, G.O.D. was built upon a different philosophical business model, designed to treat game developers in a more *just* way. In particular, this means paying higher royalties, more creative freedom, and less rigid contracts.

This chapter highlights G.O.D.'s roots, their clients and goals, and how they aim to revolutionize the gaming industry well into the 21st century.

Roots

Mike Wilson came up with the idea to start Gathering of Developers when he was still the official "biz guy" at id Software, then and now one of the top independent game developers in North America. Unless you've been living under a rock for the past five years, you probably know that this talented team of programmers and artists was responsible for the first-person perspective 3D shooter revolution with *Wolfenstein 3D* and the mega-successful *Doom* and *Quake* action series.

At that time, their publisher was GT Interactive, a then-small company whose products were a Fabio screen saver and a Richard Simmons "Deal a Meal" CD-ROM! Then id Software's *Doom 2* became one of the first real PC gaming breakthrough titles, selling over two million units (even before Cyan's *Myst* was released). This title, plus other blockbusters from this southern studio, turned GT Interactive into a billion-dollar initial public offering, the largest IPO of 1995, in fact. According to Wilson, they were paid what were considered fair royalties at the time, but in retrospect, they were "horribly low" if you consider that *Doom 2* generated over $80 million in revenues.

And thus, the idea for G.O.D. was born...

Mission

G.O.D.'s goal is to become the premier publisher and worldwide leader in the delivery of commercially successful game software, designed for both the computer and console platforms. Just how do they plan on accomplishing this? CEO Mike Wilson answers, "By securing long-term relationships with the industry's top independent development talent."

With this approach, G.O.D. aims to establish a new status quo for developer/publisher relations based on a number of mandates: fair treatment of developers; royalties based on title sell-through; a title approval process that incorporates the judgment of development experts in the computer gaming industry; and management's successful experience in providing marketing, operational, and financial expertise.

The G.O.D Difference

Wilson believes that the most critical functions of the publisher are to identify development talent and secure long term relationships with these "hit-makers." Ironically, says Wilson, "these are also the most difficult functions for publishers, even (and sometimes especially) for the largest publishers. The reason for this stems from two things: distrust of the developers for *traditional* business people, and a poor understanding of developers and their needs." He expands:

> G.O.D. takes advantage of its management's unique understanding of these problems, as well as the management's close relationships to the industry's top talent. Unlike other publishers, the company launched with a lineup of long-term development deals that are truly unparalleled in the industry.

Wilson says he wants G.O.D. to be recognized as the leader in developer relations and gamer relations, and hopes others will follow suit in doing so successfully:

> We have no desire to publish games for non-gamers. We want to publish the ones that those who live and breathe games will recognize as brilliant artistry from professional game developers. Now if, in doing this, we prove our point that a publisher can be successful by maintaining mutually beneficial relationships with respected artists, rather than by taking over their companies or robbing them of their intellectual property, or keeping them so broke that they can't negotiate, then we hope the industry will take note. If we're left alone to work under this model, so be it, but I think it's more likely that we signal the start of a very important trend for all publisher/developer relations. At the least, we will ensure that developers are informed about what they're worth and what they can expect to be able to negotiate based on that worth.

Are business relationships really that one-sided between developers and publishers? President and director of new business development Harry A. Miller answers:

> [Developers] are currently strong-armed by publishers, misinformed as to industry standards, misled due to their lack of business savvy in some instances, due to their ideals about partnership in others. The strategy has been to pay very meager advances and royalties, keeping developers "barefoot and pregnant," unable to negotiate or to shop around because of the uncertainty that comes from being economically dependent on that next milestone payment. Only a healthy, independent developer with proper business representation and good information to work with can strike a deal properly. Our strategy is to keep those developers informed so that, when they do reach that point, they know that they can turn to us for a relationship that will ensure that their work reaches their fans with minimum hassle and maximum integrity.

➤ G.O.D. announced in January of 1999 that they will co-present the first annual Game Developers Conference (GDC) "Independent Games Festival" along with Miller Freeman, Inc. This festival is designed to promote interactive entertainment as an art form, and provide a forum for independent game developers from around the world to showcase their work, receive recognition, and meet potential publishers. Read more about this in Chapter 25.

Games and Distribution

Many other publishing companies believe G.O.D.'s mission statement sounds fine on paper, but there are enormous distribution and marketing costs they must factor into their budget. G.O.D. insists this has all been accounted for. For one, Take 2 Interactive is distributing the first 10 G.O.D. titles through its BMG subsidiary in Europe, the U.S., and Canada, and they use the same retail channels as everyone else. This includes CompUSA, Wal-Mart, Best Buy, Electronics Boutique, Babbages/Software Etc., Computer City (now owned by CompUSA), FRYs, etc. Wilson says about 10 accounts make up 90% of sales in our industry, plus G.O.D. has smaller distributors that specialize in "mom and pop" operations to handle the rest, and another arrangement for direct sales over the Internet (although this is still a small fraction of total sales).

G.O.D. launched with six red-hot development studios under their belt. These are, in no particular order: 3D Realms (responsible for the popular *Duke Nukem* series); Ritual Entertainment (*Sin* and *Quake: Scourge of Armagon*); PopTop Software (headed by industry veteran Phil Steinmeyer), Terminal Reality (*Monster Truck Madness* series for Microsoft, and many others); Epic Games (creators of the smash 3D shooter *Unreal*); and newcomers Edge of Reality (currently porting *Monster Truck Madness II* for the Nintendo 64). Heading Edge of Reality is Rob Cohen, who left Iguana after serving as lead programmer on the 1.5 million-selling *Turok: Dinosaur Hunter*.

G.O.D.'s first two releases were Epic Games' *Jazz Jackrabbit 2* and PopTop Software's *Railroad Tycoon II*, with both titles receiving critical acclaim.

Left, a gameplay from Railroad Tycoon II (PopTop Software); right, the lovable side-kick Spaz from Jazz Jackrabbit II (Epic Games). (Used with permission by Gathering of Developers)

➤ For more information about G.O.D., their board of directors, and their impressive lineup of 1999 and 2000 titles, drop into www.godgames.com. Who knows—maybe you and your development team may be touched by the hand of G.O.D. one day!

CHAPTER **23**

Design Schools

As evident by their entries in this book, dozens of successful game designers, programmers, and artists believe some level of advanced schooling is an important asset, and serves as a solid foundation on which to build a career in the interactive entertainment industry. In fact, many project leaders and producers will not employ someone unless they have a degree relating to their specialty (such as a university/college computer science diploma for programmers). There are hundreds of such courses for programmers, artists, animators, musicians, and sound engineers, but very few that focus specifically on how these disciplines relate to computer or console *gaming*. And it comes as no surprise that there's even less that's strictly on game *design*.

This chapter takes a look at a few schools and courses that cater to individuals who want to make a living as a developer in the computer or console gaming industry.

DigiPen Institute of Technology (www.digipen.edu)

Jason Chu, Registrar of DigiPen Institute of Technology takes some time out of his schedule to chat with us about what this unique school has to offer.

First, a bit of history. DigiPen Corporation was founded by Claude Comair in Vancouver, British Columbia, Canada in 1988. Its beginnings were as a company that provided services in 3D computer animation and special effects to the entertainment industry. Comair and company recognized that there was a tremendous shortage of 3D computer animators, and decided to do something about it. DigiPen started to offer educational programs for artists to become 3D animators.

In 1991, they had a meeting with Nintendo of America (NOA) and discussed the possibility for DigiPen to offer educational programs in video game programming. This idea became reality in September of 1994, when they started the computer game programming program, supported by NOA. According to Chu, they realized that this program was the only one of its kind in Canada or the U.S. It was a two-year program; however, games were becoming more complex to program when the trend shifted to 3D. Therefore, DigiPen expanded the course to a four-year bachelors degree program. In February, 1998, DigiPen opened a larger campus in Redmond, Washington.

Chu explains that video games are essentially interactive simulation programs in real time, hence the name they chose for the discipline: Bachelor of Science Degree in Real-Time Interactive Simulation.

This curriculum currently consists of 9 levels of mathematics, 2 levels of physics, 4 levels of computer animation, 23 levels of computer science, and 4 complete projects in game implementation. The degree, in total, consists of 154 credits. DigiPen also offers a two-year associate degree program and a high school summer course.

In the fall of 1999, DigiPen will debut a new program for animators: an Associate of Applied Arts Degree in 3D Computer Animation. And there are talks of offering a masters and Ph.D. degree in the near future as well.

Asked why someone who wants to learn about game programming or 3D animation would attend DigiPen, Chu answers in light of the current curriculum on programming:

> This is a highly specialized educational program in the area of game programming. As far as we're aware, we are currently the only degree-granting institution in the world dedicated to video game programming. If one is committed to becoming a game programmer as a career, this is the right school for the training.

➤ For more information, such as course overviews, full descriptions, prerequisites, student lists, galleries, and tuition/financial assistance info, visit www.digipen.edu on the World Wide Web.

The photo above was taken during the ribbon cutting ceremony for the official open house of the Redmond, Washington, campus on Feb. 18, 1998. Left to right: Washington State Governor Gary Locke; President of Nintendo Minoru Arakawa; and the founder of DigiPen, Claude Comair. Below, a classroom of students working on a project. (Used with permission by Jason Chu)

Full Sail (www.fullsail.com)

Another high-tech college with a program dedicated to game design is Full Sail in Winterpark, Florida. Their motto is "real world education," and game design is but one of the digital media programs offered. The Game Design Degree Program was established to teach students the skills necessary to design and create single and multiplayer computer games for networks, PCs, and dedicated gaming consoles.

The course starts at an introductory level, beginning with basic mathematical and programming techniques and a sweeping chronological perspective of the computer gaming industry in order to study and identify market trends that determine successful gaming hardware and software. This preface provides the foundation needed for the heart of the course: math and physics, programming in C++, artificial intelligence techniques in modeling opponent behavior, coding multiplayer games, and ultimately a game project and significant clock hours on the PC.

Full Sail has a career placement assistance department to arrange post-graduate internships in game development companies.

➤ For a free catalog or a more thorough description of each of the 14 modules in the 58-week game design program, drop into Full Sail's home page at www.fullsail.com.

➤ Tim Cain, the game designer responsible for the best-selling RPG Fallout, is planning to co-teach a class on game design at the University of California at Irvine in the spring of 1999. The curriculum had not been ironed out in time to be included in this book, but Cain's course will contain modules including 3D programming and OpenGL.

NBCC Miramichi (www.miramichi.nbcc.nb.ca)

This Canadian school, on the eastern side of the country, offers a program in "electronic game design technology." This branch of New Brunswick Community College (NBCC) teaches apprentice game designers how to design, script, and develop various categories of electronic games.

According to the course calendar, the focus of this 80-week (six semesters) program is to prepare students to develop interactive entertainment and educational software products (also known as "edutainment"). Modules within semesters include computer programming, game mechanics, game design, graphics and animation, software testing, marketing, and a handful of related electives. Considerable emphasis is placed on learning by doing. In fact, an essential requirement for the completion of the course is for students to develop a product "deemed marketable by the industry and the college."

➤ For more information, visit the following address on the Web:
www.miramichi.nbcc.nb.ca/nbccmira/our_programs/frames/elec_game_des.html

Other Schools to Consider

The following is a list of additional schools and links to consider for amateur game designers, programmers, and animators alike:

- Art Institutes International (AII)
  www.aii.edu
- The Bell Centre for Creative Communications at Centennial College
  www.bccc.com
- The Center for Advanced Digital Applications at New York University
  www.sce.nyu.edu/cada
- The Center for Digital Imaging and Sound
  www.artschool.com

- Centre National d'animation et de Design
  www.nad.qc.ca
- Cogswell Polytechnical College
  www.cogswell.edu
- DeVry Institute of Technology
  www.devry.edu
- Eastern Business Computer Institute, College of Applied Arts and Technology
  www.ebci.ca
- Herzing Institute
  www.herzing.edu
- L'Institut d'informatique de Québec
  www.iiq.qc.ca
- Marycrest International University
  www.mcrest.edu
- MIT Artificial Intelligence Laboratory
  www.ai.mit.edu/
- National Centre for Computer Animation at Bournemouth University
  http://ncca.bournemouth.ac.uk/
- Pratt Institute
  www.pratt.edu/ad/cgim
- Rochester Institute of Technology
  www.rit.edu
- San Francisco State University
  www.cel.sfsu.edu/MSP/msp.html
- School of Communication Arts
  www.ncsca.com
- School of Computer Science and Cognitive Science Research Centre
  www.cs.bham.ac.uk/~axs
- School of Computing at Middlesex University
  www.cs.mdx.ac.uk/cg/
- University of Abertay Dundee
  www.tay.ac.uk
- University of California, Los Angeles
  www.ucla.edu
- University of Michigan
  http://ai.eecs.umich.edu/ugclasses.html

23

- University of North Texas
  www.cs.unt.edu
- University of Southern California
  www.usc.edu/dept/cs/degree_programs/
- ViaGrafix
  www.viagrafix.com

Note >> A special thanks goes to Alex Dunne, editorial director of *Gamasutra* (www.gamasutra.com) for assistance in compiling this list.

And remember to check the listings in your town. The 21st century is just around the corner, so you can expect many more schools to pop up around the world devoted to game design, programming, computer graphics, and interactive sound engineering.

CHAPTER **24**

Game Design Resources on the Internet

This book may cover a lot of ground in a number of areas, but by no means is it the final word on game design and how to break into this bustling industry. The Internet is an outstanding medium for both novice and seasoned designers and other game developers to learn, interact, and contribute as a member of the thriving gaming community. The purpose of this chapter is to present a number of enlightening stopovers while surfing the information highway.

 Note >> Throughout this entire book, dozens of URLs and handy Usenet newsgroups have been offered for further and future reference, but this chapter is dedicated to more general game design.

The following Web sites and Usenet newsgroups are listed alphabetically.

Computer Game Design

www.neversoft.com/christer/GR/design

This e-zine, maintained by Christer Ericson, contains a collection of essays and links to a number of members of the interactive entertainment industry. Example features include "A Crash Course in Game Design and Production," "Designing Online Puzzle Games," "Project AI," and "Elements of Videogame Style." This page contains no graphics, so it will load remarkably fast.

Computer Role-Playing Game Designer

www.ultranet.com/~melkior/crpg/index.htm

Available here are a number of sequential design documents written by Steve Crocker on creating a successful CRPG (computer role-playing game). The goals, rules, programming info (C++ as the reference), and user-interface proxy are covered.

DevGames.com

wwww.devgames.com

As the name suggests, DevGames.com is a Web e-zine devoted to the development of computer games. And what a resourceful site it is! Sections include news, feature articles, editorials, Q&A, helpful books, and other resources. Some good reads include "The DirectX Programmer's Q&A," "The Basics of Game AI," "2D vs. 3D," the many development diaries for some of today's and tomorrow's hit games, and Microsoft articles on tackling Windows and Direct3D programming. Don't pass this one up.

Gamasutra

www.gamasutra.com

Gamasutra is simply one of the best game design Web sites, covering a wealth of topics, from programming to graphic design, sound engineering to music, even areas dedicated to the production, legal, and business angle of the gaming industry. For each section, there's regularly updated news, editorials, interviews, columns from experts in the industry, job classifieds, free utilities and source code, and much, much more. In short, make this your startup page on the Web.

Alex Dunne, the editor-in-chief of *Game Developer* magazine, is also the editorial director for Gamasutra.com, also a Miller-Freeman publication.

Game Design

http://members.aol.com/anarchyxi/gamedev.htm

This game designer's home page discusses some milestones in the video gaming industry and suggests the best ways to begin a project. Designing the game's story, genre, and playing perspective are on the top of the list, with many examples for illustration.

Game Design Newsgroup

rec.games.design

To keep abreast on all the latest happenings, to exchange ideas or ask queries yourself, the rec.games.design newsgroup on Usenet is a must for game designers to visit at least a few times a week.

Common posts include "An idea for a new multiplayer game," "Any game musicians out there?" and "Need help in creating rules for…"

The rec.games.design FAQ is available at www.qucis.queensu.ca/home/dalamb/Games/design/design.html.

Game Design @ Gameslice

www.gameslice.com/vgd/index.shtml

Formerly known as Video Games Design at www.videogamesdesign.com, this informative Web site is separated into four areas: game design, code (programming), graphics, and sound. Each section provides handfuls of interviews with famous game designers and developers, and a number of well-written and inspiring feature articles on the industry. At the end of this chapter, the editor of Game Design has a few words to share about this e-zine and the Web as a game designer's haven.

Game Developer Magazine

www.gdmag.com

Game Developer magazine is undisputedly the ultimate monthly bible devoted to game designers and developers. Edited by the creative force behind Gamasutra, Alex Dunne, *Game Developer* magazine and its online counterpart are a comprehensive look at the entire game development spectrum. At the Web site, users can subscribe to the magazine, search for back issues, or link to sister site Gamasutra for exclusive content.

24

Although this chapter focuses on Internet resources for game designers and developers, Game Developer magazine is a must-read monthly publication, whether you're just starting out in the industry or are a veteran game developer. (Used with express permission by editor Alex Dunne)

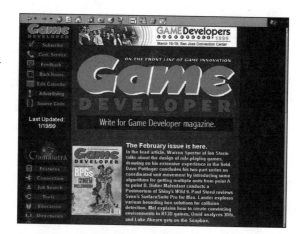

Game Developer Resourcium

www.resourcium.com

Since its inception in 1996, the Resourcium has served thousands of amateur and professional game developers with reviews and links to the best game development resources available on the Internet. It looks and operates like a standard search engine, with a directory and query box to type in keywords.

Game Development Search Engine

www.game-developer.com

Think of this Web site as the definitive search engine and directory to many of the game developer sites on the Internet. This includes news sites, articles, interviews, source code, graphic utilities, and much more. Visitors can either use the query box to type in a keyword or select a directory of interest and browse the links from there. Awesome!

As you can see by this screen grab, the Game Development Search Engine is a handy Web site to bookmark in your browser. Visitors can search the extensive database by perusing the directory or by typing keywords. (Used with express permission by Dungeon Crawl Software)

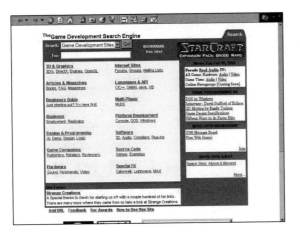

24

Gameslice

www.gameslice.com

Simply one of the best "behind the scenes" Web sites for those who want to know what's happening in the computer gaming industry. Editor Geoff Keighley has his finger on the pulse of the biz and delivers news, reviews, hard-hitting editorials, and feature interviews and company profiles to his many readers.

Gaming Insider

www.gaminginsider.com

For all the gossip and delicious rumors in the gaming industry, you can trust "BitchX," an anonymous reporter with "an ear to the ground and a sharp tongue at the ready!" What does this have to do with game design? Nothing, really, aside from the fact that you may be able to get the dirt on someone you may eventually work beside!

Happy Puppy: The Biz

http://happypuppy.com/biz/index.html

The mega-popular Happy Puppy Web site runs an exceptional page dedicated to the gaming industry. Sections include Developer Den, Game Companies, Job Listings, Classified, and more. The bulk of this page contains hundreds of hand-picked links to other game design, programming, art, and sound design resources.

I Have No Words and I Must Design

www.crossover.com/~costik/nowords.html

This well-written and thought-provoking article was originally published in 1994 in *Interactive Fantasy*, a British role-playing game journal. The lengthy essay analyzes games and game design in varied components and covers topics such as goals, resource management, game tokens, decision making, and a handful of suggestions to increase a game's strength. The article is available in English, Japanese, or Korean.

Loony Games

www.loonygames.com

One of the newest Web sites on game design and development to emerge over the past couple of years is Loony Games, presented by Next Generation Online (www.next-generation.com) and published/hosted by Blue's News (www.bluesnews.com), the most popular action game Web hub on the net.

Loony Games houses many feature stories and regular columns written by some of the industry's finest game designers, programmers, and artists. Examples include "The History of Shareware," "What It's *Really* Like to Program for a Next-Generation Console," and hand-drawn texture tutorials, to name a few.

➤ The popular Gamecenter e-zine (listed at the end of this chapter) has published a seven-chapter feature story titled "Game Design 101: Designing a Game from the Polygons Up." Grab yourself a coffee or soda and head on over to www.gamecenter.com/Features/Exclusives/Design.

Murphy's Rules

http://kovalic.com/Murphys/Murphys.html

Call it the "Funniest Home Videos" for the gaming industry, but Murphy's rules are ones that don't make sense, or "holes" found in computer games. Visitors can read the history of this site, jump right in and read the lengthy list (and their significance), or can submit their own. There's also a humorous cartoon devoted to some of the larger holes found.

So, You Want to be a Computer Game Developer

www.makegames.com

Diana Gruber's well-written and wonderfully laid-out step-by-step guide to breaking into the business covers everything from self-promotion to working with other people to the nature of the industry. A large area is devoted to writing your first and second games, plus a list of helpful books to ease the programming pain.

24

Sweet Oblivion

www.sweetoblivion.com

Welcome to the "total game development resource." This sleek and content-rich Web site offers the latest and greatest in game design and development with daily news, insightful feature stories, a game workshop, downloadable files, an online store, and links to other worthwhile articles on the Internet. Their goal is to become "the complete resource for aspiring game programmers and developers." Definitely one to visit today.

Ultimate Gaming Resource - Company Directory

www.ugr.net/listings/listings.htm

Hundreds of computer and console game developers and publishers are listed here in alphabetical format. All entries contain the link to their official home page, plus many of them have their phone number, address, and e-mail contact information for those looking to send in a résumé or work sample. This is definitely a page to bookmark.

Essential Gaming E-Zines

The following is an alphabetical list of some of the top PC and console gaming e-zines on the World Wide Web:

- Adrenaline Vault
  www.avault.com
- All Games Network
  www.allgames.com
- Computer Games Online
  www.cdmag.com
- Computer Gaming World
  www.gamespot.com/cgw
- Console Domain
  www.consoledomain.com
- Future Games Network
  www.futuregames.net
- Game Revolution
  www.game-revolution.com
- Gamecenter
  www.gamecenter.com
- GamePen
  www.gamepen.com
- GamePower
  www.gamepower.com
- GamePro
  www.gamepro.com
- Games Domain
  www.gamesdomain.com
- Gamesmania
  www.gamesmania.com
- Gamespot U.K.
  www.gamespot.co.uk
- Gamespot
  www.gamespot.com

- Gamestats
  www.gamestats.com
- Happy Puppy
  www.happypuppy.com
- Imagine Games
  Network
  www.imaginegames.com
- Meccaworld
  www.meccaworld.com
- Next Generation
  www.next-generation.com
- Online Gaming Review
  www.ogr.com
- PC Gamer
  www.pcgamer.com
- PC Games
  www.pcgames.com
- PC Multimedia &
  Entertainment
  www.pcme.com
- UGO Alliance
  www.ugo.com
- Videogames.com
  www.videogames.com
- Fastest Gaming News
  Online
  www.fgnonline.com
- Electric Playground
  www.elecplay.com

Robin Ward, GameSlice's Game Design

Robin Ward is the editor for the Game Design Page at GameSlice and is a freelance writer for other sites, including Gamasutra. He joins us here to chat about what GameSlice's Game Design page has to offer, and to provide his thoughts on the Web as a medium for budding game designers.

Once upon a time I started up a site dedicated to game design, called videogamedesign.com—despite the word "video" being in the title, it really focused on all aspects of computer game creation. The specialty was interviews with top game designers, programmers, and artists, with questions that weren't like "What's your favorite food?"—they were about balance, design, and how to get into the industry.

Needless to say, there was quite a demand for that kind of thing, and the site got a decent amount of traffic. Later on, after updates became a little slow due to personal difficulties, Geoff Keighley of GameSlice offered to let me set up the site as a section of GameSlice.com. So now it resides at www.gameslice.com/vgd, and has all of our old interviews and articles, along with a few new ones that we post from time to time. We also have a FAQ that answers some commonly asked questions about game creation—specialty schools, how to get an idea created, etc.

The game industry attracts many people, but few people actually know how games are made. So when we interviewed designers, programmers, musicians and artists, we asked them specifically the types of questions that people ask us. Such as "How can I work at your company?" or "Is game design art?" So instead of features about whether the latest game features lightsourcing or x players at once, we have creation-related questions. And people really find that useful.

Also, we try and reply to every single email received. I can't claim to have replied to them all (some eventually get lost), but I'd say almost all of the people who send mail will get a reply. And not a one-liner, either. It will answer their question to the best of our ability.

I remember when I wanted to learn stuff about games a few years back, and all the sites I emailed didn't bother replying, even if I said "PLEASE REPLY." That really annoyed me. So I try to do it better.

24

What exactly can readers get from the site?

> Readers will probably find the answers they're looking for when it comes to game development. There's a lot of people in the world who want to develop games, but it's hard to find out how people actually go from regular Mr. John Doe to a high-profile developer.

In closing, Ward says "We can tell you how some of the best game designers did it, what the best path into game design is, and how to get there."

Rick Vandervoorn, GameJobs.com

Rick Vandervoorn is an associate publisher at the CyberActive Media Group. He has these words to say about GameJobs.com and the purpose of the site:

> GameJobs.com is a comprehensive listing of companies involved with the video games industry, with a direct link to the appropriate human resources page for each company. Gamejobs.com came as an online extension of the print version housed in *GameWEEK* magazine. The vision for GameJobs.com (which we're working toward) is for it to become a full-function searchable interactive database for games-related and other high-tech job openings.

Vandervoorn says the Internet has changed the industry for budding game designers in several ways. He explains:

> First, it makes it easier for aspiring game designers to get hired. With services like GameJobs.com, the Internet helps to bridge the communications gap between successful game developers/publishers and budding game designers. Aspiring designers can unobtrusively make contact with game developers, plus the Internet (or, more accurately, the World Wide Web) can act as a forum to display the aspiring developer's work, which in the long run contributes to making it easier for the budding developer to get noticed and hired by a developer/publisher.

> Second, the Internet/Web makes it easier for the budding game designer who can't get hired by a developer/publisher or who wants to strike out on his/her own to market his/her creation. The Internet/Web provides a storefront for the aspiring developer who wants to market a game to gamers around the world. With the advent of selling and distributing games on the Web, a presence at retail is no longer necessary.

➤ Be sure to visit GameJobs.com at, you guessed it, www.gamejobs.com.

CHAPTER **25**

Key Conventions, Organizations, and Awards

In today's information age, it's possible for members of the gaming industry to work virtually anywhere in the world. With electronic file transfer via the Internet and relatively cheap overnight deliveries from courier services, there's no reason why game programmers, artists, and musicians need to work in the same room together, although there are obvious advantages in doing so.

However, if you're trying to get a job at a development company or attempting to get your game picked up by a publisher, or you want to keep an eye on what your competitors are up to, it's highly recommended that you get out there to meet and greet the gaming community in the flesh. In fact, in this book, many game designers recommend getting out there to talk face to face, because this makes a much better impression than dealing with someone via email or over the telephone. Therefore, the first half of this chapter deals with all the gaming industry's top conventions, trade shows, and conferences around the world. Each listing explains what the show is all about and who it's best suited for, and provides a link to the official World Wide Web site for that show. The second part of this chapter lists a number of essential organizations in the industry you may want to belong to, including various academies and associations that cater to different facets of the gaming industry.

Conventions and Trade Shows

Electronic Entertainment Expo (E3)

The Electronic Entertainment Expo (E3) is the largest and most extravagant event in the gaming industry. Period. In 1999, the fifth year of this annual mega-event, close to 50,000 members of the international computer gaming, video gaming, and edutainment industry will flock to see—or display—what may be the hottest products of the year. E3 is not only a gathering for exhibitors to showcase their upcoming gaming software and hardware to the media and retailers (over 2,000 new products were shown in 1998), but also a place for enlightening conferences and workshops hosted by the top names in the business. E3 is strictly a trade event; therefore, only professionals from the industry are allowed to attend.

And what a party it is! Techno music blasts through the booths, multiplayer games take place over 40-foot video screens, celebrities are present to rub elbows, larger-than-life mechanical creations of favorite video and computer game characters appear, and concerts at night feature famous bands sponsored by the likes of Sony, Nintendo, and Eidos Interactive (to name a few).

The event usually takes place at the end of May each year. It spent its first two years in Los Angeles, then moved to Atlanta for two years and went back to L.A. for 1999. For more information, visit www.e3expo.com, but also be sure to check out www.e3.net or www.e3daily.com.

Game Developers Conference (GDC)

Another extremely important conference for game designers to attend is the Game Developers Conference (GDC). This annual show takes place in the late winter/early spring and has something to offer for all roles of the industry: programming, visual arts, sound and music, production, general game design, and even the business and legal side of the gaming industry.

The four-day event is loaded with keynote speakers, tutorials/workshops, seminars, contests in each field, awards, and exhibitors. Keynote topics and speakers for the 1999

GDC included Interplay's Brian Fargo on "Surviving 15 on the Frontlines of the War," Sega's Bernie Stolar on "Redefining Game and Hardware Development through Evolution," Tommy Tallarico on "Music in Video Games: The Art of the Deal"—and many more. The official Web site is at www.gdconf.com.

In 1999, the Game Developers Conference added a new special sideshow and festival. Read on…

GAMEXecutive

The first ever GAMEXecutive trade conference took place at the 1999 Game Developers Conference. This is a two-day trade event for CEOs; strategists; executives in marketing, sales, distribution, retail, and finance; venture capitalists; and others involved in the business side of the billion-dollar interactive entertainment industry. At GAMEXecutive, industry experts discuss and analyze statistics and a wide variety of business trends for both software and hardware for the PC and console systems. A full list of speakers and their topics can be seen at www.gamexecutive.com.

Independent Games Festival

The second new addition to the annual GDC is the Indie Games Festival, sponsored by the Gathering of Developers (G.O.D.). This event is intended to promote interactive entertainment as an art form and provide a forum for independent game developers from around the globe to show their work, receive recognition, and meet with potential publishers and/or distributors.

25

Indie designers can compete for prizes and the opportunity for their games to be submitted to the G.O.D review board for publishing consideration. Categories are based on platform: PC, Macintosh, Sony PlayStation, Nintendo, or online games, plus awards are also presented for technical excellence, art, audio, game design, and audience choice. For festival info, rules, and application procedures, interested developers should go to www.indiegames.com.

Is this the gaming industry's answer to the Sundance Film Festival?

Electronic Consumer Trade Show (ECTS)

The ECTS is Europe's premier gaming conference, held every fall in London, England. Game developers and publishers from Europe and around the world display their top interactive products (software and hardware) for the fourth quarter and the following year. Like E3, ECTS is a glitzy trade show, but for members of the industry only. And it's on a much smaller scale, too—less than 2,000 attendees. Every year ECTS also hosts an awards ceremony for the top interactive entertainment products of the year. For more information, punch in www.ects.com while surfing the Web.

Milia Games

Held in Cannes, France, is a spectacular annual event: Milia, the International Content Market for Interactive Media. In 1999, Milia began a separate entity exclusively reserved for the gaming industry, dubbed Milia Games. New game showcases, title announcements, keynote speeches and conferences, and the Milia Games awards ceremony are but a few of the festivities here. There's also a developer's day, with hundreds of freelance programmers, graphic and sound designers, and scriptwriters invited from around the world. In short, this event caters to the entire gaming industry, including designers, publishers, and distributors. Access more information on this event at www.milia.com.

SIGGRAPH

For computer graphic artists and animators, SIGGRAPH is one of the most important conventions of the year. Its main purpose is to promote "theory, design, implementation, and application of computer-generated graphics and interactive techniques to facilitate communication and understanding." The three-day event includes dozens of conferences and workshops, exhibits by software and hardware companies, and a career resource center for aspiring computer graphics specialists. To learn more about SIGGRAPH as an organization and/or the annual conference, visit www.siggraph.org.

GamesCon

Since E3 and ECTS are for the gaming trade only, GameCon is meant to be a "traveling E3" that will host quarterly conventions in major cities across North America—but for all gamers. GamesCon consists of three sections over as many days: exhibitors are there to preview upcoming gaming software titles and hardware technology, a major LAN (local area network) party is held for hundreds of simultaneous players to compete for prizes, and workshops and seminars are provided by key members of the gaming industry. The official URL for GamesCon is www.gamescon.com.

GenCon

Held in Milwaukee each year, GenCon is a gaming convention for role-playing game (RPG) enthusiasts. Although I couldn't locate an official Web site for this annual show, WebCasts from previous years are available at www.evilgeniuses.org/gaming/archive/index.html.

Comdex, CES, MacWorld Expo, Toy Fair

While wrapping up this half of the chapter, it should be noted that Comdex (www.comdex.com), the Consumer Electronics Show (www.cesweb.org), MacWorld Expo, and the various international toy fairs may also be good places to attend throughout the year as a game designer. They're not nearly as crucial as E3, GDC, or ECTS, but you may find inspiration or make good contacts with other members of the gaming industry.

➤ The Flights of Fantasy Awards has been recognizing outstanding console and computer game talent since 1995. Awards are given for areas of excellence such as art direction, lighting/texturing, story, innovation, character design, character animation, best promotional campaign, music, sound, and so on. Be sure to visit www.flightsoffantasy.com for the complete list of nominees and winners over the past few years.

Organizations

Academy of Interactive Arts and Sciences (AIAS)

The Academy of Interactive Arts and Sciences (AIAS) was founded in 1996 as a not-for-profit organization dedicated to the advancement and recognition of the interactive arts and sciences. As stated in its bylaws and published on the Web site, this is the formal mission of the academy:

- Promote and advance common interests in the worldwide interactive community.
- Recognize outstanding achievement in the creation of interactive content.
- Conduct an annual awards show and enhance the image and awareness of the interactive arts and sciences.

25

The annual awards show mentioned above takes place during the annual Electronic Entertainment Expo (E3). For membership information, news, events, and award winners, visit the AIAS at www.interactive.org.

International Game Developers Association (IGDN)

The International Game Developers Network (IGDN) is a grassroots not-for-profit membership association for the game developer community. Its primary focus is to serve members by providing and sharing resources that are not easily accessible anywhere else. This includes finding people, finances, publishers, attorneys, software, or hardware. This association also publishes a newsletter and hosts conventions for developers to congregate. The official Web site is at www.igdn.org.

Software & Information Industry Association (SIIA)

The Software Publishers Association (SPA) and the Information Industry Association (IIA) merged on January 1, 1999, to form a new trade association representing the software and information industry: the Software & Information Industry Association (SIIA).

Their mission statement, in part, is as follows:

> [...]unite the software code and information content industries into a power-
> ful global consortium. This union of code and content in the digital age
> delivers unmatched industry advocacy, business development, research, and
> education to the nearly 1,500 SIIA member companies.

Some of the SIIA's efforts go toward anti-piracy, government affairs, and many other
programs, publications, conferences/symposiums, and awards. Two of their popular
awards events are highlighted below. (Tap into www.siia.net for more information about
the SIIA.)

Codie Awards

One of the oldest annual awards ceremonies held for the software industry is the Codies.
There are 39 categories under different award groupings: general, online, enterprise,
business/home office, consumer, games, and software for schools. Awards within the
games category go to the best new adventure/role-playing game, best new arcade/action
game, best new sports game, best new strategy and simulation game, and best new
multiplayer online game. For a list of rules and past winners, visit
www.siia.net/conf/codieawards/.

Marketing Achievement Awards

There are two events under this heading, including the best software packaging award
and the "Immy" awards for the industry's finest in marketing achievement. For details,
see www.siia.net/conf/marketawards.htm.

Computer Game Artists Association

This membership association exists to form a community of computer game artists that
interact with (share, learn, teach, and influence) each other and their industry. Find out
more about what they are and how they work at www.vectorg.com/cga.

Interactive Digital Software Association (IDSA)

Formed in 1994, the Interactive Digital Software Association (IDSA) is the only U.S.
association exclusively dedicated to serving the business and public affairs interests of
companies that publish console and computer games for video game consoles, PCs, and
the Internet. Today, their members account for more than 85 percent of the billion-dollar
interactive entertainment software sold in the United States. In short, the IDSA offers
services to gaming publishers, such as a robust anti-piracy program, government relations, business and consumer research, and First Amendment and intellectual property
protection efforts. The official IDSA Web site can be accessed at www.idsa.com.

Computer Games Developers Association (CGDA)

The CGDA is dedicated to serving the interests of the worldwide computer game development community by offering a number of benefits and services. Find out about benefits and joining this membership association at www.cgda.org.

American Association of Artificial Intelligence (AAAI)

Founded 20 years ago, the American Association for Artificial Intelligence (AAAI) is a not-for-profit society devoted to advancing the scientific understanding of the mechanisms underlying thought and intelligent behavior and their embodiment in machines. Their aims include increasing public understanding of artificial intelligence (AI), improving the teaching and training of AI practitioners, and seeking funding for important developments. As outlined at their official Web site (www.aaai.org), there are many benefits for members, including conferences, symposia and workshops, magazines, and more.

Entertainment Software Rating Board (ESRB)

You may have seen a sticker in the corner of most computer game boxes that says "ESRB" accompanied by an age rating. The Entertainment Software Rating Board is an independent group that, with the support of the industry, has developed a standardized rating system for interactive entertainment software products, and now Web sites as well. The ESRB ratings are designed to give consumers information about the content of an interactive video or computer entertainment title and the ages for which it's appropriate. For more info and the various age ratings, visit www.esrb.com.

25

Interactive Entertainment Merchants Association (IEMA)

The IEMA is a not-for-profit organization serving the business and public affairs needs of interactive entertainment product retailers. Their mandate? To assist retail and distributor members of the IEMA by increasing their current and future effectiveness, longevity, and profitability. IEMA holds a convention as well; the official Web site for both the association and convention is at www.theiema.org.

Recreational Software Advisory Council on the Internet (RSACi)

This not-for-profit organization aims to inform the public about adult content in electronic media, "by means of an open, objective content advisory system." The RSACi system provides consumers, especially concerned parents, with information about the level of sex, violence, and offensive language (vulgar or hate-motivated) in software games and Web sites. Find out more about the RSACi at www.rsac.org.

European Leisure Software Publishers Association (ELSPA)

This organization was founded in 1989 to establish a collective identity for the European computer and video games industry. ELSPA is concerned with the publishing and distribution of interactive leisure and entertainment software, working to promote the interests of all its members, as well as addressing issues that affect the industry as a whole. Point your browser to www.elspa.com to learn more.

Project Bar-B-Q

Hosted by George "The Fat Man" Sanger and sponsored by Cirrus Logic, this annual conference is meant to serve as a think tank for computer musicians and sound engineers to solidify their opinions and put those opinions to work for the good of the manufacturers, developers, and primarily the consumers of computer/audio products. The Web address is www.fatman.com/bbq.htm.

APPENDIX

Biographies

Alas, we have come to the end of the book. It's time now to learn a little more about the fine folks who have offered their discerning words of wisdom.

Though a few of our sages in the gaming industry were unable to supply a bio, most are listed here, in alphabetical order for easy reference. And perhaps one day you too will be listed in a book like this.

Akemann, Peter—Treyarch Invention

Peter T. Akemann, Ph.D., is a managing member of Treyarch Invention and project lead on *Die by the Sword (DBTS)*. He created the VSIM animation system that drives most of the animation in *DBTS*. The keyframed sequences in the game (mostly in the movies) were done by several contract animators (mostly Mike McCarthy of Interplay); Treyarch has no animators on staff.

Arnlund, Kurt—Accolade

As a programmer at Accolade, Arnlund is currently working on the action title *Slave Zero*, but prior to this project he programmed a number of hit games, including *MechWarrior 2: NetMech*, *Interstate '76*, *The Interstate '76 Arsenal*, *The Interstate '76 Nitro Pack*, and *Heavy Gear 2*.

His future aspirations are many, but he says he'd like to continue to work on creative projects that don't just push the technological limits of the available hardware, but also give game players new experiences that are different from anything they've seen before. Says Arnlund, "I love the challenge of taking something that's been done in every game before it and thinking up a way to make it more spectacular than anything that has ever been seen." He'd also like to get more involved in game design and would like to pitch and start a project where he's more of a contributor toward the design.

Backman, Ted—Valve Software

As an artist and animator at Valve Software in Kirkland, Washington, Ted Backman worked on their first title, *Half-Life*. Now that *Half-Life* is done, he's busy poring over possible artistic reference material. "It's a hard thing to try to clear your mind of two years' worth of work and start fresh on a new project." Every night, he finds himself drawing and looking at a wide range of material, just to try to infuse some new ideas into his creative process. In the future, he hopes to be able to create intriguing game worlds, compelling characters, and engaging scenarios in many game genres.

Bailey, Kelly—Valve Software

Kelly Bailey is a senior game designer and music and sound effects engineer at Valve Software. Kelly did all of the music and sound effects for *Half-Life*, and spent the 1998 summer and fall working on *Half-Life* game design. Earlier in the development of *Half-Life*, he wrote the code to allow characters to speak, and implemented the software DSP system that provides reverb and echo effects. Kelly's most recent musical background includes several years of singing, song writing, and playing guitar in local bands in the Seattle area. Although his initial work at Valve was full time on engineering, early in the project he presented a five-song demo CD to the company and found himself happily responsible for the game's full soundtrack.

Bain, Sinjin—PyroTechnix

Sinjin Bain is the studio manager at PyroTechnix, a wholly owned subsidiary of Sierra On-Line. He cofounded PyroTechnix (originally named Computer Presentations, Inc./CPI) over 10 years ago as a computer graphics and disk-based marketing and animation company. Although PyroTechnix' primary thrust was business software, they pioneered a 3D authoring environment called True3D, and have been involved in a number of game-related projects with various licensors. Since being acquired by Sierra in 1998, they have released the very successful game *Return to Krondor*.

Bates, Bob—Legend Entertainment

Bob Bates is Legend Entertainment's studio head, and he shares the duties of running the organization with Mike Verdu, who has been his partner at Legend since they founded the company in 1989. Bates' game-writing career started at Infocom in 1986, where he wrote two text adventures: *Sherlock! The Riddle of the Crown Jewels* and *Arthur: The Quest for Excalibur*. Since starting Legend, he has also written *TIMEQUEST*, *Eric The Unready*, and, most recently, *John Saul's Blackstone Chronicles*.

Altogether, he has written, co-designed, or produced over 20 games that have won more than 30 industry awards, most notably the 1992 Adventure Game of the Year award for *Eric The Unready*.

Bernal, Mark—Bungie Software

As lead artist and art director at Bungie Software, Bernal has worked on *Myth 2: Soulblighter*, *Myth: The Fallen Lords*, and *Marathon 2*. His future aspirations are to continue to create entertaining, top-of-the-line "A list" games and to explore and develop the technical and creative aspects of computer games.

Biessman, Eric—Raven Software

As project coordinator and lead designer for Raven Software, Eric Biessman has worked on *Heretic: Shadows of the Serpent Riders*, *Hexen*, *Hexen: Death Kings of the Dark Citadel*, *CyClones*, *Hexen 2*, and *Heretic 2*. During his tour of duty with Raven, the team that he has worked with has won numerous awards, including Most Valuable Product and Best Shareware for *Heretic*, and several industry awards, such as the Spotlight Award (Spotty) from the Computer Games Developers Association. These games have also always done well in the eyes of the reviewers and the public, which is the highest award that anyone can ask for.

The only thing that he can see in his future, says Biessman, is that he will continue to work on great games: "If this means that I continue with my current position, great! If it means that I continue in a different capacity, like producer, that would be fine too. Regardless, I have chosen this field for a career and I hope to have a long and prosperous one."

Bleszinski, Cliff—Epic Games

Cliff Bleszinski is a 24-year-old game designer who has been working in the industry since the age of 17. He originally began developing adventure games for Epic Games, and later found his calling in the realm of action-adventure titles. In 1993, Cliff designed *Jazz Jackrabbit*, commonly referred to as "the Sonic the Hedgehog of the PC," which went on to become a huge hit. Not one to rest on his laurels, Cliff immediately began working on a Jazz sequel and a little 3D shooter called *Unreal*. One of the original four developers for *Unreal*, it was Cliff's responsibility to oversee and assist with all level design on the game, as well as to contribute to the game's overall design and direction. He's probably most well-known for the infamous "Skaarj Introduction" and the terrifying first level "Vortex Rikers" in *Unreal*, which set a new standard for cinematic immersiveness; both were hailed as some of the most memorable moments in gaming history.

Cliff is now developing *Unreal Tournament*, an action title that takes place in the *Unreal* universe, pitting the player against the hardest (and most devious) criminals in all the galaxy in the ultimate test of Deathmatch skills.

Broussard, George—3D Realms

George Broussard is a partner and president of 3D Realms. Their past products include *Terminal Velocity* (developed by Terminal Reality), *Duke Nukem 3D*, and *Shadow Warrior*. They're currently working on *Duke Nukem Forever*, and have a small hand in *Max Payne* (being developed by Remedy Entertainment in Finland). Duke has been ported to every platform imaginable, and now they're starting to license original Duke games, such as *Duke Nukem: Time to Kill* (PSX) and *Duke Nukem: Zero Hour* (N64), while they continue to focus on PC games. Their future goals are to stay lean and mean and focused on a couple of quality 3D titles at a time, and continue to grow the company and their franchises.

Bumgardner, Chip—Interplay Productions

Chip Bumgardner has worked on many games as a producer, including *Chessmates*, *Lost Vikings 2*, *Earth 2140*, *Dragon Dice*, *Max 2*, and the *Caesar's Palace* series. He's currently working on a sequel to the popular game *Conquest of the New World*, *Star Trek: New Worlds*, and *Caesar's Palace II* for the PC, Sony PlayStation, and Dreamcast platforms.

Caracciolo, Carol—Acclaim Entertainment

Carol Caracciolo is the quality assurance manager at Acclaim, whose past products include *Mortal Kombat II*, *Turok*, *Quarterback Club*, *All-Star Baseball*, *NBA Jam*, *WWF: Raw*, *WWF: Warzone*, *Alien Trilogy*, *Revolution X*, and more. She founded Quality Assurance at Acclaim four and a half years ago with a staff of only three testers. She is currently maintaining a staff of approximately 75 over two full-time shifts, 7 days a week.

Castle, Louis—Westwood Studios

Louis Castle is the executive vice president and cofounder of Westwood Studios. For the past 13 years, he has worked as designer, executive producer, programmer, artist, and art director. In 1994, Castle brought *The Lion King* to Super Nintendo, and in 1995, he brought free parking to the Internet with the *Monopoly CD-ROM*. In 1997, Castle unleashed *Lands of Lore: Guardians of Destiny* and *Blade Runner*. His background in fine arts and computer science helps him maintain an artistic vision for Westwood's products throughout the turbulent and explosive growth of the software industry.

Charne, Jim—Academy of Interactive Arts and Sciences

Jim Charne is president and executive director of the Academy of Interactive Arts and Sciences (www.interactive.org). Before joining the Academy, Jim maintained an interactive entertainment and music industry law practice in Santa Monica, California. He has also served as vice president legal and business affairs and general counsel for a large East Coast-based console software studio, produced entertainment and personal productivity software for Activision, served on the corporate staff of the Technology Acquisitions Group of Merrill Lynch & Co., Inc. in New York, and worked in the music industry as a national marketing department head for CBS Records (now Sony Music) and as in-house counsel for Arista Records. Jim is admitted to practice law in California, New York, and New Jersey, and has spoken at industry conferences presented by E3 Expo, Computer Game Developers Conference, California Lawyers for the Arts, and Digital Hollywood.

Cloud, Kevin—id Software

Kevin Cloud is an artist for id Software, plus part owner of id along with Adrian Carmack and John Carmack. He started with id during the development of *Wolfenstein 3D*. Prior to id, Cloud worked as a computer artist and editor at Softdisk, a small monthly on-disk magazine that provided users with five to seven programs per month along with regular columns, editorials on the industry, etc. As id has grown and developed, Cloud has spent the last few years wearing a number of different hats and involving himself in the day-to-day operations of the company. Lately, he's tried to put those duties aside and focus more of his attention on improving as an artist.

Coallier, Steven—Electronic Arts

Steven Coallier is currently the software development manager for an in-house development group (Scoreboard Productions) at Electronic Arts' Redwood Shores location, which is also the corporate headquarters.

He began in the industry as a tester for Sierra On-Line, but became a programmer for them fairly soon afterward and ended up porting more than 20 of their graphic adventure games to the Amiga computer. His time at EA has had a lot of variety to it—he's shipped a PC first-person shooter, *Shadowcaster*, which was actually the first game to ship using the *Doom* engine; a PlayStation port of *Wing Commander III*; and two versions of *NCAA March Madness*, a college basketball game for the PlayStation. Next up for Coallier is the sequel to their new boxing game, *Knockout Kings*.

Cochrane, Bryce—Electronic Arts

At 28, Bryce Cochrane is the lead artist for the *NHL* series (PC/PSX/N64) at Electronic Arts (Canada). Serving in capacities ranging from testing and map design to lead artist, modeling, and animation, Cochrane has also produced work for all sorts of platforms—NES, Saturn, 3DO, Genesis, PC, N64, and others. Past games include *James Bond Junior*, *Terminator*, *Bob*, *Wayne's World*, *Crash Test Dummies*, *Ren and Stimpy's Videots*, *NHL All-Star Hockey*, *MTV Sports*, *Foes of Ali*, *Phoenix 3*, *Perfect Weapon*, *Triple Play 99*, *NHL 98*, *NHL 99*, and *NHL 2000*.

Cook, Vance—Sierra On-Line

Vance Cook has been developing golf simulators for about 10 out of the last 12 years. It has consumed a significant portion of his life so far. He worked at Access Software for about six years with many other talented developers on several projects, most notably *Links* and *Links386 Pro*. He left Access Software about six years ago to fulfill his lifelong goal of starting his own company, and founded Headgate, Inc. After dabbling in business productivity products for a few years, Cook came back to golf simulators again and ended up selling the company to Sierra On-Line, where he has been happily employed for the last three years.

Corea, Nicholas—Electronic Arts

Nick Corea is a computer graphic artist at Electronic Arts. His impressive résumé includes *Virtual Pinball* (all art), *US Navy Fighters* (terrain, cockpits, 3D shapes, some user interface), *Marine Fighters* (lead artist, terrain, 3D shapes, cockpits), *US Navy Fighters 97* (lead artist, some 3D shapes), and *WWII Fighters* (lead artist).

Corea wanted to design video games as a young teenager and made several pinball games with Bill Budge's *Pinball Construction Set* on the Atari 800. In 1983, he sent them to EA with a letter saying he wanted to design games for them. He soon discovered "girls, skateboarding, and an Amiga 2000." A "surfboard-shaper-friend's-brother" was the art director for video games at Disney, so Corea started working as a freelance artist in 1991 for Disney (Buena Vista Software) in Burbank, California, on a product called *Un-Natural Selection*. The work included a lot of user interface work and claymation. The producer left Disney for EA and offered a contracting job with Bill Budge on a new pinball project for the Sega Genesis (ten years after his letter!). He then came to work for EA a year later, on a permanent basis. *USNF* had room for a 3D artist, and luckily he had a chance to touch every type of art on the project. When the sequel started, he was chosen as lead artist.

On the *WWII Fighters* project, it was an opportunity to push the art. The hope now, says Corea, would be to someday become an art director of several projects.

Desiderio, Vince—Running With Scissors

Vince "Desi" Desiderio is the CEO of Running With Scissors. Their first release was the controversial *Postal*, and *Flesh & Wire* is next. *Postal* won numerous awards and accolades, with Desi's favorites being called "the #1 worst thing in American society" by U.S. Senator Joseph Leiberman of Connecticut (#2 was Marilyn Manson and #3 was Calvin Klein underwear ads), and being awarded Best Packaging by SPA, an ironic award since it was taken off the shelves of the major retailers after the first month.

Dorf, Barry—Electronic Arts

Barry Dorf was an assistant producer for the *Madden* series since 1998, and moved over to do online projects. He helped designed *The Edge* and is now in the process of designing several of EA Sports' new *Fantasy Football* and *Madden Football Interactive* Web sites. He came from working in TV in Los Angeles, and EA is the first video game company he worked for. Pretty good first call.

Freeman, Chad—Dreamforge Intertainment

Chad Freeman is a lead programmer at Dreamforge Intertainment, Inc. Past products include New World Computing's *Anvil of Dawn*, SSI's *Warwind*, and *Sanitarium,* published by ASC Games. His future aspirations are to create a game that surpasses *Sanitarium* in both gameplay and storyline.

Fristrom, Jamie—Treyarch Invention

Jamie Fristrom is a senior programmer at Treyarch in California. Previously he worked on *Magic Candle II*, *Magic Candle III*, *Bloodstone*, *Seige*, *Wheel of Fortune* (DOS and Windows), *Beat The House* (Windows), *Die by the Sword*, and most recently, *Limb From Limb*.

Gough, Charles—Bungie Software

Charles Gough, a.k.a. Chucky, is a programmer for Bungie Software Products, Inc., in Chicago. He has been a paid programmer since January of 1998, when he left college early to come work for Bungie, but he's been programming on and off since he was around nine, when his father showed him the basics of AppleSoft Basic on the old Apple IIe. Gough's past products were a "bunch of dinky unfinished shareware games that would have won numerous awards and accolades had the public ever known of them." He's currently working on an unannounced action game that will "take the world by storm in the spring of 2000 and move Bungie farther along the road of global domination."

Green, Mark A.C.—Psygnosis

Mark A.C. Green is currently the production and design liaison for Psygnosis' Leeds studio. Until late 1998, he was the lead designer on one of the projects (*Global Domination* for PC and PSX), and has since moved on to a wider role, with more dealings with marketing and input on all games that come out of the Leeds studio. He started in the games industry back in the summer of '93, for a company called Lore Design. They worked on the soon-forgotten Atari Jaguar and released *Highlander*, which was the second Jaguar CD game, and the first game on any platform to use an optical motion-capture system. Because the company was small, Green played a huge variety of roles, varying from tester through designer and motion analyst to project coordinator (even trainee programmer at one stage!). It was this range of experience that gave him his grounding in the *art* of designing games.

As for the future, Green guesses, "It's what we all dream of—that fantasyland where developers are given enough time to create the game that they want. We all have our visions of the 'perfect' game, and it would be great to reach a position where I can make mine happen."

Grimani, Mario—Ensemble Studios

Mario Grimani is an AI specialist at Ensemble Studios. Some of his past products include *Monty Python and the Quest for the Holy Grail*, developed by 7th Level, and *Dominion: Storm Over Gift 3*, developed by ION Storm. Currently, he's working on computer player AI for *Age of Empires II: The Age of Kings*. Grimani expects to continue working on AI for real-time strategy games for a while.

Hall, Tom—ION Storm

Tom Hall is a game designer and president of ION Storm. He was also a cofounder of id Software, and then later ION Storm. Hall is originally from New Berlin, Wisconsin. After getting a programming degree from the University of Wisconsin, he turned his game-making hobby into a dream job. His history includes the *Commander Keen* series, *Wolfenstein 3D*, *Spear of Destiny*, *Doom*, *Duke Nukem II*, *Rise of the Triad*, *Terminal Velocity*, and now the 3D sci-fi RPG, *Anachronox* (pronounced uh-NAH-kruh-nox).

Hess, Torsten—Blue Byte Software

As project manager and graphic artist at Blue Byte Software, plus a freelance graphic artist, Hess has worked on a few games for the company—most notably and recently, *Incubation* (storyboarding) and *Settlers III* (project manager), and will be involved in the expansion packs for the game.

Horling, Bryan C.—Freeverse Software

Bryan C. Horling is a shareware programmer for Freeverse Software, and a computer science graduate student who studied multi-agent systems. He has written *Burning Monkey Solitaire* for the Mac and PC, *Jared* and *Virtual Viagra* for Freeverse, and is in the process of finishing *Mr. Relaxer*. In the future, he plans on updating the Mac version of *Burning Monkey Solitaire* for Freeverse, and possibly incorporating Internet play into it. He may also write another "toy" program for them, involving a monkey that sits onscreen and says/does random things throughout the day.

House, Sean—Electronic Arts

Sean House is an associate producer at Electronic Arts for the *Madden NFL Football* series on the PC. His aspirations include "moving up the proverbial ladder, taking on more responsibility, and developing new and innovative entertainment software."

Householder, Matt—Blizzard Software

Matt Householder has learned a lot over the years about game design and the production process on nearly any type of platform: coin-op (he witnessed the creation of *Q-Bert*), consoles (going back to the ColecoVision and including NES, Game Boy, SNES, Genesis, 3DO Multiplayer, and PSX), and home computers (Apple II, C64, DOS—going all the way back to CGA graphics, Amiga, Atari ST).

Householder started out programming coin-op games in 1981 and finished his first game, *Krull*, an action/RPG, in 1983. In 1984, he converted *Moon Patrol* to the ColecoVision (including doing most of the art and sound effects himself), and produced many original computer games for Epyx during 1985-88, including *Winter Games*, *World Games*, and *California Games* (which he created, designed, and directed). Since then, he has produced games with varying (mostly little) success for Activision, Epyx (again), DTMC (defunct), and 3DO. He joined Blizzard North to produce *Diablo II* and recruit game developer employees—programmers, artists, and sound/music artists.

Hudgins, Marc—Yosemite Entertainment

Marc Hudgins is an art director and game designer for Yosemite Entertainment, a division of Sierra On-Line. "Too many to list" was Hudgins response when asked to describe his past projects, but some of the highlights include *Quest for Glory 1*, *3*, and *4*, *Slater and Charlie Go Camping*, *The Realm*, *King's Quest 7*, and most recently, *Babylon 5*.

Jackson, Allen —Origin Systems

Allen Jackson is a software engineer at Origin Systems who has helped program a number of action titles and space simulations: *Crusader: No Remorse*, *Crusader: No Regret*, *Wing Commander Prophecy*, and *Wing Commander Prophecy: Secret Ops*. He primarily works on the higher-level game code, including interface, Win32 GUI applications, game-defined objects, and networking.

Jaquays, Paul—id Software

Paul Jaquays is a game designer at id Software, Inc., also serving as a level designer for *Quake II*. His current project is game and level design for *Quake III: Arena*. Previous computer/electronic game projects include script and map layouts for Interplay's *Lord of the Rings, Volume 1*, design for Expx's *4x4 Off Road Racing*, "script doctor" for *Bard's Tale IV* from EA, concept and co-design (with Joe Angiolillo) for *Wargames* for the ColecoVision and ADAM computer, the *Pac-Man* tabletop arcade from Coleco, and the *Donkey Kong* tabletop arcade from Coleco.

His previous jobs are an interesting mix, including staff cover artist and then director of graphics for TSR, Inc. (publisher of *Dungeons & Dragons*); freelance illustrator, game designer and editor; director of product development for Penguin Products; director of game design for Coleco Industries, Inc., and game designer and illustrator for Judges Guild.

Jaquays' other projects worth noting are role-playing game adventures: *Dark Tower*, *Caverns of Thracia*, *Book of Treasure Maps I*, *Hellpits of Nightfang*, *Griffin Mountain* (with Rudy Kraft and Greg Stafford), *The Savage Frontier*, and *The Shattered Statue*. He designed the concept for and wrote the first three books in the *Central Casting* character development book series and produced *City Books 4–6* for Flying Buffalo, Inc. Jaquays is on the development credits for *Marvel Super Heroes* dice game from TSR (he also did all the dice icon artwork), and illustrated numerous adventure game products and created the art look for the *Dragon Dice* game. He also directed the design and development of all Coleco's non-educational video games.

Future aspirations? "Keep having fun making games."

Jensen, Jane—Sierra On-Line

Jane Jensen is an award-winning game designer at Sierra On-Line whose past products include *EcoQuest: Search for Cetus* (co-designer), *King's Quest VI* (co-designer), *Gabriel Knight: Sins of the Fathers* (designer and series creator), and *Gabriel Knight: The Beast Within*. Jensen's current project in development is *Gabriel Knight: Blood of the Sacred, Blood of the Damned*. She has also written and published two novels: *Gabriel Knight: Sins of the Fathers* and *Gabriel Knight: The Beast Within*, which are obviously based on the plot of the games. She has an original novel (i.e., not game-based) called *Millennium Rising*, coming out from Del Rey in the fall of 1999, and another original book due on the Del Rey contract which should be published by the end of 2000.

Her future aspirations are to continue to do books and games, although she will probably continue to move into a more independent role with the games, where she writes the design and perhaps the major dialogue scenes but doesn't participate as much during the development process. She finds the day-to-day production process more managerial and "grunt-workish" than she really cares for, and prefers to focus on writing.

Johnston, Matthew Lee—Microsoft Corp.

Matt Johnston is the audio lead at Microsoft. As a youth, he was always into music and sound. A common afternoon would find him on the floor with headphones listening to the production subtleties of Pink Floyd's "The Wall," or sitting in a tree listening to the different Hawaiian bird species share their stories. Countless hours were also spent playing his Atari 2600 and riding his bike down to the "Fun Factory" to play *Crazy Climber*, *Cliffhanger*, *Astro Fighter*, or whatever was new, with stolen money from his parents' "money jar." In 8th grade, he became obsessed with computers after seeing the movie "Wargames." Performing on his Apple IIe, he managed to orchestrate worldwide notoriety through moments of video game software piracy, more than a few phone system phreaking opuses, and a cacophony of bulletin board operation.

His parents had always explained the "hardships" of being a musician, and insisted he find something like his computer interests to fall back on. In college, he discovered a place called the "computer music lab," where two of his three obsessions seemed to exist in harmony. He spent the entirety of his interdisciplinary education either working with the Buchla Modular synth or Sound Designer 1.0 in the lab, or acting as music director at the college radio station, KAOS. Back in the "house of doom," his roommates and he were "blowing smoke, drinking malt liquor, and trying hard to kick each other's nads on the Genesis, NES, or the 2600." All of this activity became the ideal preparation for his current position as resident juvenile delinquent at Microsoft.

Projects Johnston has worked on at Microsoft include *Flight Simulator 95* and *98*, *Microsoft Golf 2.0, 3.0, 98*, and *99*, *3D Movie Maker*, *Cinemania 96*, *Reader's Digest Complete Do-It-Yourself Guide*, *Monster Truck Madness 1* and *2*, *CART Precision Racing*, *Combat Flight Simulator 1.0*, and *MS Digital Phone*.

His future aspirations include working on more hardware projects, preserving quiet places, and collaborating with Lauryn Hill on some interactive music.

Kahn, Adam—Acclaim Entertainment

Adam Kahn is a PR manager at Acclaim Entertainment. Before he joined Acclaim in the winter of 1998, he worked at Shandwick International, a PR firm, on the Microsoft Games account.

Kirk, Geoff—Humongous Entertainment

Humongous Entertainment's sound designer and sound effects programmer, Geoff Kirk, has worked on many titles, including *Pajama Sam*, *Putt-Putt Travels Through Time*, *Spy Fox*, *Freddi Fish 3*, *Pajama Sam 2*, *Putt Putt Enters the Race*, and *Freddi Fish 4*. He has also contributed background music for a couple of bonus levels in *Pajama Sam's Lost and Found* and the background music for the "Happy Fun Sub" in *Spy Fox*. Kirk is also a musician, but says, "I don't think this is necessary to become a good sound effects programmer."

In college, he studied a number of topics that helped him in his work at Humongous. He learned "classic" analog synth programming on instruments like the Arp 2600, and also basic recording techniques. He also learned tape editing, which in those ancient days was done with a razor, and experimented with such things as making long loops of tape with drums or other sounds on them and using them in various compositions. Later on, he worked for Muzak splicing tapes together, and while he was there used to make small tape loops with various silly things on them, which also helped develop some of the skills he uses today editing sounds together. During this time, he began building a small personal studio at home and learning about MIDI, the various types of digital synthesizers, and sampling. The greatest preparation for what he's doing today, says Kirk, was the time spent when he was very young watching cartoons, especially the old Warner Brother's Bugs Bunny. "They used music as a sound effect in a way that is still rather revolutionary. The background music on those old cartoons is also very cool and ahead of its time."

His future aspirations are to contribute more background music to games and to work on games that aren't just for young children.

Koberstein, Joe—Raven Software

Joe Koberstein is an artist at Raven Software and has been in the game industry about five years, working in California, Japan, and Wisconsin. He's currently in game development, but has also worked in publishing, advertising, and marketing of video games. Past employers include *GameFan* magazine, subsidiaries of Activision (Raven Software), marketing groups for Disney and Sony PlayStation (Ascii Entertainment), as well as his own freelance agency, Kdesign.

Laidlaw, Marc—Valve Software

Marc Laidlaw is a writer/level team coordinator for *Half-Life* and a game designer at Valve Software. His published novels include *The 37th Mandala* (winner of the International Horror Guild Award for Best Novel of 1996), *Kalifornia*, *The Orchid Eater*, *Dad's Nuke*, *Neon Lotus*, and *The Third Force: A Novel of Gadget*. Future aspirations are to continue to hone the cutting edge where game design meets storytelling.

Land, Michael—LucasArts

Michael Land is the sound department manager and a member of the music team at LucasArts Entertainment and has contributed to many award-winning and best-selling products through the years: the entire *Monkey Island* series, *The Dig*, *X-Wing*, *TIE Fighter*, *Indiana Jones and the Fate of Atlantis*, and *Day of the Tentacle*. His future aspiration is simply to continue writing music.

Lanzinger, Franz—Actual Entertainment

Franz Lanzinger is the chairman of Actual Entertainment. Franz worked as a programmer and game designer at Atari Games Inc. and Tengen. He left in 1990 to cofound Bitmasters, where he was president until April of 1995. He then founded Actual Entertainment with Mark Robichek and Eric Ginner.

A terrific video game player, he held the world record for the arcade version of *Centipede* for six months in 1981. On September 19, 1997, Franz achieved further fame when Gamasutra selected him as their Geek of the Week! He is a bridge life master and broke 90 at Sunnyvale Municipal Golf Course on one of his better days. On top of all that, Franz programmed and designed a few games you might have heard of: *Crystal Castles* (coin-op, original), *Toobin* (NES, conversion), *Ms. Pac Man* (NES, conversion), *Krazy Kreatures* (NES, original), Rampart (NES, SNES, conversion), *Championship Pool* (SNES, original), and *NCAA Final Four Basketball* (SNES, original). He also designed *Ms. Pac Man* (Genesis, conversion), *Championship Pool* (Genesis, NES, Game Boy, original), and *NCAA Final Four Basketball* (Genesis, original).

Larkin, Tim—Yosemite Entertainment

Tim Larkin is a senior sound designer at Oakhurst, California's Yosemite Entertainment. His current project is lead sound designer and design audio implementation schemes on J.R.R. Tolkien's *Middle Earth*. He has also scored sound for the opening movie and cut-scenes for *Quest for Glory V*. Before moving on to Yosemite Entertainment, Larkin served as lead sound designer and composer at Brøderbund, where he was the lead sound designer for *Riven: The Sequel to Myst*. This included creation of sound effects for over 900 individually rendered movies and animations, and close to an hour of interactive ambience. Also at Brøderbund, Larkin composed and produced music and/or sound design for the *Carmen Sandiego* series, *Rugrats*, *Warbreeds*, and more. Before that, Larkin produced and engineered sound and music for numerous TV themes, industrial videos, commercials, multimedia, and album projects.

Levelord, The (Richard Bailey Gray)—Ritual Entertainment

According to his published bio, The Levelord is originally from New Haven, Connecticut. He has served a tour of duty in the U.S. Navy and attended several institutions of higher learning, from which he earned a technical degree in business-oriented programming and a degree in computer engineering. He has been doing level design since 1994.

The Levelord designed half of the levels for *Duke Nukem 3D* (The Abyss, Incubator, Warp Factor, Spin Cycle, Lunatic Fringe, Raw Meat, Bank Roll, Flood Zone, L.A. Rumble, The Movie Set, Rabid Transit, Fahrenheit, Hotel Hell, and Tier Drops). The latest release of *Scourge of Armagon* includes his levels The Lost Mine, Research Facility, The Crypt, Tur Torment, and The Edge of Oblivion.

This is where the Levelord's bio ends, but he then went to Ritual Entertainment and was lead level designer for Activision's *Sin*.

Levesque, Adam—Blue Fang Games

Adam Levesque is currently the president of Blue Fang Games. He formerly worked at Papyrus, where he served as a 3D artist on *IndyCar Racing*, a producer/designer on *NASCAR Racing 1* and *2*, an executive producer on all Papyrus products, and general manager of the Papyrus division. He started Blue Fang Games last year to branch out into other game genres. He's currently working on *Dragon Hoard*, a strategy/RPG in which the player takes on the role of a dragon.

Lewis, Susan—ThinkBIG

Susan Lewis is the president of ThinkBIG, a company dedicated to representing and promoting the interests of client development and publishing companies. Publishers she has "closed deals" with Electronic Arts, Acclaim, Fox Interactive, Atari Games, and BMG Interactive. Lewis deals with virtually every publisher out there, and her company has been featured in *Wired*, *Game Developer*, *SF Chronicle*, *Gamecenter*, *Salon*, and *Screen Magazine* (Germany) and on the television program TV.Com/CNET. She was invited to speak at E3 1997 ("The Art of the Pitch," with Bryan Neider, VP of Electronic Arts) and at GDC 1998 ("The Art of the Pitch," with Ed Zono, President of Zono Games).

Linn, Bill—Linn Public Relations, Inc.

Bill Linn is a longtime game industry public relations veteran. Before starting his agency in mid-1997, Linn spent seven years as the senior in-house public relations counsel for Sierra, The Imagination Network, and Accolade. He has worked on many of the game industry's best-known and best-selling products, including *King's Quest*, *Leisure Suit Larry*, *Daryl Gates' Police Quest*, *Hardball*, *Jack Nicklaus Golf*, *Prince of Persia*, *Riven*, *Uprising*, *Warlords*, and *Test Drive*. In all, he has launched more than 100 PC multimedia, console, and Internet games. Before joining the game industry, Linn spent several years promoting everything from politicians to concerts and worked as a journalist for several major newspapers.

A gamer at heart, Linn approaches product public relations by integrating his passion for interactive entertainment with his professional training and experience. He grew up playing everything from *Pong* and *Coleco Football* to *M.U.L.E.* and *Leisure Suit Larry*. Today, he devotes many hours to playing games on the PC, PlayStation, Nintendo 64, and at video arcades.

Linn's client roster includes some of the industry's leading companies: Sierra, THQ, Brøderbund, The 3DO Company, and ASCII Entertainment.

Lupidi, Tony—Electronic Arts

Tony Lupidi is an art director for Scoreboard Productions, an in-house development company at Electronic Arts. He has shipped two games—*March Madness '98* and *March Madness '99*—college basketball simulations on the PlayStation game platform.

Lupidi comments, "From my viewpoint, we are right on the verge of the emergence of a new, more interactive form of mass media. Some of the technologies driving this new media are 1) real-time 3D display hardware as a consumer technology (à la *Voodoo*, TNT); 2) broadband networks (cable modems for the masses); and 3) continued development of faster and cheaper computers.

The film industry has over 100 years of history and a successful formula for making money, and thus has neither the incentive nor imagination to develop interactive media. That is the reason I have switched careers from doing TV and film animation to working in the video game industry. If you look at the history of the development of new media, there is always a period at the beginning of intense experimentation, innovation, and risk taking before successful formulas are derived. As a creative type, this is the most exciting time since you have the fewest constraints placed on you. I want to participate in this next step in media."

McCart, Michael—Ensemble Studios

The way Michael McCart got his job at Ensemble Studios as their Webmaster is inspiring to anyone with a fan site. McCart ran the popular *Age of Empires: Heaven* Web site, hosted by Gamestats, and was snagged from

Ensemble Studios because they were pleased with his talent and dedication. That's the short answer. The longer one is available at Michael McCart's home page at www.electrosonic.net.

McGrath, Michael—Dynamix

Michael D. McGrath is an engineer/programmer at Dynamix/Sierra. His past products include *Netrek* (public domain), *Extreme Warfare* (Trilobyte), and *Red Baron 3D* (Dynamix). Current projects include *Desert Fighters* and *Aces of the Pacific II,* and future plans include a rewrite of *Netrek*, plus sci-fi flight/combat sims and conquest titles.

Meier, Sid—Firaxis Games

Sid Meier is the chairman and director of creative development at Firaxis Games. Called the "father of the computer gaming industry," his career is a story of "firsts." He created the first combat flight simulator, *F15 Strike Eagle*, in the early '80s, which has sold well over a million copies and inaugurated the flight simulation industry. His *Silent Service* was the first submarine simulation. The innovative *Pirates!*, a unique blend of historical sim, arcade action, strategy, and role-playing, opened the doors to a plethora of genres. *F19 Stealth Fighter* was the first flight sim to incorporate an infinite mission generation system, a mainstay of recent flight sims, and an element of strategy that made it one of the most popular flight games ever. Sid's recent titles, such as *Railroad Tycoon* and *Civilization*, ushered in the new era of "god games" that started yet another new genre in computer gaming. Having won every major award in the industry, Sid continues to be on the leading edge of entertainment software.

Meijers-Gabriel, Ellen—Oddworld Inhabitants

As composer/sound designer at Oddworld Inhabitants, Ellen Meijers-Gabriel has written music and designed sound effects for both of the development studios' products, *Oddworld: Abe's Oddysee* and *Oddworld: Abe's Exoddus.*

Her first interaction with music was when she was about six years old and living in Holland. She studied piano for about 12 years before/until she developed a problem with her shoulders that prevented continuing her normal practice routine. This inability to practice meant that she could no longer pursue her goal to become a pianist and was now faced with what to do with her life. Wanting to stay in music, she chose to pursue other less physically-intense aspects of music. As soon as she accepted this decision, she enrolled in a masters program in musicology. Even before finishing the program, she was drawn to the technical side of music, so she concurrently started a music technology program at a different school. She enjoyed the technical side so much that she then began a master of arts program in interactive multimedia at The Royal College of Art in England. Immediately after graduating, Meijers-Gabriel was offered the opportunity to start working on games for a company in America.

Future aspirations include doing sound design and music for feature films; she would also like to further explore morphing techniques and synthesizing sounds from scratch, as opposed to changing existing sounds. To do this, she hopes to use tools like Kyma, Software DSP languages like MSP, and physical modeling synthesis, among others.

Meyers, Michael—Acclaim Entertainment

Michael Meyers is the director of product public relations at Acclaim Entertainment. He was involved in or in charge of the PR launches for *Turok: Dinosaur Hunter, Turok 2: Seeds of Evil, NFL Quarterback Club '98* and *'99, All-Star Baseball, Extreme-G, NBA Jam '99, WWF: Warzone, Jeremy McGrath Supercross*, and many others.

Miyamoto, Shigeru—Nintendo

Shigeru Miyamoto is the general manager of entertainment analysis and development at Nintendo Co. Ltd., Kyoto, Japan. The following is a list of all 50 games he's worked on, from 1981 to the present. He served as producer on most of these, but in a few cases as director or supervisor. In chronological order, they are *Donkey Kong, Donkey Kong Jr., Mario Bros., Popeye, Super Mario Bros., Wild Gunman, Duck Hunt, Hogan's Alley, Excite Bike, The Legend of Zelda, Volley Ball, Super Mario Bros. 2, Zelda II-The Adventure of Link, Ice Hockey, Super Mario Bros. 3, Kirby's Adventure, Super Mario World, Pilot Wings, F-Zero, Sim City, The Legend of Zelda: A Link to the Past, Super Mario Kart, Star Fox, Super Mario All Stars, Stunt Race FX, Super Donkey Kong, Earth Bound, Kirby's Dream Course, Super Mario World 2, Yoshi's Island, Super Mario RPG, Kirby Super Star, Radar Mission, Kirby's Dream Land, Wave Race, The Legend of Zelda: Link's Awaking, Kirby's Pinball Land, Donkey Kong, Mario's Picross, Kirby's Dream Land 2, Kirby's Blockball, Mole Mania, Super Mario 64, Pilot Wings 64, Wave Race 64, Mario Kart 64, Star Fox 64, Yoshi's Story, 1080 Snowboarding, F-Zero X*, and *The Legend of Zelda: Ocarina of Time.*

At the 1998 Electronic Entertainment Exposition, Miyamoto was honored as the first inductee into the Academy of Interactive Arts and Sciences Hall of Fame. His future aspirations are to continue to assist in the creation of new and exciting gameplay experiences for Nintendo.

Moe, Richard—Humongous Entertainment

Richard Moe is a project lead for Humongous Entertainment, "a confusing title which means basically that I design, produce, and implement games from the ground up." His area of expertise is programming—for all Humongous games, they work in a proprietary language called SCUMM, which was developed by the company cofounder Ron Gilbert. Some of the titles Moe has worked on as designer and programmer are, in ascending chronological order, *Junior Field Trips: Let's Explore the Airport, Pajama Sam in There's No Need to Hide When It's Dark Outside, Backyard Baseball*, and most recently *Putt-Putt Enters the Race.*

Newell, Gabe—Valve Software

Gabe Newell is the managing director at Kirkland, Washington's Valve Software. Their debut product, *Half-Life*, has won numerous print and online "Game of the Year" awards, as well as "Best PC Game" at the 1998 E3 from UGO.

Nichols, Mike—Surreal Software

Mike Nichols is a VP, creative director, and founder at Surreal Software. He started in this industry about 10 years ago. One of his first projects was *NY Warriors* in 1989 for the Amiga, coin-op, and PC (back when it was CGA and EGA only). Since then, he's worked for several companies as an artist and designer, having put out some 20 or more products. Nichols' last employer was Boss Game Studios, where he was the lead designer for *Spider* on the PlayStation.

Nichols' responsibilities at Surreal include managing the art teams and contributing to shape the future of Surreal and the type of products they want to create—not to mention creating art for the products themselves. Surreal is first and foremost a games developer. They don't carry egos or the notion of becoming the biggest game company in the industry. Their aspirations are simple: "Work hard at creating what we love—games."

O'Connor, Paul—Oddworld Inhabitants

As lead game designer at the Oddworld Inhabitants development studio, Paul O'Connor headed up *Oddworld: Abe's Oddysee* and *Oddworld: Abe's Exoddus* for the Sony PlayStation and PC. He has been a game designer in either a freelance or staff capacity more or less continuously since 1981, designing computer games, video games, board games, and role-playing games. He has also worked as a freelance writer, primarily writing comic books for Malibu and Marvel Comics.

Ostergard, Genevieve—Sierra Studios

Genevieve Ostergard, a senior PR manager at Sierra Studios, has been in the computer games business for four years and in PR for six. She started at Interplay as an assistant communications manager doing PR for MacPlay and the console divisions. Six months later, she was promoted to communications manager and proceeded to spearhead PC and console games PR for Interplay. After Interplay, she was a senior account executive for the Shandwick PR agency, handling the Microsoft Games account.

Prior to her game PR experience, she did PR for Ziff-Davis Press, the former book publishing division of the most successful computer magazine publisher in the world.

Pardo, Rob—Blizzard Entertainment

Rob Pardo is a producer/designer at Blizzard Entertainment. His credits include *StarCraft* and *StarCraft: Brood War*, and at Interplay he was a producer on the titles *Whiplash*, *Casper*, and *Tempest X*. His primary goal is to continue to produce and design AAA-quality games with Blizzard Entertainment.

Patmore, Alan—Surreal Software

Alan Patmore is the president and design director at Surreal Software. He is also the lead designer on *Drakan*. He has been an avid game player/designer since he was eight.

Perry, David

David Perry is behind some of our industry's most beloved games, such as the *Earthworm Jim* series and *MDK*. He invites all who are interested to read his extensive bio at www.shiny.com/company/meet_dp.htm.

Pfeifer, Kurt—Cavedog Entertainment

Before he was lead programmer on *Good & Evil*, Cavedog Entertainment's Kurt Pfiefer worked on *Total Annihilation*, *Duke Nukem* (Saturn port), *Microsoft Soccer*, *Powerslave*, *DinoPark Tycoon*, and *Magic School Bus Across the Solar System*.

"I think my bowling team won first place when I was twelve. Does that count as an accolade?"

Prince, Bobby—Bobby Prince Music

Bobby Prince is a composer/sound designer for bobby prince Music (his logo has the *b* and the *p* as half notes).

Past products include *Commander Keen*, *Wolfenstein 3D*, *Duke Nukem II* and *3D*, *Doom* and *Doom II*, *Zorro*, *Axis & Allies*, plus many early shareware games and other retail products. Back in 1991, Prince was fairly active on the MIDI/Computer Music section of Prodigy. This was before the Internet was the common mode of communications. One Saturday in April, a fellow by the name of Scott Miller posted a note asking to hear from people who were interested in writing music for computer games. A couple of weeks before that, he had downloaded the original *Commander Keen* and was extremely impressed with it. He didn't know at the time that Scott's new company, Apogee Software, had distributed *Commander Keen*, and Scott didn't mention that in his note. He figured that he was a wanna-be but responded anyway. The next day, Scott called him up and when he mentioned *Commander Keen*, Prince knew that he'd like to work with him. He hired him, "music unheard." Several months later, he received a call from John Romero of id Software and began working on the music for the second *Commander Keen* series. As they say, the rest is history. Future aspirations are "to continue to have fun the rest of his life."

Pritchard, Matt—Ensemble Studios

Matt Pritchard has been a graphics programmer for a number of gaming titles (in chronological order): *Dragon Quest Pi*, *Overload*, *Age of Empires*, *Age of Empires: Rise of Rome*, and *Age of Empires II: Age of Kings*.

Resnick, Josh—Pandemic Studios

Josh Resnick is the president of Pandemic Studios, but prior to starting his own development studio he produced *Mechwarrior 2*, directed *Dark Reign*, and oversaw the production of *Battlezone*. He has been in the industry for nearly five years, after starting at Activision as an associate producer.

Reynolds, Brian—Firaxis Games

Brian Reynolds began his career in computer gaming at Microprose Software, collaborating closely with Sid Meier on the design of *Sid Meier's Colonization*. He went on to design *Civilization II*, which topped the charts with sales of over one million copies worldwide. A founding partner of Firaxis, one of Reynolds' particular specialties is artificial intelligence. Addicted to strategy games himself, Brian is on a never-ending quest to "make the computer play as well as I do." Brian brings a rich and varied background as a summa cum laude graduate in the fields of history and philosophy from the University of the South, Sewanee, Tennessee. His computer wizardry is self-taught.

Riley, Hugh—Bethesda Softworks

Hugh Riley is a senior artist at Bethesda who has worked on dozens of games over the past 12 years on most home computer formats, both as a freelancer and, more recently, in-house.

Rippy, Chris—Ensemble Studios

Chris Rippy is the sound director at Ensemble Studios. Thus far at Ensemble he has helped develop two games: *Age of Empires* and *Age of Empires, the Rise of Rome Expansion Pack*. As a musician, Rippy says he "kind of stumbled" into the gaming world. Games had always been a hobby, but he never thought that he could combine two things that he enjoyed—sound and games—and make a good living at it. His brother, David Rippy, has worked with Ensemble Studios' president Tony Goodman for a number of years, and eventually word got out that Tony would be starting a game company. Well, David would be doing the music, and they asked Chris Rippy to join in and do the sound effects. With a background in radio and a history in recording studios, it was a natural fit (and a lucky one). "That was in 1994," says Rippy, and he's "been humming along ever since."

Robinson, Seth—Robinson Technologies

This 24-year-old CEO of Robinson Technologies, Inc. is also co-owner of Nexgen Gaming, a retail network gaming facility located in Salem, Oregon. Products under Seth Robinson's belt include *Legend of the Red Dragon 1* and *2, Planets: The Exploration of Space*, and most recently, *Dink Smallwood*.

Robinson Technologies, Inc. has been selling shareware for over 10 years. At the time of this interview they had been subcontracted by ManMachine (published by Macmillan Digital Publishing) for work on a couple of new games. *Dink Smallwood* has been written about in many game magazines, including *PC Gamer* and *PC Games*, and is considered to be one of the highest-quality shareware RPGs in cyberspace.

Roseman, Stuart—nineCo

As CTO of nineCo, Inc., producers of *Gamesville*, Stuart Roseman has overseen the production of many online multiplayer games: *The Bingo Zone*, *Picturama*, *AceyDeucey*, *Crystal Ball*, *Gridiron Madness*, *Pop Quiz*, *$100 CatchUp*, *CoverAll*, and *E-mercial*.

Ruttmann, Haiko—Blue Byte Software

As music director for Blue Byte Software, Haiko Ruttmann's job is to compose, arrange, and produce music for computer games and product videos, to create sound effects, and to coordinate and produce voice recordings. He started his career 10 years ago as a freelancer for the computer gaming industry. His work can be found in the following titles: *TwinWorld*, *Tom & the Ghost*, *Historyline 1914–1918*, *Battle Isle I*, *II*, and *III*, *Great Courts I* and *II*, *The Settlers I*, *II*, and *III*, *Chewy ESC from F5*, *Dr Drago*, *Schleichfahrt*, *Extreme Assault*, *Ugh!*, and *Incubation*.

Saladino, Michael—Presto Studios

Michael Saladino is a lead programmer for Presto Studios, but has been in the game industry for the last four years. The first two were spent with a small startup company named Mobeus Designs, where he was responsible for creating the 3D graphics engine. He then found himself at Volition, the creators of *Descent*, where he worked as one of two graphic engine developers at the company. He was later promoted to lead programmer on a racing game, and eventually moved on to Presto Studios, where he now works as one of their engine programmers and lead on a new project that's still in the design phase. In four short years, he has had the luck to work on many different projects in many different capacities.

Sanger, George (The Fat Man)—Fatman Music

The Fat Man, or George Alistair Sanger, has been composing music for games since 1983. Along with Team Fat, his legendary team of three other cowboy composers, he is internationally recognized for having created music for over 130 games, including such sound-barrier-breaking greats as *Loom*, *Wing Commander I* and *II*, *The 7th Guest I* and *II*, *NASCAR Racing*, *Putt-Putt Saves the Zoo*, and *ATF*. He wrote the first general MIDI soundtrack for a game, the first direct-to-MIDI live recording of musicians, the first Redbook soundtrack included with the game as a separate disk, the first music for a game that was considered a "work of art," and the first soundtrack that was considered a selling point for the game.

Team Fat is the original out-of-house source for music for games. More than once they have set trends and raised the bar for what is expected musically from games, significantly increasing sales of hardware and software. On a 380-acre ranch on the Guadalupe River, The Fat Man hosts the annual Texas Interactive Music Conference and BBQ (Project BBQ), the computer/music industry's most prestigious and influential conference.

Schilder, Kevin—Raven Software

Kevin Schilder is the manager of the audio department at Raven Software in Madison, Wisconsin. He is one of two people on staff who handle all the duties of sound design, music composition, and audio production for their games.

With 30 years of experience in the music field and degrees in music performance and education, Schilder's background includes a wide variety of musical styles. Before working at Raven, he worked in the retail music industry and taught music in public schools for six years. He has been associated with Raven Software since its inception, but formally employed with the company since 1994. Projects include *Black Crypt* on the Amiga (all music), *Cyclones* (some sound effects), and all music and sound effects on *Heretic*, *Hexen*, *Necrodome*, *Hexen II*, *Portal of Praevus*, *Mageslayer*, *Take No Prisoners*, and *Heretic II*. He was also creative director on *Take No Prisoners*.

He became involved in doing game music by association with Brian and Steve Raffel, the founders of Raven Software. As a friend, he offered to work on some music for their first game attempt, *Black Crypt*. Schilder's broad music background, interest in computers, love of fantasy/science fiction movies and computer games, as well as a desire to compose keep him interested in the field.

Schnurr, Carl—Red Storm Entertainment

"My mom claims I started playing games in the womb… if only I could remember the rules." Carl Schnurr is bringing counter-terrorism to harrowing 3D life by overseeing the production of Tom Clancy's *Rainbow Six*. Carl is a stickler for research; in preparing the realistic movements of the characters, he led the rest of his production team to a real-life shooting range, where they learned the nuances of combat.

Before joining the company, Schnurr was vice president of game development for Fringe Multimedia, Inc., a Chapel Hill, North Carolina-based software and Web site development startup. While there, Carl oversaw the production of games and educational titles, as well as the development of TheBlip.com, an award-winning Web site. His gaming experience also includes having written numerous role-playing game supplements for White Wolf's popular *Ars Magica* game.

Outside of the gaming world, Schnurr's background is just as unique: he has written manuals for shuttle astronauts and holds a Ph.D. and master's degree in physics from Duke University and a B.S. in physics from the University of Texas at Austin. He is now so experienced in counter-terrorist activities, President Clinton might want to take notice. "But I'd hesitate to mention to him the singing telegrams and the ren-fest gigs that I used to do." Then again, maybe not.

Sheldon, Lee—Southpeak Interactive

Lee Sheldon is a senior writer and game designer at SouthPeak Interactive. From most recent to oldest, Sheldon has worked on "an action/adventure game based on a major license, but still shrouded in secrecy," *20,000 Leagues: The Adventure Continues, Dark Side of the Moon, Temujin,* and *The Riddle of Master Lu.* Prior to writing and designing computer games, Sheldon was a writer and producer in television with over 200 produced credits, everything from Hanna Barbera cartoons to the daytime soap "The Edge of Night" to primetime series from "Charlie's Angels" to "Star Trek: The Next Generation." Sheldon was nominated for awards twice by the Mystery Writers of America and once by the Writers Guild of America.

Shelley, Bruce C.—Ensemble Studios

Bruce C. Shelley is a senior game designer at Ensemble Studios; his impressive past computer game co-design credits include *Railroad Tycoon, Covert Action, Civilization, Age of Empires, Age of Empires II: Age of Kings,* and a new RTS game yet to be named.

Simpson, Toby—CyberLife Technologies

Toby Simpson is the creative director for *Creatures* products at CyberLife Technology Ltd., based in Cambridge, England. He was producer of *Creatures 1, Creatures 2,* and now *Creatures 3,* and has written two published white papers and several books—two of which are all about the *Creatures* products and cover the science behind it all. Simpson feels he is part of something very exciting, and that this approach of biologically inspired bottom-up modeling systems is the one most likely to yield the technologies necessary for massive shared-space virtual worlds of the future.

Smith, Brandon—Cavedog Entertainment

Brandon Smith is a communications manager at Cavedog Entertainment and has been involved in *Total Annihilation* (and all the expansion packs) and *Total Annihilation: Kingdoms.* "In a past life," he worked on *Gex: Enter the Gecko, Blood Omen: Legacy of Kain, MDK, X-COM: Apocalypse, Worms 2,* and many more.

Stellmach, Timothy J.—Looking Glass Studios

Tim Stellmach is a senior game designer at Looking Glass Studios. His role on *Thief: The Dark Project* was lead designer, for which he was responsible for training and managing junior designers and overseeing the design of gameplay systems and missions. Previous products include *Ultima Underworld, Ultima Underworld II, System Shock,* and *Terra Nova.* His main aspiration right now is to transform *Thief* from a successful project into a successful series, "thus securing Looking Glass the well-deserved adulation of the masses."

Street, Greg—Ensemble Studios

Dr. Greg T. Street is a game designer at Ensemble Studios. He worked on the *Age of Empires: Rise of Rome* expansion pack and is currently finishing up *Age of Empires II: The Age of Kings.* His responsibilities include designing campaigns and random map types, and he also helps contribute to unit and civilization balance, as well as providing historical background when needed.

He got the job by answering the help wanted section of Ensemble Studios' Web page. Before working at Ensemble, he was a marine biologist at the University of South Carolina. He had no professional game industry experience—"See, it IS possible," he says—but his education, writing talent, historical breadth, and extensive gameplay experience got him the job.

Suarez, Gonzo—Pyro Studios

Gonzo Suarez started in the video games industry around 1984–85, programming *Goody* for the Sinclair Spectrum, Amstrad CPC, MSX, Atari ST, and Commodore Amiga, at the company Opera Soft. It was distributed abroad by Alligata Soft. After that first title came *Sol Negro*, *Mot*, *Crazy Billiards*, and *Arantxa Super-Tennis*. Around 1989–90, the Spanish video game industry collapsed, and he moved to other types of software, such as graphic design applications. In 1996, together with a group of colleagues (most of whom are now part of the *Commandos* team), he built the company Arvirago Entertainment and created the design for the video game *HeadHunter*, for which Javier Arévalo programmed a technology prototype. They pitched the project to companies like SCI, with no luck. In January 1997, with Ignacio Pérez, they created Pyro Studios; thus *Commandos: Behind Enemy Lines* was born. In an alpha state, the game was sold to Eidos.

Tallarico, Tommy—Tommy Tallarico Studios

Tommy Tallarico is the president of Tommy Tallarico Studios, Inc., the largest multimedia post-production audio company on the planet. He also hosts the "Electric Playground" weekly TV show. In total, Tallarico has worked on 140 games, yielding a total of $25 million in sales. Past products include *Prince of Persia*, *Global Gladiators*, *The Terminator*, *Cool Spot*, *Aladdin*, *Robocop vs. Terminator*, *Earthworm Jim 1* and *2*, *Skeleton Warriors*, *MDK*, *Treasures of the Deep*, *Wild 9*, and *Test Drive 4* and *5*, to name just a few. Current projects are *Tomorrow Never Dies*, *Messiah*, and *Pac-Man 3-D*. He has been in the industry for eight years and has won 19 awards.

Tallarico explains how he got started in the business:

"I'm originally from Springfield, Massachusetts. When I was a kid I always wanted to move to southern California to be a musician (doesn't everybody!). Anyway, when I turned 21 I left Massachusetts and drove across country to Southern Cal. The only thing I really knew out here was Hollywood, so I drove to Hollywood. I didn't have a place to stay, didn't know anybody, didn't have a job, and oh yeah, I didn't have any money!!! So I showed up in Hollywood, took a look around, and said, 'What the hell is this!!!' Those of you who have been to Hollywood, you know what I'm talking about. Hollywood isn't exactly the way they portray it on TV; it's pretty much a dump. I said to myself, 'Self, there's no way I'm living here!!' The only other thing I knew in California was Disneyland, so I stopped some bum on the street and asked him where Mickey Mouse lived. He pointed me about 45 minutes south to Orange County. When I got to Orange County, I said, 'Now this is more like it!'

"So I picked up a newspaper and got a job the very next day selling keyboards at Guitar Center. (I was sleeping either in my car or on Huntington Beach at this point, so I was looking for anything I could find—I knew about music and keyboards, so what the hell.) The next day I started work and believe it or not, the very first person I waited on happened to be a producer for a new software company starting up called Virgin Mastertronic. I've loved music my whole life; I've been playing piano since I was three years old. My second love has always been video games. Never in my whole life did I ever think of putting my two loves together, until that day. I became the first tester at Virgin the next day. (A tester was somebody they paid to play games and find bugs in the programs.) There were only about 15 people at Virgin at the time, so they didn't need a full-time musician. When the first opportunity arose for music (*Prince of Persia* on the Game Boy), I jumped on it. I would sit down with the programmers and technicians every chance I got to learn about the machines. I know nothing about programming or any of that kind of stuff. I just know music. I think that has become a plus in my career—I mean, think about it, how do you program the blues or rock 'n' roll, that's just something you feel! Anyway, I worked on *Prince of Persia* for free on the weekends and after work, and the VP of the company was so impressed he made me the music guy!"

Taylor, Chris—Gas Powered Games

Chris Taylor is the president of Gas Powered Games. He started in the video games business 11 years ago; his first game was called *Hardball II*, a sequel to the very successful game by Bob Whitehead. The company that he worked for, Distinctive Software, was very well known for the game *Test Drive*. Taylor worked on *Test Drive II* for a month or so to help out when it fell behind schedule. As Taylor recalls, "Those were what we lovingly refer to now as the 'good old days.'" When he shipped *Hardball II*, it was "like giving birth—anyhow, the first one is always the toughest." The game went on to sell in the neighborhood of a hundred thousand units and won an SPA award for the best sports product of the year. "Back in those days there wasn't much in the way of awards, so we made a big deal out of it," says Taylor.

After *Hardball II*, he went straight to work on a game called *4D Boxing* with Jay MacDonald. Taylor reminisces: "He was the one who really understood what motion-captured data could bring to a game. I learned a lot from working with him and we had a great time working on that game." The next significant title was *Triple Play*, even though he was often heard saying he would never do another baseball game again. "It was actually a much better experience than I would ever let on." He then did a port of *Virtua Stadium Baseball*, and shortly afterwards hooked up with Ron Gilbert and began work on *Total Annihilation*. "This was the game that I hoped would change a lot of things… including my will to live and continue in this business," remembers Taylor.

Taylor then left Cavedog/Humongous to start his own company, Gas Powered Games, which has recently signed a publishing deal with Microsoft.

Taylor, Chris—Interplay Productions

Chris Taylor is a senior game designer at Interplay Productions. He was lead designer for *Stonekeep* and *Fallout*, a campaign designer for *MAX 2*, and his current project is *Star Trek: Starfleet Command*.

Thomas, Chance—Yosemite Entertainment

Chance Thomas is a multiple-award-winning composer (Emmy, Telly, Addy, Aurora) and music producer with a background in the advertising industry. His credits include such household names as McDonald's, Nissan, Tupperware, Rexall, the Salvation Army, the N.B.A. (*Utah Jazz*), and many others. His music has been broadcast throughout every television market in America, and across five continents.

Chance works in the entertainment software industry under an exclusive contract with Sierra On-Line to create music for their Yosemite Entertainment division. His interactive credits include creating and producing Sierra's first live orchestral score, their first rock single, and their first game soundtrack album. He was among the first to design a highly interactive music system based on digital audio streams, as opposed to MIDI. His games include *Quest for Glory V, SWAT 2, The Realm, J.R.R. Tolkien's Middle-Earth,* and *Navy SEALs.*

Chance is involved in a proactive effort to raise awareness for the quality and profile of music in games. He is lobbying the Academy of Interactive Arts and Sciences (AIAS) to provide greater opportunity and recognition for composers and musicians. He writes articles and speaks out in the press on the virtue of high fidelity sound coupled with highly interactive music design. Perhaps most notably, he catalyzed and leads the current movement for a game music Grammy award.

Chance is a former entertainer, and has toured extensively as a lead singer and keyboardist. He has also performed as a solo pianist, entertaining such well-known personalities as Tom Cruise, John Travolta, Bruce Willis, and Sarah Vaughn. He is a cum laude Baccalaureate of Brigham Young University's School of Music, and a scholastic All-American.

Toschlog, Matthew—Outrage Entertainment

Matthew Toschlog is the president of Outrage Entertainment, a development studio currently developing *Descent 3*, to be published by Interplay Productions. In their previous incarnation as Parallax Software, they developed *Descent* and *Descent II*. Toschlog started in the game industry in 1996, working at Sublogic Corporation on *Flight Simulator* and *Jet* for the 68000 machines (Amiga, Atari ST, and Mac). Prior to forming Parallax Software in 1993, he was project leader on *Car & Driver*, a racing game published by Electronic Arts, and he also made a small contribution to Origin Systems' *Ultima Underworld*.

Vogel, Jeff—Spiderweb Software

Jeff Vogel is the president of Spiderweb Software, Inc., a two-person (plus many freelancers) software company in Seattle which produces and sells shareware fantasy games for the Macintosh and Windows platforms. They've been designing games for five years now, and their annual sales are well into six figures at this point. They developed the *Exile* trilogy, *Blades of Exile,* and *Nethergate* in-house, and they also distribute *Ocean Bound,* a small, clever game for the Macintosh. Their games have been reviewed by practically every major gaming magazine, and *Exile III* won "Shareware Game of the Year" from *Computer Gaming World.* And, of course, as Vogel says, "We often get the most flattering award, which is $25–35 of people's hard-earned money."

Walls, David—Hasbro Interactive

David Walls is the creative director at Hasbro Interactive and has been for the last two years. He designs and directs design for most of Hasbro Interactive's games. Recent products are *Frogger, Centipede, Game of Life, Jeopardy, Wheel of Fortune, Clue,* and the *Tonka* series, to name a few. Future aspirations are to continue making top-quality games for Hasbro Interactive, and along the way, add some original games to the mix.

Willits, Tim—id Software

Tim Willits is the lead level designer for id Software, where he has been employed for the last three years. His early experience with id and their products was *Doom*. When he first played *Doom*, he knew it was something special, something different. Later, when he discovered that he could create his own *Doom* levels, he knew creating virtual worlds was something that he wanted to do. He worked on a series of maps called the Raven series. These were *Doom II* single as well as Deathmatch maps built to be played together.

At that time, luckily, id was looking for some contract maps for a product called the *Doom II Masters Levels*. They contracted Willits and he quickly started working for them. Also at that time, Rogue Entertainment needed a full-time map designer to work on a game called *Strife*, which they hired Willits for. He came to Texas and started his career a few doors down from id working full time for Rogue. As chance would have it, id soon needed another full-time level designer, so he left Rogue and went to work for id directly. He worked on the *Ultimate Doom* title and helped them finish *Quake*. He then became the lead designer on *Quake II* and currently is busy working on *Quake III: Arena*.

Wilson, Jay—Monolith Productions

Jay Wilson is a game designer at Monolith Productions. The products he worked on are as follows: *Blood* (lead level designer), *Blood: Plasma Pak* (lead level designer), *Blood 2: The Chosen* (project lead) and *Blood 2 Add-on* (project lead).

Zuk, Jon—Raven Software

Jon Zuk is a designer (and more recently, lead designer, on *Heretic II*) at Raven Software. Past products include *Take No Prisoners* (designer), *Hexen II: Portal of Praevus* (lead designer) and *Heretic II* (lead designer). He is very happy working at Raven and can see himself there for a long time.